1986

# INFLATION MANAGEMENT

# INFLATION MANAGEMENT

**100 PRACTICAL TECHNIQUES
FOR BUSINESS AND INDUSTRY**

HOWE C. STIDGER
RUTH W. STIDGER

**A Wiley-Interscience Publication**

**JOHN WILEY & SONS,** New York • London • Sydney • Toronto

*Library of Congress Cataloging in Publication Data:*

Stidger, Howe C   1936–
  Inflation management.

  "A Wiley-Interscience publication."
  Includes bibliographies and index.
  1. Industrial management and inflation.   I. Stidger,
Ruth W., 1939–   joint author.   II. Title.
HD69.I6S74      658.1′5      76-8927
ISBN 0-471-82485-2

Printed in the United States of America

10 9 8 7 6 5 4 3 2

**TO OUR PARENTS**

# PREFACE

*Inflation Management* has been prepared as a guide to help business executives cope more effectively with the problems and dislocations associated with an economic environment characterized by persistent, long-term inflation.

The book does not attempt to answer questions of *why* spiraling inflation has occurred in recent years, *who* is responsible for it, or *what* governments can do or should be doing about it; dozens of texts have already been written on these subjects. Rather, *Inflation Management* takes the view shared by many leading economists—that tenacious inflation will be a worldwide phenomenon in the foreseeable future—and sets out methods to help businessmen adjust to this condition, learn to live with it, and maintain profitability in spite of it.

The 100 techniques covered in the book have been drawn from a broad range of sources and represent some of the best management thinking that has evolved in recent years to combat inflation at the company level. Although founded primarily on American business practices, the text also includes inflation-controlling techniques that have proven effective for businesses in Germany, Japan, Great Britain, Canada, the Netherlands, Brazil, and other countries.

The book presents inflation-offsetting ideas for nearly every important business function—money management, purchasing, wage and salary administration, production, sales, accounting, electronic data processing, budgeting, personnel, and so on. Being broad in scope, the text is intended primarily as a compendium of steps that can be initiated by upper management to increase profitability by lessening the impact of inflation on company operations. Additionally, executives responsible for managing the key business areas just named should find the book valuable in controlling inflation-related costs within their particular spheres of interest. The book should be of interest to executives at all management levels wishing to gain an overall grasp of the business problems caused by inflation and measures that can be taken to alleviate them.

In keeping with its sourcebook format, *Inflation Management* lists the 100 techniques alphabetically and gives a brief description of each method under its heading. The reader can thus study the book in its entirety, or peruse the headings and descriptions to pick out only the topics pertinent to his or her business area. The cross-referencing section on page xiii lists all techniques related to the same key business functions. For those wishing to explore specific ideas in greater detail, a suggested further reading list is included for each method.

HOWE C. STIDGER
RUTH W. STIDGER

*New York, New York*
*May 1976*

# CONTENTS

NOTE:  For a listing of all techniques relating to each of eight key business areas see INDEX BY MANAGEMENT FUNCTION, page xiii.

# INDEX BY
# MANAGEMENT FUNCTION

The 100 techniques outlined in *Inflation Management* should all be of interest to upper-level executives and general management. Additionally, many of the techniques that cover specific business functions—such as personnel, purchasing, and sales—should prove valuable to executives charged with managing these key business areas.

The following cross-reference index provides the *chapter numbers* of all techniques contained within the book that relate to eight major functional areas of management concern. The appearance of the same number under more than one heading indicates that the technique has multiple applications.

| Production and Manufacturing Management | | | Administrative and Office Management | | | Financial Management and Accounting | | | Purchasing and Materials Management | | |
|---|---|---|---|---|---|---|---|---|---|---|---|
| Chapter Numbers | | | Chapter Numbers | | | Chapter Numbers | | | Chapter Numbers | | |
| 1 | 5 | 7 | 6 | 7 | 10 | 2 | 3 | 6 | 1 | 7 | 8 |
| 8 | 9 | 10 | 17 | 18 | 19 | 7 | 11 | 12 | 11 | 12 | 15 |
| 11 | 12 | 15 | 20 | 22 | 24 | 13 | 14 | 16 | 16 | 18 | 19 |
| 16 | 18 | 19 | 26 | 27 | 28 | 18 | 19 | 20 | 20 | 21 | 22 |
| 20 | 21 | 22 | 29 | 31 | 32 | 21 | 23 | 24 | 23 | 26 | 27 |
| 23 | 26 | 27 | 33 | 35 | 36 | 25 | 26 | 29 | 29 | 30 | 31 |
| 28 | 29 | 35 | 39 | 40 | 41 | 30 | 32 | 34 | 35 | 37 | 38 |
| 37 | 38 | 39 | 45 | 46 | 48 | 35 | 38 | 39 | 39 | 40 | 41 |
| 45 | 48 | 53 | 51 | 54 | 56 | 40 | 42 | 43 | 46 | 47 | 48 |
| 54 | 56 | 62 | 59 | 60 | 61 | 46 | 47 | 48 | 49 | 50 | 53 |
| 63 | 64 | 65 | 62 | 63 | 64 | 49 | 50 | 55 | 55 | 60 | 61 |
| 67 | 68 | 69 | 67 | 68 | 69 | 57 | 58 | 65 | 64 | 65 | 73 |
| 71 | 73 | 75 | 70 | 71 | 73 | 66 | 70 | 73 | 75 | 76 | 77 |
| 76 | 77 | 78 | 77 | 78 | 82 | 74 | 76 | 77 | 87 | 88 | 91 |
| 83 | 85 | 86 | 83 | 85 | 86 | 80 | 82 | 84 | 97 | 99 | 100 |
| 87 | 89 | 91 | 87 | 89 | 93 | 87 | 88 | 92 | | | |
| 94 | 95 | 96 | 94 | 95 | 96 | 94 | 97 | 99 | | | |
| 97 | 98 | 99 | 98 | 99 | 100 | | | | | | |
| 100 | | | | | | | | | | | |

| Sales and Marketing Management | | | Personnel Management | | | Data Processing Management | | | Design and Engineering Management | | |
|---|---|---|---|---|---|---|---|---|---|---|---|
| Chapter Numbers | | | Chapter Numbers | | | Chapter Numbers | | | Chapter Numbers | | |
| 1 | 12 | 16 | 3 | 4 | 6 | 5 | 9 | 12 | 1 | 5 | 12 |
| 19 | 20 | 21 | 19 | 20 | 28 | 15 | 16 | 17 | 18 | 23 | 29 |
| 24 | 27 | 30 | 31 | 33 | 35 | 31 | 59 | 60 | 37 | 53 | 62 |
| 31 | 38 | 39 | 36 | 39 | 45 | 62 | 63 | 64 | 73 | 75 | |
| 41 | 44 | 45 | 51 | 54 | 56 | 65 | 70 | 73 | | | |
| 47 | 52 | 55 | 60 | 61 | 62 | 82 | 89 | 93 | | | |
| 56 | 58 | 62 | 63 | 67 | 68 | | | | | | |
| 63 | 65 | 66 | 69 | 71 | 72 | | | | | | |
| 70 | 72 | 73 | 73 | 78 | 85 | | | | | | |
| 77 | 78 | 79 | 86 | 87 | 89 | | | | | | |
| 81 | 83 | 86 | 93 | 95 | 96 | | | | | | |
| 87 | 90 | 92 | 98 | 99 | 100 | | | | | | |
| 94 | 97 | 99 | | | | | | | | | |
| 100 | | | | | | | | | | | |

# SECTION 1

## ALTERNATE MATERIALS
## AND DESIGNS

*Discusses raw material prices with respect to inflation and supply/demand and provides guidelines for cutting costs through materials and design alternatives.*

The unprecedented peacetime materials shortages that hampered manufacturers during the recent inflationary periods forcefully brought home a condition that many economists had been preaching about for years: availability of many basic raw materials may be restricted in the years ahead. Even if the flow of materials is sufficient to meet demand, most prices will be significantly higher than those of the past decade.

The messages for manufacturers are clear: wherever possible, switch to materials that will be least affected by future shortages and the resulting supply/demand price hikes, and design them into existing and new products.

### THE PROBLEMS

Economists disagree on what caused the recent raw material shortages. One school believes that it was the first strong indication that world population and economic expansion are finally beginning to tax limits of world production and resources. These experts believe that shortages will be a recurring phenomenon from now on—that shortages of raw materials and soaring prices are here to stay.

At the other extreme, a second group believes that shortfalls were caused by a number of random, temporary occurrences unfortunately converging at the same time. They do not expect worldwide shortages to become a way of life and blame recent problems on the following factors.

#### Inadequate Capacity

Because of sagging profits during the 1969–1970 recession, many of the basic materials and processing industries did not expand capacity enough in the early 1970's.

### Demand

For the first time in the postwar era, all industrialized nations of the world were expanding production in unison. This put an unprecedented peacetime strain on basic raw materials and suppliers, culminating in shortages.

### Price Controls

Controls applied by governments kept raw material prices artificially low, spurring high consumption and stockpiling in anticipation of rising prices once controls were lifted. At the same time, controls flattened profits of raw material producers, curtailing expansion investment.

### The Energy Crisis

Superimposed on the foregoing problems, the energy crisis was the straw that broke the camel's back. Increases in energy costs and inadequate supplies of fuel and petrochemical feedstocks caused a "domino effect" among industries; primary suppliers failed to deliver to secondary suppliers, who in turn were forced to default with their own customers.

The truth regarding future availability of raw materials probably lies somewhere between these two extremes. However even the most optimistic forecasters see no return to lower price levels. Production may be able to close the demand gap over the next decade, but prices will continue to increase for a number of reasons.

### Present Undercapacity

Because of long lead times required to expand existing facilities and build new plants, many of the basic materials industries will be working at near-capacity levels for at least the next few years. Suppliers of chemicals, paper, fertilizers, oil, and some metals will be hard pressed to keep up with orders. Demand for these materials will pull prices up.

### Synchronous Worldwide Economies

There is a growing tendency for economies of the world's industrialized nations to expand and contract at the same time. Previously it was common for some countries to have overheated economies while others were experiencing recessions. Since the early 1970's, however, expansions have been moving in harmony, as have contractions, throughout the world. This may be the result of trade interdependence. Whatever the cause, if this trend continues, the need for raw materials by the world's industrialized nations will cause prices to continue to rise sharply during each economic upswing.

### Cartels

The success of the Organization of Petroleum Exporting Countries (OPEC) in forcing a fourfold increase in oil prices has caused dozens of other primary-producing nations to take note, and a new economic nationalism is becoming increasingly evident. Cartels have been openly discussed by nations producing nonfuel minerals such as copper, bauxite, iron ore, and mercury. In some cases individual exporters have announced unilateral price hikes on minerals—Morocco on phosphate rock and Jamaica on bauxite, for example. Supplies of other minerals including nickel, tin, platinum, and chromium, are also held by relatively few countries. Since the United States is becoming increasingly dependent on imported mineral supplies, concerted efforts by these developing nations to raise prices would have an important effect on raw material costs.

**Table 1 Estimated Ocean Bed Surface Deposits and Known Global Deposits of Mineral Resources**

| Mineral resource | Estimated ocean bed surface deposits[a] | | Approximate known global deposits[b] | |
|---|---|---|---|---|
| | Tons (millions) | Estimated length of supply at present rate of use (years) | Tons (millions) | Estimated length of supply at present rate of use (years) |
| Aluminum | 43,000.00 | 1,130 | 1,170.00 | 31 |
| Cobalt | 5,200.00 | 260,000 | 2.18 | 110 |
| Copper | 7,900.00 | 925 | 308.00 | 36 |
| Gold | 5.00 | 5,500 | 0.01 | 11 |
| Iron | 207,000.00 | 480 | 100,000.00 | 240 |
| Lead | 1,300.00 | 370 | 91.00 | 26 |
| Manganese | 358,000.00 | 43,400 | 800.00 | 97 |
| Nickel | 14,700.00 | 15 | 147,000.00 | 150 |
| Petroleum | 12,000.00[c] | 6 | 60,000.00[d] | 31 |

[a] *United Nations Survey of Ocean Bed Mineral Resources.*
[b] *U.S. Bureau of Mines Report on Mineral Facts and Problems.*
[c] Offshore petroleum only.
[d] Estimated weight.

### Mineral Depletion

Finally, on a longer-term basis, there is the very real possibility that some of the world's basic minerals will be running dangerously near depletion before new technology can be developed to tap further supplies. Scientists are generally in agreement that vast quantities of raw materials are stored under the ocean floor and in other currently inaccessible places beneath the earth's surface. The problem is to mine them, and this will be prohibitively expensive in the foreseeable future. Although there is some disagreement about exact amounts of mineral reserves that can be mined with current technology, Table 1 gives an indication of the extent of the problem. It is clear that several key minerals—aluminum, copper, gold, lead, and petroleum—will be exhausted, or nearly so, by the end of the century. If new technologies have not been found to tap other sources of supply, prices of these minerals will skyrocket as available quantities are depleted.


## THE IMMEDIATE OUTLOOK

Against the overall background just outlined, what is the near-term outlook for key materials affecting industry? What can be expected in the way of shortages and/or price increases over the next few years? According to latest data, the situation can be summed up as follows.

### Petrochemicals

Shortages are not likely to ease in the near future, as expansion tries to catch up with demand. Supplies of the industry's basic chemical product, ethylene, probably will not balance with demand until the end of the decade. Ethylene's price, which has quadrupled in recent years, will continue to rise. OPEC decisions will exert a strong influence on pricing.

### Aluminum

Aluminum supplies should be sufficient for the remainder of the 1970's and beyond, although prices will continue to rise. The tripling of prices in recent years has given impetus to production expansion programs, and capacity by 1978 will be up at least 20 percent over late 1974 levels.

### Cement

Shortages of cement are a distinct possibility, since demand will grow at a 3 percent annual rate through 1980 and industry is not geared to expand rapidly enough to meet this demand. Supplies and prices will depend largely on the strength of the housing market.

### Steel

Supply of steel will probably keep abreast of demand, the result of massive expansion programs and ample supplies of raw materials. Prices will continue to rise, largely because of increased energy costs.

### Forest Products

If the housing market expands significantly over the next few years, shortages and spiraling prices will almost certainly occur again in the lumber industry. Plagued for some time by insufficient capital for expansion, the industry cannot meet strong demand.

Even though billions of dollars are being spent on a crash expansion plan, pulp and paper suppliers are still running at capacity levels and are unlikely to meet demand for several years. Prices will rise accordingly.

### Energy

The United States will remain heavily dependent on foreign energy supplies well into the 1980's, and pricing will be strongly influenced by overseas decisions. There will be stepped-up domestic exploration and development in oil and gas industries, while coal will make a strong comeback as an energy source. Even so, demand will grow faster than domestic supplies until at least 1980. One key energy problem is natural gas, which is now imported in ever-increasing quantities. As with oil, this dependence on foreign supplies could have severe consequences if producers decide to raise prices sharply. Furthermore, no immediate relief from this dependence is in sight. By 1980 nearly one-sixth of the natural gas used in the United States will be derived from foreign sources.

## ALTERNATIVES

Spurred by anticipated inflationary prices and possible future shortages, increasing numbers of manufacturers are searching for substitute materials to use in place of traditional ones. There will be no headlong rush into new materials until future supplies and price trends stabilize somewhat, but more research is being directed toward determining the effects of alternate materials on products and production. Many of these substitutes will be used in the future.

Substitutions are already in use in some industries. In the food industry, for example, meat extenders increasingly reflect the low cost of textured vegetable protein compared with meat protein. Synthetic flavors are also being utilized extensively. For instance, candy manufacturers are searching for cocoa substitutes to replace this high-priced commodity. Sugar price increases have turned many food processors to high-fructose corn syrup— nearly 50 percent cheaper—for sweetening.

In manufacturing, a switch from oil to coal as an energy source is rapidly accelerating. By 1980 production of coal should be up nearly 60 percent from 1974 levels. Supplies are extensive.

Aluminum has been used as an alternate material, although this trend has slowed now because of price and supply uncertainties. Automobile manufacturers, for example, find cost advantages because of aluminum's lower weight, compared with steel. The material's future in many components seems assured if supplies and prices stabilize. Many experts feel that the aluminum industry can add capacity more quickly than can steelmakers, and that once large orders start coming from Detroit, the industry will commit itself to a rigorous expansion program. This will increase availability to a broad range of substitute applications.

Higher metal prices in the building industry have caused contractors to increase use of wood and cement products. Wood housing framing increasingly replaces aluminum systems. In new office buildings, concrete panels often replace aluminum. Wood cost advantages have been extended by developments within the industry. Low-cost particleboard and hardboard production has been stepped up signficantly, further undercutting the cost of metals. Particleboard surfaced with veneer provides a good, low-cost substitute for other materials in the manufacture of counter tops, tables, TV cabinets, and so on. New, stronger types of the material can be substituted for other wood materials, such as more expensive plywood.

Plastics, a key alternate material, will continue to offer price advantages despite higher feedstock costs. In the building industry, plastic materials are replacing aluminum in window frames, copper in piping, and wood for exterior sidings. A new type of load-bearing brick wall is being constructed of quarry scrap bonded with plastic resin.

In other industries plastic is replacing a broad range of materials. Glass-reinforced plastics will be extensively used in automobiles in the next few years. Metal price rises will further encourage use of plastics, including nylon, polycarbonate, acetal, and thermoplastic polyester, which are being marketed as alternatives to metal. Plastics can also replace expensive zinc in die castings and in areas where polyethylene competes with paper.

## DESIGNING FOR ALTERNATIVES

For the reasons already given, the costs of raw materials will increase more rapidly in some areas than others. At the same time, the supply of some materials will become more critical. Certain energy sources will be more expensive for use in manufacturing than their alternatives.

Some industries cannot make broad-scale substitutions in materials or energy sources. It makes economic sense, however, to evaluate materials used in products, substituting less expensive materials when possible. Evaluation must include both existing products and those still in developmental stages, since it is easier to design in cost-effective materials before production than to make substitutions later.

To begin the evaluation, list each product's raw materials and project future prices and supply availability. Identify materials with supply or cost problems and establish possible substitutes. Alternatives may not always exist. However, modern technology is constantly finding new ways to utilize materials. Industry consultants may be able to provide information about material alternatives that are emerging.

If substitute materials are available, cost/supply advantages may be obvious or rather hazy. For example, it may be possible to substitute a certain material at a lower cost, but availability of future supplies may be difficult to ascertain. Judgments must be made, weighing these factors after all available information has been gathered.

### Responsibilities

Four corporate areas should be included in the study of possible materials substitution. These are design, purchasing, production, and marketing. The first two work directly to find alternatives that cost less and to name possible applications. Production and marketing advise on production feasibility and consumer acceptance.

Decisions made at the design stage have the most far-reaching effects on substitution profitability. Design engineers should:

- Use less expensive materials wherever possible.
- Reduce amounts of expensive essential materials.
- Reduce energy used in production.

In many cases design engineers are not kept informed of price/supply trends in raw materials. This results in a tendency to rely on parts, materials, and processes that have been used in the past.

The purchasing department is first to know about cost changes and/or shortages in materials, and the purchasing director should initiate design alternatives or substitution evaluation programs. The purchasing function can warn designers about future cost/supply problems and recommend possible alternatives. This responsibility should include involvement in new product design, as well as purchasing recommendations for existing products.

Goals in substitution programs should include:

- Use of renewable rather than nonrenewable resources.
- Development of long-life products.
- Use of less material.
- Use of less production energy.
- Use of materials with good long-term prospects in terms of cost and availability.

Materials decisions should focus on a long-term view. For example, plywood might appear attractive as a material alternative to metal in some frame or support applications. Plywood production is heavily dependent on natural gas, however, and the profitabilities and consequences of future gas shortages and prices would have to be evaluated.

The life cycle of a product is a key consideration in weighing alternatives. Material cost and supply changes that are likely to occur during the company's manufacture of the line must be considered at the design stage. Even after production begins, purchasing should continue to evaluate alternate materials that might prove even better or more economical. Toward this end, the knowledge and experience of vendors can often be tapped to contribute to design alternative programs.

## SUGGESTED FURTHER READING

Block, F. E., "Raw Materials Shortages: Are They Cyclical or Long Term?" *Financial Analysts Journal,* November 1974, pp. 20–26.

"Coping With Shortages," *Business Week,* September 14, 1974, pp. 56–58.

Donohue, J., "Vertical Integration Can Ease Supply Woes," *Purchasing,* March 4, 1975, pp. 34–35.

Dowst, S., "Don't Let Designers Be Deadheads," *Purchasing,* March 18, 1975, pp. 69–70.

Meitz, A. A. and B. B. Castleman, "How to Cope With Supply Shortages," *Harvard Business Review,* January 1975, pp. 91–96.

"Shortages Shake Things Up," *Purchasing,* September 3, 1974, pp. 42–43.

# SECTION 2

## ANTI-INFLATION CHECKLIST

*Gives tactics usually found effective for most businesses operating in an inflationary environment.* [1]

Although individual company situations may require additional and/or different approaches, the tactics in this checklist can be helpful in accomplishing the following objectives:

1. Accelerating cash receipts and reducing receivables.
2. Delaying cash disbursement and increasing payables.
3. Obtaining cash and investing for growth and/or yield.

| Objectives | | | Tactics |
|---|---|---|---|
| 1 | 2 | 3 | Coordinate marketing, production, and financial responsibilities to minimize surprise cash needs and surpluses. |
| 1 | 2 | 3 | Improve cash management staff and/or systems capabilities. |
| | | 3 | Review all banking arrangements with respect to current needs, benefits, and costs. |
| | | 3 | Consolidate accounts to reduce aggregate minimum balances. |
| 1 | | 3 | Use automatic transfer accounts and take advantage of bank wire systems and electronic funds transfer arrangements. |
| 1 | 2 | 3 | Reconsider needs and cost effectiveness of cashier functions at all locations. |
| | | 3 | Plan investment of temporary excess cash, including participation in money management funds, and so on. |
| 1 | 2 | 3 | Plan for extra borrowing, loan commitments, sale of receivables, credit purchases, and so on, to fill temporary shortages. |

[1] *Coopers & Lybrand Newsletter,* Vol. 16, No. 11, November 1974, New York, pp. 2–3.

| Objectives | | Tactics |
|---|---|---|
| | 3 | Review fixed investments, joint ventures, properties, and so on, for growth or yield potential and liquidation possibilities. |
| | 3 | Review litigation and other claims receivable for favorable early cash settlement potential. |
| | 3 | Evaluate sales pricing for possible increase and/or charges to customers for presently free options. |
| 1 | | Establish or tighten due dates and/or terms for all sales or other money sources; provide interest or penalty charges on late or deferred customer payments. |
| 1 | | Strengthen credit and collection function. |
| 1 | | Include provisions for advance, partial, or progress payments in sales terms. |
| 1 | | Reevaluate effectiveness and rate of cash discount offered to customers to induce early payment. |
| 1 | | Minimize frequency or likelihood of error in order filling or delivery, and speed adjustment of mistakes. |
| 1 | | Reduce delay in order fulfillment to allow quicker invoicing. |
| 1 | | Ensure invoicing promptly upon delivery; for example, shorten billing cycles. |
| 1 | | Enhance invoice clarity and minimize billing errors and/or omissions, particularly in addresses. |
| 1 | | Reevaluate customer and product mix for emphasis on sales with faster cash conversion. |
| 1 | | Speed up collection efforts and begin them earlier. |
| 1 | | Provide preaddressed return envelope with invoice to speed reply mail and identification. |
| 1 | | Provide separate turnaround remittance advice to speed payment identification for collections control and deposit. |
| 1 | | Speed up preparation and dispatch of deposits to coordinate with bank clearing schedules. |
| 1 | | Use lockbox services to obtain instant deposit. |
| 1 | | Streamline efforts to recover for checks returned unpaid. |
| | 2 | Reevaluate purchases to reduce unit cost and/or order quantities. |
| | 2 | Curtail product line; avoid replenishment of slow-moving, high-cost items. |

| Objectives | | | Tactics |
|---|---|---|---|
| | 2 | | Use supplier's inventory; buy on order whenever feasible. |
| | 2 | 3 | Balance inventory investment risks and costs with anticipated availability and price-level effects. |
| | | 3 | Reevaluate make-or-buy and lease-or-buy options for maximum growth or yield from cash used. |
| | | 3 | Review standard costs for currency to assure recovery of current costs. |
| | 2 | | Negotiate better terms on purchases and other commitments, especially where delivery/construction is delayed. |
| | 2 | 3 | Review insurance coverage, premium payment timing, and loan availability. |
| | 2 | | Review feasibility of tax options to defer tax payouts; for example, depreciations, LIFO inventory, loss reserves, and installment sales. |
| 1 | 2 | 3 | Time year-end transactions for gain and loss offsets to reduce current tax payments. |
| | | 3 | Offer new or treasury shares to stockholders in lieu of dividend payout. |
| | 2 | | Provide noncash/deferred benefits in executive and employee compensation plans. |
| | | 3 | Limit need for cash advances to employees, salesmen, agents, and so on; for example, by providing fast reimbursement, use of charge accounts, and drafts. |
| | | 3 | Use drafts for large volumes of small payments so that cash is required only when drafts are presented. |
| | 2 | | Make selective use of cash discounts. |
| | | 3 | Time cash transactions to take advantage of grace periods, weekend interest, and so on. |
| | | 3 | Avoid undue future price commitments or provide escalator clause in sales contracts. |

## SUGGESTED FURTHER READING

*Coopers & Lybrand Newsletter,* Vol. 16, No. 11, November 1974, New York, pp. 2–3.

# SECTION 3

## ASSET FORMATION

*Outlines the European wage plan in which a portion of wage settlements are paid in deferred company savings bonds.*

Asset formation is a wage plan that not only helps control wage costs during an inflationary environment but simultaneously increases employee involvement in company goals and objectives. The plan is used in small to medium-sized firms in Switzerland, Italy, Holland, Germany, and France, and will undoubtedly increase in popularity if persistent inflation continues.

Under the asset formation plan, company savings bonds become a mandatory portion of wage settlements. The portion varies, of course, dependent on the size of the settlement and negotiations between labor and management. The bonds are not redeemable by employees for a specified number of years, and thus can be used for capital financing by the company in the interim. This feature is especially important because of both the scarcity and expense of capital financing during inflationary periods.

Experience has shown that use of the plan heightens worker involvement with the company, since the employees, in effect, have a stake in the business. This involvement can be made even greater by paying interest on bonds based on productivity increases.

In addition to benefiting the company, use of the asset formation plan can have a positive effect on a nation's overall economy. By postponing payment until a later date, the system takes money out of the economy and reduces consumer demand (employee demand) for goods and services. This, in turn, can be instrumental in slowing the rate of inflation.

**SUGGESTED FURTHER READING**

*Financial Times,* London, March 14, 1974, p. 18.

# SECTION 4

## ATTRITION/TERMINATION MODEL

*Presents a model to indicate the most cost-effective way to reduce personnel.*

The economic dislocations caused by persistent inflation often call for reductions in staff. During recent inflationary periods some companies were forced by rising costs, sluggish sales, and dwindling profits, to reduce headcount by as much as 25 percent. Often these layoffs are on a short-term basis and employees are rehired as business picks up. With the contracted markets and material shortages predicted for the next decade, however, managers will have more problems related to reducing manpower for prolonged periods of time.

The method of headcount reduction through normal attrition or termination can have a major effect on profitability. The following simplified case history presents an attrition/termination model[1] that can be used to determine the most cost-effective method of reducing staff as a result of worsening business conditions.

### BUILDING THE MODEL

In this example a company employing 500 professionals must reduce operating expenses by 15 percent. Fixed overheads dictate that headcount must be cut by 100. It is expected that 400 professionals will be needed during each of the 3 years following the reduction. Is it most cost effective to terminate the 100 employees immediately, let natural attrition reduce the number by 100 over a period of time, or use a combination of these methods? In building the model, the costs for different combinations of termination and attrition are calculated to allow the company to choose the least-cost alternative.

---

[1] Adapted from Richard Traum, "Reducing Headcount Through Attrition and/or Termination: A Cost-Effective Model," *Personnel,* January/February, 1975, pp. 18–24.

## Termination Costs

Short- and long-term costs must be calculated. The short-term costs (Table 2) in this example equal 12 months of the average annual salary of the employees in the group—$15,000. These costs include the following.

*Separation Pay.* When terminated, each professional receives one week of separation pay for each year of service. Average for the group is 2½ months.

*Stock Vesting.* The company contributes 10 percent of an employee's salary in its stock to a retirement fund. If "terminated without cause," the employee receives the firm's contributions. The cost of vesting due to termination is calculated as 3 months' salary.

*Early Retirement.* Older employees receive a special retirement program, which includes a premium for the difference between their normal retirement income, including social security, and their early retirement income, without social security. The premium, prorated among the entire group, equals 3 months' salary.

*Unemployment Benefits.* Employees unable to quickly find new jobs collect unemployment insurance, increasing unemployment insurance rates for the firm in the future. Increased rates on active employees are calculated at one month's salary per terminated employee.

*Accrued Vacation.* Payment is made for accrued vacation, as well as all

**Table 2  Termination Costs per Employee**[a]

| Cost | Months' salary | Cost per employee (average salary = $15,000) |
|---|---|---|
| Separation pay | 2½ | $ 3,125 |
| Stock vesting | 3 | 3,750 |
| Early retirement | 3 | 3,750 |
| Unemployment insurance | 1 | 1,250 |
| Accrued vacation | 1 | 1,250 |
| Notice of termination | ½ | 625 |
| Miscellaneous | 1 | 1,250 |
| | 12 | $15,000 |

[a] *Source:* Traum, "Reducing Headcount Through Attrition and/or Termination," *Personnel,* January/February, 1975, p. 20. Reprinted by permission of the publisher from *Personnel,* January/February 1975. © 1975 by AMACOM, a division of American Management Assn.

vacation for the following year. Average cost to company: one month's salary.

*Notice of Termination.* Two weeks' notice of termination is given, during which little work is done.

*Miscellaneous.* Executives with contracts receive individualized separation pay, outplacement office expenses, and benefits continued for 3 months. Average cost to company: one month's salary.

Long-term termination costs are mostly for replacement. Replacement costs hinge on the firm's turnover rate—in this case 12 percent. With 400 professionals, one would expect 4 employees (1 percent) to leave the following month, requiring 4 replacements. These replacement expenses must be calculated as part of termination costs, since if employee reductions took place through attrition, those in positions earmarked for elimination could replace others who left.

The cost of hiring compared to internal placement is $6825, calculated as follows.

*Cost of Hiring.* Recruiting agency fee and interview travel expenses: 3 months' salary ($3750).

*Relocation.* Relocation costs, prorated over all hires: 1½ months' salary ($1875).

*Training.* Value of time lost in formal training and adjustment period for new employee: one month's salary ($1250).

Thus, total replacement costs equal 5½ months' salary, or $6825. It is assumed that the $6825 (to be spent in the future) has a current value of $6000. This is based on the assumptions that the average employee would be hired 11 months after the decision to reduce headcount and that the cost of money would be 15 percent; $6000 invested today at 15 percent yields $6825 in 11 months.

Total average termination cost per employee is thus $15,000 for termination plus $6000 future replacement cost, or $21,000.

### Attrition Costs

The cost of keeping each of the 100 professionals on the payroll is $18,000 ($15,000 salary plus $3000 for benefits).

If the decision was made to reduce headcount by 90 through termination and 10 by attrition, subsequent turnover would be about 4 per month. The cost of attrition is calculated as follows: 4 employees leave after one month (4 man-months' salary), an additional 4 leave after 2 months (8 man-months' salary, and 2 more leave after 3 months (6 man-months' salary).

Table 3   Attrition/Termination Alternatives[a]

| Termination | Attrition | Termination cost | + | Attrition cost | = | Total cost |
|---|---|---|---|---|---|---|
| 100 | 0 | $2,100,000 | | $ 0 | | $2,100,000 |
| 90 | 10 | 1,890,000 | | 27,000 | | 1,917,000 |
| 80 | 20 | 1,680,000 | | 90,000 | | 1,770,000 |
| 70 | 30 | 1,470,000 | | 192,000 | | 1,662,000 |
| 60 | 40 | 1,260,000 | | 330,000 | | 1,590,000 |
| 50 | 50 | 1,050,000 | | 507,000 | | 1,557,000 |
| 40 | 60 | 840,000 | | 720,000 | | 1,560,000 |
| 30 | 70 | 630,000 | | 972,000 | | 1,602,000 |
| 20 | 80 | 420,000 | | 1,260,000 | | 1,680,000 |
| 10 | 90 | 210,000 | | 1,587,000 | | 1.797,000 |
| 0 | 100 | 0 | | 1,950,000 | | 1,950,000 |

[a] *Source:* Traum, "Reducing Headcount Through Attrition or Termination," *Personnel,* January/February, 1975, p. 22. Reprinted by permission of the publisher from *Personnel,* January/February, 1975. © 1975 by AMACOM, a division of American Management Association.

The cost of the 18 man-months' salary and benefits at $1500 per month ($18,000 per year) is $27,000.

## ATTRITION/TERMINATION MODEL

Using the calculated costs of $21,000 for terminating each professional and $1,500 per month per professional until attrition provides openings, models can be set up to show the total cost of any attrition/termination combination (Table 3). Consider an example.[2]

Ninety professionals are terminated and 10 are reduced through attrition. The total cost is equal to the termination cost plus the attrition cost. The termination cost is calculated by multiplying the cost of terminating one professional, which is $21,000, by 90 professionals, which equals $1,890,000. The attrition cost for 10 professionals has been previously calculated at $27,000. The formula is

$$\text{total cost} = \text{termination cost} + \text{attrition cost}$$
$$= \$1,890,000 + \$27,000$$
$$= \$1,917,000$$

[2] Traum, "Reducing Headcount Through Attrition and/or Termination" *Personnel,* January/February, 1975, p. 22. Reprinted by permission of the publisher from *Personnel,* January/February, 1975. © 1975 by AMACOM, a division of American Management Assns.

By reviewing the different combinations, it appears that the best decision, taking no other variables into account, is to terminate 50 and permit 50 to leave through attrition. The cost would equal $1,557,000, which is $543,000 less than terminating 100 professionals, and a significant cost reduction.

Stated simply, if it were to cost $21,000 to terminate a professional, it would be worthwhile to use up to $21,000 for his salary and benefits until he either replaced someone else or left on his own as part of normal attrition. If he were partially productive, it would be worthwhile to wait longer.

## SUGGESTED FURTHER READING

Chambers, P., "Easing the Pain of Large-Scale Redundancies," *International Management,* January 1975, pp. 26–29.

Traum, Richard, "Reducing Headcount Through Attrition and/or Termination: A Cost-Effective Model," *Personnel,* January/February, 1975, pp. 18–24.

# SECTION 5

## AUTOMATION

*Discusses automation and its role in combating inflation through increased productivity. Provides guidelines for automating manufacturing processes.*

During inflationary periods wages tend to rise faster than normal, as employees demand increases to maintain their standards of living. If these wage demands are met without proportionate increases in productivity, a strain is put on profits. For this reason, it is axiomatic that one of the best ways to overcome the effects of inflation is to increase productivity—the output per employee per hour.

Although there are a variety of management tools to help achieve production increases—incentive programs, psychological motivation, behavioral control, and work study programs—the best method in many instances is the automation of work processes. At base, automation cuts the number of employees needed to perform a certain task, thus reducing wage costs. Even more important, however, automation raises production potential beyond the purely human capabilities of manufacturing personnel. A man working on a production line can produce only a limited amount, even under optimal conditions; there are human physical limitations to what he can do. The speed of automated equipment, on the other hand, is restricted only by current technology and ingenuity of design. Potential output is not limited by physical capabilities of manufacturing personnel. During inflationary times, therefore, a strong argument exists for investigating all phases of production with an eye toward intelligently automating as many processing steps as possible. The stress here is on "intelligently," for if the wrong processes are automated, the results can be disastrous. The following material provides guidelines for deciding which processes can be profitably automated and gives the steps required to see the job through.

### THE POTENTIAL

Potential cost savings and/or productivity increases through the use of automation are enormous in most manufacturing enterprises. Contrary to

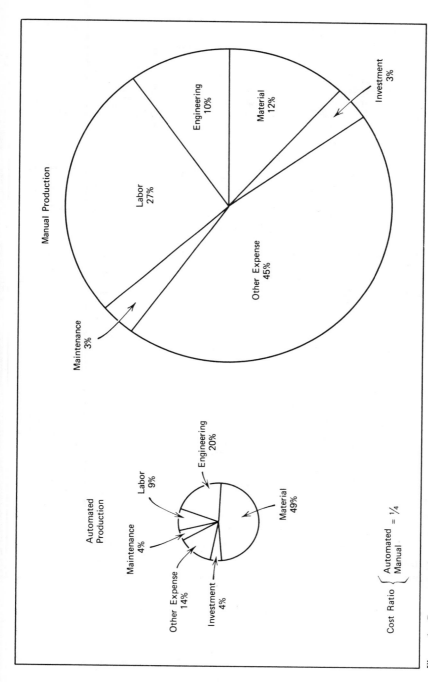

**Figure 1** Cost comparison of similar components: automated versus manual production operation at capacity level. (*Source:* Luke, *Automation for Productivity,* Wiley, New York, 1972, courtesy Western Electric Co.)

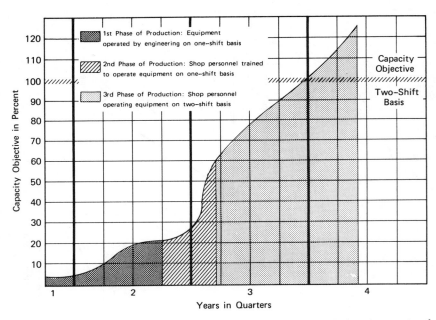

**Figure 2** Production output of the product in Figure 1. (*Source:* Luke, *Automation for Productivity,* Wiley, New York, 1972, courtesy Western Electric Co.)

commonly held beliefs, it has been estimated that "no more than 10 to 15 percent of our plants can be considered automated with extensive modern facilities."[1] In fact, several countries—notably Japan and Germany—have "imported" a wealth of American automation technology since World War II, and some foreign industries are now ahead of the United States in this vital area. The higher productivity made possible by their use of technology has been largely responsible for the exporting success of these countries during the past decade.

Examples of potential cost savings through automation are numerous. One study revealed that in materials handling $10 worth of human work can be duplicated by a few cents worth of electrical power when automated equipment is used.[2] Since it has been estimated that materials handling accounts for an average of 22 percent of United States manufacturing wage costs, the potential savings in this one area alone are tremendous.

Another study, conducted by Western Electric Company, determined that the production cost of a product was reduced to one-fourth the manual

[1] Hugh D. Luke, *Automation for Productivity,* Wiley, New York, 1972, pp. 269.
[2] Electric Industrial Truck Association, Pittsburgh, 1971. (Now Industrial Truck Association.)

labor cost when automated production facilities were installed (see Figure 1). Labor costs alone dropped from 27 to 9 percent.

Naturally such savings are not achieved overnight but are the result of much planning, time, effort, and financial commitment on the part of management. Figure 2 presents the time scale used to achieve the cost reduction shown in Figure 1; 2½ years were required from the time the automated system was installed until full savings were realized.

## THE ECONOMICS

The economic viability of automating a work process is determined by two factors: cost and existing workers.

### The Cost

Analysis must be made of all costs incurred in automating and operating a process versus the cost of manual production using less sophisticated equipment. In making these calculations, the following formula is often used:

$$A +/- L = OM$$

Here $A$ is the cost of automation. It is determined by adding the total cost of the automated system and the estimated operating cost during the system's lifetime, then dividing this total by the system's estimated lifetime.

The $L$ is the human labor using existing equipment. It is determined by adding estimated labor costs and operating cost for the time period used in $A$ and dividing this total by the number of years used in $A$.

The optimal method, $OM$ is the more economic of the two alternatives.

### Existing Workers

Decisions must be made about the future of workers displaced by automation. Will they be retrained for other jobs? Will they upgraded or downgraded? Will they become unemployable?

These are very real economic considerations, since in many cases management will find that labor agreements prohibit the dismissal of workers even when they are displaced by automated processes. Some large unions even have contract clauses that require employee approval before installation of automated equipment. These and other employee considerations must be weighed in calculating the profitability possible through automation.

In some cases buy-out agreements can be used to help overcome the problems just mentioned. Under such agreements, management grants to employees certain concessions (e.g., early retirement at full pay) in exchange for installation of automated processes. Another alternative is retraining displaced employees at company expense.

Often, better employees can be upgraded to operate automated equipment. This is generally a successful practice. The productivity of such employees usually increases because of greater job challenge, providing a productivity benefit in addition to the higher output of the new system.

Automation can also be economically advantageous in reducing required supervisory personnel, according to Floyd C. Mann, an industrial social psychologist. His studies show that automation reduces labor costs by requiring fewer supervisors, since the workers in the smaller group of retained personnel are usually more highly skilled. For example, if a supervisor is needed for each 10 employees in a factory employing 100 laborers, the supervisory staff numbers 10. If automation reduces the total number of workers to 10, the operation will require just one full-time supervisor—or perhaps none at all if the remaining employees are sufficiently skilled to report to the next higher management level.

### THE GOALS

As stated earlier, the automation of production processes must be carried out with intelligence and caution. Perhaps the most important step in converting to automated equipment comes at the very beginning—in defining goals that automation is to achieve.

Experience in a broad range of industries has shown that automation is most cost effective when unnecessary processing steps can be eliminated or when an automated system offers better adaptability to a continuous manufacturing process. Caution should be used to ensure that automation of processes does not simply produce a brilliantly engineered production line that has no marked effect on lowering the cost of goods produced. The end goals of higher productivity and/or lower unit production costs must always be kept rigidly in mind. The checklist in Table 4 outlines the types of results that should be expected from successful automation.

### EVALUATION OF PROCESSES

Not all types of processes can or should be automated, since some are best suited to manual operation. Processes that inherently demand a great deal

Table 4   **Results of Successful Automation**[a]

| Production | Increases total quantity |
|---|---|
| | Increases output per worker |
| | Increases rate of production |
| Labor | Decreases unskilled labor |
| | Increases skilled labor |
| | Improves worker conditions, relations, and attitudes |
| | Increases safety |
| Product | Decreases manual handling |
| | Decreases unit costs |
| | Increases quality |
| | Increases uniformity |
| Profits | Reduces costs |
| | Increases net earnings |

[a] *Source:* Luke, *Automation for Productivity,* Wiley, New York, 1972, p. 26.

of manual dexterity are often beyond the scope of complete automation—at least with current technology—and attempts to force automated processes into such operations usually prove fruitless and costly. However many manual or handcrafted operations have now been successfully converted to automation through modification of product design to match automated process capabilities. In other words, design of manually produced goods may offer little scope for automation; but if a product is redesigned, incorporating automated processing capabilities, chances of successful automation may be good.

Another important factor is compatibility of all automated production elements. The system must be considered in its entirety, and timing cycles of each of the production processes must be compatible with the others. The goal of automation is continuous operations, and this can be successfully accomplished *only* when the separate stages are integrated into a closely controlled system with compatible time cycles. Many entire systems have had to be scrapped because improper initial evaluation had resulted in one element having a production level that was well below the rest of the system. It makes little sense to invest in equipment for station A that can turn out 1000 parts an hour if the rest of the system can only absorb 500 parts an hour. To be financially viable, every process step must meet the time cycle requirement of the total system, as well as the functional aspects of production.

Automation of processes carries two different levels of financial risk, depending on complexity of work.

### Low Risk

Little risk is involved when automation is fairly straightforward, using proven, well-defined, well-understood, easily controlled processes. The track record in this type of automation has been established, and it is usually a matter of adapting the processes and equipment to a new operation. The financial risks in installing such a system, properly researched and evaluated beforehand, are minimal.

### High Risk

High-risk systems include those involving processes that have never been automated and call for new technology, original equipment, and untried processes. Before management considers such systems, it must obtain the very best technical advice available, from inside and outside the company, and must be willing to assume the financial risk inherent in technical pioneering. The risks may be high; however experience has shown that the innovators who made significant automation breakthroughs in the past are most often today's high-productivity companies and industry leaders.

## OBJECTIVES

The goal of automation is not simply mechanizing a plant's production processes for automation's sake. Rather, it is the increasing of productivity and profits. Properly planned and installed, automation can accomplish any or all of the following objectives.

### Increased Production

Even when working at maximum capacity, manual production methods may not be able to turn out quantities of goods required to respond to market demand. Although it is sometimes possible to expand facilities and increase the number of workers, these steps may be accompanied by lack of quality control or greatly increased costs. With anticipated high demand, it is often better to investigate innovative new methods of increasing production, an area well suited to automation.

### Reduced Costs

Production costs can be reduced through automation in a number of ways, each adding to profitability. Basically, automation increases the productivity per worker. This lowers per-unit cost and makes it possible to reduce the price of products—or at least to hold the line if price increases are inevitable. This can result in the capture of a larger market share. Lower per-unit production costs and/or increased sales are reflected in a company's profitability, and an upturn in profits leads to better worker wages and an increase in capital available for investment.

Production costs, reduced through automation, can enhance profits in other ways. The success of a new product often depends on market acceptance of its price. Automation can help ensure the lowest price possible. Additionally, automated equipment can help pull an overpriced product into line with less expensive competitors.

On the production line, automation usually reduces material costs through more accurate machining and assembly operations, limiting scrap.

Automatic storage equipment can be instrumental in reducing the cost of maintaining and handling raw material and/or product inventories. Additionally, reduced setup times possible with automated equipment make shorter runs feasible, also cutting inventory costs.

### Better Quality Control

One of the key advantages of automated processing systems is uniform quality. The presence of the human element means that manual production operations are not only less accurate than automated operations but produce much greater variation in product quality. The use of automated equipment reduces faulty processing spoilage and, perhaps even more important, delivers a more consistently reliable product to the marketplace. Moreover, recently developed automatic inspection machines built into the production line can inspect products with greater speed and accuracy than would ever be possible relying on human inspection. This provides another assurance of continued product quality.

### Improved Working Conditions

Many operational steps in modern production processes are hazardous or detrimental to the health of human workers. In such cases the use of automated equipment not only reduces production costs but has very real benefits in the area of employee relations. Automated controls for machine tool operations, for processes generating toxic emissions, and for other dangerous areas reduce insurance costs while pushing up employee morale.

Automation can also be used to reduce worker boredom caused by repetitive, tedious processes. When routine jobs are automated, workers can be

freed for more interesting, stimulating responsibilities, with results of lowered absenteeism and improved performance.

### New Products

Automation often can be the deciding factor in bringing out new, unique products. Many products in the marketplace today would never have appeared without the help of automation. It would have been impossible to produce them in the quantities and qualities required. Modern computers are a good example. Without automated, computerized manufacturing equipment, it would be impossible to turn out the highly sophisticated data processing equipment in use today. This new equipment, in turn, will be used to produce even more sophisticated hardware in the future, continuing an upward spiral of technological advancement. With each improvement in automation technology, new tools and systems emerge, making possible still other new, unique products.

## AUTOMATING EXISTING FACILITIES

Although it is usually better to "start from scratch" when automating a processing system, this does not necessarily mean that old plants must be torn down and new ones built. It is often possible to improve existing operations. Table 5 provides guidelines for solving existing production problems

**Table 5   Attacking a Production Problem with Automation[a]**

1. Identify and define the existing problem.
2. Outline desired objectives.
3. Collect information concerning all areas (i.e., production requirements, costs, product design) pertinent to the automation project.
4. Generate various approaches that would achieve the results sought.
5. Define the system capabilities that would be necessary to implement each approach.
6. Develop standards with which to assess the design concepts, including such things as how the new system or systems will interface with existing operations, total investment required, return on investment, and applicability to long-range production and enterprise goals.
7. Decide on one approach.
8. Specify the equipment and components that will best implement the chosen concept.

[a] *Source:* Luke, *Automation for Productivity,* Wiley, New York, 1972, p. 34.

with automation. In addition to the steps outlined in Table 5, the following points should be noted in seeking to upgrade existing operations to more automated processes.

### Determine the Basic Production Flow

At the outset, disregard the variety of production steps and concentrate on the overall process flow pattern. Generally the flow falls into one of three basic types:

- One material in, one product out.
- Several materials in, one product out.
- One material in, several products out.

Of these three flow patterns, the first—*one material in, one product out*—is generally the easiest to automate. The processing steps follow a relatively simple straight-through pattern, rather than combining interrelated production steps at points along the line.

### Pinpoint Highly Repetitive Labor Operations

Operations that require workers to repeat the same tasks over and over usually can be automated and should be noted wherever they occur in the production process. Automation of these processes will not only result in faster, more accurate production but will free bored workers for more self-fulfilling jobs.

### Pinpoint High Throughput Operations

Automation is most effective with high throughput operations that can be run continuously. Look for processes that require a minimum amount of setup time and can handle several types of similar materials and/or products. These continuous operations will produce the highest returns when automated.

### Pinpoint Processing Steps that Require Similar Time Cycles

When each of a number of separate processing operations requires about the same amount of time, there is a good possibility of combining all the steps into an automated system. Many of the most successfully automated systems in use today were designed using this strategy.

### Pinpoint Bottlenecks

In many instances total production capacity is held back by one or more bottleneck processes that prevent the rest of the system from operating at efficient levels. These bottlenecks should be eliminated or the work mechanized to flow at a level compatible with the rest of the line.

### Improve Product Design

Often relatively minor modifications in product design greatly facilitate automated processing. Learn what automation can and cannot do with your existing product line; then make product modifications where possible, to take advantage of existing automation technology.

### Evaluate Production Sequences

Substantial automation savings often can be realized by changing the sequence of processing steps. In many operations the existing sequence was built gradually and follows no overall plan. An evaluation of the overall process may reveal possible sequential changes that will make automation simpler and less costly.

## STARTING FROM SCRATCH

If a completely new automated process is to be designed, all phases of the operation should be fully analyzed to avoid costly mistakes. An entirely automated process is more than a series of interrelated machines, and skillful management in planning and design is essential. Additionally, implementation of the chosen plan should be placed in the hands of specialists.

Following are some important considerations when designing a new, automated system.

### Assembly

Parts of a product being assembled in an automated process must be of high quality and high uniformity, and they must have fairly close tolerances. Automated equipment is designed to perform a specific task with a certain-sized part. If parts vary widely in uniformity or quality, the automated function will not be satisfactory. In steps that require assemblage of nonuniform parts or materials, a manual operation should be used. This problem often can be overcome through product design changes, building in parts uniformity compatible with automation.

### System Factors

An automated system is basically the combination of several production operations into one continuous unit. The most profitable automated system is one that contains the lowest possible number of production operations, eliminating all but the absolutely necessary production steps. The fewer production steps required, the lower the equipment cost, the lower the operating cost, and the shorter the process cycle needed to turn out products. In planning a new system, strive for a design that eliminates all unnecessary steps and combines as many steps as possible into functional units.

### Controls

The type of product manufactured usually dictates the method of automated equipment control. When tolerances are not critical, manual controls can be used. An automated process required to roll steel to ±0.0001 inch, however, calls for the sensitivity of a computerized control system. The method of control should be incorporated into system planning from the beginning.

### Plant

Although new automated systems are best installed in plants especially designed for the purpose, it is often possible to make profitable use of an existing building if certain guidelines are followed.

The building should be in good enough condition to last for a number of years, since the substantial amounts of money spent on installing automated equipment should not have to be duplicated later. The building must be appropriately designed and big enough to allow for the flow pattern of the automated system; it should also provide ample room for required storage of materials and/or finished products. Future expansion plans should be taken into consideration. Does the facility provide space for anticipated volume increases in the years ahead? Does the building design permit extension or modification of the automated process to meet increased demand?

The building must allow for certain automated production requirements, such as adequate power supply and means of waste and sewage disposal.

Also consider whether the automated system best lends itself to a single or multistoried building.

Automated processes are less successful when forced into unsuitable facilities. If an old building is to be used, be sure that it is adequate and flexible enough for the job.

## AUTOMATION IN THE OFFICE

Automation has made less progress in office operations than in manufacturing, although studies show that the potential for increased productivity and cost savings are greater in the office. Modern electronic data processing (EPD) equipment, which is being constantly adapted to office work areas, increasing productivity wherever it is wisely applied, is largely responsible for this potential.

As in manufacturing processes, studies must determine the economic viability of switching from manual to automated systems. The break-even point of automation has lowered in recent years with the increased availability of computer time-sharing programs. These programs make it possible for small- or medium-sized firms to rent just as much or as little computer time as they need. This has vastly broadened the range of companies that can profitably make use of automated office systems.

Generally offices have depended on automation to help them handle greatly increased volume, rather than to reduce numbers of employees. Cost per item of data handled is thus reduced, and as a rule a smaller supervisory staff is required.

An important side effect of EDP is that as its use increases, the types of skills required in both offices and plants become more alike; for example, both groups need employees to control computerized equipment. Personnel specialists predict that this similarity will decrease future labor costs to some extent, the result of a large common pool of available workers.

## SUGGESTED FURTHER READING

Luke, Hugh D., *Automation for Productivity,* Wiley, New York, 1972.

Morris, T. D., "Automation Technology—Key to More Productivity," *Computers and People,* November 1974, pp. 12–14.

"Robot Market to Hit $1 Billion by 1985," *Industry Week,* September 16, 1974, p. 58.

## BRAZILIAN EXPERIENCE

*Outlines techniques used by the Brazilian government to negate the effects of inflation on business and society.*

Prices in many South American countries began to rise rapidly after World War II, accelerating to hyperinflation in the 1960's. By 1964 inflation in Brazil had reached 90 percent annually, and the economic fabric of the country was in shreds.

Faced with this situation, the government introduced one of the most innovative and far-reaching economic programs ever attempted in a major country. The goal of the program, which is still in effect, is to reduce and correct the effects of inflation, as well as to stimulate economic growth. The way in which company accounts were presented was completely changed. Perhaps most importantly, the place and the function of money was altered.

In the second decade of the plan the inflationary rate in Brazil was reduced by 80 percent and the country enjoyed record economic expansion. Currently the trade situation is sound, productivity continues to rise at about 10 percent annually, and the country is more prosperous than before. In tandem with other nations, Brazil suffered economic difficulties resulting from the oil embargo and the recent world recession. It is too early to gauge the final impact of these problems. Unquestionably, however, business and society in Brazil have learned to survive and thrive *with* inflation; inflation has been running at more than 20 percent throughout the country's dynamic growth period. For this reason, many other countries have adapted elements of the Brazilian system in recent years. Their techniques for dealing with inflation are worth studying, and we now present highlights of these inflation-correcting economic reforms, with particular emphasis on techniques used by industry.

### PROGRAM HIGHLIGHTS

Basic to Brazilian economic reforms was the belief that worldwide inflation had become a fact of life. The strategy chosen involved accepting the condition of inflation and finding ways to live with it.

Another basic rule was that no one would be in a worse position because of the loss in purchasing power of money. Toward this end, the following inflation-adjustment measures have been applied:

• Businesses are required to regularly adjust the value of their fixed assets, depreciation, and working capital, based on an officially calculated wholesale price index. "Index-linking" has also been applied to government bonds, long-term mortgages, public utility rates, insurance, pensions, savings deposits, and even to legal judgments for damages.
• The coefficient for inflation adjustment (the index-linking rate) is determined by the Minister of Planning. Timing of adjustments varies from case to case, and there has been a tendency in recent years to use specific price indicators for different transactions.
• Minimum wage rates are adjusted annually according to the rate of inflation. The wage rates vary geographically throughout the country. It has not been necessary to use general controls over all wages.
• Prices on selected items considered basic necessities are controlled by the government. Many foodstuffs are in this category, and some industrial prices are also controlled.
• To remain competitive in international trading, Brazil adopted a minidevaluation policy of frequent but small devaluations, called the *crawling peg technique*. Each devaluation—usually less than 2 percent—is based on the rise in domestic price levels minus the rate of inflation in the United States. The policy has effectively neutralized the impact of inflation on exports and on short-term speculative movements of capital.
• Tax obligations are maintained through inflation adjustment, and fines and interest charges on unpaid taxes are index-linked. The technique has significantly reduced delinquency, which was prevalent before 1964.

### Interest Rates

In Brazil, a distinct separation is made between the interest rate and the inflationary rate. Interest is negotiated by the banks, and inflation is accessed by the government. Banks and government together determine how much a borrower must pay for his loan, but the factors are separated in preparing his accounts. Thus although the basic interest rate on a loan remains constant, the index-linked inflationary rate varies with each government adjustment.

### Bonds

Government bonds are index-linked to ensure that they do not lose purchasing-power value as inflation pushes prices upward. Bond value is computed in terms of purchasing power, using purchase date as the base price. The inflationary rate may be computed on the day of issue for short-term bonds. Long-term bonds reflect actual depreciation calculated by the Central Statistical Office. (The practice of issuing index-linked bonds is becoming more popular with governments and corporations in other parts of the world. Floating-rate notes have been developed in the United States and Europe in response to the reluctance of institutions to invest in fixed-rate bonds. If inflation rates remain high, index-linked bonds undoubtedly will become more widely used as inflation-proof financing vehicles.)

### Debt Collection

All commercial debts in Brazil are indexed every 28 days, adjusting the original amount to its real value. The technique is also used to protect against losses in purchasing power of uncollected debts. Thus if inflation increases 2 percent a month, the amount due from earlier billings will increase 2 percent a month. The index rates are calculated by the government. Use of the method has resulted in prompt payment of bills to avoid indexed increases. (Some European companies are also employing index-linked invoices, adjusting the amount due on a monthly basis. Usually the Cost of Living or Wholesale Price Index is used.)

### Wages and Taxes

Brazilian wages are index-linked and are automatically adjusted upward every year to reflect inflationary increases. Likewise, the threshold at which income tax becomes payable is periodically adjusted. This prevents lower-income workers from being pushed into higher tax brackets as their wages increase. (Every country in Europe has now introduced a system of indexing wages to keep pace with inflation.) In other countries, cost-of-living increases are often a part of union agreements. Economist Milton Friedman, a strong proponent of wage indexing, views the technique as a deterrent to inflation:[1]

The argument for indexing wages is primarily that it will make it easier to slow down inflation. If a businessman agrees on a wage bargain with his workers when on both sides they expect a 10 percent inflation rate, and then actual inflation is 6 percent, the real wages the employer pays are higher than he had planned. He will therefore have to reduce his production to adjust to this higher wage. If wages were indexed, then his real wage bill will be what he expected. So the case for indexing wages is that it reduces the side effects—the costs—of slowing down inflation.

[1] "Ending Inflation—A Matter of Will," *The Guardian,* London, September 19, 1974, p. 20.

### Home Loans and Savings

Mortgage interest rates are adjusted annually in Brazil to compensate for cost-of-living increases. At the same time, savings accounts earn inflation equalization payments on top of interest and also qualify for extra federal income tax deductions. These measures have been instrumental in channeling of $19 billion into Brazil's home financing system in the past decade. The number of private savings accounts in the country increased from 220,000 in 1968 to more than 5 million in 1974. Twelve million accounts are forecast by 1977. Brazilian savings accounts earn about 8 percent annually, plus an indexing adjustment payment, comparable to the yearly increase in the cost of living.

### Fixed Assets, Depreciation, and Working Capital

Fixed assets, depreciation, and working capital are all revalued annually for tax purposes, making it possible for Brazilian industry to plan its investments with confidence.

The problems for industry without such revaluations are manifold. Two-thirds of the assets of many manufacturing firms are in the form of stock and work in progress. There may be a thousand automobiles going through a company's assembly lines, or several miles of sheet plastic being processed. The same amount of work in progress may have been in the factory a year ago, but because of inflation, it is more valuable now. Without revaluation of assets, the company is taxed as if it had made an additional profit.

Likewise, an industrialist who buys a new machine is expected to depreciate it and accumulate funds to replace it on the assumption that his new machine will cost no more than the old one. In fact, prices of new machines are rising rapidly. If the price increases at 20 percent annually and corporation tax is levied at 50 percent on profits, a firm must earn profits four to five times as great as the historic cost of its depreciating equipment just to stay in business.

The Brazilian technique of annual revaluations produces a sophisticated system that alleviates problems for industrialists and lets them cope with a 20 percent inflationary rate with little difficulty.


## THE RESULTS

In addition to overcoming the effects of inflation, the measures adopted in Brazil have had far-reaching social consequences. For the most part, these have been good.

• Social welfare levels appear to have been greatly improved. Real income of workers has not been depreciated by inflation since 1967.
• Employment has expanded steadily.
• Housing for low-income families is more readily available and more reasonably priced than in the past.
• Growing government revenues have made possible massive expansion of education, transportation, health, and other government/institutional facilities.

Perhaps even more important, the Brazilian experience provides a number of valuable economic lessons for dealing with inflation.[2]

• It is feasible to discard the illusion that stable prices are the normal pattern.
• Inequitable impacts of inflation can be largely neutralized by the use, economy wide, of monetary correction devices.
• A policy for neutralizing inflation permits a nation to concentrate on reducing unemployment, on speeding economic growth, and on resolving critical social problems through resulting increases in government revenues.
• The process of economic expansion, particularly in an economy with considerable excess capacity, can itself be a significant anti-inflationary force because of the resulting possibilities for higher productivity. economies of scale, and improved technology.

## SUGGESTED FURTHER READING

Bathon, Greg, "Consumer Behavior in Brazil Under the Pressure of Constant Inflation," *Consumer in Crisis*, J. Walter Thompson Co., Chicago, October 1974, pp. 18–21.

Bowden, Lord, "Brazil's Dramatic Recovery," *The Guardian*, London, July 9, 1974, p. 16.

DeVoe, R. F., Jr., "Under the Southern Cross: The Role of Monetary Adjustment in Brazil's Economic Miracle," *Financial Analysts Journal*, September, 1974, pp. 32–34.

Getzelman, J. C., "Financial Analysis in an Inflationary Environment," *Management Accounting*, March 1975, pp. 31–35.

"Indexing: The Brazilian Solution and the U.S. Economy," *Monthly Labor Review*, November 1974, pp. 57–58.

Robinson, Christopher H., "Living with Inflation—Brazilian Style," *Tempo*, Vol. 21, No. 1, 1975, pp. 18–20.

Robock, Stefan H., "We Can Live with Inflation," *Harvard Business Review*, November 1972, pp. 20–32.

---

[2] Stefan H. Robock, "We Can Live with Inflation," *Harvard Business Review*, November 1972, p. 32.

# SECTION 7

## BUDGETING

*Sets out budgeting techniques geared to an inflationary environment.*

Budgeting problems are compounded during periods of inflation. Since profits are under pressure, it is more important than ever that budgets be forecast accurately and then maintained. Against this, however, rapid and unanticipated increases in prices and costs make it extremely difficult to hold budgets once they have been established.

In this situation, how can managers commit themselves to yearly budgets when no one knows for sure what is on the economic horizon? How can a purchasing agent stay within budgetary bounds when a piece of equipment quoted at $50,000 costs $55,000 by the time the purchase order is processed? How can capital financing expenses be budgeted when interest rates rise almost weekly?

The following guidelines for budgeting techniques in a time of rapid price change should give a degree of protection against inflation and other volatile business conditions.

### AVOID LONG-TERM COMMITMENTS

One of the basic strategies of inflation budgeting is the avoidance of long-term commitments whenever possible. In an inflationary environment, a 6-month commitment should be the maximum. Within the company, managers should not commit themselves to budgets that agree to provide goods or services to other departments for a prolonged period at a fixed price. Similarly, companies should avoid getting locked into long-term, fixed-price contracts with customers.

### STANDARD COSTING

One of the primary rules of budgeting is that individuals should be held responsible *only* for controllable budget items. This becomes difficult in an inflationary environment, since rapid price changes, long delivery times,

**Table 6   Budget Responsibility for Cost Variance**[a]

| Standard raw material cost per unit | | | | Actual raw material cost per unit | | |
|---|---|---|---|---|---|---|
| | | | versus | | | |
| standard quantity | × standard price | = standard cost | actual quantity | × actual price | = actual cost |  |
| 110 pounds | × $1.68 | = $184.80 | 108 pounds | × $1.75 | = $189 |  |

Total variance          −$4.20 (unfavorable)

Budget responsibility
   Purchasing: price variance × quantity
      −$0.07 × 108 pounds =                          −$7.56 (unfavorable)
   Production: quantity variance × standard price
      +2 pounds × $1.68 =                             +$3.36 (favorable)

[a] *Source:* Merz, "New Ways to Budget in a Time of Rapid Price Change," *Administrative Management,* November 1974, p. 28. Excerpted from *Administrative Management,* © 1974 by Geyer-McAllister Publications, Inc., New York.

shortages of raw materials, and other factors mean that formerly controllable budgetary items become uncontrollable. In this situation, certain elements of standard cost systems—often used by manufacturing firms to control product costs—can be used to help control administrative costs.

Standard costing calls for budgeting in both physical units and dollars. The method separates budget responsibility for the usage of goods or services from uncontrollable price changes due to external inflation, as the following example shows.[1]

After a careful examination of historical trends, of expected price changes, planned changes in production methods, and the like, a manager decides that to make each unit of his product, 110 pounds of fiberglass resin costing $1.68 per pound should be used. If the purchasing agent goes ahead and buys the resin, the standard raw material cost is then $184.80 per unit. But say the actual cost of the resin really was $189, and that 108 pounds were actually used, at a cost of $1.75 per pound. Then, the standard cost system pats the production foreman on the back (he saved two pounds), but slaps the wrists of the purchasing agent (he paid seven cents per pound too much). More specifically, as the computations in Table 6 show, the total unfavorable variance of $4.20 is seen as the result of a favorable variance of $3.36 and an

[1] Excerpted from *Administrative Management,* copyright © 1974 by Geyer-McAllister Publications, Inc., New York. (C. M. Mertz, "New Ways to Budget in a Time of Rapid Price Change," *Administrative Management,* November 1974, p. 26.)

unfavorable variance of $7.56. The favorable variance of $3.36 is attributed to the production foreman, while the unfavorable variance of $7.56 is assigned to the purchasing agent.

Some administrative costs can be similarly divided in fixing budget responsibility. For example, electricity or gas for an office can be budgeted in kilowatt-hours or cubic feet, rather than naming a set dollar amount. The office manager's performance is judged by whether he keeps within the budgeted quantities, since his budget is unaffected by utility company price increases.

Of course a price responsibility must be set somewhere when budgets are expressed in terms of physical usage instead of dollars. In some budgets expenses incurred when goods or services are acquired can be differentiated from those arising once the acquired items are in use. In these cases, the purchasing department should assume price responsibility.

In recent years, however, material shortages and the inflationary environment have created expenses for which no one can realistically assume budget responsibility. In these instances there is really only one practical alternative: uncontrollable costs should be passed along to customers through price increases.

## INDEXED BUDGETING

Some companies have adopted the practice of tying budgets to various price indexes or other economic indicators. Most commonly used is the Wholesale Price Index or the Gross National Product Implicit Price Deflator. Budget performances are measured against changes in these indexes. If the budget in a business is dependent on market activity—new housing starts or new car sales, for example—the budget can be tied to specific industry economic indicators. Companies using indexed budgeting usually do not set a firm budget for the year. Generally, fixed budgets are set for only the upcoming quarter, and adjustments are made every 3 months to take into account changes in the economic situation.

## ABC BUDGETING

A recent innovation in budgeting is the adaption of ABC analysis, a technique commonly used by manufacturers to control inventory.

When applied to budgeting, an A type of cost is one in which a small change in price or usage would produce a large change in profit, a B cost change in price or usage would have a moderate impact on profits, and a C cost change would not seriously affect profitability.

In ABC budgeting each budget item is ranked according to its profit impact as an A, B, or C—that is, critical, important, or slightly important. A system is then formulated to watch and control A costs very closely, B costs less closely, and C costs casually. In this way emphasis is placed on controlling the costs that most significantly affect overall profit performance.

### PERSONNEL

In many cases companies should consider increasing allocations of people in areas that are crucial to meeting budget goals. This is because today's economic environment calls for more professionalism and concerted effort in certain functions that were formerly considered routine.

For example, the collection of receivables is critical during an inflationary period; interest rates are high, the value of uncollected dollars goes down in real terms each month, and poor credit risks are much more prevalent.

Traditionally, billing and collecting have been considered routine clerical functions, performed as a minor adjunct to the business. Today, however, consideration should be given to upgrading the level of management and perhaps increasing the number of employees involved in the accounts receivable operation.

The same holds for purchasing. Escalating prices and material shortages have made purchasing far more complicated than it was a few years ago. This function now demands a higher degree of professionalism—and perhaps more people—to maximize budgetary cost effectiveness.

### SUGGESTED FURTHER READING

Curran, M. W., "How Bracket Budgeting Helps Managers Cope with Uncertainty," *Management Review,* April 1975, pp. 4–15.

Gibson, R. F., "Don't Let Budget Panic Sink Long-Range Plans," *Industry Week,* March 10, 1975, pp. 23–28.

Merz, C. M., "New Ways to Budget in a Time of Rapid Price Change," *Administrative Management,* November 1974, pp. 25–27.

Mullis, E. N., Jr., "Variable Budgeting for Financial Planning and Control," *Management Accounting,* February 1975, pp. 43–45.

Murray, T. J., "Tough Job of Zero Budgeting," *Dun's Review,* October 1974, pp. 70–72.

# SECTION 8

## BUFFER STOCK

*Outlines a method of stabilizing raw materials costs and availability.*

The buffer stock technique can be instrumental in procuring needed raw materials at lower costs or ensuring continuity of materials during periods of fluctuating price and supply. Most often, buffer stock plans are operated by governments, but the recent inflationary environment has caused many industrial companies to make use of the technique.

For reasons of supply and demand, raw material and commodity prices can fluctuate markedly over the period of a year. Businesses using the buffer stock technique wait until the price of a needed material reaches a "floor" price, then purchase large quantities of the material to stockpile. When average prices are being asked for the material, the firm continues to buy needed quantities from the market. If prices go past a preestablished "ceiling," however, the firm uses its inventoried hoard of buffer stock to avoid paying the inflated price.

The technique can be instrumental in ironing out price/availability fluctuations but obviously can be employed only in the case of materials that can be stored at relatively little cost.

### SUGGESTED FURTHER READING

Davis, William, *Money Talks,* Coronet Books, London, 1974, p. 42.

"Is Our Cupboard Bare?" *Forbes,* September 15, 1974, p. 31.

Stockpile Urged to Foil Foreign Price Ploys," *Purchasing,* September 17, 1974, p. 5.

# SECTION 9

## CAPACITY PLANNING
## AND SCHEDULING

*Outlines a computerization technique to reduce labor costs and increase productivity.*

Capacity planning and scheduling is a management tool that can prove especially profitable during an inflationary environment in making use of equipment and labor, reducing the cost of down or slack time, and minimizing overtime payments. The computerized technique not only reduces labor costs, but can be instrumental in improving productivity and critical in offsetting inflationary effects on company operations.

Production data, machine and labor capacity, delivery dates, and so on, are fed into the computer and correlated automatically. The resultant output gives optimum scheduling of both equipment and labor to achieve the most cost-effective production.

In practice, capacity planning and scheduling are usually done by stage, ranging from short-term, day-to-day scheduling, through monthly or quarterly planning projections, to long-range strategies in which computerized evaluation of data helps management make decisions about capital equipment outlays and plant additions.

Through use of computer time-sharing, small and medium-sized firms can now make use of capacity planning and scheduling techniques, which were formerly feasible only for large-scale manufacturing facilities.

**SUGGESTED FURTHER READING**

Orlicky, J., *The Successful Computer,* McGraw-Hill, New York, 1972.

Plossl, G. W. and O. W. Wright, *Production and Inventory Control—Principles and Techniques,* Prentice-Hall, Englewood Cliffs, N.J., 1970.

# SECTION 10

## CAPACITY STUDIES

*Outlines systematic analysis of equipment and processes to achieve greater productivity and/or cost reductions.*

Capacity studies are undertaken to uncover possible economies that can be achieved through better utilization of existing machinery and equipment. Use of such studies can result in higher productivity and/or reductions in cost, both important elements in offsetting the effects of inflation on company operations.

When analyzing a specific machine or operation, capacity studies ask the following questions:

- Can the equipment or process be eliminated?
- Would greater efficiency or cost savings result if the equipment or process were placed somewhere else in the plant or office?
- Are there other jobs or operations that could make use of the equipment or machinery when it is not serving its primary purpose?
- Does the equipment require a full-time, trained operator? If so, are current operators properly trained to make maximum use of the equipment?
- Are substitute operators available for emergency use, or must the equipment stand idle if the normal operator is absent?
- Could greater productivity be achieved if an incentive plan was instituted for the equipment operator?
- Could production be increased if preproduction tasks (sorting of materials, preparation of supplies etc.) were carried out in some other way, permitting the operator to make full-time use of the machine?

Experience has shown that most firms, by carefully formulating capacity studies in advance and comprehensively analyzing each piece of equipment and/or process, can achieve significant savings in many operations.

### SUGGESTED FURTHER READING

Cemach, H. P., *Work Study in the Office,* MacLaren & Sons, London, 1969.

# SECTION 11

## CAPITAL EQUIPMENT ANALYSIS

*Sketches importance of analyzing capital equipment expenditures during inflation and summarizes three analysis techniques.*

Capital equipment analysis is the evaluation of potential investment in equipment to determine whether it is less costly to purchase new equipment or to continue to operate with the old. The analysis process takes on added importance during inflationary periods because internally generated funds are under pressure and outside sources of money for capital expenditures are usually scarce and/or expensive. All investments in new equipment must be weighed more carefully than usual against expected return.

Analyses of proposed capital equipment expenditures must take into account a number of factors, the most important being the extent to which production rates, labor and fringe benefit costs, maintenance costs, and down time can be reduced by the new installation. The reduction of these costs must be measured against the prorated installed cost of the new equipment, possible increased power costs, buy-out agreements with unions, and lost interest on the capital investment. Buying decisions are usually based on an analysis prepared by a firm's financial staff and based on information submitted by the manufacturing, engineering, and purchasing departments.

The three most widely used capital equipment analysis approaches are MAPI formulas, the payback period technique, and discounted cash flow.

### MAPI Formulas

The Machinery and Allied Products Institute (MAPI) has developed numerous formulas to determine the most cost-effective purchase of equipment. Prepared formulas in worksheet form are used to compare advantages and disadvantages of existing equipment and proposed purchases.

### Payback Period Technique

As the name implies, the company using the payback period method makes projections to determine the length of time the capital investment will take to pay for itself, based on savings that will result from its installation. If the time period is feasible, the investment is made. If several new-equipment or new-process options are available, the choice is based on the installation having the most rapid payback period.

### Discounted Cash Flow

With discounted cash flow the annual return for the proposed equipment is determined and the capital expenditure is authorized only if the rate of return meets or exceeds established company standards—usually 20 to 25 percent after taxes.

During inflationary periods, all three of the techniques must take into account inflation-related data, such as anticipated inflationary increases in price of the equipment if the purchase is postponed, decline in real value of the money used to pay back the lending institution, and higher-than-normal financing costs.

## SUGGESTED FURTHER READING

Ammer, Dean S., *Materials Management,* Irwin, Homewood, Ill., 1968.

Bey, R. P., "Evaluation of Capital Budgeting Procedures Under Uncertainty," *Journal of Finance,* March 1975, pp. 227–228.

Chen, A. H. and A. J. Boness, "Effects of Uncertain Inflation on the Investment and Financing Decisions of a Firm," *Journal of Finance,* May 1975, pp. 469–483.

Grossman, E. S., "Getting a Better Bead on a Leading Indicator," *Conference Board Record,* March 1975, pp. 2–6.

# SECTION 12

## CASH CONSERVATION

*Pinpoints cash conservation opportunities in the areas of general management, marketing and distribution, manufacturing, engineering, and financial administration and taxes.*

During times of unstable economic conditions—and especially during inflationary periods—cash conservation becomes critical. Money becomes tight, and even when it is available the cost of borrowing becomes exorbitant. Cash flows are affected by slow payments for goods received and services performed. In many instances poor business conditions cause outright defaults among customers, meaning that the company must absorb losses.

To help overcome these and related cash problems, cash conservation techniques should be employed to assure full utilization of all untapped potential sources of money within the company. The following provides guidelines for maximizing cash conservation during periods of persistent inflation.[1]

### WARNINGS AND OPPORTUNITIES

Most companies have untapped potential sources of money, but these often go unrecognized until unstable economic conditions force management to seek additional funds. Generally impending cash problems can be foreseen by alert financial executives. Some symptoms that should serve as warnings are as follows:

- A deteriorating cash position.
- Expanded borrowings.
- High interest payments.
- Current or anticipated reductions in business activity levels.
- Decreasing profits or incurrences of losses.
- A buildup of inventories.

[1] Adapted from Hugo Swan, "Cash Conservation," *Management Accounting,* August 1975, pp. 14–16.

- A decrease in turnover of accounts receivable.
- A failure to take advantage of purchase discounts.
- Insufficient funds for new plant equipment.

Cash conservation opportunities exist in many areas of operations: general management, marketing and distribution, manufacturing, engineering, and financial administration and taxes. If a company has any of the symptoms just listed, cash conservation measures should be called into play. All facets of the business should be questioned, even if decisions to implement some of the measures prove difficult.

## General Management Actions

Cash conservation programs should begin in general management. Sell or eliminate unprofitable or marginal product lines, divisions, plants, or departments. All ramifications of such actions should be fully analyzed before such decisions are taken, of course, but firm action should be implemented when the facts reveal that decisive steps are needed to prevent continued cash drains.

All data processing activities that cannot be cost justified should be curtailed. Often lack of data integrity in computerized systems forces individual departments to keep manual records. These records are often duplicated in different formats elsewhere and picked up to produce computer printouts; thus in effect the computer is being used as a typewriter. Challenge whether computers or computer peripherals can be eliminated and whether planned systems installations should be deferred or eliminated.

Capital appropriation procedures should be examined, and planned capital expenditures should be viewed critically. Decisions for such outlays made during a normal economy may no longer be valid. Many divisional general managers circumvent corporate capital expenditure policies by permitting a large capital expenditure request (requiring approval at corporate level) to be broken into several smaller project requests that can be approved at divisional level. Division procedures, expenditures, and projects should be audited, and a stringent cash management program should be implemented to prevent such occurrences.

Pricing strategies should be improved. Accurate knowledge of costs and cost changes is needed for making good, strategic decisions regarding what markets to enter, what jobs to bid, and when to institute price increases. A reevaluation of pricing strategies is frequently needed to cover cost increases (expected to occur between the bidding of a job and the billing of the customer). Often escalation clauses in the contracts will suffice.

Capital and debt structure should be examined. Highly leveraged companies are particularly vulnerable to cash drains in times of low profits and high interest rates. Dividend payments should be challenged, deferred compensation plans considered, and all long-term plans examined. Plans should be constantly revised under the direction of key management decision makers.

### Marketing and Distribution Actions

In the marketing and distribution functions, the first consideration for cash conservation is the culling of marginal outlets and warehouses. Policies should be reviewed regarding timeliness of deliveries to customers, methods of deliveries, and warehouse locations. One company located four efficient warehouses near airports, slightly increased air freight shipments, closed down and sold 15 smaller, inefficient warehouses, cut inventories substantially, decreased "back orders," and paid for the changes in 2 years.

Marketing plans should be updated for increased effectiveness and attainability, since manufacturing and financial planning depend directly on marketing plans, as do effective cash planning, management, and conservation. Advertising and promotional efforts should be reviewed with regularity, since changes in the economy may call for increased, decreased, or drastically modified company programs.

Effectiveness of salesmen should be reviewed, as well as controls over the activities and expenses of sales personnel. Determine whether the company's sales training programs, sales incentives, call controls, and expense controls need to be improved to increase sales volume and cash intake. Investigate the feasibility of speeding sales-order entries and subsequent shipments and billings to improve the company's cash position. Examine the possibility of telephoning or wiring orders taken at remote locations rather than mailing them to the outlet.

Consider the use of outside representatives rather than in-house salesmen. Increasing the number of outside representatives is a fast way of increasing the sales force without incurring a large cash outlay to keep additional salesmen in the field.

The major factor to analyze when conserving cash in structuring the selling arm is the effect on profits and cash flow, not the selling cost per sales dollar. Another cash conservation consideration is the timing of sales commission payments. An increasing number of companies are conserving cash by paying a portion or all of the sales commission when the invoice is paid, rather than when the order is taken. This increases the salesman's incentive to encourage the customer to pay quickly.

### Manufacturing Actions

Inventory turnover is one of the most important cash conservation considerations in the manufacturing area. Inventory reduction is frequently a promising source of cash. Examine this opportunity by the following routes.

• Question order quantities and reorder points. Many companies fail to change these when the business activity level or interest rates change.
• Use material requirements planning techniques.
• Challenge excess freight-in costs.
• Use better sales forecasting methods.
• Accelerate the purchasing-production-shipping process by using different scheduling rates (controlling shop order inputs vs. outputs to shrink queue times, analyzing bottlenecks, implementing corrective-action decisions, and using tighter purchase "bring in" scheduling rules).

A productivity audit should be performed to determine whether people are working at a reasonable pace, and attempts should be made to identify potential excess staffing.

"Make-or-buy" decisions should be examined, and subcontractors' fees should be challenged. Many of these decisions are made when a plant is operating at or near capacity, and under unstable conditions it may become more economical to reschedule the work in-house.

Review cost-reduction suggestion programs. Team-building sessions featuring discussions of cost reduction, organization improvement, and quality problems hold great potential for cash conservation. Team-building can improve productivity significantly because it tends to improve worker and management attitudes.

Overtime costs should be reviewed. Excessive overtime costs during times of reduced business activity often are a symptom of other managerial problems or of poor production controls.

### Engineering Actions

Engineering actions are difficult to challenge because, together with R & D, they represent the company's future products. However all large engineering projects should be carefully examined with an eye toward cash conservation, and consideration should be given to postponing all nonessential projects. Defer R & D activities until they can be justified by an increase in expected business activity levels. New model changes should be reduced to a minimum, and cost-justification procedures should be examined for nonessential engineering changes, to ensure that such changes reduce costs.

### Financial and Tax Actions

When money is tight, financial and tax actions to conserve cash are extremely important. The following techniques can be beneficial:

- Make greater use of cash forecasting, budgeting, and reporting.
- Establish an aggressive centralized cash management program.
- Send invoices immediately.
- Use lock boxes and regional collection centers for receipts, to reduce loss of income from funds delayed in the mail.
- Employ an aggressive collection policy.
- Establish maximum balances for each bank.
- Invest all available funds, including those in the "float" between banks.
- Make vendor payments late in the day, permitting cash to be used during the early part of the day.
- Make payments by bank drafts, to extend the cash withdrawal period.
- Improve control over intercompany and interdivisional cash transfers.

Purchase orders accompanied by a bank draft (not to exceed a specified maximum dollar amount) can be used for small purchases. This reduces clerical costs in accounts payable. Also, determine whether short-interval scheduling of clerical work will increase office efficiency and reduce costs. In addition, consideration should be given to savings from vendor discounts versus income from use of the money.

Credit terms to customers should be reviewed to make sure they are enforced by the cashier's operation.

Cost estimating procedures for pricing purposes should be questioned. Consider fixed versus variable costs, values added through the production process, and costs of holding inventories during the process. Often it is advisable to take the estimating of product costs out of the sales department. Too often, the desire to make the sale affects the sales department's judgment regarding true costs.

Cost and ratio trends for the last 3 years should be reviewed and compared against 6- and 12-month forecasts. Challenge any significant differences affecting the cash flow.

Consideration should be given to adoption of the last-in, first-out (LIFO) inventory method, which results in lower income calculations and income tax payments during inflationary periods. Investment tax credits should be maximized by making certain that all engineering, negotiating, and installation charges for appropriate assets are considered. Review capitalization versus expense policies, and review depreciation methods and asset lives. Make certain that inventory levels are low on assessment dates for state and local property tax purposes.

## SUGGESTED FURTHER READING

Battle, T. Q., "Critical Eye on Cash," *Director*, September 1974, p. 321.

Swan, Hugo, "Cash Conservation," *Management Accounting*, August 1975, pp. 14–16.

# 13

## CASH MANAGEMENT

*Discusses dynamic cash management as a means of countering erosionary effects of inflation on idle funds.*

Cash management takes on new importance during periods of spiraling inflation. With money losing value in real terms almost daily, idle cash depreciates rapidly. A company that holds $1 million in cash during 12 percent annual inflation finds that the money's real value is less than $900,000 in current purchasing power at the end of a 12-month period. Even more important, idle cash is not earning money. During an inflationary period—more than at other times—it is critical that cash be treated as an asset required to earn a reasonable return.

Not only can good cash management keep idle funds from losing value, it can put them to work, as contributors to profits. This section outlines recent thinking for optimum investment of idle cash during inflationary periods.[1]

### THE TRADITIONAL VIEW

Cash management has traditionally been charged with providing funds for day-to-day company operations. Two accounting approaches have evolved to determine the amounts of cash that will be required: the source and application of funds technique and the receipts and disbursements method. Both techniques have shortcomings with respect to generating revenue from idle cash. The first method does not provide detailed information on daily or weekly cash movements. The second method requires so much detail and time that it is impractical and difficult to control on a prolonged basis.

Both of these approaches are accounting oriented and have traditionally been used to forecast company operational cash requirements. They are not investment oriented, and many firms have lost potential investment revenue through use of the methods. Since there are obvious disadvantages to keep-

[1] Adapted from Paul J. Beehler, "Cash Management Forecasting for Profit," *Management Advisor*, July/August, 1973, pp. 40 ff. Copyright © 1973 by the American Institute of Certified Public Accountants, Inc.

ing either too much or too little cash on hand, new approaches are needed that view cash as a dynamic asset and an income source.

Ideally, cash management in an inflationary economy uses daily forecasting of cash balances. Idle funds can then be invested to return additional income. Outstanding funds should be charted to facilitate appropriate long-term cash investments.

## INVESTMENT-ORIENTED CASH MANAGEMENT

Investment-oriented cash management involves three primary decision areas:

- Financial considerations in developing a cash management program.
- Choice of optimizing technique to be used.
- Choice of the forecasting model to predict cash balances.

### Financial Considerations

For long-term success, a cash management program must be grounded on solid internal and external financial procedures, including the following:

- Concentration of corporate funds.
- Establishment of a line of credit.
- Determination of use and cost of borrowed funds.

*Concentration of Funds.* Firms may receive funds from a widespread geographical area. These funds must be centralized for three main reasons:

- To provide control of total corporate cash resources.
- To concentrate responsibility for management and investment of corporate funds.
- To generate cash consciousness within the corporation at all levels.

Probably the best method of centralizing funds is to arrange for wire transfers from local banks to one central collecting bank. Experience has shown that charges for such transfers are more than offset by revenue generated by way of consolidated funds.

Consolidation of accounts payable can have significant financial benefits too. If accounts payable are centralized, the firm can control payments to make maximum investment use of its cash resources. For instance, if no discount is given for prompt payment of a specific account payable, disbursement can be withheld until the due date. Such money is held in the company's account up to 60 days longer than it would have been if immediate payment had been made, and it generates income, since the funds can be invested during the holding period. Additionally, if accounts payable are centralized, the need for operating cash is reduced at the local level.

Fund consolidation also aids investment. Although cash amounts that would be held by individual operations might not be large enough to justify investments, pooling of funds open up short-term investment opportunities not available at the local level.

*Line of Credit.* Overly optimistic forecasts of available funds may occur from time to time. A line of credit should be established with the bank holding the firm's centralized fund, to cover deviations from projections. The cost of this line of credit varies and is somewhat negotiable. Generally cost is based on maintaining compensating balances—between 10 and 20 percent of the total line of credit.

The size of the line of credit required depends on experience with the cash forecasting model. Over a period of time, experience will indicate the upper limit needed for the line of credit. Adjustments to the model should be made accordingly, to limit future inaccurate forecasts.

The line of credit is used simply for short-term borrowing when cash forecasts fall short and more cash is invested than is actually available. It provides a safety factor.

*Cost of Borrowed Funds.* When cash that has been invested exceeds cash on hand, money should be borrowed from the line of credit for the short-term period required. Interest charges on these borrowings usually range from the prime rate to prime rate plus 1 percent.

In considering costs for short-term borrowing, the important factor is not how much is borrowed but how frequently borrowing occurs. If a consistent pattern of borrowing emerges, the forecasting model should be reviewed to determine causes of deficits in cash income.

The company should determine the point at which it considers borrowing excessive. This decision usually involves the degree of increased profitability from the cash management program, compared to the costs of borrowing.

### Optimizing the Cash Management Program

Optimum goals to be achieved by a profit-oriented cash management program vary from company to company. Such goals depend on the balance of risk and related profit a company expects to experience, and they are hinged to the firm's business objectives. A conservative firm with a strong cash position, for example, will probably keep borrowing of all types to a minimum. In such a case, the conservative firm must expect to suffer lost opportunity costs in the form of underinvested funds.

On the other hand, an aggressive company that invests all funds available each day will undoubtedly make occasional overestimates of the funds available. The company must then draw on its line of credit. Resulting costs of borrowing are an expense of optimizing for the aggressive firm.

In cash management optimization, then, the decisive factor is corporate philosophy regarding investment of funds. Corporate decisions affect the cash management program in the following key areas:

• Formulating company policy regarding overdrafts.
• Defining the maximum allowed borrowing (either in total dollars or frequency of borrowing).
• Establishing size of the line of credit.
• Establishing investment criteria.
• Ability and willingness to alter internal cash handling policies.

As a basic guideline, the maximum amount to be borrowed should reflect the point at which borrowing additional funds will not generate sufficient investment income to cover the cost of borrowing. Size of the line of credit, however, has an important effect on profits stemming from the cash management program. It effectively determines how much cash can be invested on any given day. With an adequate line of credit, larger long-term investments *without* reserve financing are possible.

Existing banking relationships will play an important role in determining size of the line of credit available to a specific company. Credit-line size should also be compatible with company objectives. Generally the larger the line of credit, the more flexible and profitable the results of the cash management program.

In making risk versus profit decisions, the following factors are of primary importance to most corporations:

Security.
Marketability of investments.
Yield.

Since the funds invested must be readily available to the corporation on a day-to-day basis (except for committed long-term funds), the combination of these factors is essential to a sound cash management program.

Some of the securities available for short- and long-range investment of funds are as follows:

U.S. Treasury bills.
Federal agency issues.

Negotiable certificates of deposit.

Commercial paper.

Repurchase agreements.

Changing company procedures to centralize cash and accounts payable on a daily basis is often the key to successful inflation cash management. Retraining of corporate field personnel is required. Centralization necessitates extensive interoffice coordination to facilitate daily fund transfers to the concentration point.

### Forecasting to Predict Cash Balances

An accurate, workable cash forecasting method is at the heart of any successful cash management program. As already indicated, traditional accounting-oriented approaches to flow of funds are inappropriate because they do not supply daily cash balance information. Quarterly projected cash requirements are necessary for major short-term planning, but they are of little value in pinpointing daily cash fluctuations that can be profitably invested.

Two major cash forecasting model types have been developed to overcome this problem: micro models and macromathematical models.

*Micro Models.*  A micro cash forecasting model is developed from the smallest unit of business activity. It forecasts the outstanding cash balance for the next day or other period. The model is used to estimate cash balances in the future. It is based on all the company's cash-related accounts. All cash income and dispersals are detailed on a daily basis.

Experience shows that micro forecasting models present some significant problems, the extent depending on the size and centralization of the company. Corporations with a wide geographical spread of operations, for example, have difficulty tracing each cash transaction on any given day. Extensive retraining of personnel and substantial data processing programming are required to develop a workable system. Disruption of existing corporate procedures at the lowest operating level, and increased clerical and administrative expenses, may create operational problems disproportionate to the benefits realized.

For these reasons, some companies find the micro forecasting approach impractical.

*Macromathematical Models.*  A macromathematical model is one that statistically forecasts the total dollars available for corporate investment. Fluctuations of cash receipts or cash disbursements are not taken into account on a daily basis. Rather, the forecast is based on average daily balances, adjusted to include recent experiences and modified to conform to corporate policies. In effect, the macromathematical model develops a set of statistics to accurately reflect the cash position of the company on a daily basis.

The main advantage of this approach is that it focuses attention on the actual number of dollars available for daily investing; emphasis is placed on the net result of cash inputs and outputs throughout the corporation. Another advantage is that macromathematical models can be computer programmed and simulated to achieve optimum forecasting. The program should be written to maintain constraints established by corporate policy assumptions about investment levels. Established management policies can be added to the system to modify financial projections.

Three problems are usually associated with macromathematical models:

• Achieving management acceptance.
• Developing internal technical expertise to plan and implement the model.
• Selecting an effective method for the company to produce reliable results for the forecast period.

In relation to the extensive work needed to develop micro models, however, the mathematical approach offers a fast, relatively efficient method of beginning a cash management program. Safeguards may be introduced in macromathematical models to reflect changing characteristics of the corporate environment—including inflationary conditions. Extent of model responsiveness can be controlled within constraints established by management.

In general, it is recommended that those wishing to develop an integrated cash management program use the macromathematical model as a starting point. Depending on corporate cash management philosophy, the macromathematical approach should optimize performance of the cash management function.[2]

Dynamic cash management, then, can be used to help overcome the erosionary effects of inflation on idle cash, as well as to generate corporate revenue. Prior to setting up a profit-oriented cash management plan, management must define parameters for the program. These corporate decisions should take into account the following:

• Ability to concentrate funds for investment.
• Acceptable types of investments, as related to their risk levels.

[2] For an excellent step-by-step guide to developing a macromathematical model, see Paul J. Beehler, "Cash Management: Forecasting for Profit," *Management Advisor,* July/August 1973, p. 40.

- Availability and use of lines of credit.
- Management philosophy on impact of long-term levels of invested funds.

Selection of the optimal forecasting model should be based on the investment requirements of the corporation. Additionally, performance should be evaluated continually, and corrective steps should be initiated when needed.

During inflationary periods, cash should be as profitably used as any other corporate resource. Dynamic cash management can convert idle cash from a liability of doing business to a working asset.

## SUGGESTED FURTHER READING

Beehler, Paul J., "Cash Management Forecasting for Profit," *Management Advisor,* July 1973, p. 40.

Betancourt, R. C., "Plan Your Own Cash Flow System," *Financial Executive,* January 1975, pp. 28–30.

Hunt, P., "Funds Position: Keystone in Financial Planning," *Harvard Business Review,* May 1975, pp. 106–115.

Seed, A. H., "Needed: Strategies to Improve Cash Flow," *Management Review,* March 1975, pp. 11–18.

# 14

## COLUMNAR WORKSHEET METHOD

*Outlines an inflation accounting technique that produces a detailed profit and loss account, as well as double-entry accounting for checking accuracy.*

The columnar worksheet method is an *inflation accounting* technique (see p. 179) for converting financial statements from historic figures to dollars expressed in terms of current purchasing power. The technique requires a slightly greater amount of work than the *net change method* (see p. 236), but has the following advantages:

• Produces a detailed profit and loss account, with the accompanying information about a company's current purchasing power profit and loss.
• Uses double-entry accounting, making it easier to check work accuracy.

The method can be most conveniently outlined by division into a number of steps.

### STEP ONE

Prepare the basic accounts for the present and immediately preceding periods. (See Tables 7, 8, and 9, prepared for a company at the end of its sixth year, with comparable figures for Year 5.)

### STEP TWO

Obtain Consumer Price Index figures for the past 6 years, ending on the balance sheet data (Table 10).

### STEP THREE

Transpose the figures that produced the Balance Sheet and the Profit and Loss Account for the present period to a worksheet having the following

**Table 7  Balance Sheet for Year 6<sup>a</sup> ($000)**

Year 5

| | | | | |
|---|---|---|---|---|
| | | **Share capital and reserves** | | |
| 500 | | Ordinary share capital | | 500 |
| 246 | | Undistributed profit | | 309 |
| 746 | | Total equity interest | | 809 |
| | | **Loan capital** | | |
| 200 | | Debenture | | 200 |
| 34 | | **Tax equalization account** | | 39 |
| | | Current liabilities | | |
| | 270 | Creditors | 300 | |
| | 35 | Proposed dividend | 40 | |
| | 70 | Current taxation | 77 | |
| 375 | | | | 417 |
| 1355 | | | | 1465 |
| | | **Fixed assets** | | |
| | 100 | Property | 100 | |
| | 10 | Less depreciation | 12 | |
| 90 | | | | 88 |
| | 700 | Plant and machinery | 800 | |
| | 270 | Less depreciation | 350 | |
| 430 | | | | 450 |
| 520 | | | | 538 |
| | | **Investments** | | |
| | 10 | Fixed interest | 10 | |
| | 10 | Equity | 10 | |
| 20 | | | | 20 |
| | | **Current assests** | | |
| | 440 | Stock | 480 | |
| | 290 | Debtors | 320 | |
| | 85 | Cash | 107 | |
| 815 | | | | 907 |
| 1355 | | | | 1465 |

<sup>a</sup> *Source: Accounting for Inflation,* London, 1973, Part II, p. 15. Reproduced and adapted by permission of The Institute of Chartered Accountants in England and Wales.

**Table 8   Profit and Loss Account for Year 6[a] ($000)**

| Year 5 | | | | |
|---|---|---|---|---|
| 1750 | | Sales | | 1920 |
| | | Cost of sales | | |
| | 400 | Stock at beginning of period[b] | 440 | |
| | 1090 | Purchases[b] | 1190 | |
| | 1490 | | 1630 | |
| | 440 | Stock at end of period[b] | 480 | |
| | 1050 | | | 1150 |
| | 431 | Expenses (other than depreciation) | | 471 |
| | 72 | Depreciation | | 82 |
| 1553 | | | | 1703 |
| 197 | | Operating profit | | 217 |
| 2 | | Investment income | | 2 |
| 199 | | | | 219 |
| 14 | | Debenture interest | | 14 |
| 185 | | Profit before tax | | 205 |
| 74 | | Tax | | 82 |
| 111 | | Profit after tax | | 123 |
| 190 | | Balance at beginning of year | | 246 |
| 301 | | | | 369 |
| | | Dividends | | |
| | 20 | Ordinary—interim | | 20 |
| | 35 | —final | | 40 |
| 55 | | | | 60 |
| 246 | | Balance at end of year | | 309 |

[a] Source: *Accounting for Inflation,* Part II, p. 16. Reproduced by permission of The Institute of Chartered Accountants in England and Wales.
[b] These items would not normally appear in the published accounts of a company. They are included to help clarify this example.

## Table 9  Columnar Work Sheet for Year 6[a]

|  | All figures in thousands of historic dollars[c] | | | | | |
|---|---|---|---|---|---|---|
|  | Balance sheet at beginning of year | Net monetary assets account | Closing items and Journal entries | | Profit and loss account for year | Balance sheet at end of year |
| Items[b] | 1 | 2 | Debit 3 | Credit 4 | 5 | 6 |
| Debentures (B) | (200) | (200) |  |  |  |  |
| Debentures (E) |  | 200 |  |  |  | (200) |
| Tax equalization account (B) | (34) | (34) |  |  |  |  |
| Tax equalization account (E) |  | 39 |  |  |  | (39) |
| Creditors (B) | (270) | (270) |  |  |  |  |
| Creditors (E) |  | 300 |  |  |  | (300) |
| Proposed dividend (B) | (35) | (35) |  |  |  |  |
| Proposed dividend (E) |  | 40 |  |  |  | (40) |
| Current taxation (B) | (70) | (70) |  |  |  |  |
| Current taxation (E) |  | 77 |  |  |  | (77) |
| Property | 100 |  |  |  |  | 100 |
| Depreciation | (10) |  | 2 | 2 | 2 | (12) |
| Plant and machinery | 700 | (100) |  |  |  | 800 |
| Depreciation | (270) |  | 80 | 80 | 80 | (350) |
| Fixed-interest investments (B) | 10 | 10 |  |  |  |  |
| Fixed-interest investments (E) |  | (10) |  |  |  | 10 |
| Equity investments | 10 |  |  |  |  | 10 |
| Stock (B) | 440 |  |  |  | 440 |  |
| Stock (E) |  |  | 480 | 480 | (480) | 480 |
| Debtors (B) | 290 | 290 |  |  |  |  |
| Debtors (E) |  | (320) |  |  |  | 320 |
| Cash (B) | 85 | 85 |  |  |  |  |
| Cash (E) |  | (107) |  |  |  | 107 |
| Sales |  | 1920 |  |  | (1920) |  |
| Investment income |  | 2 |  |  | (2) |  |
| Purchases |  | (1190) |  |  | 1190 |  |
| Expenses |  | (471) |  |  | 471 |  |
| Debenture interest |  | (14) |  |  | 14 |  |
| Tax on profits of the year |  | (82) |  |  | 82 |  |
| Subtotals |  |  |  |  |  |  |
| Gain on net monetary liabilities |  |  |  |  |  |  |
| Dividends—ordinary interim paid |  | (20) |  |  | 20 |  |
| Dividends—ordinary final proposed |  | (40) |  |  | 40 |  |
| Equity interest (B) | (746) |  |  |  |  | (746) |
| Subtotals |  |  |  |  |  |  |
| Retained profit for year |  |  |  |  | 63 | (63) |
| Gain on net monetary liabilities |  |  |  |  |  |  |
| Totals (Dr + Cr) | 1635 | 2963 | 562 | 562 | 2402 | 1827 |

[a] Source: Accounting for Inflation, Part II, pp. 18–19. Reproduced and adapted by mission of The Institute of Chartered Accountants of England and Wales.

**Table 9** (Continued)

| | All figures in thousands of dollars of current purchasing power (12/31/6)[c] | | | | | |
|---|---|---|---|---|---|---|
| Conversion note 7 | Balance sheet at beginning of year 8 | Net monetary assets account 9 | Closing items and Journal entries | | Profit and loss account for year 12 | Balance sheet at end of year 13 |
| | | | Debit 10 | Credit 11 | | |
| 1 | (212.0) | (212.0) | | | | |
| 2 | | 200.0 | | | | |
| 1 | (36.0) | (36.0) | | | | (200.0) |
| | | | | | | |
| 2 | | 39.0 | | | | |
| 1 | (286.2) | (286.2) | | | | (39.0) |
| 2 | | 300.0 | | | | (300.0) |
| | | | | | | |
| 1 | (37.1) | (37.1) | | | | |
| 2 | | 40.0 | | | | |
| 1 | (74.2) | (74.2) | | | | (40.0) |
| | | | | | | |
| 2 | | 77.0 | | | | (77.0) |
| 3 | 129.0 | | | | | 129.0 |
| 3 | (12.9) | | 2.6 | 2.6 | 2.6 | (15.5) |
| 3 | 857.7 | (102.9) | | | | 960.6 |
| 3 | (339.3) | | 96.2 | 96.2 | 96.2 | (435.5) |
| 1 | 10.6 | 10.6 | | | | |
| 2 | | (10.0) | | | | 10.0 |
| 4 | 12.9 | | | | | 12.9 |
| 5 | 468.2 | | | | 468.2 | |
| 6 | | | 483.4 | 483.4 | (483.4) | 483.4 |
| 1 | 307.4 | 307.4 | | | | |
| 2 | | (320.0) | | | | 320.0 |
| 1 | 90.1 | 90.1 | | | | |
| 2 | | (107.0) | | | | 107.0 |
| 7 | | 1975.7 | | | (1975.7) | |
| 7 | | 2.1 | | | (2.1) | |
| 7 | | (1224.5) | | | 1224.5 | |
| 7 | | (484.7) | | | 484.7 | |
| 7 | | (14.4) | | | 14.4 | |
| 8 | | (82.0) | | | 82.0 | |
| — | (997.7) | | | | | |
| | 1875.9 | | | | | |
| | | | | | → (9.7) | |
| 9 | | (20.6) | | | 20.6 | |
| 10 | | (40.0) | | | 40.0 | |
| — | (878.2) | | | | | (878.2) |
| — | | (3051.6) | | | | |
| | | 3041.9 | | | | |
| — | | | | | 37.7 | (37.7) |
| — | | 9.7 ← | | | | |
| | 1875.9 | 3051.6 | 582.2 | 582.2 | 2470.9 | 2022.9 |

[b] B = beginning of year; E = end of year.　　　[c] Parentheses indicate credit.

Table 10    Consumer Price Index[a, b]

| Year | Average | End | Increase during year |
|---|---|---|---|
| 1 | 102.0 | 104.0 | 4% |
| 2 | 106.2 | 108.2 | 4% |
| 3 | 110.5 | 112.5 | 4% |
| 4 | 114.8 | 117.0 | 4% |
| 5 | 119.4 | 121.7 | 4% |
| 6 | 125.4 | 129.0 | 6% |

[a] *Source: Accounting for Inflation,* Part II, p. 17. Reproduced by permission of The Institute of Chartered Accountants of England and Wales.
[b] January 1 of Year 1 = 100.

columns: Balance Sheet at the beginning of the period, Net Monetary Assets account, Closing Items and Journal Entries, Profit and Loss Account for the period, and Balance Sheet at the end of the period.

The first six columns of Table 9 show the workings of Tables 7 and 8 transposed as outlined in the preceding paragraph. The same columns have been used for both debits and credits; debit figures are plain, credit figures are in parentheses. Totals at the foot of each column represent the total of the debits and also the total of the credits. Debit subtotals are plain, credit subtotals in parentheses.

The Net Monetary Assets column is like a cash account. It links the Balance Sheet at the beginning of the reporting with the Profit and Loss Account for the period and the Balance Sheet at year's end. All balances and transactions involving monetary assets and liabilities are entered here, as are balances, receipts, and payments in cash.

Three closing journal items must be taken into account:

• The Profit and Loss Account must be debited ($2) and Cumulative Depreciation (Property) in the Balance Sheet must be credited ($2). This represents property depreciation for the period.
• The Profit and Loss Account must be debited ($80) and Cumulative Depreciation (Plant and Machinery) in the Balance Sheet must be credited ($80). This represents plant and machinery depreciation for the period.
• The Balance Sheet must be debited ($480) and the Profit and Loss Account must be credited ($480). This is the stock at the end of the reporting period.

## STEP FOUR

Items in the Balance Sheet at the beginning of the period (Column 1) must be converted into "real value" dollars in terms of current purchasing power at the end of the period. The new figures are entered in Column 8.

To convert historic dollars to "real value" dollars, each figure is multiplied by the index at the end of the reporting year, then divided by the index at the time of the original transaction. Thus a sample is as follows:

$$\$200 \times 129 \div 121.7 = \$212$$

where $\$200.0$ = figure to be converted

$129.0$ = index at end of year

$121.7$ = index at beginning of year (time of original transaction)

The notes in Table 11 will aid in fully understanding the methods used in

**Table 11  Notes for Column 7, Table 9**[a]

1. Monetary item at beginning of year, conversion factor therefore $129.0/121.7 = 1.060$.

2. Monetary item at end of year, therefore no conversion required.

3. Nonmonetary item, see Table 12.

4. Nonmonetary item acquired 1/1 of Year 1, therefore conversion factor = $129.0/100.0 = 1.290$.

5. Nonmonetary item acquired evenly over last 3 months of Year 5, index to use is calculated as follows:
the appropriate index is the average of the index at the beginning and end of the last quarter.
The index at 10/1/5 is $(119.4 + 121.7)/2 = 120.6$.
The index at the midpoint of the fourth quarter is $(120.6 + 121.7)/2 = 121.2$.

6. Nonmonetary item acquired evenly over last 3 months of Year 6.
Index to use is calculated as follows:
Index at 10/1/6 is $(125.4 + 129.0)/2 = 127.2$.
The index at the mid-point of the fourth quarter is $(127.2 + 129.0)/2 = 128.1$.

7. Transaction during Year 6. It is reasonable to assume that this transaction occurred evenly throughout the year, therefore use average index for year, which is 125.4. Conversion factor is therefore $129.0/125.4 = 1.029$.

8. This is assumed to occur at the end of the year to ensure that the tax charge is the same in both the historical and current purchasing power accounts. Conversion factor therefore = $1.000$.

9. Paid on 6/30/6. Conversion factor therefore = $129.0/125.4 = 1.029$.

10. Payable at end of year, conversion factor therefore is $1.000$.

[a] *Source: Accounting for Inflation,* Part II, p. 20. Reproduced and adapted by permission of The Institute of Chartered Accountants in England and Wales.

**Table 12  Analysis of Cost and Cumulative Depreciation[a, b]**

| Year of acquisition | Cost ($H) | Cumulative depreciation to end Year 5 ($H) | Cumulative depreciation to end Year 6 ($H) | Factor | Cost ($C) | Cumulative depreciation to end Year 5 ($C) | Cumulative depreciation to end Year 6 ($C) |
|---|---|---|---|---|---|---|---|
| Property | | | | | | | |
| Beginning of Year 1 | 100 | 10 | 12 | 129.0/100.0 = 1.290 | 129.0 | 12.9 | 15.5 |
| Plant and Machinery | | | | | | | |
| Beginning of Year 1 | 400 | 200 | 240 | 129.0/100.0 = 1.290 | 516.0 | 258.0 | 309.6 |
| 2 | 50 | 20 | 25 | 129.0/106.2 = 1.215 | 60.8 | 24.3 | 30.4 |
| 3 | 100 | 30 | 40 | 129.0/110.5 = 1.167 | 116.7 | 35.0 | 46.7 |
| 4 | 50 | 10 | 15 | 129.0/114.8 = 1.124 | 56.2 | 11.2 | 16.9 |
| 5 | 100 | 10 | 20 | 129.0/119.4 = 1.080 | 108.0 | 10.8 | 21.6 |
| Subtotal | 700 | 270 | 340 | | 857.7 | 339.3 | 425.2 |
| 6 | 100 | | 10 | 129.0/125.4 = 1.029 | 102.9 | | 10.3 |
| Total | 800 | | 350 | | 960.6 | | 435.5 |

[a] *Source: Accounting for Inflation*, Part II, p. 13. Reproduced and adapted by permission of The Institute of Chartered Accountants in England and Wales.

[b] $H = thousands of historic dollars; $C = thousands of dollars of current purchasing power at the end of Year 6.

converting each group of figures in Column 8. Column 7 shows which note is most applicable to each item. When converting the figures for property and plant and machinery—and cumulative depreciation on these assets— their acquisition dates must be determined and the appropriate index figure used. These workings have been set out in Table 12.

Total equity interest is *not* converted because it is a balancing item, as explained in Step Seven.

### STEP FIVE

The items in the Net Monetary Assets Account (Column 2) are next converted into dollars in terms of current purchasing power at the end of the year. These "real value" figures are then entered in Column 9. The balances at the beginning of the year need only be copied from Column 8. The balances for the end of the year can be copied from Column 2, since all the items are monetary and their real value and current purchasing power are equal at year's end. With two exceptions, the appropriate indexes for converting the remaining figures are the year-end index (129) and the average index for the year (125.4). Sales, for example, are converted

$$\$1920 \times 129 \div 125.4 = \$1975.12$$

The two exceptions are the final ordinary dividend and the tax on profits. These occurred at the end of the year, rather than evenly throughout the year, and no conversion is required.

It is unlikely that the "real value" debits and credits in Column 9 will equal each other, as they did with historic figures in Column 2. Adjusting this discrepancy is discussed in Step Seven.

### STEP SIX

Next items in the Closing Items and Journal Entries columns are converted into "real value" dollars in terms of current purchasing power at year's end. These items relate to depreciation during the reporting period and stock at the end of the reporting period. The conversion is accomplished as follows:

#### Depreciation

Depreciation can be calculated in two ways:

• By applying the normal depreciation percentages to the current purchasing power figure for the asset's cost at year's end.

• By calculating the difference between the cumulative depreciation figures at the beginning and end of the year (see Table 12).

### Stock

See Note 6 in Table 11.

### STEP SEVEN

As indicated in Step Four, the Balance Sheet at the beginning of Year 6 will not balance when all the items—with the exception of total equity interest—have been converted from historic dollars to "real value" dollars. It is necessary to insert a figure in Column 8 that will make the column balance. This figure represents the dollar value of the total equity interest at the beginning of Year 6 expressed in terms of current purchasing power. Enter the figure also in Column 13, the Balance Sheet at the end of the year.

As stated in Step Five, the Net Monetary Assets column will not balance after conversion from historic dollars to "real value" dollars. This difference is the gain (or loss) on net monetary liabilities, as indicated at the end of Column 9. Being a gain, it is credited in Column 12, the Profit and Loss Account for the year. Had it been a loss, it would have been debited to the Profit and Loss Account.

### STEP EIGHT

Taking the items from Columns 8, 9, 10, and 11, add and subtract them according to the debit and credit signs and enter the results in Column 12 or 13, whichever is appropriate. The Profit and Loss Account balance ($37.7) represents the retained profit for the year. It should be credited to the Balance Sheet, balancing Column 13.

### STEP NINE

The last step is simply the setting out of the figures from Columns 12 and 13 into a traditional format. This has been done in Tables 13 and 14. Historic dollars and dollars in terms of current purchasing power are set adjacent to each other to clearly show the results of conversion.

**Table 13   Balance Sheet for Year 6** [a, b]

| Item | $H | | $C | |
|---|---|---|---|---|
| Total equity interest | | 809 | | 915.9 |
| Loan capital | | | | |
| Debenture | | 200 | | 200.0 |
| Tax equalization account | | 39 | | 39.0 |
| Current liabilities | | | | |
| Creditors | 300 | | 300.0 | |
| Proposed dividend | 40 | | 40.0 | |
| Current taxation | 77 | | 77.0 | |
| | | 417 | | 417.0 |
| | | 1465 | | 1571.9 |
| Fixed assets | | | | |
| Property | 100 | | 129.0 | |
| Less depreciation | 12 | | 15.5 | |
| Net | | 88 | | 113.5 |
| Plant and machinery | 800 | | 960.6 | |
| Less depreciation | 350 | | 435.5 | |
| | | 450 | | 525.1 |
| Investments | | | | |
| Fixed interest | 10 | | 10.0 | |
| Equity | 10 | | 12.9 | |
| | | 20 | | 22.9 |
| Current assets | | | | |
| Stock | 480 | | 483.4 | |
| Debtors | 320 | | 320.0 | |
| Cash | 107 | | 107.0 | |
| | | 907 | | 910.4 |
| | | 1465 | | 1571.9 |

[a] *Source: Accounting for Inflation,* London, 1973, Part II, p. 22. Reproduced and adapted by permission of The Institute of Chartered Accountants in England and Wales.
[b] $H = thousands of historic dollars; $C = thousands of dollars of current purchasing power at the end of Year 6.

**Table 14   Profit and Loss Account for Year 6[a, b]**

| Item | $H | | $C | |
|---|---|---|---|---|
| Sales | | 1920 | | 1975.7 |
| Cost of sales | | | | |
|    Stock at beginning of period[c] | 440 | | 468.2 | |
|    Purchases[c] | 1190 | | 1224.5 | |
| | 1630 | | 1692.7 | |
|    Stock at end of period[c] | 480 | | 483.4 | |
| | 1150 | | 1209.3 | |
| Expenses (other than depreciation) | 471 | | 484.7 | |
| Depreciation | 82 | | 98.8 | |
| | | 1703 | | 1792.8 |
| Operating profit | | 217 | | 182.9 |
| Investment income | | 2 | | 2.1 |
| | | 219 | | 185.0 |
| Debenture interest | | 14 | | 14.4 |
| | | | | 170.6 |
| Net gain resulting from effects of inflation on company's net monetary liabilities | | | | 9.7 |
| Profit before tax | | 205 | | 180.3 |
| Tax | | 82 | | 82.0 |
| Profit after tax | | 123 | | 98.3 |
| Dividends | | | | |
|    Ordinary—interim | 20 | | 20.6 | |
|    Ordinary—final | 40 | | 40.0 | |
| | | 60 | | 60.6 |
| Retained profit for year | | 63 | | 37.7 |

[a] *Source: Accounting for Inflation,* London, 1973, p. 23. Reproduced by permission of The Institute of Chartered Accountants in England and Wales.

[b] $H = thousands of historic dollars; $C = thousands of dollars of current purchasing power at the end of Year 6.

[c] These items would not normally appear in the published accounts of a company. They are included to help clarify this example.

## SUGGESTED FURTHER READING

*Accounting for Inflation* (Parts 1 and 2), The Institute of Chartered Accountants in England and Wales, London, 1973.

Battle, T. Q., "Accounting for Inflation," *Director,* January 1975, p. 26.

Davidson, S. and R. L. Weil, "Inflation Accounting," *Financial Analysts Journal,* January 1975, pp. 27–31.

Monroe, A. L., "Experimenting with Price Level Reporting," *Financial Executive,* December 1974, pp. 38–40.

Vancil, R. F. and J. N. Kelly, "Get Ready for Price-Level-Adjusted Accounting," *Harvard Business Review,* March 1975, pp. 6–8.

Weston, F. T., "Adjust Your Accounting for Inflation," *Harvard Business Review,* January 1975, pp. 22–24.

# SECTION 15

## COMPUTER APPLICATIONS
## IN PURCHASING

*Outlines new uses of computerization to assist purchasing in an economy of inflation and shortages.*

For two decades increased computerization of various purchasing functions has resulted in significant cost savings and efficiencies for most large companies. In a volatile, inflationary economy, however, using computers for purchasing presents difficulties not encountered during normal times.

Traditionally, computers have been used by purchasing departments to limit inventories, maintain large vendor history and rating cards, calculate optimal order sizes, and so on. But during periods of inflation and shortages, lead times on which computer models are based often become totally unpredictable. Additionally since computer models assume stable future prices, they normally recommend minimal order sizes. Because of price increases during inflation, however, optimal order sizes may be significantly larger than those recommended by the computer model.

Vendor rating files can also become unreliable. Vendors themselves lose control in an uncertain economic situation and hesitate to quote firm prices if they cannot be guaranteed. They too have lead-time problems. In this situation computerized vendor standards for timeliness and quality may be rendered inoperative.

For these reasons, and because the purchasing function becomes especially critical during periods of persistent inflation, new computer applications are being developed to respond to changing demands in the economy. In many cases all that is required is new emphasis on already existing applications that have not been widely implemented.

This section outlines a number of new computer applications that can be instrumental in helping the purchasing function operate more efficiently in an inflationary economy.[1]

---

[1] Adapted from Robert B. Fireworker, "Computer Applications in a Volatile Economy," *Journal of Purchasing,* Spring 1975, pp. 5–12.

## LEAD TIMES AND SHORTAGES

Several computer solutions are available for coping with problems associated with long lead times and shortages. If production scheduling requirements and customer orders are systematically fed into the computer, the machine can decide how promptly to translate a requisition order into a purchasing order. Second, the system can allow for advanced query of scheduled orders the buyer anticipates at a later date. This effort can be enhanced if the production-planning department routinely fills out a materials requirement form when it plans future schedules.

This system provides several advantages. It maintains a smooth production flow by not interrupting work in process because of material unavailability or delay. Additionally, it provides better coordination between purchasing and production in the areas of materials substitution and delay in transit. If purchasing is given sufficient advance notice of future materials requirements and is asked to requisition an item rising rapidly in price, it may be able to suggest suitable material alternatives that will meet the quality standards of the product. Furthermore, if the substitution requires product redesign, there may even be sufficient lead time for engineering to carry out needed changes.

### DELIVERY DELAYS

Advance scheduling can also help alleviate problems caused when materials are delayed in transit. With the system, purchasing has lead time to check the status of all outstanding orders due but not yet received by production. If delay is anticipated, purchasing can notify production, to allow rescheduling. Or, if the goods have been received but are being only temporarily delayed by routine inspections, purchasing can inform production that a scheduled run can proceed as planned.

### PERT-TYPE SCHEDULING

A scheduling system based on the program evaluation and review technique (PERT) can help to overcome long lead time and shortage problems. The system can be computerized to identify the shortages that are critical and require prompt attention. The system becomes even more useful if the data base is indexed by commodity as well as supplier. If the PERT scheduling system indicates that a commodity's lead time exceeds its critical point and that material will be unavailable when needed, a coded commodity data base can be used to show the major features of the product—composition, size, durability, and so on. Possible substitutions can then be indexed. For example, if a certain type of rivet has been ordered but will arrive late, computerized commodity coding can suggest substitutions having shorter lead times.

The coding system may also be used to reflect corporate policy. For instance, if a great many routine commodities do not involve any inspection delays upon receipt, the code can indicate this, causing these commodities to be sent directly to production.

A computer data base indexed by supplier's name can also be developed, to help rectify late delivery complaints. A supplier who is presented with a constantly updated record showing all late deliveries should become particularly conscious of the need for promptness.

## PRICE CONSIDERATIONS

Erratic price fluctuation, one of the greatest problems faced by purchasing in an inflationary environment, has created a need for frequently updated price forecasts, substitution studies, variance reports to accounting, and follow-up of prices of recent purchases from different vendors. All these can be most efficiently accomplished by computerization.

For purchasing, any negotiations for long-term contracts depend on a reasonable estimation of future costs. Additionally, since many companies spend most of their operating cost on raw materials, it is critical that the sales prices be set to allow for probable future prices for raw materials. Also, make-or-buy decisions are heavily influenced by future price considerations.

The computer can identify best production strategy resulting from price forecasts of materials in a specific product. Forecasts can also be based on a broad series of leading or lagging economic indicators. Fluctuations in many of them can be weighted to reflect specific commodity price forecasts of interest to purchasing. The procedure can even be broken down by commodity, using different indicators and/or weights to forecast prices for various commodities.

Last, an interrelationship of variables can be programmed to yield an econometric forecast. Simulations for alternative economic conditions can be performed to detect their overall impact on future prices.

Substitution studies, with respect to price fluctuations, require coordination between purchasing and engineering. As soon as purchasing anticipates a significant price rise in a component specified by engineering, it can check the commodity-indexed data base for possible substitute parts less adversely affected by impending price increases. Possible substitutions can be submitted to engineering for evaluation. If a substitution is found that is agreeable to engineering and production, a purchase order for this commodity can be programmed to override the former, more costly one.

## PRICE FORECASTS AND ACCOUNTING

Adequate price forecasts and detailed records of actual costs can aid accounting in the form of variance reports. This is especially true when firm prices on contracts are unavailable, for then projected cash flows can be erroneously high.

In such cases purchasing can run a computer check on all accounts payable data against the previously assumed standard costs. This reveals variances before accounting realizes that a deviation has occurred. A forecasting system of this type can also project future commitments in upcoming contracts. This information can help accounting forecast more accurate cash flows.

## PURCHASING/DISTRIBUTION COORDINATION

Many of the innovations in purchasing are the result of increased computerization by distributors. Pressed to cut costs and provide more efficient customer service, more distributors are making use of a wide variety of computer applications. The future will bring considerably more coordination between the computerization efforts of purchasing and distribution. Some of the more important applications are covered next.

*Profit Margin per Item Analysis.* In the past, most distributors had only a vague idea of each item's continually changing profit margin. Recent price fluctuations have made this problem even more critical. Often the distributor has not been able to grant price concessions simply because of lack of updated profit margin information.

Recent computer applications, however, make analysis of profit margin per item much more scientific. This should benefit purchasing by making closer price breaks more feasible.

*Purchaser/Manufacturer Communications Link.* A computer link between purchaser and distributor lets the distributor rapidly update and consolidate orders for specific products. Minimum order volumes and maximum waiting time for any customer's order can be easily programmed, enabling the distributor to negotiate with the manufacturer from a position of strength based on volume. In periods of shortages, this can help the distributor obtain a fair share of the manufacturer's production for his purchasers.

*Advanced Allocations.* Through terminal connections to the inventory records of large-volume purchasers, a distributor can maintain inventory management data on his customers' buying needs and habits. The distributor's computer can then issue automatic checks and order requisitions on behalf of customers, allowing adequate lead times. This advance allocation benefits both purchaser and distributor. The purchaser gains in a shortage crisis because his requirements have already been allocated. The manufacturer, in turn, is better equipped for his production and planning needs. The distributor benefits through not having to carry such large inventories to meet customer needs.

*Analysis of Product Turnover Rates.* The distribution operation is essentially based on turnover, and a product that moves quickly off a distributor's shelf deserves a lower price. Until computerization, however, it was impossible to reflect the turnover rate on each item, and distributors were forced to work with a few broad markup categories. Recent computer applications have increasingly documented product turnover rates, and inventory management files of the distributor can now include product turnover rates on the entire stock carried. This should result in more equitable pricing in the future.

*Analysis of Product Turnover Rates for Major Customers.* Through computerization, distributors can maintain accurate data on major customer usage rates. The large customer for a given product should be given a price concession to reflect his volume. If the distributor's files are indexed by commodity and purchaser, the needed data are available to grant the discount. Criteria for the size of the discount can also be computed in relation to the volume of each product, insuring a systematic price discounting procedure that best reflects true costs.

## SUGGESTED FURTHER READING

Fireworker, Robert B., "Computer Applications in a Volatile Economy," *Journal of Purchasing,* Spring 1975, pp. 5–12.

# SECTION 16

## COMPUTER MODEL

*Presents a computer model to help select coherent product mixes, manufacturing processes, market strategies, and prices, to safeguard company profits from inflationary erosion.*

The pressure that inflation exerts on company profits is obvious. If a fixed revenue declines in value while costs escalate, profits are squeezed.

The company operating in an environment of sharply rising costs can defend itself from this squeeze in a number of ways. The defense strategy presented in this section[1] is based on a computerized model developed from the experience of several international corporations that have learned to operate in countries in which runaway inflation has posed a critical threat to business.

### GAUGING A CORPORATION'S RATE OF INFLATION

A corporation's personal rate of inflation is determined by two factors—the change in the price index of its inputs and the change in the price index of its outputs, or products.

Inputs typically include labor, raw materials, and imported products—the components that make up a company's costs. Outputs are the components that make up a corporation's sales revenues.

The indexes of these two components are the critical variables management should examine when studying the impact of rising prices on its strategies. Since profits are simply the difference between sales revenues and costs, profits are squeezed when inflation affects costs more than revenues. If both indexes are equal, the company's cash flow and profit margins are protected from inflation. If prices inflate faster than costs, the output index might well exceed the input one, and profits would rise.

To control the impact of inflation, then, a company must keep these two indexes in proper balance. This is what the computer model helps management accomplish.

[1] Adapted from Bernard A. Lietaer, "Prepare Your Company for Inflation," *Harvard Business Review,* September/October, 1970, pp. 113–125.

**Table 15  Computation of a Company's Inflation Indexes in France[a]**

| | Thousands of units $a_i$ | September 1970 price (francs), $b_i$ | September 1971 price (francs) | September 1971 index, $c_i$ | Input inflation index (weighted averages of product input) |
|---|---|---|---|---|---|
| Product A (100,000 produced) | | | | | |
| Local labor (man-hours) | 5 | 200 | 220 | 110 | |
| Local raw materials (lb) | 10 | 500 | 700 | 140 } 123.33[b] | |
| Imported raw materials (lb) | 10 | 300 | 300 | 100 | 126.61[c] |
| Product B (250,000 produced) | | | | | |
| Local labor (man-hours) | 20 | 200 | 220 | 110 | |
| Local raw materials (lb) | 25 | 600 | 800 | 133 } 128.16 | |

| | Thousands of sales units | Present price (francs) | Future price (francs) | Future index | Output inflation index (weighted averages of product output) |
|---|---|---|---|---|---|
| Product A | | | | | |
| Local market | 50 | 120 | 144 | 120 | |
| Export market | 50 | 120 | 120 | 100 } 110 | |
| Product B | | | | | |
| Local market | 100 | 100 | 100 | 100 | |
| Export market | 100 | 100 | 100 | 100 } 100 | 103.24 |

[a] *Source:* Lietaer, "Prepare Your Company for Inflation," *Harvard Business Review,* September/October, 1970, p. 116.

[b] Computed as $\sum_{i=1}^{3} a_i b_i c_i \left[ \sum_{i=1}^{3} a_i b_i \right]^{-1}$.

[c] Computed as $\sum_{i=1}^{5} a_i b_i c_i \left[ \sum_{i=1}^{5} a_i b_i \right]^{-1}$.

Table 15 illustrates the computation of these two indexes for two products, A and B, made in France by an American firm. Both indexes are for the same time period and for the same volume of products manufactured and sold. The following assumptions are used for a one-year period:

- The cost of local labor will rise 10 percent.
- The costs of raw materials will rise 40 percent for product A and 33 percent for product B.
- Import and export prices will remain stable.
- The sales price of product A can be increased by 20 percent in the local market.
- The government will freeze product B's price at present levels for the next year.

Using these assumptions, the input inflation index in Table 15 is 126.61, and the output inflation index will be only 103.24. Obviously profits on products A and B are in danger. What can management do to maintain profit margins?

## CONTROLLING THE IMPACT

As outlined previously, management must guarantee that the sales receipts on products are higher than the replacement costs. Four strategies are available.

### Increase Prices

When there are no price controls, the easiest and most obvious solution is to increase prices. Unfortunately, the method is often self-defeating, for it contributes most to the total inflation of the economy.

### Rearrange Suppliers and Markets, Locally and Abroad

If a company is operating in a country plagued by sharply rising inflation, it could start purchasing abroad, in areas where there is less inflation. At the same time, efforts could be made to sell more in the operating country, where prices are rising. If the inflationary situation reverses itself, suppliers and markets might again be shifted, but in the opposite direction. Of course import and export regulations might be imposed, and the shifts would have to be performed within such limitations.

### Adapt Production Processes to Minimize the Inflation of Inputs

New processes with varying types or amounts of raw materials or labor can be adopted to cut costs. Automation has been the classic response when labor cost increases exceed other inputs.

### Modify the Product Mix of the Corporation

If profits on a particular product are being consistently reduced, production of the item can be slowed and the productive capacity used for more profitable areas. This strategy attacks a company's personal inflation rate at its source. In deciding what to make and how to sell it, a firm, in sum, fixes its own corporate inflation rate.


### PROBLEMS

During persistent inflation a company may have to maintain profitability by the simultaneous use of all four of the techniques just described. Moreover, the options can become very complex, as can be seen by returning to the example of the American firm in France.

Obviously product B should be dropped entirely as a defense against inflation, since its input inflation index will rise to 128.16 while its sales price is frozen.

However other factors are involved. The product may keep 80 percent of the labor force occupied; heavy investment has been made in facilities and machinery; market position may be lost indefinitely, and so on. Or, if production capacity was shifted from product B to product A, the market may not be able to absorb the additional quantities of product A. The company could start producing a new product—but which one? Made by what process? Offered for sale where?

Additionally, there are uncertainties about inflation rates, costs, and market demand. Not all these entities can be forecast with absolute assurance, and the firm would have to take this factor into account.

Finally, a company's freedom to change its product mix is hampered by a wide range of regulations and constraints. Export-import regulations may restrict raw material imports. Or, there could be monetary exchange limitations. Union regulations—or company social concern—may prevent the dismissal of any laborers. Also, there is the fundamental question of "What industry are we in?" A company must consider the practical, mechanical restraints on its modifications of product mix.

Regrouping a company's product mix generally is complicated by three factors.

• The interlocking web of decisions, made in the past, that constitute a company's general policy and product-management strategy.
• The uncertainty of the information and forecasts on which the regrouping must be based.
• The government regulations, company goals, and other restraints to fashioning the new grouping.

The computer model that follows brings these factors under management's control.

### THE MODEL

The model adjusts product mix to maximize the expected market value of company production and to minimize the expected variable replacement costs of this production. Thus it maximizes the expected profit margin.

At the same time the model minimizes the unpredictability of total earnings. This variability could be the result of the uncertainty of forecasted inflation, costs, or market response.

The "expected market value of production" is defined as the dollar receipts generated by the sales of the products in the export as well as the local markets.

The definition of "variable replacement costs" is less obvious, since it depends on the time period that the model considers. This period is the span between the time management decides on a product strategy and the time revenues are received. Thus it includes the ordering of raw materials, the production cycle, the inventory period, the sales, and the credit terms of sales. In addition, any costs that are changing according to the quantity of products turned out during this time period must be considered variable costs.

In short, the model considers *all* the variable expenses required to reproduce the product in that future period when cash will be received to be costs of the product. The model will select the product mix that will minimize the total variable replacement cost.

The "minimization of earnings variability" is more complicated still. A strategy is optimal when it corresponds to the highest expected profit margins of a given level of variability in earnings. Thus there is no single optimal strategy, but an infinite set of them.

At one extreme is the product mix strategy that gives the lowest possible

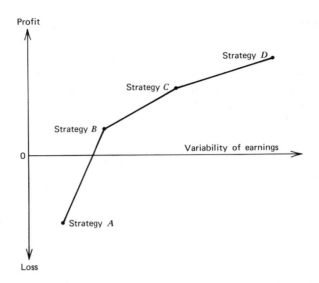

**Figure 3**   The efficient frontier of corporate strategies. (*Source:* Lietaer, "Prepare Your Company for Inflation," *Harvard Business Review*, September/October, 1970.)

uncertainty about earnings; it typically corresponds to a product mix for which production costs are very predictable and stable, and the market is reliable and well known. As might be expected, the profit margins are seldom remarkably high.

At the other extreme is the product mix strategy with the highest possible profit expectations but much less certainty of earnings. In between, there are strategies that trade off expected profit margins against the reliability of earnings flows. Among all these options, management can select the one best suiting its own conception about the proportionate value of safety and profit opportunity.

Mathematically, all the optimal solutions can be represented as a line on a graph, as in Figure 3.

The product mix involving the lowest risk, or the lowest variability in earnings (strategy A) actually has a negative expected profit margin—a loss. More aggressive strategies (B and C) have a higher profit potential but also higher variability. The most aggressive product mix (strategy D) has a sizable expected profit margin but a substantial uncertainty in the cash flow.

## MODEL INFORMATION REQUIREMENTS

Information required for the model includes standard data on all the variables already outlined. To use the model, the following steps must be taken.

• Management must determine the total planning horizon and divide it into time periods. The planning horizon will be at least as long as the longest product cycle—that is, the time between ordering of raw materials and the receipt of cash from sales. Time periods are merely convenient fractions of this total planning horizon. For example, if the longest product cycle is 1½ years, management could select a total planning horizon of 2 years with four 6-month time periods.

• Management must list all the possible products the company is willing to make. Then for each product it must list a set of practical alternative production processes, along with the product's particular input requirements and mechanical restraints. For example, a manufacturer's list of potential products might include ventilators made from different materials and pumps of varying types (Table 16). A product list ordinarily involves many more items and more complex combinations of raw materials.

• Management must determine the general inflation rate predicted for the planning horizon and forecast the likely increase due to inflation for each input cost.

To do this, management must obtain forecasts of a basic common infla-

**Table 16   List of Potential Products of a Light Equipment Manufacturer**[a]

| Product | Process | Material | Pounds/ 100 units produced | Labor nan-days/ 100 units produced |
|---|---|---|---|---|
| Ventilator, | Plastic molding | Plastic | 350 | 2 |
| type Z | Injected aluminum | Aluminum | 600 | 3 |
|  | Welded plate | Steel plate | 500 | 35 |
|  | Stamping | Steel plate | 400 | 5 |
| Pump, type X | Castings | Iron | 800 | 20 |
| Pump, type Y | Castings | Iron | 600 | 30 |

[a] Source: Lietaer, "Prepare Your Company for Inflation," Harvard Business Review, September/October, 1970, p. 119.

tion index of the whole economy for each of the time periods of the model. This could be the Consumer Price Index, the GNP deflator, or any other price index that is suitable. These forecasts must provide three inflation rate values for each time unit: (*a*)the minimum inflation rate possible, (*b*)the inflation rate most likely to occur, and (*c*)the maximum inflation rate possible. For example, management could forecast a basic inflation of between 5 and 10 percent, with a most likely rate of 7 percent.

Determining the inflation of individual input costs is not easy. Management must develop estimates of the *basic* price of each input at the beginning of each period—that is, of the price of the input *before* inflation—along with the sensitivity of this price to the overall inflation.

Suppose, for example, that the cost of a specific class of labor is likely to be $10/hour at the beginning of the third period, with a projected maximum of $11/hour and a projected minimum of $9/hour. Furthermore, suppose management expects the cost of labor to go up exactly as fast as the overall inflation during this period.

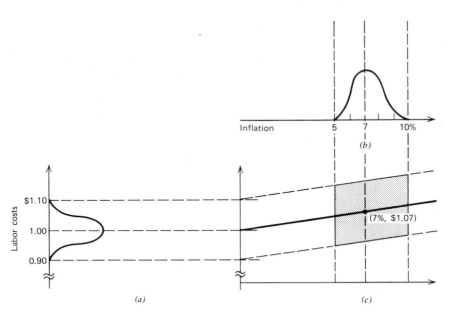

**Figure 4**   Inflation and labor costs—third period. (*a*) Basic cost of this labor in the third period. (*b*) General inflation in the third period. (*c*) Area of actual labor cost for the third period. (*Source:* Lietaer, "Prepare Your Company for Inflation," *Harvard Business Review,* September/October, 1970.)

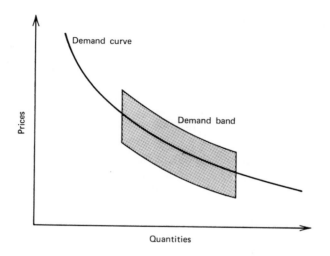

**Figure 5** Demand band. (*Source:* Lietaer, "Prepare Your Company for Inflation," *Harvard Business Review,* September/October, 1970.)

Figure 4 presents the data to be entered on labor costs in the third period. The *expected* cost of labor at the *end* of the period is $10.70 ($10 expected basic cost, plus 7 percent inflation). However the combined effect of the uncertainties of the cost at the beginning of the period and of the inflation rate during the period could result in an actual cost anywhere within the black area of Figure 4c.

For all inputs—labor, local raw materials, and imported goods—graphs like Figure 4 should be prepared for each time period.

• Management must prepare market demand curves for each product during each period. These curves describe the relationship between the price of each product and the quantity sold. The information needed does not have to be as precise as that usually required for demand curves. A "demand band" would perhaps be a more accurate description, because the model requires only a reasonable range of quantities and prices for each product. Uncertainty about this range can also be taken into account. Economists would use the precise demand curve appearing in Figure 5, but the model requires only the demand band (shaded area).

• Management must list all the restrictions under which the product mix has to be modified—mechanical constraints, company policies, government regulations, and so on.

## RESULTS AND APPLICABILITY

All the foregoing data are fed into the computer, which produces the full range of optimal corporate strategies, printing out the expected profits and variability of earnings associated with each one.[2]

When management decides to apply this approach to protect a company against inflation, the first step is to compute the input and output indexes as shown in Table 15. These computations reveal vulnerability of the corporate cash flow to rising prices.

If this vulnerability is substantial, management's next step is to decide whether the corporation's business lends itself to a formal mathematical model of this type. The ideal types of industry for the model are those employing batch processes (i.e., the same type of equipment and labor can produce a variety of different end products), for it is then relatively easy to modify product mixes and adapt new production processes.

In other industries some of the decision variables become irrelevant. But even for companies in these industries, the pricing and import-export decisions can be complex enough to warrant formal input-output analysis, though not necessarily by way of a computer model.

### Multinational Applications

Inflation rates differ widely from country to country at any given time. Using the model permits corporations having a number of production and marketing facilities in different countries to take advantage of these inflation differentials. The model can be readily expanded to include production facilities in a large number of countries and to optimize the production location for each product, while taking into account differential inflation rates, transportation costs, regulations for exporting, and related foreign exchange controls, as well as the company's productive and marketing capacities in the different locations.

### SUGGESTED FURTHER READING

Lietaer, Bernard A., "Prepare Your Company for Inflation," *Harvard Business Review*, September/October, 1970, pp. 113–125.

---

[2] For step-by-step examples of how the model is applied using actual company data, see Lietaer, pp. 120–124.

## COMPUTER PRODUCTIVITY

*Outlines nine ways to improve computer productivity to offset the effects of inflation and to avoid capital investment in a larger system.*

Computerization is one of the key elements of offsetting the effects of inflation on a company. In office operations data processing equipment can be instrumental in handling greatly increased workloads with little or no increase in staff. In manufacturing facilities computerization is usually at the heart of automation programs designed to increase efficiency and decrease payrolls, both key to fighting inflation. In nearly every business, EDP can serve in some way to increase productivity, lower costs, and cut numbers of employees.

In recent years computerization of business operations has expanded at a record pace. This demand—plus inflation—has caused the price of data processing equipment to rise sharply. For this reason, more and more managements are investigating methods of getting increased productivity out of existing EDP equipment, rather than automatically upgrading to newer and bigger hardware. Nine techniques for increasing computer productivity can lower data processing costs and should be investigated before taking on the expense of a new, larger system.[1]

### FACILITIES MANAGEMENT

With facilities management (FM), an outside firm is brought in under a contract to assume responsibility for the company's data processing facilities. Advantages to the organization can be numerous: a quick solution is provided when EDP departments are not producing as expected by management, FM can result in better technical expertise, costs are often lowered, and management can concentrate on running the organization instead of the new technology of data processing.

[1] Adapted from Dr. Edward O. Joslin, "Nine Alternatives to a New Computer," *Journal of Systems Management,* November 1974, pp. 38–41.

Facilities management works best for service-type organizations in which procedures are fairly standard and applications are static; in particular, it has proven useful in the banking, insurance, credit card, and medical fields.

## EXTRA SHIFTS

A computer system should be used 600 to 650 hours a month. If less machine time would be required, productivity might be increased by the use of extra shifts, instead. For some small systems the staffing cost for extra shift utilization may be more than the cost of a system with increased capability. For medium- to large-scale systems, however, the staffing costs for extra shift utilization should be less than the cost of increased capability.

## AUDITING OF WORKLOAD

Any process or program that can be discontinued or run less frequently makes the computer available for other programs that are perhaps more critical. For this reason existing workloads should be audited to find out why each process is used, for whom it is used, whether existing frequency is necessary, and how much the sponsor of the process is willing to spend to continue to receive the results he is getting. Workload audits often reveal unnecessary process patterns.

## LEVELING WORKLOAD PEAKS

Often there is a discrepancy between peak workloads and normal work-loads. If a system is being used 24 hours a day for the last 4 days of every month and only 8 hours a day the rest of the month, perhaps the peak workload can be spread out over the full month. Persuading system users to accept their outputs at different times of the month can be difficult, but it can often be accomplished. One effective method is use of an internal charge that is substantially higher at the end of the month.

## REDESIGN OF CRITICAL PROGRAMS

Many organizations are still running processes designed for first-generation computers on their upgraded third-generation equipment. Although these processes have been modified to run on the newer systems, they have not been resystematized to run efficiently. Running time often decreases 50 to 90 percent when programs are redesigned for the new system. These time savings are especially important for critical programs that are run hourly or daily and consume large portions of the monthly run time. Merely improving these critical programs frequently alleviates the need for enlarging the present system.

## EQUIPMENT AUGMENTATION

When trying to increase productivity from existing computers, hardware and/or software monitors should be used to locate bottlenecks in the configuration. If programs create tie-ups, programming segments can be corrected and checked again. If segments of the existing configuration are the problem, present equipment can be augmented with additional or better equipment. Types of equipment that should be considered include more units of the same type, replacement of existing units by more efficient ones, and adding another system.

## NEW SOFTWARE

Often productivity can be increased by augmenting the software supplied with the existing system. Various software houses offer operating systems and FORTRAN or COBAL compilers that are superior to those available from the hardware vendor. The more efficient programs may reduce running time by as much as 10 to 20 percent.

## SERVICE BUREAUS

When complex programs or special capabilities are required, in-house computers can be supplemented with the facilities of an outside service bureau. Buying service bureau capabilities has several advantages.

• It usually costs far less to handle peaks through a service bureau than to add new equipment.

• Complex programs can be run without the company having to invest in its own equipment.

• Service bureau costs are usually reasonable, since the facilities generally have surplus computer time and sell it for what they can get.

## TIME-SHARING SERVICES

If demands for faster response, greater computational capability, or faster accessing of data bases become excessive, real-time capability may be needed. In this case it is often possible to augment the present system with commercial time-sharing services. There are disadvantages to this method—downtime, limited input-output speeds, confidentiality, and costs—but time-sharing does permit buying only the time and computer power needed. In many instances it is a cost-effective way of increasing productivity without capital investments.

## SUGGESTED FURTHER READING

Austin, J. E., "Educating Management in the Use of Information Systems," *Advanced Management Journal,* Spring 1975, pp. 37–42.

Gildersleeve, T. R., "Organizing the Data Processing Function," *Datamation,* November 1974, pp. 46–50.

Had, N. and J. G. Burch, Jr., "Getting More from Your Computer," *Datamation,* November 1974, pp. 60–62.

Joslin, Dr. Edward O., "Nine Alternatives to a New Computer," *Journal of Systems Management,* November 1974, pp. 38–41.

"Managing the Data Center," *Data Management,* October 1974, pp. 21–25.

Multinovich, J. and H. A. Kanter, "Organizing the MIS Department," *Journal of Systems Management,* April 1975, pp. 36–41.

# SECTION 18

## CONSERVATION OF ENERGY

*Sketches a program for holding down inflated energy source costs and provides examples of savings that can be achieved.*

It has become increasingly apparent that traditional sources of energy and associated raw materials will be in short supply in the foreseeable future. These shortages will result in inflationary energy source price increases as supplies are outstripped by demand.

Faced with this situation, many leading companies are taking steps to reevaluate their basic strategies, objectives, and approaches to dealing with energy source costs. The following planning framework can be used by companies in such reevaluation programs; examples are furnished to show what some firms have done to offset energy source price increases.

### AN ENERGY SOURCE PLAN

Business operations over the next decade will be characterized by what has been called the "conservation ethic." The years ahead will be a period of relatively slow growth, and completely new methods of production will be formulated to conserve raw materials and energy. Whole new business areas will be developed for identifying and evaluating alternative programs required by the new strategy. The following four-step program can be useful in meeting these challenges.

#### Initiate a Fact-Finding Audit

A thorough examination should be made of all business operations to locate opportunities for energy source cost savings. Special emphasis should be placed on functions most affected by shortages (also see *Energy Analysis,* pp. 129). The audit should ask the following questions.

*Is it possible to eliminate the existing approach?* Dow Chemical, for example, replaced an inefficient heat-transfer system and cut steam consumption in half. Installation costs were recovered in less than a year.

**89**

*Is it possible to combine operations?*   Steel companies have found they can save up to 40 percent of energy costs by smelting and fabricating in one operation. Previously, ore was smelted into ingots, cooled, and reheated at a later date for fabrication.

*Is it possible to substitute a more cost-effective method?*   With anticipated shortages and price increases in natural gas and oil, many firms are rediscovering coal as an energy source. Virtually unlimited supplies and competitive pricing will make coal even more popular in the decades ahead.

### Draw Up an Action Plan

After a thorough audit of operations, a strategic action plan should be formulated, detailing possible alternatives and listing key objectives. The plan should spell out both short and long-term proposals for change and should include each functional area of the business.

### Select Programs to Achieve Objectives

Optimal programs to achieve objectives in the action plan should be defined, evaluated, and slotted into the framework just outlined. Once this is done, duplications and conflicts with other business objectives can be eliminated. Cost effectiveness of the various proposals can be measured using conventional program management and budgeting techniques.

### Implement the Plan

When the plan is final, savings targets should be specified, the program explained to all concerned, and the campaign launched. Careful monitoring should be maintained to ensure compliance with program strategies and to pinpoint trouble spots.

### WILL IT WORK?

Like any cost-control strategy, an energy conservation program is only as effective as management's determination to make it work. Properly conceived, implemented, and monitored, such programs can usually show significant beneficial results. Following are some examples.[1]

[1] *Source:* Logan M. Cheek and Stephen P. Toadvine, III, "The Energy Crisis as a Profit Opportunity," *Advanced Management Journal,* October 1974, pp. 38–39.

- In research and engineering, Alcoa recently patented a new smelting process that will eliminate 30 percent of the electric power required to make aluminum.
- In manufacturing, Union Carbide cut energy per pound of product up to 20 percent by burning fuel residues, installing larger heat exchangers, installing air-intake regulators, and adopting more than 200 other efficiency measures. The total savings was $8.4 million.
- DuPont has limited its increases in energy consumption to 10 percent since 1967, even though production has increased more than 50 percent. DuPont claims that almost any plant with an annual energy bill exceeding $500,000 can reduce fuel costs 7 to 15 percent.
- In facilities design and maintenance, Eastman Kodak is designing new buildings to eliminate large areas of glass, installing solar bronzed glass, and building a new 2-acre warehouse that will require 30 percent less heat than existing buildings.
- In financial planning and controls, Wang Laboratories, St. Regis Paper, and Johns-Manville are instituting controls over energy consumption as a fact-finding tool to identify opportunities. The idea is to institute "Btu accountability" against a preagreed, planned level or a historic baseline. Electrical consumption at Wang has been reduced to between 93 and 61 percent, and natural gas to between 85 and 49 percent of established baselines.

Energy savings have not been limited to larger companies, where significant economies are normally expected. Examples from these smaller firms are also noteworthy.

- L. S. Jones Timber Products Company instituted a variety of measures to reduce fuel in its manufacturing, logistics, and administrative functions, effecting energy savings ranging from 24 to 75 percent.
- Enterprise Products is employing new welding machines with solid-state controls that save 30 to 40 percent over tube-control equipment in electricity costs.
- Harvard University instituted a buildings and grounds master operating plan that reduced requirements for steam, electricity, oil, and gas by 3 billion Btu during just one winter month.
- Overlook Hospital in Summit, New Jersey, constructed two additional wings without having to increase boiler capacity, even though boilers were operating at nearly peak loads before the additions were completed. Recycled waste heat was used, saving costs equal to approximately 20 percent of the estimated new construction costs.

These achievements were largely prompted by necessity. Until 1973 energy consumed only 5 cents of every manufacturing dollar, and aggressive conservation efforts were not profitable. Since that time, the average cost of a million Btu has soared from 20 cents to more than a dollar. This new situation makes strategies of energy conservation much more cost effective.

## PROBLEMS

The biggest problem usually encountered in installing meaningful energy-saving measures is organizational inertia. There is a widespread belief that the energy crisis will pass and operations can return to normal. The fallacy in this, of course, is that even if supplies are brought into line with demand, inflated prices are here to stay. To remain competitive, all companies will eventually have to adopt energy-conserving techniques, rather than simply passing along their higher costs as price increases.

The following guidelines can be used to help overcome skepticism about the reality of the crisis and the sense of futility often encountered in attacking the problem.

*Appoint a Coordinator.*   One man should be made responsible for the entire energy-conservation program and given the authority to act decisively. He can be a full- or part-time employee, depending on organization size. (Monsanto has a full-time vice president of energy and materials management.) Task forces should be avoided because they represent a diffuse number of vested interests that will hamper action.

*Stamp out Skepticism.*   Armed with hard logic and facts, the coordinator should aggressively "sell" management and the rank and file on the necessity of instituting energy-saving strategies to save costs and remain competitive.

*Convince Top Management.*   Solid data showing potential profit improvements that can come through better energy use should win top management's commitment to the program. Do not assume this, however. Regular communication of specific opportunities and risks are needed to allow top management to make the critical decisions. Without top support, the program will be endangered.

*Monitor and Control.*   Major changes within an organization pose threats and direct challenges to existing processes, work patterns, and organizational structures. Lip service may be paid to energy-conservation techniques, but skeptics may revert to old patterns after programs are initiated. Follow-up and control are required to ensure compliance with new operations.

# SUGGESTED FURTHER READING

Cheek, Logan M. and Stephen P. Toadvine, III, "The Energy Crisis as a Profit Opportunity," *Advanced Management Journal*, October 1974, pp. 35–42.

"Industry Cut Energy Use Substantially in '74," *Industry Week*, April 7, 1975, pp. 18–19.

Kolbe, R. A., "Waging the War Against Scarcity," *Purchasing*, March 18, 1975, pp. 49–51.

"Manager's Guide to Energy Conservation," *Industry Week*, April 14, 1975, pp. 40–41.

"Six Projects Seek More Efficient Electricity Use," *Commerce Today* (now *Commerce America*), May 26, 1975, p. 18.

Tanerini, R. G., "Gas Flow Computer Cuts Demand Penalties by $3000 per Month," *Pipeline and Gas Journal*, November 1974, p. 46.

## CONSUMER PRICE INDEX (CPI)

*Outlines use of the CPI as a yardstick for measuring the effects of inflation on retail prices and provides index figures since 1960.*

The Consumer Price Index and Retail Prices of Consumer Goods and Services are compiled by the Bureau of Labor Statistics (BLS) of the federal Department of Labor.

The index is a statistical measure of changes in prices of 400 selected goods and services bought by families of city wage earners and clerical

**Table 17    U.S. Consumer Price Index for Cost of Living**[a] (Index: 1967 = 100)

| Year | All items | Food | Apparel and upkeep | Housing Total | Rent | Medical care | Reading and recreation |
|------|-----------|------|--------------------|---------------|------|--------------|------------------------|
| 1960 | 88.7 | 88.0 | 89.6 | 90.2 | 91.7 | 79.1 | 87.3 |
| 1961 | 89.6 | 89.1 | 90.4 | 90.9 | 92.9 | 81.4 | 89.3 |
| 1962 | 90.6 | 89.9 | 90.9 | 91.7 | 94.0 | 83.5 | 91.3 |
| 1963 | 91.7 | 91.2 | 91.9 | 92.7 | 95.0 | 85.6 | 92.8 |
| 1964 | 92.9 | 92.4 | 92.7 | 93.8 | 95.9 | 87.3 | 95.0 |
| 1965 | 94.5 | 94.4 | 93.7 | 94.9 | 96.9 | 89.5 | 95.9 |
| 1966 | 97.2 | 99.1 | 96.1 | 97.2 | 98.2 | 93.4 | 97.9 |
| 1967 | 100.0 | 100.0 | 100.0 | 100.0 | 100.0 | 100.0 | 100.0 |
| 1968 | 104.2 | 103.6 | 105.4 | 104.2 | 102.4 | 106.1 | 104.7 |
| 1969 | 109.8 | 108.9 | 111.5 | 110.8 | 105.7 | 113.4 | 108.7 |
| 1970 | 116.3 | 114.9 | 116.1 | 118.9 | 110.1 | 120.6 | 113.4 |
| 1971 | 121.3 | 118.4 | 119.8 | 124.3 | 115.2 | 128.4 | 119.3 |
| 1972 | 125.3 | 123.5 | 122.3 | 129.2 | 119.2 | 132.5 | 122.8 |
| 1973 | 133.1 | 141.4 | 126.8 | 135.0 | 124.3 | 137.7 | 125.9 |
| 1974 | 147.7 | 161.7 | 136.2 | 152.2 | 131.1 | 150.5 | 133.8 |
| 1975[b] | 162.8 | 178.1 | 142.2 | 167.7 | 138.0 | 170.9 | 144.7 |

[a] *Source:* U.S. Department of Labor, Bureau of Labor Statistics.
[b] Eight months.

Table 18 Decline in Purchasing Power of the
Dollar, Measured by Consumer Price Index[a]

| Year | Purchasing power of dollar |
|---|---|
| 1967 | 1.000 |
| 1968 | 0.960 |
| 1969 | 0.911 |
| 1970 | 0.860 |
| 1971 | 0.824 |
| 1972 | 0.798 |
| 1973 | 0.752 |
| 1974 | 0.677 |
| 1975[b] | 0.614 |

[a] *Source:* U.S. Department of Labor, Bureau of
Labor Statistics.
[b] Six months.

workers. It measures only the *changes in prices,* telling nothing about
changes in the kinds and amounts of goods and services families buy, the
total amount families spend for living, or the differences in living costs
across geographical areas.

The Bureau of Labor Statistics recently completed a major revision of
the Consumer Price Index and Retail Price Indexes. The principal improvements made in the indexes in the course of the revision are as follows:

• The weighing factors and the price data base have been updated.
• Certain improvements in statistical procedures have been introduced.
• More comprehensive indexes have been developed, including single
workers living alone and families of wage earners and clerical workers. A
separate new series for families is still provided for comparison to the old
series.
• In the future, the BLS plans to compile and publish separate city indexes
for all metropolitan areas that had populations of 1 million or more in 1960.

The basic index concepts have not been changed as a result of these revisions. The national index still measures average changes over time in prices
of goods and services bought by urban wage earners and clerical workers.
The same statistical formula is employed in the index calculations, and the
reference base period has been shifted to 1967 = 100. The essential historical continuity of the revised index has been maintained back to 1913.

The changes in weights, in samples, and in techniques of measurement simply make the index a more efficient and precise measure.

The Consumer Price Index is, of course, the key yardstick in measuring the effects of inflation on retail prices. Computation determines how current prices compare to prices charged for the same items in past years. The comparison is expressed as an index of how current prices compare to prices charged in 1967. If in a given month, for example, it costs $135 to buy the same goods and services that $100 would have purchased in 1967, the CPI for that month would be 135.

Table 17 sets out the Consumer Price Index for all items and for selected goods and services since 1960. Table 18 shows the decline in the purchasing power of the dollar since 1967, as measured by the CPI.

### SUGGESTED FURTHER READING

Bronstein, R. J., "Cost of Living and Salary Administration," *Personnel,* March 1975, pp. 11–18.

*Handbook of Basic Economic Statistics* (monthly), Economic Statistics Bureau, Washington, D.C.

*Statistical Abstract of the United States* (yearly), U.S. Bureau of the Census, Washington, D.C.

Scheibla, S., "Figures Do Lie: Flaws in the Consumer Price Index Prompt a Major Revision," *Barrons,* January 6, 1975, p. 5.

## CONSUMER PRICE INDEX—
## SELECTED LARGE CITIES

*Sets out changes in the Consumer Price Index in 20 large cities in the United States since 1960.*

Knowledge of the rate of inflationary increases in specific geographical locations can be helpful in many ways. In wage negotiations, for example, managements in areas with below-average rates of inflation can show employees that demands for pay increases to match the rise in the national Consumer Price Index are not justified because local prices have not risen so rapidly (see *Salary Administration,* pp. 333). Or, companies planning to move their operations or set up a new plant will want to pay special attention to locations least affected by inflation, since both construction and local labor costs will probably be cheaper. Firms transferring executives between cities or hiring out of state may want to take local indexes into account in making salary decisions.

Table 19 sets out the Consumer Price Index since 1960 for selected large cities in differing geographical areas of the United States. Inflationary increases in retail prices range from a low of 156.2 in Portland, Oregon, to 165.2 in the New York City area.

### SUGGESTED FURTHER READING

*Handbook of Basic Economic Statistics* (monthly), Economic Statistics Bureau, Washington, D.C.

*Statistical Abstract of the United States* (yearly), U.S. Bureau of the Census, Washington, D.C.

**Table 19  Consumer Price Index for Selected Large Cities[a] (1967 = 100)**

| Year/Month | Atlanta | Baltimore | Boston | Chicago | Cincinnati | Cleveland | Detroit | Houston | Kansas City | Los Angeles |
|---|---|---|---|---|---|---|---|---|---|---|
| 1960 | 89.3 | 89.1 | 86.5 | 90.7 | 90.0 | 90.6 | 88.2 | 89.2 | 86.9 | 88.5 |
| 1961 | 89.7 | 89.9 | 87.7 | 91.2 | 90.4 | 91.4 | 88.7 | 89.7 | 88.0 | 89.6 |
| 1962 | 90.5 | 90.6 | 89.6 | 92.2 | 91.3 | 91.7 | 88.9 | 91.4 | 89.4 | 90.6 |
| 1963 | 91.4 | 92.0 | 91.4 | 93.0 | 92.2 | 92.7 | 89.8 | 92.3 | 90.3 | 92.0 |
| 1964 | 92.8 | 92.9 | 92.7 | 93.4 | 93.7 | 93.2 | 90.5 | 93.7 | 92.5 | 93.7 |
| 1965 | 94.0 | 94.4 | 94.5 | 94.7 | 94.4 | 94.7 | 92.6 | 94.8 | 95.5 | 95.7 |
| 1966 | 97.0 | 97.7 | 97.7 | 97.4 | 97.2 | 97.2 | 96.7 | 97.5 | 98.0 | 97.5 |
| 1967 | 100.0 | 100.0 | 100.0 | 100.0 | 100.0 | 100.0 | 100.0 | 100.0 | 100.0 | 100.0 |
| 1968 | 104.0 | 104.1 | 104.1 | 104.3 | 104.8 | 105.9 | 104.3 | 104.3 | 104.0 | 103.9 |
| 1969 | 110.2 | 110.5 | 110.0 | 109.9 | 109.8 | 111.9 | 110.6 | 111.0 | 109.6 | 108.8 |
| 1970 | 116.3 | 117.0 | 116.5 | 116.3 | 115.7 | 119.3 | 117.4 | 116.8 | 115.8 | 114.4 |
| 1971 | 121.7 | 123.4 | 122.8 | 120.8 | 120.7 | 125.3 | 121.7 | 120.9 | 120.5 | 118.5 |
| 1972 | 125.8 | 126.5 | 126.8 | 124.3 | 125.1 | 126.5 | 126.2 | 124.9 | 124.3 | 122.3 |
| 1973 | 134.6 | 135.9 | 133.7 | 133.0 | 132.9 | 134.0 | 135.5 | 131.3 | 131.0 | 130.0 |
| 1974 | 148.5 | 152.4 | 148.7 | 146.1 | 146.3 | 147.9 | 149.1 | 147.8 | 144.2 | 142.5 |
| 1975 March | 158.5 | 162.9 | 159.0 | 155.6 | 156.0 | 157.7 | 157.2 | 161.4 | 154.8 | 154.2 |

| Year/Month | Minneapolis | New York | Philadelphia | Pittsburgh | Portland | St. Louis | San Francisco | Scranton | Seattle | Washington, D.C. |
|---|---|---|---|---|---|---|---|---|---|---|
| 1960 | 89.0 | 87.3 | 88.4 | 90.5 | 87.1 | 87.7 | 87.8 | 86.9 | 87.9 | 87.7 |
| 1961 | 89.9 | 88.1 | 89.4 | 91.3 | 88.1 | 89.0 | 88.9 | 85.7 | 89.3 | 89.0 |
| 1962 | 91.0 | 89.4 | 90.1 | 92.1 | 88.5 | 90.0 | 90.3 | 89.8 | 90.6 | 89.8 |
| 1963 | 92.3 | 91.3 | 91.8 | 93.1 | 90.2 | 90.9 | 91.5 | 91.0 | 92.1 | 91.3 |
| 1964 | 93.2 | 92.8 | 93.8 | 94.3 | 92.2 | 92.6 | 92.9 | 92.7 | 93.4 | 92.8 |
| 1965 | 94.5 | 94.3 | 94.7 | 95.8 | 94.6 | 94.1 | 94.7 | 94.1 | 94.5 | 94.1 |
| 1966 | 96.8 | 97.5 | 97.3 | 98.3 | 97.6 | 97.2 | 97.1 | 97.4 | 97.1 | 97.3 |
| 1967 | 100.0 | 100.0 | 100.0 | 100.0 | 100.0 | 100.0 | 100.0 | 100.0 | 100.0 | 100.0 |
| 1968 | 104.6 | 104.3 | 104.8 | 104.7 | 103.5 | 104.0 | 104.5 | 104.1 | 104.1 | 104.7 |
| 1969 | 109.9 | 110.8 | 110.4 | 110.4 | 108.8 | 109.2 | 110.2 | 109.5 | 109.2 | 111.2 |
| 1970 | 117.5 | 119.0 | 117.8 | 116.4 | 113.2 | 115.2 | 115.8 | 116.3 | 114.0 | 117.6 |
| 1971 | 121.7 | 125.9 | 123.5 | 121.5 | 116.1 | 119.6 | 120.2 | 121.4 | 116.2 | 122.7 |
| 1972 | 125.2 | 131.4 | 127.0 | 125.0 | 119.2 | 122.5 | 124.8 | 125.9 | 119.7 | 126.9 |
| 1973 | 132.0 | 140.9 | 136.6 | 131.9 | 126.2 | 130.1 | 132.2 | 134.6 | 127.4 | 134.9 |
| 1974 | 148.3 | 156.3 | 151.6 | 147.3 | 142.8 | 142.2 | 144.4 | 151.5 | 141.5 | 150.1 |
| 1975 | | | | | | | | | | |
| March | 156.0 | 163.6 | 161.1 | 157.0 | 154.0 | 152.4 | 156.0 | 161.8 | 152.5 | 158.4 |
| June | 161.0 | 165.2 | 163.5 | 161.0 | 156.2 | 156.7 | 158.6 | 163.8 | 157.0 | 160.7 |

a *Source:* U.S. Department of Labor, Bureau of Labor Statistics.

SECTION **21**

## CONTRACT NEGOTIATION

*Outlines methods of negotiating and drawing up contracts to provide maximum protection from inflationary price rises.*

Periods of inflation usually cause increased problems in negotiating contracts with suppliers.

First, inflationary economies are often accompanied by shortages in raw materials as companies place orders that are larger than usual to hedge against future price hikes. This results in a sellers' market, with suppliers holding most of the negotiating cards.

Second, suppliers become reluctant to enter into fixed-price contracts during rapid inflation because of uncertainty about their own future costs. When prices of raw materials are rising almost daily, sellers seek to protect themselves with flexible contracts based on costs at time of shipment, rather than at time of contract.

Although most buyers are sympathetic to valid, anticipated price rises that stem directly from increases in the prices of raw materials, it is still necessary to negotiate for the very best contract terms, pinning down as many details as possible. Even more important, extra diligence is needed to ensure that any price rises on the final invoice are *only* the result of increased raw material costs and that the supplier is not using the economic situation as an excuse for profiteering.

The following provides guidelines for negotiating contracts with suppliers during inflationary periods. Sample clauses that can be inserted into contracts to protect purchasers against unanticipated—perhaps unwarranted—price increases, are included.

### NEGOTIATING TECHNIQUES

At the outset of negotiations, strive for a firm, fixed-price contract. This should be the goal of every purchasing agent during inflationary times, and it provides the best protection against future price rises. Often the right contract can be achieved by entering a long-term agreement, since the size of the order may give the buyer a wedge for price leverage. Additionally, long-term contracts can be instrumental in obtaining needed materials; suppliers generally give large, long-term customers first priority.

If suppliers balk at entering fixed-price contracts, the following techniques can be used to help overcome supplier-slanted contract terms.

### Cost/Price Studies

Rather than giving in to each price increase, make suppliers justify every hike by demanding cost/price analyses. Find out exactly why and how their costs have risen to verify that price increases are justified and not simply extra profit. Examine all figures carefully. For example, a supplier may ask for a 15 percent increase in price because his raw material costs have gone up 15 percent. An examination might show, however, that the material content of his product only represents 25 percent of the cost. This means he is only entitled to a 4 percent increase, rather than 15 percent.

### Justification of Timing

In addition to insisting that price rises be justified because of material cost increases, make suppliers justify price-hike timing as well. Refuse to pay increased charges on goods produced before the supplier incurred additional material or labor costs. Most often, this problem arises with distributors who raise prices on goods already in stock at the time of price increases. Find out exactly when items were produced and pay no more than is justified by production cost at that time.

### Purchase for Suppliers

Many large firms have lowered their costs by buying raw materials and allocating them to their supply sources. Large-quantity purchases are strong negotiating tools in getting lower prices, and the method is also an important means of ensuring the availability of raw materials.

### Create Competition

Even in a sellers' market, the creation of a competitive environment can be instrumental in keeping suppliers' prices in line. Try to have multiple sources of supply (at least two) to play off against one another. If established suppliers become too demanding with their contractual terms, look for new ones. Often changing suppliers is a good idea even if there is no price advantage; this move is a demonstration of strength and shows suppliers that other options are available. This is especially important if suppliers balk at providing detailed analysis of price increases.

### Product Analysis

It is possible to set up contracts in which certain aspects of the price are firm, and others flexible. If the products contain quantities of a commodity, such as steel or copper, these amounts can be determined and made a flexible part of the contract. The up and down price swings of these commodities can be easily checked using published indexes, and buyers can ascertain exactly how much more—or less—they should be charged because of commodity price fluctuations.

### Adequate Notice of Increases

Provision should be made in the contract for adequate notice of any price increases, as well as the right to approve all hikes. These terms are standard clauses in most order forms, but they should be accompanied by the right to cancel the order if the terms are not met. If unwarranted or unexplained price increases appear on invoices, the invoices should be returned to the supplier by the accounts payable department. Make suppliers fully justify any prices or rises not included in the contract.

### CONTRACT CLAUSES

The best method to guard against unwarranted or unanticipated price increases is to button down all terms of purchase at the signing of the contract. This is especially important during inflationary periods, since often the provisions of standard contracts are inadequate to protect buyers against the various price escalations that characterize an inflationary economy.

A number of steps can be taken to give existing contracts legal teeth.

• The standard terms and conditions printed on order forms can be revised to plug loopholes suppliers might use during inflationary periods to skirt contract commitments.

• Rubber-stamped or typed-in clauses can be put on the face of orders to spell out important elements that are part of the contract agreement. These changes can be made as an interim step if the key elements have not yet been incorporated into standard terms on the back of order forms, or to emphasize the existence of key clauses in standard terms or conditions.

• Special clauses can be formulated as part of custom-designed contracts when dealing with specific situations, such as unusual commodities or new, unknown suppliers. These clauses should be framed with formulas that limit price escalations or make them easily measurable.

Of the many types of clauses for protecting buyers during inflationary periods, three are especially important:

• Clauses that give the buyer the right to approve all price increases before shipment.

**Example.** "This order must be filled at or below the price set forth on the face of the order. In the absence of a stated price, the order cannot be filled at a price higher than that previously quoted or charged unless written permission is given by the buyer."

• Clauses that assure firm prices for the time period covered by the order.

**Example.** "Order price is firm for duration of the order."

• Clauses that require the seller to furnish documented cost/price increases.

**Example.** "Order must be acknowledged with firm net prices. Price increases are not acceptable without fully documented cost justification and approval of the buyer."

In addition to these three key clauses, a wide variety of other types are used to forestall unexpected price increases. Some set a percentage limit on price hikes. Some limit escalation to government-published index rises. Some keep suppliers competitive by stating that if two or more vendors offer lower prices, the contract can be terminated unless the existing supplier requotes at a competitive price.

Any clause going into a contract should be drafted by legal advisors; the following examples, however, illustrate the types that can be used to limit price increases in eight common situations. Of course it is not always possible to get suppliers to accept such conditions unaltered, but the clauses can often be used as a basis for negotiations that will bring about a contract acceptable to both buyer and seller.

| Purpose of Clause | Sample |
|---|---|
| To limit price escalation to material costs. | "Seller may not increase the price except to the extent of material cost increases after date of order. Documentation of such increases must be provided." |

| Purpose of Clause | Sample |
|---|---|
| To secure price increase approval. | "Seller may not increase the price without buyer's approval prior to shipment. If new price is not approved, buyer may terminate the order." |
| To limit price escalation to orders shipped after a certain date. | "Seller may not increase the price of goods prior to ____ months from date of order." |
| To hold cost increases to a maximum percentage. | "Seller may not increase the price in excess of ____% of the original quoted price." |
| To ensure that price increases are justified. | "Purchaser will be allowed to examine supplier's records and other pertinent data concerning cost of materials and labor to verify cost increases." |
| To limit price increases to government index increases. | "Increase or decrease in the contract price shall be limited to the increase or decrease in the _____ Index, as published by the U.S. Department of Commerce. Supplier must notify the buyer within ____ days of such increase or decrease, and proposals for contract price adjustments must include supporting documentation." |
| To limit increases to market prices published by the supplier. | "Seller guarantees that order prices are not higher than supplier's published prices at date of contract and/or delivery." |
| To set a price escalation limit. | "Supplier's price may be adjusted upward for inflation only to ____% per year." |

## SUGGESTED FURTHER READING

Dowst, S., "Contract Negotiation in a Seller's Market," *Purchasing,* October 8, 1974, pp. 55–58.

Dowst, S., "Tighter Terms Mean Better Buys," *Purchasing,* December 17, 1974, pp. 63–64.

"How a Fixed-Price Contract Derailed Pullman," *Business Week,* March 17, 1975, p. 56.

"How to Write a Shortage Contract," *Business Week,* November 23, 1974, p. 38.

Kelly, E. J. and L. R. Scheewe, "Buyer Behavior in a Stagflation/Shortages Economy," *Journal of Marketing,* April 1975, pp. 44–50.

# SECTION 22

## CONTRACYCLICAL BUYING

*Sets out cost savings that can be realized through out-of-season purchasing.*

Many industries are seasonal or cyclical, either working to capacity to fill huge backlogs of orders or sitting with idle plants because of lack of business. Buyers who purchase goods made by these industries can often negotiate sizable discounts if they make their purchases during the slack season. This "contracyclical buying" can be an effective method of holding purchasing costs to a minimum to help offset the effects of inflation.

Some purchasing departments have developed a deliberate policy of negotiating long-term contracts during their vendors' slack seasons. The vendors know that the business slowdown is cyclical and that theoretically there is no need for price reductions, yet an empty factory has a depressing psychological effect. The result is that sellers are usually much more willing to grant price discounts during the slack season than when the factory is working to capacity, even though delivery dates on orders are identical.

One midwestern purchasing agent claims to save 5 percent annually by placing his orders for mill supplies in August, a dead month for the industry. Although his suppliers know they will be delivering against the purchase order all year, the psychological insecurity of the slack month results in the granting of discounts.

### SUGGESTED FURTHER READING

Ammer, Dean S., *Materials Management,* Irwin, Homewood, Ill., 1968.

# 23

## COST REDUCTION

*Outlines 12 techniques for identifying cost reduction
potentials to aid in maintaining profits during inflation.*

Cost reduction is not the same as cost control, and the distinction between the two should be kept firmly in mind by businesses seeking to lower costs to cope with an inflationary environment.

*Cost control* is concerned with reducing costs to the level of established standards, whereas dynamic *cost reduction* involves lowering the established standards themselves—a difficult job when continued inflation is anticipated. In the case of cost control, the standards are targets to shoot at, but in cost reduction the standards are suspect. Cost control emphasizes the past and present, whereas cost reduction emphasizes the present and future. Generally cost control efforts are limited to items that have standards or budgets. In cost reduction efforts are applied to every section of the business, regardless of whether standards exist.

As an example, assume a company engineer has used only motion-time analysis (MTA) to set a standard for an eyelet press operation of 3 hours per 1000 pieces at a base wage of $2.50 per hour. Under the cost control approach, as long as the direct labor costs for this operation do not exceed $7.50 per 1000 pieces, the operation is considered to be under satisfactory control. Another engineer however, might take a cost reduction approach and suggest changes in the machining speed, manning, tooling, tolerances, or materials to permit the standard to be reduced to 2½ hours per 1000 pieces, or $6.25 per 1000. The standard has now been lowered; and as long as only time study is used, the cost accounting department, having adjusted the standard cost sheet, will remain satisfied if direct labor costs do not exceed $6.25 per 1000 pieces.

But suppose the cost reduction approach is further applied and a methods analyst is hired. He may find that by putting the part on an automatic screw machine, direct labor cost can be reduced to $4.75 per 1000. Again, the cost accounting department changes its standard cost sheets. Then another analyst finds that the ±0.0005 inch tolerance on the part is overdesigned, tighter than required for product reliability. The specifications are changed to ±0.005 inch, and direct labor cost becomes $4.00 per 1000. Continuing the search, it is discovered that the part can be made of plastic and injection molded in the company's plastics department at lower cost. Finally, the cost reduction team finds the plastic part can be purchased from an outside supplier at a delivered price of $2.00 per 1000.

The example could be continued ad infinitum—possibly designing the part out of existence—but from a *cost control* standpoint, cost accounting would have been satisfied with a direct labor cost of $7.50 per 1000 pieces. The *cost reduction* approach did not accept that standard, and the cost was materially reduced.

Managements devote considerable attention and resources to the problem of cost control. Such activities as general accounting, budgeting, cost accounting, industrial engineering, and even data processing have been used in cost control methods and techniques. In many organizations, however, comparatively little effort has been expended on true cost reduction, particularly on a continuing, full-time basis.

In an inflationary business environment—characterized by rising labor and materials costs, tight money, the need for productivity increases, and a squeeze on profits—cost accounting and cost control are not enough. A company with good cost control is not necessarily cost efficient. To achieve really significant savings, true cost reduction methods must be employed.

The following outlines 12 techniques[1] for identifying cost reduction potentials that can be beneficial in improving business efficiency to offset the effects of a volatile economy.


## MAJOR VERSUS MINOR COSTS

All businesses have a distinctive cost structure or cost profile. Usually the cost profile expresses every cost element as a percentage of sales dollars or cost of sales. When labor and raw materials costs account for two-thirds of the total factory cost, it is obviously fruitless to concentrate efforts on minor cost items such as insurance, which represents 0.1 percent of factory cost. The emphasis should logically be on manpower and materials. Many companies spend too much time and effort on minor items while excluding major cost areas.

---

[1] Adapted from Joel L. Roth, "Cost Reduction Begins Where Cost Control Ends," *Management Advisor,* May–June, 1974, pp. 32–38. Copyright © 1974 by the American Institute of Certified Public Accountants, Inc.

### PARETO'S PRINCIPLE

A distinction should be made between the "vital few versus the trivial many," more formally known as Pareto's principle of maldistribution, or the 80:20 rule. The economist Vilfredo Pareto observed that wealth is distributed through society in such a way that a small percentage of the population controls a very large proportion of the wealth. The principle can be applied to the business organization in many ways. For example, a small percentage of products usually accounts for a large percentage of revenues. A small number of customers usually accounts for a large percentage of sales. Most substandard work can be traced to a few operators or a few machines. When initiating cost reduction programs, emphasis should always be placed on the vital few.

## CONTROLLABLE VERSUS NONCONTROLLABLE COSTS

At any given level of an organization, the manager has control over certain costs and no influence at all over others. He must learn to distinguish between the two and concentrate on reducing controllable costs, rather than wasting efforts on cost factors he cannot influence.

This is not to suggest that some costs are not controllable. It is axiomatic that every single cost element is controllable at some level of the organization. If the cost is not controllable by a manager at one level, it is controllable by someone up the line. It is important to direct each manager's attention to the costs that can be controlled at his level.

### FIXED VERSUS VARIABLE COSTS

Managers generally think of variable expenses as controllable and fixed expenses as noncontrollable; they think of variable expenses as susceptible to cost reduction and fixed expenses as relatively irreducible. This is not always the case, however. The following examples illustrate how fixed costs can be converted into controllable, reducible costs.

• Building depreciation is generally included in factory overhead and regarded as fixed at a given location. However, this expense can be regarded as reducible with geography. The cost or occupancy cost for a given size building can vary as much as 50 percent over different locations.
• Maintenance labor is usually a fixed cost, yet these expenses can be both controlled and reduced. For example, one firm that employed a nine-man

painting crew in the maintenance department found that after hiring an industrial painting contractor who was used only when needed, the crew could be reduced to two men. Not only were substantial direct economies realized, but the contractor was willing to work evenings and weekends, eliminating disruption in production and office operations. A fixed cost, the painting crew, was converted to a variable expense.

## UNIT COSTS

Unit costs are one of the most useful indicators of cost reduction potential. The unit fixed cost of a product—that is, the fixed portion of the unit cost— is variable inversely with volume. The variable unit cost is fixed with volume. This means that a very sound cost reduction result is obtained when greater volume can be achieved from an existing production unit, whether it be man, machine, building, or the conversion of unused productive resources into usable ones. As production goes up, the fixed unit cost will decline and the variable unit cost will remain the same. Consequently the total unit cost will go down.

## STATIC STANDARDS

Study of existing budgeted standard costs often reveals that some figures have changed very little or not at all in years. This usually suggests that a particular cost or operation has not been closely scrutinized for some time and probably should be reevaluated. Such reassessment is especially critical with standard materials during periods of rapid inflation; substitutions can often present large cost reductions.

## BUDGET VARIANCE

Variances from standard, as shown in periodic variance reports or operating statements, can be significant indicators of cost reduction potential. For example, a continuing negative labor variance, if analyzed properly, might be traced to excessive overtime. This, in turn, could lead to the installation of new equipment, addition of more manpower, or a change in production scheduling techniques. It is just as important to analyze a positive variance or a gain variance. For example, if an operating manager has found a methods improvement and lowered his cost, the change may be applicable elsewhere in the company.

## PROFITABILITY ANALYSIS

A regular "profitability measure" should be taken of each business segment. Too often, business managers fail to demand or receive a regular income statement or return on investment (ROI) evaluation of the various key components of their business. For example, sales vice presidents should get a gross income statement by branch, by distributor, by salesman, by product line, by territory, or by customer. Plant managers should have a balance sheet or an ROI measure of the major product lines going through their plants if they are responsible for a number of different product lines.

Too many managers do not receive or request this type of information. In one company, for example, five unrelated product lines aggregated $10 million in annual sales. Although the company did not maintain internal product-income statements, an estimate of product line performance was made. When outside consultants were called in, it was found that one of the five lines had lost an estimated $3.5 million over the preceding 8 years. This amount also represented a disproportionately high percentage of total investment. Such knowledge, of course, is critical if costs are to be reduced.

## MAKE VERSUS BUY

Although the make-or-buy technique is well known, many companies do not avail themselves of its cost-reducing potential. Instead managements tend to attempt to produce everything possible "in-house," believing that this will increase burden absorption, when in fact it might be more economical to reduce the burden than to absorb it. In one example, a manufacturer of electromechanical products maintained a sizable production machine shop and other fabricating operations, even though the shop operated on an average of about 15 percent of capacity. He also maintained a sizable parts inventory, since the cost of setup in some cases justified 3 years' production. It was found that by making minor redesigns, many of the parts would conform to industry standards and could be purchased directly from suppliers and distributors at lower cost. As a result, the machine shop and fabricating departments were virtually dismantled, parts inventories were cut sharply, and costs were reduced significantly.

## STANDARDIZATION

Like make-or-buy decisions, the technique of standardization is well known but not so often practiced. Standardized parts, materials, machines, equipment, processes, and so on, should be utilized wherever possible to avoid high costs inherent in uniqueness. Any company that has numerous lengthy materials bills, for example, is probably a candidate for standardization analysis. Nor are the benefits of standardization confined to manufacturing. One large finance company negotiated separate automobile loans every time a customer walked into the office, eventually leading to more than 84,000 different automobile financing contracts. An analysis of these instruments showed that every one could be handled within one of 12 standard contract conditions or terms. The resulting standard contract led to a significant reduction in paperwork, clerical labor, and data processing costs.

## INTRACOMPANY PRICING

In an attempt to use the profit center concept, numerous companies distort their internal operating results. Transfer pricing is often based on arbitrary or artificial management policies, producing depressed results for efficient profit centers and inflated results for inefficient operations. In a metals mining company, for instance, all the mines were treated as a profit center and all the concentrates from these mines were consumed within the company by its own mills and smelters. Mine revenues were computed on the basis of prevailing comparable market prices. So long as the mines, in aggregate, showed a profit, management was satisfied. But investigation showed that four of the mines in the company were extremely costly and inefficient, since the ores could be purchased on the open market far more cheaply than they could be produced in these mines. The more efficient mines had hidden the inefficiencies.

## COMPETITIVE ANALYSIS

A great deal of insight can be gained from public and quasi-public information about particular industries and competitive companies within the industries. For example, many industry groups prepare operating ratio statistics and other data, as do the IRS and a number of other agencies. This information can often be helpful in pinpointing areas within company operations that hold potential for cost reduction. For example, a cosmetics company was losing money steadily. Analysis of the registration statements, prospectuses, and other data available on some of the more successful companies in the industry quickly revealed that the firm's costs of sales were in line with more successful competitors, as were direct sales and administrative expenses. However certain selling expenses, such as promotion, demonstrator's salaries, and other selling costs, were double those of similar companies. This led to a pruning of the customer mix, a revision of promotional allowances, an alteration of trade channels—and a considerable reduction of costs.


## SUGGESTED FURTHER READING

"Companies Scurry to Cut Costs," *Business Week,* November 30, 1974, pp. 22–23.

Craig, Q., "Cost Control: Whose Job?" *Management Accounting,* March 1975, pp. 22–24.

"Despite Strong Profits, Inflation Is Spurring Cost-Cutting Efforts," *Industry Week,* September 9, 1974, pp. 78–80.

Merz, C. M., "Inflation and Cost Control," *Administration Management,* January 1975, pp. 20–21.

Neuman, J. L., "Make Overhead Cuts that Last," *Harvard Business Review,* May 1975, pp. 116–126.

Roth, Joel L., "Cost Reduction Begins Where Cost Control Ends," *Management Advisor,* May–June, 1974, pp. 32–38.

Segar, A. M., "Reducing Manufacturing Costs," *Management Review,* May 1975, pp. 46–48.

# 24

## CREDIT AND COLLECTION CHECKLIST

*Outlines 10 methods to improve efficiency of credit and collection efforts.*

Credit and collection efforts should be stepped up during inflationary periods to improve cash flows, minimize risk of losses due to insolvencies, and protect against the loss in purchasing power of uncollected funds. Accounts receivable, which often represent the company's largest single asset, can be crucially important in holding the line against rising costs and eroding profits.

An efficient credit and collection function can prevent the costs of carrying a few extra days' sales on the receivables books. For example, suppose a large manufacturing company's annual sales are $730 million, or $2 million a day, and the company's credit manager has kept receivables days' sales outstanding at 40 days. A competitor in the same industry with identical volume has 50 days' sales on the books. The credit manager of the first company has furnished the firm with $20 million more in cash with which to pay bills, expand, declare dividends, or use in other ways that are most profitable. Equally important, the competitor may be forced to borrow to overcome the $20 million differential. The cost at 7 percent (conservative during inflation) would be $1.4 million annually. Additionally, restrictions might be placed on the company's operating freedom as a condition of borrowing.

The following checklist[1] provides methods of sharpening credit and collection techniques to help ensure maximum profitability of accounts receivable.

[1] From Glen Schiller, "How to Sharpen Your Credit and Collection Efforts," *Credit and Financial Management,* September 1975, pp. 14–15. Adapted with permission of Credit and Financial Management magazine (September 1975) c 1975 by the National Association of Credit Management.

## INCREASED FOLLOW-UP

Closer follow-up on collections is one of the best methods of cutting down on capital tied up in accounts receivable. A study should be made to determine which firms account for the major portion of outstanding bills. Some may have to be carried for valid business reasons, but they should be isolated and the reasons for tolerating them challenged.

With those remaining, interfacing between the collections department and the sales manager should be used to pinpoint customers that need stricter treatment. It may be decided that some customers are simply not worth keeping, and they should be dropped immediately. These decisions can be made by comparing profitability against risk involved as well as past paying history. Marginal customers should be put in a special category to be watched closely. Some of these will offer profitable business if properly handled, but the potential of significant losses exists if such accounts are not promptly collected.

## CREDIT POLICY

Periodic reviews of new account credit policy should be made to keep abreast of changes. Changes occur in the economic outlook, market conditions within the industry, seasonal aspects, inventory, and the employment situation. There are also changes in the prospects of an individual customer or potential customer.

All these are important factors affecting new account credit policy. Policies regarding payment terms, follow-up procedures, and credit reports should be reviewed regularly.

## REGULAR CONTACT

Slow-paying customers should be contacted regularly and often. A well-organized procedure should be developed for making, recording, and following through on contracts with slow-paying accounts. Often credit managers with a good knowledge of the industry and their accounts know when certain customers receive payments from their customers. This is the best time to make contact for money due.

### SELL FOR CASH

Accounts receivable can often be tightened and cash flows stimulated by simply selling more products for cash. Consider setting a minimum dollar amount for credit shipments. Ask for cash in advance on smaller orders, or ship COD.

### COLLECTION BUREAUS

Inevitably some accounts require the efforts of collection bureaus. If not, company credit policy is probably too tight and profitable sales may be lost. Results produced by various outside collection agencies should be checked and compared. The National Association of Credit Management maintains throughout the United States a network of collection bureaus with a good record of producing a high percentage of collections at low cost.

### LOCK BOXES

Companies that sell nationally are increasingly using bank lock boxes to reduce the "float" of customer payments in the mail and to get money into bank accounts with the least possible delay.

### BILLING PRACTICE

Billing practices should be speeded wherever possible. Most often, billing should be at the time of shipment. Since any backlog in invoicing means a delay in payment by the customer, billing should be streamlined when there is room for improvement.

### DISCOUNT POLICY

During inflation many companies liberalize their discount policies or turn to a cash discount because it is cheaper in the long run than borrowing short-term funds from banks to finance a large portfolio of receivables. This route can be especially effective when price increases are being announced.

## DISPUTED BILLS

Often disputed bills get put aside for later action and are temporarily forgotten. Generally, however, the older they get the harder they are to settle, and trouble should be avoided by giving customers a full explanation when any unusual bill is issued. Prompt attention to disputed bills helps ensure that cash is flowing and working, not tied up somehow.

## FINANCING

Some credit executives have been successful in expediting payment from their customers by helping them obtain financing. Assistance and advice in obtaining equity, capital, and short-term funds—if the credit manager can give it—not only relieves the burden on accounts receivable but also generates goodwill and provides good customer service.

## SUGGESTED FURTHER READING

Brock, L. A., "Tact in Credit Writing," *Credit and Financial Management,* September 1974, pp. 28–29.

Connolly, H. J., "So You Want to Increase Collections," *Credit and Financial Management,* September 1974, pp. 14–15.

Korn, B. P., "Leveraged Leasing: A New Way to Manage Credit," *Credit and Financial Management,* September 1974, p. 34.

Schiller, Glen, "How to Sharpen your Credit and Collection Efforts," *Credit and Financial Management,* September 1975, pp. 14–15.

Smith, C. P., "Automating of Collections," *Credit and Financial Management,* May 1975, pp. 10–11.

Stamm, D. E., "System Speeds Debt Collection," *Journal of Systems Management,* December 1974, pp. 7–9.

# SECTION 25

## DAILY INCOME FUNDS

*Surveys daily income "money market" mutual funds and their use in short-term investing during inflationary periods.*

Stock and bond markets are usually depressed during periods of accelerating inflation, and idle cash loses value almost weekly. For these reasons, businesses often show increased interest in "money market" investments, including such securities as certificates of deposit, commercial paper, United States Treasury bills, and other short-term investments.

Persistent inflation has been largely responsible for the recent appearance of mutual funds that invest primarily in securities of this type. Many of these funds declare daily dividends and pay dividends on a monthly basis.

The following survey[1] outlines the main features of these emerging types of mutual funds, which will undoubtedly play an increasingly important role in corporate cash management as inflation continues.

### FEATURES

"Money market" mutual funds offer corporate investors the usual mutual fund advantages of diversification and portfolio management in this specialized securities market. Additionally, many funds have liquidity features that make it possible for businesses to invest larger cash amounts than formerly might have been prudent.

A fund's performance is affected by the objectives desired. Some investors are looking for maximum liquidity, while others are primarily concerned with high income or the preservation of invested capital. A fund that invests solely in government securities, for example, generally will not produce as high a return as a fund specializing in certificates of deposit or commercial paper. This is because of the relative degrees of risk inherent in these various types of securities.

[1] *Source: Coopers & Lybrand Newsletter,* Vol. 16, No. 11, November 1974, New York, pp. 4–7.

### Purchasing

There are no fees involved in purchasing shares in most of the funds that have appeared to date. All funds require minimum initial investments, however, and most specify the maintenance of a minimum balance. The number of shares an investor receives when purchasing into a fund depends on the amount invested and the net asset value per share. As Table 20 indicates, minimum investments range from $1000 to $50,000.

### Holding the Investment

The funds usually invest in money market obligations having maturities of less than one year. Maturity dates are staggered to ensure that portions of the portfolio mature every business day, providing cash for normal redemptions.

Safety is maintained by placing restrictions on the investments in which funds may participate (see Table 21). Additionally, most money market funds are managed by well-known investment advisors, as Table 20 reveals.

Since the securities involved have relatively stable market values, yield is the key performance factor. Yields are determined primarily by the money market but are reduced by the fund's expenses. Dividends are declared daily, but frequency and form of payments varies from company to company, as shown in Table 22. In many cases dividends are automatically reinvested by the funds, and cash can be obtained only by redeeming shares. Dividends are taxable to the shareholder, regardless of whether shares are redeemed.

### Redeeming

As Table 20 indicates, several redemption procedures are in use. Most funds have some form of expedited redemption procedure to keep money at work. Two funds surveyed offered a check-writing feature that allows the shareholder to draw a check on the fund's bank to the order of any person (including the shareholder) in an amount exceeding a prescribed minimum. The shareholder continues to receive dividends declared on the shares to be redeemed until the check is presented to the bank for payment.

Some funds permit the exchanging of money market shares for shares of other funds managed by the same investment advisor. Still another plan provides for automatic withdrawals of a fixed monthly amount, similar to an annuity.

**Table 20  Daily Income Funds—Characteristics[a]**

| Fund | Management company (adviser) | Advisory fee percent of average net assets (%) | Minimum shareholder investment | | | Redemption procedures[c] |
|---|---|---|---|---|---|---|
| | | | Minimum initial investment | Minimum additional investment | Account lower limit[b] | |
| Anchor Daily Income Fund, Inc. | Anchor Corporation | 0.5 | $ 2,500 | $ 500 | $1,000 | R, ER, CW, AW |
| Association Liquid Reserve Fund, Inc. | Stateside Asset Management Corp. | 0.5 | 5,000 | 1,000 | 1,000 | R, ER |
| J. P. Cabot Short-Term Fund, Inc. | J. P. Cabot Advisory Corp. | 0.5 | 5,000 | 1,000 | 500 | R |
| Current Interest, Inc. | Funds, Inc. | 0.5 | 1,000 | 100 | 250 | R, ER, EP |
| Daily Income Fund, Inc. | Reich & Tang, Inc. | 0.5 | 5,000[d] | 1,000 | 1,000 | R, ER, AW |
| Dreyfus Liquid Assets, Inc. | The Dreyfus Corp. | 0.5 | 5,000[d] | 1,000 | — | R, ER, EP |
| Fidelity Daily Income Trust | Fidelity Management & Research Co. | 0.3[e] | 5,000 | 1,000 | 1,000 | R, ER, CW, EP, AW |
| Holding Trust | Fundpack Management Inc. | 0.5 | 1,000 | 1,000 | — | R, ER |
| Money Market Management, Inc. | Cash Management Research Corp. | 0.5 | 1,000 | 100 | 250 | R, ER, EP, AW |
| The Reserve Fund, Inc. | Reserve Management Corporation | 0.5 | 1,000 | 1,000 | 1,000 | R |
| Scudder Managed Reserves, Inc. | Scudder, Stevens & Clark | 0.5 | 5,000[d] | 1,000 | 500 | R, ER, EP |
| STCM Corporation | STCM Management Company, Inc. | 0.5 | 1,000 | 1,000 | — | R, AW |
| Temporary Investment Fund, Inc. | Provident National Bank | 0.35[f] | 50,000[g] | 1,000 | — | R |

[a] *Source: Coopers & Lybrand Newsletter*, Vol. 16, No. 11, November 1974, New York, p. 5.

[b] Account may be liquidated if redemption causes the account value to fall below these lower limits.

[c] Types of redemption procedures available: R = regular, ER = expedited redemption procedure available, CW = check-writing procedure available, EP = exchange privilege, and AW = automatic withdrawal plan available.

[d] Except that amounts forwarded by a securities dealer may be $1,000 per account.

[e] Does not include service fee of $2.50 per month charged directly to the shareholder's account.

[f] Includes transfer agent, dividend disbursing agent, and custodian fees for services provided by adviser.

[g] Fund may not be purchased by individuals.

**Table 21 Daily Income Funds—Limitation on Type of Investments[a]**

| Fund | Obligations issued by domestic banks having | Commercial paper as | | | |
| --- | --- | --- | --- | --- | --- |
| | | Rated | | Unrated (Having unsecured debt that is rated) | |
| | | Moody's | Standard & Poor's | Moody's | Standard & Poor's |
| Anchor Daily Income Fund, Inc. | $250 million of total assets | Prime | A | A | A |
| Association Liquid Reserve Fund, Inc. | $100,000,000 of equity | Prime-1 | A-1 | Aa | AA |
| J. P. Cabot Short-Term Fund, Inc. | One billion dollars of total assets | Not specified in prospectus | | | |
| Current Interest, Inc. | One billion dollars of total assets | Prime-1 | A-1 | Aa | AA |
| Daily Income Fund, Inc. | One billion dollars of total assets | Prime-1 | A-1 | Aa | AA |
| Dreyfus Liquid Assets, Inc. | One billion dollars of total assets | Prime-1 | A-1 | Aa | AA |
| Fidelity Daily Income Trust | $100,000,000 of equity | Prime-1 | A-1 | Aa | AA |
| Holding Trust | $200,000,000 of total assets | Prime-1 | A-1 | Aa | AA |
| Money Market Management, Inc. | Not specified in prospectus | Not specified in prospectus | | | |
| The Reserve Fund, Inc. | Not specified in prospectus | Not specified in prospectus | | | |
| Scudder Managed Reserves, Inc. | One billion dollars of total assets | Has its own credit-rating system | | | |
| STCM Corporation | Not specified in prospectus | Prime | A | A | A |
| Temporary Investment Fund, Inc. | Not specified in prospectus | Prime-1 | A-1 | Aa | AA |

[a] *Source: Coopers & Lybrand Newsletter*, Vol. 16, No. 11, November 1974, p. 6.

**Table 22  Daily Income Funds—Dividend Characteristics[a]**

| Fund | Frequency of declaration | | Frequency of payment | | Form of payment | | |
|---|---|---|---|---|---|---|---|
| | Income | Capital gains | Income | Capital gains | Cash only | Shares only | Either shares or cash at shareholder option |
| Anchor Daily Income Fund, Inc. | Daily | Daily-Short-term | Monthly | Daily-Short-term | | | X |
| Association Liquid Reserve Fund, Inc. | Daily | Annually | Daily | Annually | | X | |
| J. P. Cabot Short-Term Fund, Inc. | Daily | Annually | Daily | Annually | | X[b] | |
| Current Interest, Inc. | Daily | Annually | Daily | Annually | | X | |
| Daily Income Fund, Inc. | Daily | Annually | Daily | Annually | | X[b] | |
| Dreyfus Liquid Assets, Inc. | Daily | Annually | Daily | Annually | | X[b] | |
| Fidelity Daily Income Trust | Daily | Daily | Monthly | Monthly | | | X |
| Holding Trust | Daily | Daily | Daily | Daily | | X[b] | |
| Money Market Management, Inc. | Daily | Daily | Monthly | Monthly | | | X |
| The Reserve Fund, Inc. | Daily | Daily-Short-term Annually-Long-term | Daily | Daily-Short-term Annually-Long-term | | X | |
| Scudder Managed Reserves, Inc. | Daily | Annually | Monthly | Annually | | | X |
| STCM Corporation | Daily | None Expected | Daily | None Expected | | X[b] | |
| Temporary Investment Fund, Inc. | Daily | Daily | Monthly | Monthly | X | | |

[a] Source: Coopers & Lybrand Newsletter, Vol. 16, No. 11, November 1974, New York, p. 7.
[b] Provision is made, however, for monthly automatic redemption of shares equivalent to the dividends declared during the preceding month.

In most cases the entire account can be liquidated if its value falls below a set minimum (Table 20). This protects funds from the relatively high cost of servicing small accounts and is in line with the overall philosophy of daily income funds to maximize their net yield.

## SUGGESTED FURTHER READING

*Coopers & Lybrand Newsletter,* Vol. 16, No. 11, November 1974, New York, pp. 4–7.

# SECTION 26

## DEFICIT FINANCING

*Outlines certain advantages of budgeting more expenses than income during an inflationary period.*

Although deficit financing is usually a method used by governments, it also has business applications that can be advantageous during inflationary periods.

Deficit financing is a policy of deliberately budgeting more expenditure than income, financed by borrowing. With governments, the practice stimulates economic activity and employment by injecting purchasing power into the economy. Conversely, budgeting a surplus of taxes collected has been a traditional government technique for stemming inflation.

For businesses operating during periods of persistent inflation, it is often wise to adopt a policy of deficit financing to purchase capital improvements—plant and equipment—that appear to be marked for rapid inflationary increases in the future. By budgeting for and purchasing the needed improvements today, inflated costs can be avoided tomorrow. Additionally, the real value of the money borrowed to finance the capital improvements will be less when payments are made at a future date. Also, productivity improvements made possible by the new equipment may be instrumental in helping the company lower its personal rate of inflation.

### SUGGESTED FURTHER READING

Bannock, G., R. E. Baxter, and R. Rees, *Dictionary of Economics,* Penguin Books, Baltimore, 1974.

## DISLOYAL BUYING

*Outlines benefits derived by purchasing from several competitive suppliers.*

Purchasing is one of the key areas in controlling a company's individual inflation index and profitability, and it becomes more important as costs of raw materials and other supplies rise rapidly during inflationary periods. If needed materials are to be obtained at rock-bottom prices, the role of purchasing personnel must change from that of "order placers" to a more innovative, aggressive posture.

A tool that can help ensure efficient, cost-effective purchasing is the practice of disloyal buying. Disloyal buying is the first step in breaking traditional buying patterns and taking advantage of the cost savings that can come from *not* being a "preferred customer."

### LOYAL VERSUS DISLOYAL BUYING

There is a kind of mystique about being a loyal buyer. Numerous studies have detailed the role played by "loyalty" in the buyer's decision process. Certainly one of the key duties of the marketing function is to create buyer loyalty for a brand, for a particular store, for a source of supply, and so on. It is assumed that the buyer will receive a tangible benefit in exchange for his loyalty toward a given product or service.

Yet there is evidence that the disloyal buyer benefits at least as much and probably more than purchasers who display consistent buying patterns. The average purchasing agent relies almost entirely on his suppliers for information regarding products and services. If he is "loyal" and consistently goes to the same supplier, he has no means of obtaining reliable information on other suppliers' treatment and prices.

Another problem occurs because volume is uppermost in the supplier's mind. The salesman does not receive bonuses or promotions on his existing core of business but on increased volume generated from new customers. These new sales, of course, must come from "disloyal" buyers, and it would be a rare business that did not give preferential treatment to aid writing of new business. Thus it is the disloyal buyer who is the beneficiary of rewards offered by businesses eager to increase sales volume. The following representative example illustrates the principle.[1]

In New York, an industrial buyer for Plastics Unlimited is informed of a need for an additional amount of a chemical necessary for production. The buyer has used one firm, Excello Chemical, for many years. Why bother with a bid? He can just go to the phone, call Excello, and tell them of his need. They know his specifications from a recent order and will be willing to provide the chemical quickly.

Joe is a buyer for a competing firm operating in the same geographical area. He finds his production line is also in need of the same chemical. Excello now gets a call from Joe. Joe's firm has never bought from Excello. However, his business volume represents a "new business" potential of significant magnitude. In fact, his total purchases possibly could equal the purchases of Plastics Unlimited.

Excello knows a price reduction is planned for next week. In order to make a favorable impression on Joe, they give him his new price in advance of the announcement. But Plastics Unlimited does not need to be given this price, because they already have demonstrated their loyalty. Of course, had they called next week, they would have been given the lower price.

After accepting delivery, both of the buyers find that one carton of the chemical has been slightly damaged. Each of the buyers makes a phone call to inform Excello of this situation. Joe gets immediate satisfaction. The claims desk informs him that a new carton will be shipped quickly. He even may be told to keep the damaged carton in case he can find use for any of it. The loyal buyer, Plastics Unlimited, is given a big thanks for their information. Since the damage is slight, Excello tells them that their call is appreciated and that immediate steps will be taken to insure that this situation does not happen again. Good old loyal Plastics Unlimited understands this and will remain loyal.

If this situation had caught Excello with just enough merchandise on hand to fill only one of the two others, what would have happened? Very likely the loyal buyer, Plastics Unlimited, would be given a call and informed that their order would be delayed or only partially filled. Loyal buyers understand.

As this not atypical example demonstrates, firms and their salesmen are often quick to extol the virtues of loyalty but less than diligent in rewarding the loyal. Sometimes the buyer is unknowing and complacently believes he is receiving preferential treatment in return for his repeated business. At other times he is blatantly ignored—for example, when concessions are given only to new customers or new subscribers. Often a loyal customer is called on less frequently, is given fewer advance tips on impending price changes, and gets less service than his disloyal counterpart.

[1] G. Hayden Green and Richard D. Nordstrom, "The Rewards from Being a Disloyal Buyer," *Journal of Purchasing*, February 1974, p. 37.

Table 23   Benefits to Loyal and Disloyal Buyers from Most Sellers[a]

| Loyal buyer benefits | Disloyal buyer benefits |
| --- | --- |
| List prices | Lower than list prices |
| Normal services | Special service consideration |
| Casual sales approach | Formal sales approach |
| Spends less time buying | Spends more time buying |
| Volume discounts based on actual purchases | Volume discounts based on potential purchases |
| Taken for granted | Special attention |
| Average delivery | Special handling |
| Normal attention to warranty or damage claims | Speedy settlement of any warranty or damage claims |
| Special deals only if offered to the industry | Special deals in addition to those offered to the industry |
| Normal credit terms | Often receives extended credit terms |

[a] *Source:* Green and Nordstrom, "The Rewards from Being a Disloyal Buyer," *Journal of Purchasing,* February 1974, p. 40.

Table 23 sums up the benefits that accrue to loyal and disloyal customers as a result of the attitude most sellers take toward the two types of buyers.

The disloyal buyer clearly comes out ahead in most situations. He gets the same price, and maybe a better one; he gets the same service, and maybe faster; he receives the same news of a price change, and maybe earlier—all by refusing to demonstrate his loyalty.

Without question, the loyal, consistent buyer deserves and should receive special consideration in return for being the important asset that he represents to any selling company. Unfortunately many marketers neglect this fact once a buying pattern is established. When this happens—and especially in an inflationary environment—purchasing personnel should consider breaking the pattern and pursuing the cost efficiencies that can come from being a disloyal buyer.

## SUGGESTED FURTHER READING

Green, G. Hayden, and Richard D. Nordstrom, "The Rewards from Being a Disloyal Buyer," *Journal of Purchasing,* February 1974, pp. 33–40.

# SECTION 28

## EFFICIENCY AGREEMENT

*Sketches a labor-management agreement for improving work methods and productivity.*

An efficiency agreement is a contract between labor and management stipulating that workers will be given a certain proportion of profits derived from improved work methods or technological changes in return for their agreeing to the introduction of such changes.

More widely used in Europe than in the United States, efficiency agreements are often the most significant factors in productivity bargaining. Changes resulting from efficiency agreements usually lead to a reduction of work force or important increases in productivity, both key elements in overcoming company inflation. Overall costs are reduced, even though individual employees' wages are increased.

Effective use of an efficiency agreement depends on management's ability to accurately forecast the cost savings and/or profit improvements that can be expected from changes in work methods. (Also see *Productivity Bargaining,* p. 277.)

### SUGGESTED FURTHER READING

*Financial Times,* London, January 18, 1974, p. 6.

## ENERGY ANALYSIS

*Provides guidelines for an energy audit to aid in energy-related decisions made in an inflationary environment.*

Energy source availability and costs will create problems for most managements in the foreseeable future. Experts in the field predict sporadic supply problems with oil, natural gas, and electricity until at least the early 1980's. Coal, though plentiful, will be of little use to most companies until manufacturing operations have been converted to take advantage of its availability. Even if fairly adequate supplies of energy are available, costs will continue to rise because of inflationary pressures due to the overall economic environment and the uneven supply/demand situation.

Faced with inevitable energy source price rises, firms must take steps to reduce energy use and/or increase energy efficiency if profit levels are to be maintained. An overall energy use plan, as well as examples of savings some companies have achieved through cost-effective energy programs, is outlined in *Energy Conservation* (p. 89). The following provides details for conducting an energy analysis study within the company to provide background for energy-related decisions.

The steps described can normally be carried out in 3 to 6 weeks, depending on the complexity of the situation and the experience of personnel. The methods involved[1] yield reliable preliminary information and should be considered by any business having energy costs in excess of $100,000 annually.

Four steps are essential in carrying out an energy analysis or audit:

- Defining the purpose of the study.
- Determining the foundation elements.
- Examining areas that are large energy users to determine reduction potential.
- Performing a financial analysis of potential reduction methods.

[1] From Ralph E. Hora, "Getting on Top of the Firm's Energy Situation," *Business Horizons,* February 1975, pp. 30–34. Copyright 1975 by the Foundation for the School of Business located at Indiana University. Adapted by permission. Mr. Hora is a member of the international management firm of A. T. Kearney, Chicago, Illinois.

## THE PURPOSE

Everyone involved with an energy analysis study must fully understand the purpose of the program, to ensure that goals and objectives remain in focus as the study proceeds.

Basically, energy analysis is carried out to provide detailed and immediate information about a company's energy situation to be used in making profitable energy-related decisions. Toward this end, several questions should be asked:

- How has energy been used in the plant?
- How will energy be used in the future?
- How much reduction in use can be effected?
- What are the direct and indirect financial incentives to reduce usage?
- What additional steps should be taken?

When these questions are answered, guidelines can be drawn for determining energy reduction potential in terms of dollars, the potential for avoiding a shutdown, crude reduction methodology, and the formulation of a plan of action. The energy analysis should not be turned into an engineering study. Detailed engineering follows the analysis, but analysis itself is a management tool—its purpose is to state unambiguously the purpose of the study, clearing the way for further steps to be taken.

## THE FOUNDATION ELEMENTS

Foundation elements give information about the current status of energy use, permitting decisions about future energy use to be made intelligently. By tracing a company's 5-year energy use history and making a 5-year projection, a  time span can be developed that depicts a plant's past and expected energy activities. The following factors are important in examining the 5-year history.

*Monthly Usage.*   How cyclical is the pattern of usage? Does one fuel augment the other so that total energy use is not cyclical?

*Costs per Period.*

*Cost per Units of Energy.*   How are trends changing? Which cost trends are decidedly increasing? Is increased usage putting the firm in a lower unit cost category?

*Production Levels.*   Annual and cyclical trends must be examined and understood.

*"Enerductivity."*   Good product per 1000 Btus of energy input. Is the trend up, down, or unchanged?

*Energy Cost as a Percentage of Product Cost.* Recognition of the changing impact of the cost of energy is the first step in obtaining commitments to take action regarding energy costs.

The 5-year projection should analyze the following factors:

*Projected Production Levels.*

*Projected Energy Requirements.* These are determined by multiplying projected units by the reciprocal of "enerductivity" in the most representative year:

$$\text{units/year} \times \frac{\text{Btus}}{\text{units}} = \text{Btus/year}$$

*Total Costs per Period.* Projected by multiplying Btus/year by anticipated future energy costs in each of the categories of energy used.

*"Enerductivity."* If future "enerductivity" rates can be expected to change because of some action, the projected energy requirements should be changed.

*Energy Cost as a Percentage of Product Cost.* Continued trend analysis of this factor helps build the case for action.

*Purchasing Factors.* Included are the following:

• Expected unit cost changes. These can be gathered by discussing future energy cost projections with utility management.
• Expected availability. This factor is as important as the cost figure because of its impact on possible curtailment.

*Other Aspects.* Other considerations include:

• Viable alternatives. Can propane be used in place of natural gas? Can sunlight be used in place of electricity? Can coal be used in place of fuel oil?
• Government impact. Can EPA or OSHA regulations be expected to have an impact on future energy decisions?

The final step in developing foundation elements is to detail current energy use by type. Figure 6 shows the ultimate goals of this step. With foundation elements established, a good base exists for future energy monitoring as well as for the next steps in analysis study.

## REDUCTION POTENTIAL

Examination of each segment of the "pie chart" in Figure 6 indicates the largest users of each of the fuels in the plant. Generally the traditional *ABC*

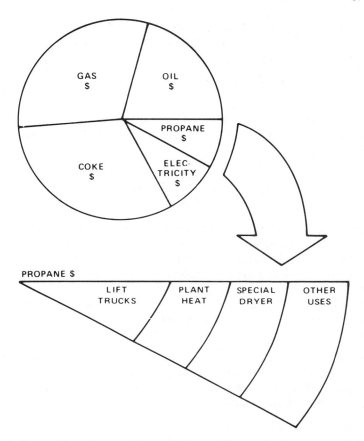

**Figure 6**   Determining energy use by type. (*Source:* Hora, "Getting on Top of the Firm's Energy Situation," *Business Horizons,* February 1975. Copyright 1975 by the Foundation for the School of Business located at Indiana University. Reprinted by permission.)

curve results: 20 percent of the equipment accounts for about 80 percent of energy use.

When analyzing each large energy-consuming operation, management should consider changing utilization patterns through use of alternative approaches: reduced fuel imput, increased equipment productivity, alternate fuels, improved technology, and so on. Thought should also be given to utilizing waste heat to dry material, generate steam, heat buildings, and/or process air, water, or products.

Strategic use of regulatory devices—thermostats, timers, peak-load-leveling devices, and pressure regulators—can also be instrumental in reducing energy waste. Scheduled preventive maintenance can also be an asset. Examples include cleaning air conditioner filters, ensuring that louvers work properly, and keeping steam traps open.

## FINANCIAL ANALYSIS

After potential methods of improving energy use and/or reducing energy requirements are found, financial analysis can be made as a first step toward decisions regarding energy action. An equation such as the following should be used:

$$\frac{\text{annual savings} - \text{annual depreciation}}{\text{total cost of project}} = \text{approximate before-tax ROI}$$

When deriving numbers needed for this calculation, it is important to determine the percentage of total fuel use that will be reduced. This factor, as well as the before-tax return on investment, will play an important part in determining future action.

## ACTION PLAN AND IMPLEMENTATION

After the four energy analysis steps have been completed, management will be in a position to formulate an action plan based on the economically available facts. If the decision is made to proceed, attention to four major elements is needed for successful implementation of the plan:

*The Tasks.* A clearly defined set of tasks and subtasks should be developed to describe precisely what is to be done.

*The Deadline.* A firm target for completion of the tasks must be set.

*The Person.* An individual with the necessary authority and skills must be assigned responsibility for completion of the tasks.

*The Leader.* A top management executive should be the driving force behind the program, requiring regular accountability reviews.

## SUGGESTED FURTHER READING

Hora, Ralph E., "Getting on Top of the Firm's Energy Situation," *Business Horizons,* February 1975, pp. 30–34.

## ESCALATION CLAUSES

*Discusses the use of escalation clauses in sales contracts to
protect manufacturers against inflationary cost increases.*

In recent years more and more companies have turned to the escalation
clause in sales contracts as a protective measure against inflation. There are
two primary reasons. First, sellers have had the upper hand in many
markets because of shortages attributable to a lack of manufacturing
capacity and inability to secure sufficient raw materials and/or
components. Second, there has been uncertainty about future inflationary
trends and the control sellers can maintain over their major costs—
materials and labor.

Because these two situations are likely to continue in the foreseeable
future, use of escalation clauses may become standard for many industries.
The following outlines the pros and cons of including escalation clauses in
sales contracts (from both the seller's and the buyer's point of view), and
describes recent trends in escalation clause usage. [1]

### THE BACKGROUND

Threatened increases in costs of materials, labor, and related items are of
greatest concern to the seller who must commit himself to a price in sales
contracts having a duration of one year or longer. In these long-term
contracts the seller may agree to supply such items as raw materials, commodities, or components over a specified period, to provide costly equipment requiring a relatively long manufacturing lead time, or to complete a
lengthy construction project.

Whatever the specific long-term sales contract, escalation clauses permit
the seller to adjust to a currently determined price, in a manner agreed to
by the buyer, to reflect changes in the seller's cost of specific items directly
or indirectly involved in product or service sold.

[1] Adapted from George S. Stothoff, "Escalation Clauses . . . Are Escalating," *The Conference
Board Record*, December 1973, pp. 23–28. © 1973 by The Conference Board.

Clauses vary from company to company and from one situation to another, but most of them include the following elements:

• A description of specific cost elements contributing to determination of the initial contract price that is subject to escalation.
• Stipulation of the index or indexes by which cost changes of these elements are to be measured.
• An indication of the frequency with which the contract price will be adjusted.
• A definition of limits of increases or decreases of cost elements subject to escalation.

As an example, the following[2] shows part of the price escalation clause used in a long-term sales contract of a heavy machinery manufacturer:

With the view of arriving at an equitable adjustment of the price herein stated in case the costs of labor and material should vary either upward or downward to an appreciable extent because of the very abnormal conditions prevailing today, the parties agree that the contract price as stated is subject to the adjustment in the following manner.

1. Labor
   (a) For the purpose of this adjustment, the proportion of the contract price representing labor is fixed at fifty percent (50%).
   (b) The above amount accepted as representing labor will be adjusted for changes in labor costs. Such adjustment to be based on the index of average hourly earnings in the blast furnace, steel work and rolling mill industry, compiled monthly by the U.S. Department of Labor, Bureau of Labor Statistics.
2. Material
   (a) For the purpose of this adjustment, the proportion of the contract price representing material is fixed at thirty percent (30%).
   (b) The above amount accepted as representing material will be adjusted for changes in material costs, such adjustment to be based on the index number of wholesale prices for group IV, metals and metal products, compiled monthly by the U.S. Department of Labor, Bureau of Labor Statistics.

Although escalation clauses have been more frequently used in contracts recently, a Conference Board survey revealed no major breakthroughs in their design. However certain industries, such as natural gas and benzene, are now using escalation clauses for the first time. Additionally, an increasing number of suppliers plan to cover steadily rising capital construction

[2] Stothoff, "Escalation Clauses," *The Conference Board Record,* December 1973, p. 26. © 1973 by The Conference Board.

costs with such clauses. This is especially true of firms committed to building added capacity to serve the needs of a relatively small number of large-volume, long-term contract customers. A few suppliers are even attempting to introduce clauses to pay replacement value of newer technology plant, for which original depreciation rates are inadequate.

Many companies are also expanding the list of items covered by escalation clauses. Examples include freight, taxes, MRO (maintenance, repair, and operating items), and overheads. Generally, however, these are short-term additions and are eliminated during stable economic periods.

### USE OF CLAUSES

Although use of escalation clauses is growing, there is much debate over the desirability and effectiveness of the method. Generally both sellers and buyers view escalation clauses as necessary evils during periods of inflation; both would rather work with fixed price contracts but are willing to adopt the clauses when necessary. The situation was summed up by a sales manager of a chemical company:

Nothing is as satisfactory for both sides as a fixed price in a long-term contract. But what are we to do? I cannot predict when the shortages of raw materials going into our products will ease up. If inflation isn't controlled, we don't know what our next labor contract will look like. And then there are possibilities that some of the indirect costs—taxes, transportation, fuel, and energy—will increase. We can't risk quoting fixed prices on contracts for 2- to 3-year deliveries except at figures that make us look ridiculous. The price escalation clause, if designed right, gives us a degree of reasonable protection. It's fair, it's understandable, and my customers only pay for what happens—not what we guess. They share equally in a risk that is mutually felt and can be openly measured.[3]

Buyers who object to use of escalation clauses usually do so on the grounds that a fixed-price contract is the only arrangement that allows accuracy in planning and meeting company objectives. Some believe that the protection afforded the seller under a price escalation clause reduces his incentive to control his costs.

Some buyers, however, claim escalation clauses can achieve lower costs. One building materials purchasing executive explains:

I can, if I insist, get a firm, fixed price in a long-term contract for a chemical we use and which is currently tight. But our supplier would crank into any fixed-price equa-

---

[3] Stothoff, "Escalation Clauses," *The Conference Board Record,* December 1973, p. 24. © 1973 by The Conference Board.

tion every single added labor, material, and any other cost he can imagine arising over the life of the contract. I dread even thinking about the figure. Far better that we accept the current market price with an escalation clause. The chances are we'll net out at a lower cost by the time the contract runs out. We'll have to pay only for what really happened—which we estimate will be less than the sum of all the possibilities invented in our supplier's sales department.[4]

It should be remembered, however, that inclusion of a price escalation clause in a contract does not necessarily mean that the seller will exercise his rights. If market conditions change or competition increases, a clause might not be invoked, even if increases in cost elements covered justify it. Escalation formulas must approximate current market demand; if a buyers' market develops, marketers looking ahead to the next order often forget about exercising existing escalation clauses.

### INCREASED PRECISION

Price escalation clauses used today are likely to be far more specific in their provisions than those used only a few years ago. Such clauses will also be based on more precise measures of cost changes and will comprise one of the most important and carefully reviewed provisions in the contract.

Some firms continue to rely on single, broad-gauged indexes for measuring cost changes (such as the Wholesale Price Index). Other companies are taking a more specific approach by using several different indexes to determine changes in different elements of cost.

The predominant trend is toward linking prices to actual changes in costs. This method is much more accurate than broad indexes in gauging cost increases based on a company's product mix and on individual orders. Additionally, many purchasers will not accept quotations based on broad-scale index escalations.

### ALTERNATIVES

During an inflationary environment, sellers and buyers find few alternatives to using escalation clauses, apart from fixed pricing. Some suppliers prefer to shorten the length of their contracts, believing it is better for buyer-seller relationships than use of escalation clauses.

Some manufacturers with contracts to deliver orders over an extended period produce the entire order at current prices and put it in inventory.

[4]Stothoff, "Escalation Clauses," *The Conference Board Record,* December 1973, p. 25. © 1973 by The Conference Board.

Careful estimates must be made in using this technique, however, to ensure that inventory costs do not exceed the labor and materials increases saved over the contract's life.

The most common alternative is probably the renegotiation of contracts. In volatile economies, both parties usually recognize that in the long run it benefits neither to have the seller locked into a financially disastrous contract. For this reason a give-and-take attitude has developed on both sides, and there will probably continue to be an above-average incidence of voluntary contract renegotiation.

## THE FUTURE

Certainly price escalation clauses provide needed protection for manufacturers against uncontrollable inflationary cost increases. Therefore the use of such clauses will become more widespread if persistent inflation continues. Some executives view the clauses as a "way of life" in sales contracts until inflation diminishes, material shortages ease, and labor costs stabilize.

Future contracts will probably give sellers more protection than in the past for individual elements of cost. For example, in a contract covering the sale of a chemical in very short supply, the clause was revised to offer its framer broader protection: its provisions now encompass labor, energy, supplies, and each raw material used in the product.

Specified maximum percentages by which the contract price or stipulated cost elements may be escalated will increase. Whereas in past years 15 percent was usually the escalation clause limit, some sellers in today's inflationary environment have stretched the limit to 20 or 25 percent. In some contracts, involving sale of products with uncertain long-term supply and price stability, "open-end" escalation limits are being written.

## SUGGESTED FURTHER READING

"Give Us Firm Quotes," *Engineering News-Record,* November 7, 1974, p. 54.

"Material Storage, Prepayment Plan Solves Escalation Clause Problem," *Air Conditioning, Heating, and Refrigeration News,* October 28, 1974, pp. 3–4.

Stothoff, George S., "Escalation Clauses . . . Are Escalating," *The Conference Board Record,* December 1973, pp. 23–28.

# SECTION **31**

## EXTERNALITY TECHNIQUE

*Outlines the monitoring of competitors' techniques, where appropriate, to reduce costs during inflation.*

The externality technique is the practice of keeping abreast of significant developments and programs in progress outside the company, especially among a firm's competitors, for the purpose of using these techniques to reduce company costs. The technique takes on added importance in an inflationary environment because some firms are more successful in controlling the effects of inflation on their business than others. By adopting methods used by successful firms, a company can often substantially reduce its own costs.

For example, constant increases in labor and materials lead to the volatile rounds of price increases that usually characterize an inflationary economy. By monitoring the prices of a successful competitor more closely than is done in normal times, a company can check that its own pricing policies retain profitability.

Other examples: a manufacturer forestalls demands for large wage increases by citing a more modest wage settlement accepted by a competitor's employees; or a retail department store actively recruits employees from a competitor having an especially effective training program, thus reducing its own training costs.

In addition to studying competitors, costs can sometimes be saved through the use of external services. During inflationary periods, for instance, mailing programs, forms printing, computer processing, distribution, and other services can often be performed more effectively and inexpensively by well-managed sources outside the company that have developed techniques to lower the impact of inflation on their operations.

### SUGGESTED FURTHER READING

Bannock, G., R. E. Baxter, and Rees, *A Dictionary of Economics,* Penguin Books, Baltimore, 1974.

"The Do-it-Yourselfers Tackle Inflation," *Industry Week,* June 24, 1974, p. 42.

# SECTION **32**

## FACTORING

*Outlines the advantages and costs of factoring accounts
receivable during inflationary periods.*

Factoring—the selling of book debts at invoice value immediately after
invoicing—has undergone significant changes in recent years. Until a
decade ago there were relatively few major independent factoring firms,
most of them operating from New York City. Since that time, however, a
number of large banks have entered the factoring field, mainly through
acquisition of the independent factors. Today nearly all leading independent
factors are subsidiaries or affiliates of major banks.

These new affiliations have sparked a rapid growth in factoring, the result
of large bank resources and the introduction of new clients through banking
organizations. Originally confined almost entirely to the textile industry,
factoring has now spread to many other fields, including electronics,
carpets, furniture, boats, poultry, and shoes. Because of certain advantages
factoring offers during inflationary periods, this growth will undoubtedly
continue in the future.

The following[1] outlines how companies can use factoring during inflation
and presents some typical costs.


### IMPROVED WORKING FUNDS

Perhaps the most important function of factoring is providing a business
with improved working funds, especially crucial during the tight money
situations typically encountered during inflation. Since the factor buys the
accounts receivable for cash, billings are turned into working funds
immediately. Since accounts receivable are converted into cash in a continuing process, a business does not have a substantial part of its working
capital tied up in the form of outstanding accounts receivable.

[1] Adapted from Langdon Van Norden, "Factoring: Cash for Your Receivables," *Administrative Management,* August 1972. Copyright © 1972 by Geyer-McAllister Publications, Inc.,
New York.

**140**

## COLLECTIONS

The purchase of accounts receivable by the factor is shown to the customer on the face of the invoice. Since the customer is instructed to make payment directly to the factor, the factor, in effect, becomes a collection department for a business. Again, this can be a distinct advantage during inflation when payments tend to be late because of poor business conditions, losing real value almost weekly.

All factors today have skilled collection personnel and are usually far more successful in collecting accounts than the average company. Most customers are anxious to maintain their credit standing when dealing with factors, since the factor may do extensive business in the customer's field; thus payments are usually prompt.

## CREDIT INSURANCE

When the factor purchases the accounts receivable, he assumes responsibility for collecting the debt. He has, in effect, approved the credit of the customer without recourse for the customer's possible insolvency. If the customer subsequently is unable to pay, the factor stands the loss. Thus the factor provides businesses with a form of credit insurance. A company that is factored need have no bad debts nor any reserve for bad debts, and this is especially advantageous during the periods of high insolvency that usually accompany an inflationary economy.

## THE COSTS

Factors charge commissions based on the accounts receivable assigned, usually ranging from 1 to 1½ percent. The cost to a business whose aggregate accounts receivable total $1 million a year would thus run between $10,000 and $15,000. Certain savings can be credited against this expense, however; the business eliminates credit losses and the need for credit reports, as well as the cost of collecting receivables.

In advancing funds to clients, factors also charge interest for the actual number of days in which funds are advanced prior to the maturity date of the invoice. For example, if a factor purchases an account receivable bearing terms of net 60 days and advances funds on the day the account receivable is created, the client is charged for 60 days' interest (plus collection days). Interest rates charged by factors are subject to variation, but generally are 2 or 3 percentage points above the prime rate.

Occasionally, however, a business can borrow at a lower rate of interest from its own bank if it enters into a three-way arrangement with the bank and the factor. The credit balance of the business with the factor is in effect assigned to the bank, which can therefore loan directly to the business, using the credit balance as collateral.

## SUGGESTED FURTHER READING

Forman, M., "Taking the Stress from Expansion," *Industrial Management,* December 1974, pp. 20–21.

Lazere, M. P., "New York: Factoring Country," *Credit and Financial Management,* December 1974, p. 33.

Van Norden, Langdon, "Factoring: Cash for Your Receivables," *Administrative Management,* August 1972, p. 34.

White, C. R., "Today's Factor: A Financial Supermarket," *Credit and Financial Management,* December 1974, pp. 16–17.

## FEDERAL WAGE AND HOUR LAW

*Presents guidelines to avoid paying unnecessary overtime wages under the Fair Labor Standards Act.*

In an inflationary environment wage costs can soar as employees push for pay increases to match or exceed cost-of-living rises. To help maintain adequate profit levels, companies must explore all avenues that promise to hold wages to a minimum.

In recent years the federal wage and hour law (Fair Labor Standards Act) has caused some confusion among employers about their legal obligations to employees. As a result, employees are sometimes paid more than the law requires. Of course there are competitive and motivational reasons for setting wage levels. But it is wise during inflationary conditions to review pay practices and personnel procedures with respect to legal options of the law. No employer wants to pay more in wages than he has to, especially when "normal" cost-of-living percentage increases reach double-digit proportions.

The following[1] provides some guidelines for reducing wage costs while staying within the federal wage and hour law.

### LUMP SUM PAY

If workloads fluctuate substantially from week to week, calling for frequent overtime, savings often can be achieved by switching employees to a flat weekly salary, rather than using an hourly rate.

For example, suppose that a clerk is put on a weekly salary of $150, regardless of the number of hours worked. During a normal week, she works 35 hours (5 days, 7 hours/day).

If a rush period requires her to work 50 hours, her base salary is still $150, or $3 an hour without overtime. Under the wage and hour law,

[1] Adapted from Lipman G. Feld, "How to Get Around the Wage and Hour Law—Legally," *Administrative Management*, December 1974. Copyright © 1974 by Geyer-McAllister Publications, Inc., New York.

**143**

however, she must be paid time and a half for each hour over 40. Accordingly, she is paid an extra $1.50/hour for the 10 overtime hours, and her total paycheck comes to $165.

If she were paid on an hourly wage basis, the overtime work would have cost the employer considerably more. Calculating her hourly rate at $4.286 ($150 divided by 35 hours), she is paid this amount until she reaches 40 hours. After 40 hours, her time and a half hourly rates are $6.429. Thus for the 50-hour work week, her total pay is $235.73 (40 hours at $4.286, or $171.44, plus 10 hours overtime at $6.429, or $64.29). The considerable difference of $70 per week between the two payment methods makes the lump sum technique well worth investigating for large offices with highly erratic workloads.

To keep within the framework of the law,

If you are going to pay on a lump sum basis, you must carefully set forth your intentions in advance in writing. You cannot jump back and forth between lump sum pay and an hourly wage to suit a particular work week. You must make the change on a permanent basis, explain it fully to employees, and record all changes in their personnel files.[2]

## UNNECESSARY OVERTIME

Because of misconceptions about what constitutes a work week, some firms mistakenly pay time and a half when it is not required by law. It is not always necessary to pay employees overtime for working more than the firm's standard work week.

For example, suppose that 25 clerks are working a standard work week of 40 hours at the rate of $3 per hour. Because of a fall-off in business, management decides to reduce labor costs and puts the clerks on a 35-hour week for several months. Each now earns $105 per week.

Suddenly business picks up and some of the clerks are returned to a 40-hour week. Mistakenly, the administrative manager pays them time and a half for the additional 5 weekly "overtime" hours. This additional pay is unjustified because the law states that time and a half must be paid only after 40 hours are worked in a week, not for hours worked over a company's standard work week, unless that standard is 40.

Again, when large numbers of workers are being improperly credited with overtime pay, the amounts spent can be substantial.

[2] Feld, "How to Get Around the Wage and Hour Law— Legally," p. 56. Excerpted from *Administrative Management,* Copyright © 1974 by Geyer-McAllister Publications, Inc., New York.

## ECONOMICAL OVERTIME

On other occasions overtime may prove to be a cost-effective practice. Suppose a firm decides it needs two employees in an evening office shift working from 5:00 P.M. until midnight. Daily cost is $42 (7 hours at $3 per hour for each person). Experience shows, however, that there is little need for staffing after 8:00 P.M. Rather than pay for the slow hours, it is better to hold over from the day shift two employees who would like to make the extra money. Working 3 hours of overtime at $4.50 per hour ($3 at time and a half), the cost to the firm is reduced to $27 per day, a sizable saving in a year's time. Even more would be saved if the overtime employees were paid on a lump sum weekly salary basis.

## WEEKENDS AND HOLIDAYS

The wage and hour law has often been misinterpreted to mean that employees must be paid overtime for work on Saturdays, Sundays, and holidays. This is not so if no more than 40 hours have been worked by an employee during a period of 168 hours—one week. If the 40 hours have not yet been reached, time and a half pay is not required by law, even on weekends and holidays.

Thus if the standard company work week is 35 hours, a company need pay only an employee's standard hourly wage for 5 hours of weekend or holiday work. Even more important, a company can have an employee who has been sick, or absent for some other reason during the week, handle weekend or holiday work. If he has been ill, for example, and has not put in 40 hours during the current work week, he can return to work at his regular rate of pay and perform duties that might otherwise have to be assigned to more costly overtime or temporary help. This is a particularly useful technique because a work week, by law, need not fall within a cyclical framework of days. It is considered to be any consecutive period of 168 hours.

## SUGGESTED FURTHER READING

"Changing Wage-Hour Rules," *Personnel Journal*, January 1975, p. 6.

Feld, Lipman G., "How to Get Around the Wage and Hour Law—Legally," *Administrative Management*, December 1974, p. 56.

Hedges, J. N., "How Many Days Make a Workweek?" *Monthly Labor Review*, April 1975, pp. 29–36.

Winter, E., "How Temporary Help Can Cut Your Payroll Costs," *Office*, December 1974, pp. 56–57.

# SECTION **34**

## FINANCING TECHNIQUES

*Outlines innovative methods for raising corporate capital during inflationary periods.*

Prolonged periods of inflation disrupt traditional channels of raising corporate capital.

During recent inflationary spirals, many creditworthy companies found themselves unable to attract sufficient long-term capital at any price. Public capital markets, both debt and equity, became all but closed to certain industries in particular, and to small and medium-sized companies in general. Safety of principal and return, high enough to offset double-digit inflation, became the predominant investor consideration.

The depressed state of the stock market during those years was also not conducive to raising new equity capital. Investor concern with inflation was reflected in declining price/earnings ratios for particularly vulnerable companies and industry groups, as well as in sharply reduced investor interest in the stock market generally.

Inflation also makes it more difficult for corporations to turn to debt markets for relief. During inflationary periods, the appeal of bonds as a corporate vehicle for raising capital is considerably lessened.

As a result of these difficulties, the capital market has responded to inflationary pressures and increased capital demands by changing the traditional forms of long-term debt instruments. The results have been debt securities that are modified to counteract the effects of inflation and the accompanying uncertain future outlook, and designed to become more attractive to individual as well as institutional investors.

The following discusses some notable new innovations in financing which are becoming increasingly important vehicles for raising capital.[1] If applied effectively, they can ease or eliminate many of a corporation's financial pressures.

---

[1] Adapted from Paul K. Kelly, "New Financing Techniques on Wall Street," *Financial Executive,* November 1974, p. 30.

**146**

## DEBT FINANCING

The major problem for capital-intensive corporations is how to keep capitalization from becoming debt heavy, resulting in lowering of the firms' bond ratings and credit status. When common equities are selling below book value, traditional sources of equity capital become prohibitively expensive, making it difficult to keep traditional debt/equity ratios in historical perspective through sole reliance on retained earnings.

### Project Financing

To solve the problem, many firms are turning to off-balance-sheet financing devices, opening a new area of investment banking techniques known generically as "project financing." Project financing combines new applications of traditional financing methods with entirely new techniques to meet interim and long-term requirements for funds.

*Documented Discount Notes.* Several off-balance-sheet short-term or interim financing methods have been devised for commercial paper or short-term private placement markets.

One such method uses the documented discount note (DDN). In financing nuclear fuel cores, for example, a trust is established by a third party and takes title to a nuclear core. It then leases the core to a utility. The dollar value of the core is thus kept off the utility's balance sheet. Typically the trust is financed with DDNs, supported by attached letters of credit from major banks. The letters of credit guarantee that payment of principal and interest will be made at maturity, by the bank if necessary. As a result, the trust obtains a credit status that permits it to sell its large amounts of debt securities to institutional investors.

Since DDNs are bank-guaranteed securities, they are exempt from the requirement imposed on ordinary commercial paper that the proceeds be used for "current transaction purposes." Consequently DDNs may be used for certain long-term transactions, such as plant construction which cannot legally be financed with ordinary commercial paper. Use of the method has saved as much as 2 percent interest compared to traditional bank construction loans.

*Leveraged Leasing.* Many new, creative applications of traditional leasing and leveraged leasing concepts are being used as intermediate and long-term financing devices. Utilities, for example, have jointly financed entire generating plants using leasing techniques. Recently a group of five utilities began joint development of a coal mining property under a leveraged lease agreement that passes along tax benefits to the third-party equity holder.

Leveraged leasing is particularly attractive to industries that have low effective tax rates and therefore do not profit significantly from the retention of tax benefits. A fairly recent innovation is application of the leveraged lease concept to pollution control financing. Here the investor receives both tax-exempt income and tax benefits that could not be fully utilized by the issuing company.

*Take-or-Pay Contracts.* The petroleum and utility industries have been particularly creative in developing new off-balance-sheet financing methods.

Certain projects, such as offshore oil ports and pipelines, make use of "take-or-pay contracts" guaranteeing that the taker will pay for the project's output at a rate that will adequately service the debt of the project, even if delivery of the output is interrupted. The offer of this type of contract is sufficient to obtain financing for the project, since the lender is assured that funds will be provided under all circumstances.

*Throughput-and-Deficiency Agreements.* The "throughput-and-deficiency agreement" is similar to the take-or-pay contract in concept, although different in form. In a pipeline project, for example, the taker agrees to accept oil shipments at a certain flow rate and at a price that will adequately service the debt of the project. If for some reason the flow is interrupted, the taker continues to make payments sufficient to maintain uninterrupted debt service.

### Pollution Control Bonds

In addition to the off-balance-sheet financing techniques just described, new direct-obligation debt instruments have been developed in recent years.

A notable example is tax-exempt pollution control financing. This is an application of the industrial revenue bond structure allowing a municipality or municipal entity to issue tax-exempt bonds to finance pollution control facilities, which are then sold or leased to a private corporation. Lease or sale payments to the corporation made by the municipality must be sufficient to pay all costs of servicing the bonds. In case of default, the private corporation's credit backs the bonds. But with tax-exempt financing, a corporation can often save from 2 to $2\frac{1}{2}$ percent in interest compared to taxable securities of similar quality.

### Floating Rate Securities

A recent innovation in debt financing is the floating rate note. This instrument has been developed in response to the reluctance of institutional investors to invest in fixed-rate bonds during a period of high inflation. The instrument protects the buyer against excessive price erosion. It has been particularly popular with individual investors because of the "put" feature that permits the investors, at their option, to redeem the note at par every 6 months.

The floating-rate security is in its infancy. Its potential attractiveness as a financing vehicle will depend on future rates of inflation. If the rate remains high, new modifications and refinements of floating-rate securities will be introduced as a marketing device to attract investor interest. One example would be to tie rates on such securities to money market or price indices other than the Treasury bill rate, which has been the pricing mechanism for the first group of floating-rate issues.

## EQUITY FINANCING

Massing a sufficient equity base is perhaps the greatest obstacle confronting companies, especially in an inflationary environment. Often retained earnings do not keep pace with debt accumulation, and at some point most companies are forced to resort to external sources of financing.

Several innovative solutions to this problem have been suggested in recent years. One approach is to rely more on preferred stock when common equity is not available at a reasonable cost. If a price/earnings ratio approximates the cost of the capital of the firm's common stock, the company can determine approximate cost of using preferred stock. For this, the firm compares the preferred dividend rate with its P/E. Obviously, the more depressed a company's price/earnings ratio, the more attractive the preferred stock alternative.

The major drawback is that at low market levels the cash flow requirement of the preferred dividend is usually substantially greater than the common dividend.

### Mutually Redeemable
### Preferred Stock

Another new technique is use of mutually redeemable preferred stock. Unlike ordinary preferred stock, which has either a sinking fund or a redemption privilege limited exclusively to the issuer, this new instrument permits redemption by the issuer or by the holder of the stock, after an initial and relatively short nonredemption period. These nonredemption periods have been as short as 2 years, but are usually 3 or more years.

This type of essentially short-term preferred stock permits the issuer to obtain equity at a slightly lower cost than ordinary preferred stock. It also gives the issuer flexibility in refunding preferred with a common issue if the stock market improves between time of issuance and the end of the nonredemption period. The holder, in turn, receives a short-term investment that will pay out at par whenever he exercises his redemption privilege. His investment is subject to the 85 percent intercorporate dividend exclusion for tax purposes. The result is a short-term investment with no market risk and a largely tax-sheltered return. To date, such issues have only been negotiated on a private-placement basis.

### Preferred Stock with Accelerated Sinking Fund Patterns

Another equity variation is a preferred stock with an accelerated sinking fund pattern designed to retire the security within 10 years of issuance and to produce an even shorter average life. This innovation again reflects today's investor unwillingness to commit funds to long-term preferred stock issues.

### Subordinated Debt

A "near-equity" alternative is the addition of a layer of subordinated debt to a company's capital structure. The benefit is the deductibility of interest charges for tax purposes, unlike preferred or common dividends. A negative aspect is lack of availability at a reasonable price, when investors are barraged by high-quality senior debt issues at high rate levels. An additional problem is that the interest on subordinated debt is included in calculation of fixed-charges coverage of a company's debt position, even though the debt may be regarded as near-equity for capital base purposes.

### SUGGESTED FURTHER READING

"Bright Spot in Business Loans: Commercial Finance and Factoring," *Banking,* March 1975, pp. 33–34.
Cohen, M., "Corporate Financial Requirements Following Inflation," *Conference Board Record,* April 1975, pp. 55–59.

Hartwell, R. W., "New Challanges for the Financial Executive," *Conference Board Record*, April 1975, pp. 60–61.

Jones, R. H., "Financial Management During Inflation," *Financial Executive*, February 1975, pp. 10–15.

Kelly, Paul K., "New Financing Techniques on Wall Street," *Financial Executive*, Vol. 30, November 1974.

Neuwirth, P. D., "Computer Forecasting—No More Surprises," *Financial Executive*, October 1974, pp. 58–60.

# SECTION 35

## FLAGS OF CONVENIENCE TECHNIQUES

*Discusses the benefits of moving company operations to areas least affected by inflationary pressures.*

"Flags of convenience" is a traditional expression referring to the practice of some shipowners of registering their vessels in countries other than their own to avoid taxes or stringent safety regulations. Because of the practice, small countries such as Liberia and Panama can boast the registration of huge merchant fleets.

With the coming of persistent inflation, the expression has taken on an enlarged meaning and refers to the practice of companies switching all or part of their operations to countries or areas that have or are projected to have the lowest rates of inflation, or to countries in which the effects of inflation are partially offset by other circumstances.

Numerous examples can be found. In recent years scores of manufacturing firms have ceased operations in Great Britain and moved to other parts of the world because of high current and anticipated inflationary rates. Many American companies that formerly imported large quantities of raw materials have set up manufacturing installations in the countries of origin of the materials, both to save inflated shipping costs and to take advantage of lower wage rates. Large numbers of firms have moved company operations from expensive urban areas such as New York to other geographical locations, saving as much as 25 to 50 percent in property, plant, and labor costs. On a smaller scale, hundreds of companies have saved significant amounts of money simply from moving from downtown locations to industrial or office locations in the suburbs.

Use of "flags of convenience" techniques depends on the company's business, material supply sources, degree of skilled labor needed, costs of disrupting business operations to relocate, employee attitudes, and so on. In many circumstances, however, the financial benefits that can be derived from switching production plants or branch offices to lower-cost areas or countries with low projected inflation rates can result in significant long-term savings.

## SUGGESTED FURTHER READING

Crawford, D., "Three Studies in Relocation," *Director,* January 1975, p. 72.

Kolbe, R. A., "Global Branch Buying Offers Savings, Certainty," *Purchasing,* May 6, 1975, pp. 62–64.

Levin, S. G., "Suburban–Central City Property Tax Differentials and the Location of Industry," *Land Economics,* November 1974, pp. 380–386.

Louviere, V., "Bigger Things for the Small Towns," *Nation's Business,* October 1974, p. 36.

# SECTION 36

## GROUP INSURANCE

*Outlines methods for evaluating group insurance programs to
assure cost effectiveness in an inflationary environment.*

Group insurance costs have soared in recent years, the result of inflationary
pressures on salaries and administrative costs in both the insurance and hos-
pitalization fields. Financial executives have come to expect increased
expenses in group insurance almost quarterly. Moreover, in light of
anticipated persistent inflation, there appears to be no end to these increases
in sight.

Recent studies indicate that fringe benefits now make up 20 to 30 percent
of the average employee's yearly income, and group insurance represents a
significant proportion of this amount. Because of the size of this expense,
companies should take steps to ensure that the group insurance programs
they offer are not only attractive but cost effective. It has been estimated
that poor insurance plan design, excess reserves held by the carrier, and
inadequate administrative procedures may be penalizing American businesses by more than half a billion dollars a year.

The following[1] sets out a number of methods companies can use to
evaluate their group insurance programs, to be sure that such programs are
financially efficient during periods of persistently rising prices.

### PLAN DESIGN

Often the overall cost of a group insurance program can be lowered by
changing certain provisions within particular plans. A number of possibilities usually exist, as follows.

#### Maternity Benefit Extension

It is not uncommon for a medical plan to guarantee maternity benefits to
women for 9 months following their termination of employment or benefits

[1] Adapted from Robert J. O'Meara and Susan Koralik, "Cutting Group Insurance Costs,"
*Financial Executive,* July 1974, pp. 70–75.

for 9 months following the termination of the policy itself. The effect of this second provision may be to build up a sizable maternity benefit reserve. Companies may believe that maternity claims incurred after the initial 9-month period are paid out of this reserve, but in fact such claims are usually paid out of current premiums. Thus a maternity benefit reserve may be held by the carrier for years.

By eliminating the extension provision, the reserve can be returned to the company for investment at a better return. For example, when the policy itself is terminated, an agreement may be made with the new carrier to provide maternity benefits during the first 9 months of the new policy. Employees lose nothing in benefits, and the maternity reserve can be used for other purposes. Savings can be significant: if a company has 5000 employees and a $300 delivery benefit, the reserve might total $130,000.

### Outpatient Care and Preadmission Testing

Group medical plans frequently provide certain benefits only if the patient is confined to a hospital. To get these benefits, individuals must be admitted to a hospital, regardless of whether a hospital stay is actually required. Large bills for hospital room and board and miscellaneous charges will be incurred, in addition to normal surgery and testing charges.

If plans are written to provide benefits for surgery performed in a doctor's office and for laboratory tests taken by the individual as an outpatient, overall claims can often be reduced.

### Preventive Medicine

Benefits for preventive medicine are commonly excluded from group insurance plans. Often cost savings can be gained by including such benefits, because the cost of providing routine physical examinations and immunizations is relatively low compared with the cost of treating major illnesses that could have been prevented or detected at an early stage. The practice conserves manpower; if a condition such as high blood pressure is detected and treated early, the productive life of an employee can be extended significantly.

### Luxury and Excessive Benefits

Benefit plans should not be designed to provide services employees would not ordinarily use if there were no insurance in force. For example, semi-private hospital rooms should be specified instead of private; benefit allowances for a particular medical service should be limited to the normal local charge for that service.

### Waiver of Premium Provision

Many group life insurance plans include a waiver of premium provision, stating that after a certain time the insurance carrier will not require a group life insurance premium for any individual in the group who becomes permanently disabled.

In most cases this waiver of premium provision is not economical. First, an incurred and unreported (I & U) reserve is usually established for the unknown liabilities. This reserve, which is held for the life of the contract, is usually between 10 and 20 percent of the annual group life premium. Second, if the premium is waived for an individual, the carrier usually puts 75 percent of the total liability carried for that individual into a disabled life reserve for the length of time the waiver is in effect.

For example, an employee having life insurance coverage of $50,000 becomes disabled, and the insurance carrier agrees to waive the premium of his or her life insurance coverage. Assuming that the monthly premium is 50¢ per $100 of coverage, the annual savings in premium will be $300. However the carrier requires the company to leave $37,500 in a disabled life reserve to cover 75 percent of the existing liability. If total life insurance premiums for the company were $100,000, the I & U reserve established earlier might be $11,000. The insurance carrier is then holding a reserve of $48,500 ($11,000 I & U plus disabled life of $37,500). Without waiver of premium, these reserves would not exist. If these funds were invested at 7 percent they would return $3395 in interest per year. The company would, of course, have to continue paying a premium of $300 per year for the disabled employee's insurance coverage, but it would be ahead by $3395 minus $300, or $3095.

## ADMINISTRATIVE METHODS

It is difficult to evaluate the administrative efficiency of an insurance company, but some estimate can be made by considering the policies of the carrier in processing claims.

First, does the insurance company audit claims to ensure that charges are reasonable and customary? If not, claims may be excessive.

Second, does the insurance carrier allow limited certification of benefits? Such requirements can lower claims. For instance, a plan might require the hospital to contact the insurance company for certification of benefits when a person is admitted. The insurance company will then certify that benefits will be paid for a specified number of days, based on a schedule of normal hospital stays. If the patient is not released at the end of that period, the hospital must ask the insurance company to certify benefits for an extended period of time. The procedure usually cuts down on prolonged and unnecessary hospital stays.

## RETENTION

Retention is the amount the insurance company charges to cover its administration costs, plus the profit it expects to receive on the contract. The amount of retention can be figured as a percentage of premium, or it can be based on the time an insurance company spends on a particular plan. Usually, however, a dividend formula based on the number of lives, types of coverage, and other elements of the plan is used to compute retention. Regardless of the method used, careful periodic analysis should be made to be sure that administrative costs do not become excessive.

Administrative costs are usually analyzed by comparing retention to total premiums. As premiums increase, the ratio of retention to premiums should normally decrease, even though the dollar amount of retention is larger. Table 24 shows how a hypothetical company's premiums, claims, and retentions might change over a 3-year period.

This company's ratio of retention to *premiums* decreased over the 3 years, but its ratio of retention to *claims* increased. Although such a pattern is not uncommon, it is an indication of administrative inefficiency. Except for claims processing, other administrative costs should be fixed over a wide range of total claims. This means that as total claims go up, the ratio of claims to retention should go down. For example, assume that fixed costs for billing, processing, and other services are $100, and variable costs for claims processing are $100 per $1000 of paid claims. At the $1000 claims

Table 24   Premiums, Claims, and Retentions Over 3 Years[a]

| Year | Total premiums | Paid claims | Retention Dollars | Retention % of premiums | Retention % of claims |
|---|---|---|---|---|---|
| 1 | $100,000 | $ 89,000 | $10,000 | 10.0% | 11.2% |
| 2 | $120,000 | $100,000 | $11,400 | 9.5 | 11.4 |
| 3 | $150,000 | $110,000 | $13,500 | 9.0 | 12.2 |

[a] *Source:* O'Meara and Koralik, "Cutting Group Insurance Costs," *Financial Executive,* July 1974, p. 72.

level, total costs are $200, or 20 percent of paid claims. If claims are $2000, total costs climb to $300, but the ratio of costs to paid claims drops to 15 percent. A similar pattern should be apparent in most cases.

Since retention is a charge for the administrative function performed by the carrier, another cost-reducing technique is to cut down on the services the company receives. One method is to combine all group insurance coverages under one carrier, thus eliminating multiple billings and duplication in data processing systems design and other services that are required for more than one carrier.

### RESERVES

Reserves can often be lowered through negotiation with the carrier, since insurance companies vary in the amount of reserve they require to back a particular liability. As a company's premiums rise year after year, the firm is placed in an increasingly strong bargaining position. When reserves become large, it is often advantageous to investigate ways of reducing them, or at least offsetting some of their financial disadvantages. The following techniques can be helpful.

#### Delayed Premiums

A company in a strong bargaining position with the carrier may be able to withhold premiums at the beginning of a plan year to offset the reserves being held. For example, if reserves are equal to 25 percent of the total annual premium, the company might simply withhold the first 3 months' premium. Any claims filed during that period can be paid out of the reserve. Since it is unlikely that the loss ratio (ratio of paid claims to paid premiums) for an established plan would be 100 percent or greater during the first 3 months of a policy year, there is little chance of exhausting the reserves. This technique, in effect, allows the use of funds held in reserve.

#### Interim Accounting

The ratio of claims paid to premium dollars—after the first plan year when reserves are being established—should be approximately 100 percent including retention charges and reserve adjustments. If the loss ratio is lower (i.e., if paid claims are lower than paid premiums), the difference is paid to the company as a dividend. Normally this dividend is based on year-end accounting, which insurance companies commonly complete about 4 months after the end of the plan year.

**Table 25    Loss Ratio in the First 6 Months**[a]

| Date | Premiums paid in current month | Total premiums paid | Total claims | Ratio loss (%) |
|---|---|---|---|---|
| August 30 | $62,500 | $500,000 | $300,000 | 60 |
| September 30 | -0- | $500,000 | $345,000 | 69 |
| October 30 | -0- | $500,000 | $395,000 | 79 |
| November 30 | -0- | $500,000 | $445,000 | 89 |

[a] *Source:* O'Meara and Koralik, "Cutting Group Insurance Costs," *Financial Executive,* July 1974, p. 74.

An insured company using interim accounting, however, can begin to check the overall loss ratio after the first 6 months of the policy year. If the ratio is considerably below 100 percent, the company, after informing the carrier, can withhold premiums until the loss ratio rises. This technique is illustrated in Table 25.

In this case the company is allowing its claims experience to catch up by not paying 3 months of current premiums. Assuming that each $62,500 monthly premium could be invested at 7 percent, the firm would realize a gain of $7665 by April 30—the date on which the dividend would have been received.

## LONG-TERM DISABILITY

Long-term disability (LTD) premiums normally do not come back as a dividend; if they are not used to pay claims, they are lost.

To reduce this loss, some companies have negotiated special premium arrangements with their carriers. For example, a carrier might agree to accept only 30 percent of the normal premium for the LTD plan. In return, the company agrees to experience rate the first 5 years of benefits. In other words, the company will pay for any long-term disability claim out of its own funds. If the normal annual premium is $30,000, this agreement could result in an annual saving of $21,000 if no claims were incurred. Long-term disability is a low-probability risk in most organizations, making this form of self-insurance viable.

## INCREASED BENEFIT ANALYSIS

When the carrier proposes increased premiums to cover an increased benefits plan, the proposal should be evaluated in terms of current plan efficiency. For example, if the current plan is paying hospital room-and-board charges at the rate of 85¢ for every dollar claimed, the plan's efficiency rate is 85 percent. If a proposal is made to improve benefits for room and board to 100 percent, the premium increase should be about 17.5 percent. An increase larger than this amount might represent an excessive premium that would be held for several months before being returned as a dividend.

## SUGGESTED FURTHER READING

O'Meara, Robert J. and Susan Koralik, "Cutting Group Insurance Costs," *Financial Executive,* July 1974, pp. 70–75.

# SECTION **37**

## HIGH–VALUE LISTS

*Outlines a systematic approach for achieving manufacturing cost reduction during inflation.*

The two basic elements in any manufacturing cost reduction program are purchases and labor. These two elements take on added importance during inflationary periods because of rapidly rising materials prices and increased wage demands by labor. Any program attempting to reduce manufacturing costs must therefore pay particular attention to these two areas.

One technique that can prove valuable to managers in helping cope with rising material and wage costs is the use of high-value lists.[1]

### COST REDUCTION ELEMENTS

The analysis of specific product costs should be preceded by the formulation of a systematic cost reduction plan composed of the following elements.

*Product Knowledge.* A thorough knowledge of all aspects of the product is a key prerequisite to cutting costs. Information should be obtained about the operational sequence, processes used, hardware, design requirements, manufacturing time, schedules, and costs.

*Utilization of Talent.* Cost reduction ideas should be encouraged, and all ideas that appear to hold promise should be investigated. All important areas of management should be included—engineering, quality control, production, manufacturing, and other members of the management team. A chairman should be appointed to spearhead cost reduction efforts and assign action items.

*Techniques.* Specialized techniques such as value engineering, work measurement, and other available resources should be utilized wherever possible.

[1] Adapted with permission from February 1975 INDUSTRIAL ENGINEERING (A. M. Segar, "Systematic Cost Reduction," pp. 14–17). Copyright American Institute of Industrial Engineers, Inc., 25 Technology Park/Atlanta, Norcross, Ga. 30071.

### PURCHASES COMPONENT

The following steps should be taken to identify costs in the purchasing component and establish a purchase high-value list:

• List every purchased item that is used in the manufacture of the end product. Include such items as nuts, bolts, resistors, and structures, as well as any labor purchased from outside operations, such as machining and assembly.
• Determine the unit cost of each purchased item.
• Determine the quantity of each item used for each end product.
• Determine the total cost of each item by multiplying the usage by the unit cost.
• Compile a list of all the purchased items in descending order of cost. This is referred to as a Purchase High-Value List. Table 26 shows a typical example.

The high-value list serves to identify the actual location of costs. For example, a screw costing 2¢ and used 1000 times represents a cost of $20.

**Table 26   Sample Purchase High-Value List[a]**

| Code, identifying part number | Description | Quantity | Purchase price of each and extended price ($) |
|---|---|---|---|
| 9378-4371 | IC DFF | 2310 | 1.800 |
|  |  |  | 4158.000 |
| 9378-4422 | Connector | 550 | 7.470 |
|  |  |  | 4108.500 |
| 9378-3151 | Resistor, fixed | 2200 | 1.830 |
|  |  |  | 4026.000 |
| 9378-2467 | Back panel | 22 | 181.000 |
|  |  |  | 3982.000 |
| 9378-2121 | Power supply | 22 | 175.000 |
|  |  |  | 3850.000 |
| 9378-1072 | Transformer | 264 | 12.400 |
|  |  |  | 3273.600 |
| 9378-4390 | IC, 4-bit | 176 | 17.880 |
|  |  |  | 3146.880 |

[a] *Source:* Reprinted with permission from February 1975 INDUSTRIAL ENGINEERING (A. M. Segar, "Systematic Cost Reduction," p. 15). Copyright American Institute of Industrial Engineers, Inc., 25 Technology Park/Atlanta, Norcross, GA 30071.

Obviously a structure costing $50 and used once represents $50. Now if we can obtain the structure for $45, we can save $5. On the other hand, if we can procure the screw for 1¢, we save $10. Thus it may not be obvious where the cost lies. Without knowing the usage and extended cost, one might not have explored the possibility of reducing the cost of a 2¢ screw.

Once compiled, the purchase high-value list often reveals that about 80 percent of the total purchase cost is contained within the first 5 to 10 percent of the items on the list. The company's cost reduction program should be built around these items. It is much easier to concentrate efforts on 50 items than on 600, and the first 10 percent of the items will produce the most meaningful cost reduction results.

## LABOR COMPONENT

The following steps should be taken to identify costs in the labor component and establish a labor high-value list:

- Establish a list of all items on which labor is performed within the company. Include assembly, machining, and inspection types of labor.
- Determine the cost of each item used in the end product by multiplying the time required for its processing (or the basis for applying the burden, if different) by the labor and burden rates for each of the burden centers—machining, assembly, testing, and so on.
- Add the burden center costs of each item and multiply the result by the total number of a particular item used for that end product. This gives the total labor and overhead costs on an item basis per product.

Table 27 Sample Labor High-Value List[a]

| Code identifying part number | Quantity system | Test unit | Assembly unit | Machine unit | Quality unit | Extended total hours | Dollars |
|---|---|---|---|---|---|---|---|
| 9378-0041 | 2 | 0 | 52.288 | 0 | 1.370 | 107.316 | 1518.54 |
| 9378-9724 | 100 | 0 | 0.753 | 0 | 0.068 | 82.100 | 1213.61 |
| 9378-7246 | 2 | 0 | 0.150 | 14.849 | 6.188 | 42.374 | 687.23 |
| 9378-8814 | 2 | 1.971 | 4.980 | 8.366 | 0.901 | 32.436 | 580.20 |
| 9378-2123 | 4 | 0 | 0.050 | 3.398 | 1.138 | 18.344 | 320.72 |

[a] *Source:* Reprinted with permission from February 1975 INDUSTRIAL ENGINEERING (A. M. Segar, "Systematic Cost Reduction," p. 16). Copyright American Institute of Industrial Engineers, Inc., 25 Technology Park/Atlanta, Norcross, GA 30071.

• List all the items used in the product in descending order of their total labor and overhead costs. This list is referred to as the Labor High-Value List. Table 27 gives a typical example.

## COMBINING THE LISTS

To achieve a maximum cost reduction, the results of each product's high-value lists are combined to obtain factory-wide or company-wide economies, as in the following example.

A structure once used, representing 32 hours, contributes $480 to cost when extended by its burden-center rates. A circuit assembly used 100 times, representing one hour each, contributes $1400 to cost when extended by its burden-center rates. Two hours less on the structure would yield a saving of approximately $30, whereas 0.1 hour less on the assembly would yield a saving of approximately $140.[2]

When all cost elements are combined and taken into account, it is often found that the top 5 to 10 percent make up 80 percent of the costs. As with purchased items, the main thrust of cost-reduction programs should be aimed at this small number of large costs. This is done by examining the high-cost items operation by operation and, working within the framework of the cost-reduction elements outlined earlier, deciding on appropriate courses of action.

## SUGGESTED FURTHER READING

Segar, A. M., "Systematic Cost Reduction," *Industrial Engineering*, February 1975, pp. 14–17.

[2] Reprinted with permission from February 1975 INDUSTRIAL ENGINEERING (A. M. Segar, "Systematic Cost Reduction," p. 17). Copyright American Institute of Industrial Engineers, Inc., 25 Technology Park/Atlanta, Norcross, Ga 30071.

# SECTION 38

## IMPLICIT PRICE DEFLATOR

*Outlines use of the GNP implicit price deflator and provides index statistics since 1965.*

Gross national product (GNP) expresses in dollars the market value of goods and services produced by the nation's economy within a specified period of time. It is almost always estimated for a calendar or fiscal year, or for a quarter of a year expressed at an annual rate.

Raw materials, components, and intermediate products are not counted separately in GNP. However their value is included in the value of finished goods sold to consumers and governments, in investment goods sold to business, or in inventory accumulation. GNP is a "gross" measure because no deduction is made to reflect the wearing out of machinery and other capital assets used in production.

The implicit price deflator (IPD) is the price index for the gross national product. Through use of the deflator, economists can compare the current GNP with what the same amount of goods and services would have cost in 1958, now the base year.

The current-dollar gross national product is divided by the same amount of goods and services expressed in 1958 dollars to arrive at the "deflator." The IPD is a three-digit number, and changes can be translated into annual percentage rates—4 or 5 percent—representing a measure of inflation. Because it is so comprehensive, the IPD is generally regarded as the best single measure of broad price movements in the economy as a whole.

From a business point of view, the IPD is an important indicator of inflationary trends in the economy, both in the United States and abroad. Along with the Consumer Price Index and the Wholesale Price Index, the IPD can be used as a basis for indexed contracts, wage negotiations, escalation clauses, bidding, and other business activities that need to take into account the impact of inflation.

Table 28 sets out the implicit price deflator for total United States gross national product since 1965.

**Table 28    Gross National Product and Implicit Price Deflator**[a]

| Period | Total GNP[b] | Total GNP in 1958 dollars[b] | Implicit price deflator for total GNP (1958 = 100) |
|---|---|---|---|
| 1965 | 684.9 | 617.8 | 110.86 |
| 1966 | 749.9 | 658.1 | 113.94 |
| 1967 | 793.9 | 675.2 | 117.59 |
| 1968 | 864.2 | 706.6 | 122.30 |
| 1969 | 930.3 | 725.6 | 128.20 |
| 1970 | 977.1 | 722.5 | 135.24 |
| 1971 | 1054.9 | 746.3 | 141.35 |
| 1972 | 1158.0 | 792.5 | 146.12 |
| 1973 | 1294.9 | 839.2 | 154.31 |
| 1974 | 1397.4 | 821.2 | 170.18 |
| I | 1358.8 | 830.5 | 163.61 |
| II | 1383.8 | 827.1 | 167.31 |
| III | 1416.3 | 823.1 | 172.07 |
| IV | 1430.9 | 804.0 | 177.97 |
| 1975 | | | |
| I | 1416.6 | 780.0 | 181.62 |
| II | 1440.9 | 783.6 | 183.88 |

[a] *Source: Economic Indicators,* Council of Economic Advisors, Washington, D.C.
[b] Billions of dollars; quarterly data at seasonally adjusted annual rates.

## SUGGESTED FURTHER READING

*Business Conditions Digest* (monthly), Bureau of Economic Analysis, U.S. Department of Commerce, Washington, D.C.

*Economic Indicators* (monthly), Council of Economic Advisors, Washington, D.C.

*International Economic Indicators* (quarterly), U.S. Department of Commerce, Washington, D.C.

*Survey of Current Business* (monthly), Bureau of Economic Analysis, U.S. Department of Commerce, Washington, D.C.

# 39

## INDEX–LINKING

*A method that automatically adjusts business transactions for inflation.*

Index-linking ties specific business or industrial transactions to a recognized monetary base or index. As the index rises during inflationary periods, so does the amount of money received from the transaction. In this way real value or purchasing power of business income is maintained.

The technique can be used to reduce inflation's erosionary effects on debt collection, capital financing, tax payments, capital assets, ordering, pricing, and wages. Additionally, sales contracts can carry index-linked clauses to protect the seller.

### HISTORY AND USE OF INDEX–LINKING

American businessmen have used index linking to protect themselves from the effects of inflation in the past. As early as 1925 the American economist Irving Fisher persuaded a manufacturing company to sell purchasing-power securities to raise needed capital. These were based on a "tabular standard" or index of the day.

Real growth of index-linking is more modern. Brazil first used the method extensively. By indexing debt collection, wages, tax bases, and capital financing, the country reduced inflation from 92 per cent in 1964 to 15 per cent in 1973. Belgium, an extensive user of indexing, has one of the lowest inflation rates in Europe.

But the most important value of index-linking is not its reduction of inflation, according to Milton Friedman. The University of Chicago economist, a major proponent of index-linking, says the method is important to business because it adjusts the effects of inflation and lets executives get on with their company's real work. "Contracts for future delivery of products, wage agreements, and financial transactions involving borrowing and lending should be indexed," Friedman says, so that "producers' wage costs and other costs will go up less rapidly than they would without indexation."

Countries other than Brazil, Belgium, and the United States are using the technique to reduce the damages of inflation to business. Index-linking is widely employed in Canada and Israel, and to a lesser extent in Britain, Australia, Finland, and other countries.

Some American Congressmen hope to use index-linking to help both business and individual taxpayers overcome inequities, due to inflation, in taxation and other areas. A bill has been put before Congress to index federal government taxes and borrowing. The measure would tie capital gains, depreciation deductions, exemptions, government bond interest rates, and personal income tax brackets to the Consumer Price Index—increasing the bases as inflation rates rise.

In this book, however, we do not discuss at length areas of index-linking that must be initiated by the government, such as the escalation of corporate tax bases. Rather, the information that follows is intended to highlight specific business and industry areas that can be protected by index linking.

### DEBT COLLECTION

During rapid inflation the buyer often finds it wise to wait as long as possible to pay bills, since the value of the amount owed decreases in real or purchasing power value. For the seller, who has immediate wage and other costs, this creates a liquidity problem to be dealt with in addition to the knowledge that money eventually received is worth less than it was at the billing date. Collection indexing was first begun by Brazilian firms. To use this method, all outstanding accounts due are adjusted to match the change in an index at the end of each 28-day period. If, for example, the base index has increased 2 percent during that period, all debts are automatically increased that proportion *in addition to any credit charges required by terms of sale*. These terms must be set out in detail in the contract. Using the method, it is to the buyer's advantage to pay before the first indexation. Collections under this system are usually prompt.

### CAPITAL FINANCING

Financing is a particularly thorny problem for business and industry during an inflationary period. Not only do governmental monetary controls restrict traditional sources of credit, but inflation itself negates the purchasing power of returns to holders of bonds and shares. Many companies have begun to retain a larger percentage of profits for expansion, further discouraging investors and, since in some cases this money is added as a production cost, actually pushing up the rate of inflation.

Indexed stock, bonds, and insurance company endowment policies can be used to increase funds for capital investment. Indexed stock may be linked to the Consumer Price Index, to the gold price index, or to the value of company property adjusted to the Consumer Price Index. Face value of shares are adjusted according to index changes. Dividend payment is not affected by indexing, thus providing the company with capital financing at a limited cash outgo. Nor is there likely to be a "reckoning someday," particularly if stock values are linked to company property values, which reflect the real value of company assets.

Indexed bonds retain the issued face value, but interest paid reflects inflation plus a base interest to encourage their purchase. For example, if the index used rises 10 percent annually, interest paid would be this percentage plus the base interest. Use of the method gives investors a positive return in purchasing power value, thus encouraging investment.

Indexed endowment policies that provide an increase of up to 25 percent each 3 years, depending on index fluctuations, are being sold now by some insurance companies. The method encourages investment of funds with these firms, which in turn are traditional capital financers for business and industry.

Loans may also be indexed to provide easier financing during inflation. First National City Bank has proposed a debt instrument that would float with the rate on Treasury bills. Other banks will probably follow suit.

### WAGES

Wage indexing is used as a means of limiting wage increases to the same percentage as price increases due to inflation. The Brazilian system indexes wages annually. The increase is based on the Consumer Price Index rise for the past 6 months and the projected index increase for the coming 6 months. This limitation of wage increases helps hold the cost line even if inflation rates are 10 to 15 percent.

Without an indexing system, workers are prone to push for unjustifiably high increases during inflationary periods. A good example is the British situation in 1974. Wage increases called for by key unions ranged from 35 to 40 percent during a period when inflation was running at about 20 percent. The unions backed these exorbitant demands by claiming that no one knew for sure where inflation would stop and insisting that the members had to be protected. If escalation clauses had guaranteed workers raises to match inflation, these claims would have had no justification, and British industry's labor costs would have been considerably lower.


## CONTRACTS

Contracts can be inflation proofed by clauses allowing increased costs to be added to the agreed price; or they can be index-linked to the Wholesale or Consumer Price Indexes. Such protection is essential to the seller during any period when costs are rising and unpredictable. For the buyer, the index-linked contract is preferable to a cost-plus agreement, since the index reflects actual market price rises. A cost-plus agreement may lead to use of excessively expensive goods, since the seller knows that the buyer will bear the cost. Additionally, indexed contracts can be used as selling tools, persuading a buyer to purchase more goods or services and pay for them now before prices are further inflated.


## ORDERING AND PRICING

Some American manufacturers are using an index-linked buying technique to protect themselves from inflation when pricing their completed products. The problem without the system is that the manufacturer never knows with certainty what his raw materials and supplies will cost. With inflation boosting these costs daily, raw material prices may be higher than originally quoted. If the manufacturer is not warned in advance, he may price his own products too low.

   With the indexing technique, the supplier of raw materials is asked to quote on a price-plus-escalation basis. Individual areas of the Wholesale Price Index (available from the U.S. Department of Labor) are used as ties. For example, if a ferrous metal price is quoted, the supplier also quotes the ferrous metal Wholesale Price Index at that time. Upon delivery of the material, a new index reading is taken and the supplier is allowed to increase the metal's price the same percentage as the index's increase. The manufacturer can accurately predict raw material costs by watching the index, ensuring that he can set his own product prices at a profitable level. Accurate, up-to-the-minute indexed cost additions are usually computed through the company's EDP system.

## SUGGESTED FURTHER READING

Bowden, Lord, "Indexing," *The Guardian,* London, July 9, 1974.

Brittan, Samuel, "Economic Viewpoint," *Financial Times,* London, July 11, 1974.

Fane, C. G., "Index Linking and Inflation," *National Institute Economic Review,* November 1974, pp. 40–45.

Friedman, Milton, "Using Escalation to Help Fight Inflation," *Fortune,* July 1974.

"How Indexing Can Ease Inflation's Pain," *Monthly Economic Newsletter,* First National City Bank of New York, October 1974, pp. 7–9.

Matthews, W. M., "Loan Indexing: A Way to Preserve Capital?" *Journal of Commercial Bank Lending,* April 1975, pp. 2–5.

Perkins, J. F. B., "How the Brazilians Learned to Live with Inflation," *The Guardian,* London, June 18, 1974.

Schnepper, Jeff, "Can Capitalism Survive Rising Inflation?" *Intellect,* November 1974.

# SECTION 40

## INDEXED LEASES

*Outlines the use of indexed cost-of-living clauses in long-term commercial leases and the implications for lessees and lessors.*

As a result of recent inflationary trends, increasing use is being made of indexed "cost-of-living" clauses in commercial leases. Their purpose is to offset the eroding effects of inflation on real estate investments with long-term leases.

Typically the rental is adjusted upward annually in relation to the increase of a recognized index, usually the Consumer Price Index. There are many variations of the cost-of-living clause, but most contain the elements of the following representative sample:[1]

The monthly base rental shall be annually increased (but not decreased) in the following manner: The base for computing the adjustment is the index figure for the month this lease commences as shown in the Consumer Price Index (CPI), *All Items,* based on the period 1967 = 100 for the Standard Metropolitan Statistical Area of Kansas City, Missouri, as revised 1964, and published by the United States Department of Labor's Bureau of Labor Statistics.

The index figure for the adjustment date shall be used to compute a percentage as it relates to the index figure on the index date. The percentage (if in excess of 100) shall be used to calculate the increase in rental payment for the period beginning on the adjustment date and continuing until the next adjustment date.

The use of cost-of-living clauses in leases can result in significant cost advantages or disadvantages depending upon whether the firm is the lessee or the lessor. The following[2] outlines the financial implications from both points of view.

[1] Reprinted from *Journal of Property Management,* September/October, 1974, p. 210 (Charles E Sutherland, "The Cost of Living Clause—A Different Perspective,"), by permission of the Institute of Real Estate Management. Copyright 1974.

[2] Adapted from Sutherland, "The Cost of Living Clause" (*Journal of Property Management,* September/October 1974, pp. 120–123), by permission: the Institute of Real Estate Management. Copyright 1974.

### LESSOR

From the lessor's point of view, indexed leases are a necessity to protect cash flows during periods of persistent inflation. The following example illustrates the eroding effects of inflation over a period of time if the rental rate remains constant.

Assume a warehouse that rents for $6000 per year is leased for a 10-year period. Operating expenses for the first year are $1000. The lessor has a mortgage of $40,000 and annual debt service of $4000. Equity in the lessor's investment is $10,000.

Table 29 indicates the drop in the relationship of cash flow to initial investment over a 10-year period assuming 6 percent cumulative inflation, which is conservative by today's standards. Note that the initial investment must be adjusted annually to reflect its true value in "inflated" dollars. This adjustment, coupled with persistent 6 percent annual increases in operating expenses, has reduced the cash flow/investment ratio from 10 to 1.8 percent over the 10 years.

Clearly a cost-of-living adjustment of some kind is needed in the lease agreement to protect the lessor from such losses. Recently increasing numbers of tenants have also come to see the financial implications for owners and have become more amenable to the inclusion of such clauses in leases. Property management specialists predict that cost-of-living escalators will

**Table 29  10-Year Projection with Fixed Rental**[a]

| Year | Annual gross rental | Operating − expenses | = No. 1 | Debt service | Cash flow | Adjusted investment | Cash flow/ adjusted investment (%) |
|---|---|---|---|---|---|---|---|
| 1 | $6000 | $1000 | $5000 | $4000 | $1000 | $10,000 | 10.0 |
| 2 | 6000 | 1060 | 4940 | 4000 | 940 | 10,600 | 8.9 |
| 3 | 6000 | 1124 | 4876 | 4000 | 876 | 11,240 | 7.8 |
| 4 | 6000 | 1191 | 4809 | 4000 | 809 | 11,910 | 6.8 |
| 5 | 6000 | 1262 | 4738 | 4000 | 738 | 12,620 | 5.8 |
| 6 | 6000 | 1338 | 4662 | 4000 | 662 | 13,380 | 5.0 |
| 7 | 6000 | 1419 | 4581 | 4000 | 581 | 14,190 | 4.1 |
| 8 | 6000 | 1504 | 4496 | 4000 | 496 | 15,040 | 3.3 |
| 9 | 6000 | 1594 | 4406 | 4000 | 406 | 15,940 | 2.5 |
| 10 | 6000 | 1689 | 4311 | 4000 | 311 | 16,890 | 1.8 |

[a] Source: Reprinted from *Journal of Property Management*, September/October 1974, p. 212 (Sutherland, "The Cost of Living Clause"), by permission of the Institute of Real Estate Management. Copyright 1974.

probably become standard in lease agreements negotiated over the next decade.

## LESSEE

From the lessee's position, the all-important factors in entering into an indexed lease are the method of adjustment, the index employed, and the adjustment intervals. If these are not carefully spelled out and understood, the tenant may find he is actually contributing significantly to increased cash flows for the owner—paying more rent than he should. This is because the owner's debt service remains constant, meaning that it goes down in real value during inflationary periods, as the following example demonstrates.

Assuming the same initial figures as outlined in the foregoing explanation, Table 30 sets out the 10-year results of 6 percent cumulative inflation, coupled with an annual cost-of-living rent adjustment (also 6 percent). The yield to the owner over the 10-year period has risen from the initial 10 percent to 26 percent. This is because the increased rental income—based on the CPI—implies a cost-of-living increase for operating expenses, equity investment, *and the mortgage debt.* In fact, the debt service remains constant, and the increase is applied entirely to the equity investment. The cash flow/investment ratio, accordingly, increases annually.

**Table 30    10-Year Projection with Indexed Rental**[a]

| Year | Annual gross rental | Operating − expenses | = No. 1 | Debt service | Cash flow | Adjusted investment | Cash flow/ adjusted investment (%) |
|------|------|------|------|------|------|------|------|
| 1 | $ 6000 | $1000 | $5000 | $4000 | $1000 | $10,000 | 10.0 |
| 2 | 6360 | 1060 | 5300 | 4000 | 1300 | 10,600 | 10.3 |
| 3 | 6744 | 1124 | 5620 | 4000 | 1620 | 11,240 | 14.4 |
| 4 | 7146 | 1191 | 5955 | 4000 | 1955 | 11,910 | 16.4 |
| 5 | 7572 | 1262 | 6310 | 4000 | 2310 | 12,620 | 18.3 |
| 6 | 8028 | 1338 | 6690 | 4000 | 2690 | 13,380 | 20.1 |
| 7 | 8514 | 1418 | 7095 | 4000 | 3095 | 14,190 | 21.8 |
| 8 | 9024 | 1504 | 7520 | 4000 | 3520 | 15,040 | 23.4 |
| 9 | 9564 | 1594 | 7970 | 4000 | 3970 | 15,940 | 24.9 |
| 10 | 10134 | 1689 | 8445 | 4000 | 4445 | 16,890 | 26.3 |

[a] *Source:* Reprinted from *Journal of Property Management,* September/October 1974, p. 21? (Sutherland, "The Cost of Living Clause"), by permission of the Institute of Real Estate Management. Copyright 1975.

## IMPLICATIONS

The implications to be drawn from the two examples are obvious. If you are an owner, you should protect yourself against the erosionary consequences of inflation by including an indexed factor in lease agreements; but the index chosen should fairly reflect true increases in costs and should not be used as a means of dramatically increasing income.

If you are a tenant, you should acknowledge that owners are entitled to periodic rental increases to keep pace with inflation; but care should be taken when entering leasing agreements to ensure that the cost-of-living increases called for do not significantly overcompensate the lessor because of his fixed-debt position.

## SUGGESTED FURTHER READING

Jones, A., "Property Leasing Check List," *Burroughs Clearing House,* October 1974, p. 30.

Sutherland, Charles E., "The Cost of Living Clause—A Different Perspective," *Journal of Property Management,* September 1974, pp. 120–123.

# SECTION 41

## INDUSTRY–PRICED MATERIALS

*Provides guidelines for obtaining discounts on items and materials that are theoretically industry priced.*

In some industries industry pricing makes it both illegal (under the Robinson-Patman Act) and unethical for suppliers to offer different prices to different customers. If a supplier offers price reductions to one customer, he must allow the same discount to all buyers of his product. This situation makes it extremely difficult to negotiate for lower prices.

However, some methods give purchasers leeway in the negotiation of fixed-price items. Since rock-bottom purchases become critical as a cost control method during inflationary periods, the following reviews opportunities available for negotiating reductions on fixed-price items.

### UNIQUE USER

If changes are made in standard specifications, the buyer can qualify as a "unique" user. Under these circumstances, the vendor and the purchaser can negotiate any terms they please. A good example is in the refrigerator field. Whirlpool Corporation makes products to sell under its own brand and also makes refrigerators for Sears to sell under its Kenmore name. Because of slight differences in specifications, Whirlpool can charge Sears less than its own wholesalers for similar merchandise bearing the Whirlpool brand. If Sears were to ask for price reductions on the Whirlpool brand, the Robinson-Patman Act would probably be violated.

### PAYMENT TERMS

Payment terms often can be negotiated with suppliers, even if prices cannot. Frequently, these terms are disguised price reductions. For example, the usual discount for prompt payment of invoices is 1 to 2 percent. In some fixed-price industries, however, buyers get trade discounts of up to 7 percent from distributors. Obviously this represents a concealed price reduction.

## CONCEALED DISCOUNTS

When a purchaser is buying from a supplier that handles both fixed-price and non-fixed-priced items, multiple orders can conceal discounts on the fixed-price materials. The buyer lists both types of items on the purchase order and deducts a previously negotiated discount on the fixed-price items from prices of non-fixed-price items.

## VENDOR INVENTORIES

Because of the high cost of inventorying, a buyer is getting the equivalent of a discount if the seller agrees to carry part of the inventory. Usual agreements guarantee that a quantity of stock sufficient for a predetermined period of use be maintained exclusively for the buyer's requirements. In addition to lowering inventory costs—warehousing, handling, clerical work, and so on—lead time is greatly reduced and materials are paid for only as they are used.

## QUANTITY DISCOUNTS

Often quantity discounts can be negotiated even though the quantities required for such reductions are not actually purchased. Suppose a 5 percent discount is given on orders of 500 units or more, but a firm only uses 50 units a month and does not want to purchase and inventory a 10-month supply. In such a case the buyer may be able to negotiate an agreement whereby the purchase order for the 500 units does not call for immediate delivery but lets the company draw on and pay for the items as needed. Thus the buyer uses only what he needs monthly, yet still qualifies for the discount.

## PACKAGING AND SHIPPING

Packaging and shipping offer numerous opportunities for reducing fixed-price costs. Specifying "f.o.b. our plant" in place of "f.o.b. shipping point" can usually bring sizable savings. Palletizing arrangements can cut costs. Shipping cartons can fill specialized requirements: specifications can be drawn for containers that can be reused by the buyer to ship goods to the company's own customers.

## SUGGESTED FURTHER READING

Ammer, Dean S., *Materials Management,* Irwin, Homewood, Ill., 1968.

# SECTION 42

## INFLATION ACCOUNTING

*Outlines basic principles of "true value" accounting techniques to offset effects of inflation on company financial statements.* [1]

An inflationary environment has a profound effect on the reporting of business operations. Historic cost principles of accounting—where all items are recorded in terms of the purchasing power of the dollar at the date of each transaction—become highly distorted when inflation is decreasing the value of money by 15 percent a year. One economic pundit has described the situation as "trying to measure the width of a room with a ruler that is getting constantly smaller." Inflation accounting attempts to alleviate this distortion by applying a standard yardstick.

Basically, inflation accounting means adjusting all accounting items by a standard index (such as the Consumer Price Index or the Wholesale Price Index) to show what the figures represent in current purchasing power (CPP). For example, a company might post a profit of $1 million one year. Assuming inflation of 15 percent annually, at the end of the next year the company must be earning profits at the rate of $1,150,000 to maintain its real or purchasing power values. If profits are less than this, the real value is declining. Inflation accounting, by linking each year's figures to a recognized index, spotlights this discrepancy and presents a much truer picture of a firm's continuing progress.

During inflationary periods, historic accounting is inadequate in four respects, as follows:

- Depreciation provisions are not realistic, since they are based on the original cost of an asset, not its current inflated value.
- Profits appear larger than they actually are to the extent that stock profits arise from general price increases.
- Holding cash becomes a liability, as high interest rates are offset by the decline in value of the money held.
- No accounting credit is given for the appreciation derived from borrowed money when the liability has been effectively reduced by inflation.

[1] Adapted from *Accounting for Inflation*, The Institute of Chartered Accountants in England & Wales, London, 1973.

Inflation accounting attempts to adjust these inadequacies on both sides of the equation and reflect more accurately a company's financial status during inflationary periods.


## THE EFFECTS

Constant revaluation of assets and liabilities, keeping them in line with current purchasing power of their original cost, affects businesses in many ways.

Most important are tax reductions resulting from the statement of earnings in real, rather than inflated terms. Most governments are becoming more open-minded about the use of index-linking to adjust tax bases, and some accept it now. Others may allow use of the new standards for computing taxes in the near future.

All profits are adjusted under inflation accounting. For example, if a company earns taxable income of $1 million in 1976 but taxes are based on currency values of 1972, the firm's "real value" taxable profit should be about $660,000, assuming a 15 percent annual inflation rate. The "false" inflated income not only increases the actual amount of tax if it is not adjusted for inflation, but may also push the company into a higher tax bracket. One study of 120 British companies showed that 72 had lower earnings using inflation accounting, 43 had higher earnings, and 5 were unchanged. The median change was $-15$ percent. More significant, however, was the percentage of tax base change *by industry* (Table 31).

Business assets are another major factor to be adjusted. If equipment value is subject to 15 percent inflation annually, depreciation should increase by the same amount. Depreciation schedules are more complicated with inflation accounting, but the benefits are usually much greater than the costs.

Liabilities, such as unpaid bills for equipment or plant mortgages, decrease during an inflationary period. Inflation accounting control of the amount of decrease frees available capital for further investment. Liabilities totaling $300,000 in 1976 will cost only $255,000 (real value) in 1977, assuming an annual inflation rate of 15 percent.

Budgeting should also reflect inflationary trends. Some companies automatically increase budget amounts by the current or anticipated rate of inflation.

Table 31  How Company Earnings Would Change with
Inflation Accounting—by Industry[a]

| Industry | Change (%) |
|---|---|
| Property | +310 |
| Entertainment, catering | +40 |
| Breweries | +35 |
| Miscellaneous (other groups) | +5 |
| Stores | +5 |
| Food retailing | +5 |
| Newspapers, publishing | −10 |
| Contracting, construction | −10 |
| Building materials | −10 |
| Banks | −15 |
| Chemicals | −15 |
| Wines and spirits | −15 |
| Light electronics | −15 |
| Tobacco | −15 |
| Food manufacturing | −20 |
| Office equipment | −25 |
| Oil | −25 |
| Household goods | −35 |
| Packaging and paper | −35 |
| Shipping | −40 |
| Miscellaneous (capital) | −40 |
| Engineering (heavy) | −40 |
| Textiles | −50 |
| Engineering (general) | −50 |
| Electricals | −50 |
| Automobiles and distributors | −60 |

[a] *Source: Accounting for Inflation,* Phillips and Drew,
Ltd., London, 1974.

## BASIC PRINCIPLES

Many accounting firms are now recommending that businesses prepare
their quarterly or annual financial reports using conventional accounting
procedures, then convert these historic dollars into approximate figures of
current purchasing power. This information is included as a supplement to
the basic accounts, giving management, stockholders, and financial analysts
a "real value" picture of the company's financial posture at the end of the
accounting period.

In converting the reports from conventional, historic figures to a CPP statement, a basic distinction is drawn between *monetary items* and *nonmonetary items*.

### Monetary Items

Monetary items are defined as assets, liabilities, or capital amounts that are fixed by a contract or statute in terms of numbers of dollars. These amounts do not vary, regardless of changes in the purchasing power of the dollar. Monetary items in the balance sheet at the end of the reporting period remain the same. Examples include cash, amounts due from debtors, amounts due creditors, and loan capital. Generally holders of monetary assets lose purchasing power during inflationary periods, whereas those having long- and/or short-term liabilities show a gain in purchasing power.

### Nonmonetary Items

Nonmonetary items are all the items that are not defined as monetary, except for the total equity interest (share capital, reserves, and retained profits). The total equity interest is considered neither a monetary nor a nonmonetary item.

Examples of nonmonetary items include such assets as stock, plant, and buildings. Holders neither gain nor lose purchasing power because of inflation, since changes in the value of the assets tend to compensate for changes in the purchasing power of the dollar. In converting accounts to current purchasing power statements, nonmonetary items are increased in value in proportion to the amount of inflation that has taken place since they were acquired or last revalued.

## PROCEDURES

Keeping in mind the distinction between monetary and nonmonetary items, and using fictitious Consumer Price Index figures, the following guidelines demonstrate how historic accounting figures are converted to dollars in terms of current purchasing power.

Since historic dollars are to be converted to "real value" dollars at the end of the period under review, converting always involves (1) multiplying by the index at the *end* of the accounting period and (2) dividing by the index at the date of the original transaction (or last revaluation, if the item has been revalued).

For example, if an asset was purchased for $10,000 when the Consumer Price Index was 110 and the index has risen to 125 at the time accounts are being prepared, the current purchasing power value of the asset would be

$$\$10,000 \times 125 \div 110 = \$11,364$$

The process of conversion involves three main divisions: the balance sheet at the beginning of the year, the profit and loss account for the year, and the balance sheet at the end of the year.

### The Balance Sheet at the Beginning of the Year

As stated previously, a distinction must be made between nonmonetary assets, monetary items, and equity interest.

*Nonmonetary Assets.* All nonmonetary assets are treated in similar fashion, as the following examples indicate.

*Fixed Assets.* If a firm has a fixed asset that cost $500 when the CPI was 110 and the index stands at 130 at the end of the accounting year, the real value equivalent is

$$\$500 \times 130 \div 110 = \$590$$

*Depreciation.* If depreciation to date on the asset just calculated is $150, this figure would be converted to current purchasing power in the same way, since historical depreciation has been calculated on the original cost of the asset:

$$\$150 \times 130 \div 110 = \$177$$

*Stock.* Assuming that a company had stock worth $15,000 at the beginning of the accounting period, that the stock was acquired fairly evenly throughout the last quarter of the previous year, that the CPI that quarter had risen from 110 to 113, and that the index stood at 120 at the time of reporting, the real value of the stock would be determined as follows:

$$\text{average index for the acquisition quarter} = 111.5$$
$$\$15,000 \times 120 \div 111.5 = \$16,143$$

*Monetary Items.* Since all monetary items are fixed by contract or statute in terms of numbers of dollars, they are, by definition, stated in dollars of purchasing power at the date of the balance sheet. However figures must be converted at the beginning of the reporting period so that they have the same real value as those at the end of the reporting period. For instance, if a company reported the following monetary items on January 1:

Debtors     $1000
Cash          570
Creditors     400

these figures would have to be converted at year's end in the following manner, assuming the CPI rose from 120 at the beginning of the year to 130 on December 31:

Debtors     $1000 × 130 ÷ 120 = $1083
Cash          570 × 130 ÷ 120 =   617
Creditors     400 × 130 ÷ 120 =   433

Monetary items do not have to be converted separately unless a detailed accounting is desired; they can be converted as a single net item.

*Total Equity Interest.*   Total equity interest is determined by subtracting liabilities from assets after both have been converted into dollars of current purchasing power for the accounting period.

### The Profit and Loss
### Account for the Year

The profit and loss account can be conveniently subdivided into four areas for conversion: transactions during the year, stock at the beginning and end of the year, depreciation for the year, and loss of purchasing power resulting from holding net monetary assets during the year.

*Transactions.*   Since transactions usually occur evenly throughout the year, the average index for the year is used in conversion. If transactions are sporadic, it may be necessary to convert each quarter's activities separately.

Assuming that the CPI rose from 120 to 130 during the reporting year, sales of $5000, purchases of $3000, and expenses of $1250 would be converted as follows at year's end:

Average index for the year = 125
Sales         $5000 × 130 ÷ 125 = $5200
Purchases     $3000 × 130 ÷ 125 = $3120
Expenses      $1250 × 130 ÷ 125 = $1300

*Stock.*   As previously outlined, stock held at the beginning of the accounting period is converted when the balance sheet at the start of the year is converted to reflect current purchasing power. Stock acquired during the accounting period is converted using the average index for the period. If stock held at the end of the period was valued at $10,000, acquired evenly over the year, and the CPI rose from 120 to 130, the conversion would be as follows:

Average index for the year = 125
Stock        $10,000 × 130 ÷ 125 = $10,400

The cost of goods sold and gross profit for the year are determined by adding and subtracting the figures for sales, stocks, and purchases, which have been separately converted to current purchasing power dollars.

*Depreciation.* To convert depreciation from historic figures to "true value" figures, the same depreciation rate is used. However it is applied *after* the cost of the asset has been converted to dollars expressed in current purchasing power value.

Thus if an asset that cost $1000 was depreciated at 10 percent a year, historic depreciation would be $100 a year. Using inflation accounting, the asset is first revalued (assuming the CPI had increased from 120 to 130 during the reporting period) as follows:

$$\$1000 \times 130 \div 120 = \$1083$$

Depreciation is then taken as 10 percent of this "true value" figure:

$$10\% \text{ of } \$1083 = \$108$$

*Monetary Assets.* Dollars lose value during inflationary periods, and holders of cash and other monetary assets lose purchasing power. If these monetary items are significant, the difference between their purchasing power at the beginning and end of the year must be shown in the current purchasing power statement. (Conversely, firms that have liabilities in fixed-money terms will gain purchasing power during a period of inflation, since repayment dollars will be worth less when the obligation is met. In effect, the debt is reduced.)

The loss in purchasing power of cash and other monetary assets that occurs during the year is calculated in two steps as follows (assuming the CPI was 120 at the beginning of the year, 130 at the end).

*Step One.*    If net monetary assets at the beginning of the year were $500, their loss in purchasing power is

$$\$500 \times \frac{130 - 120}{120} = \$42$$

*Step Two.* If net monetary assets at the end of the year were $750, the increase in net monetary assets during the year was

$$\$750 - \$500 = \$250$$

Inflation has eroded these assets for an average of half a year. The index at the end of the year is 130 and the average for the year is 125. The loss in purchasing power is thus calculated

$$\$250 \times \frac{130 - 125}{125} = \$10$$

The total loss in purchasing power over the year of the firm's net monetary assets is therefore

$$\$42 + \$10 = \$52$$

### Balance Sheet at the End of the Year

Like the balance sheet at the beginning of the year, the year-end balance sheet is divided into three areas: nonmonetary assets, monetary items, and total equity interest.

*Nonmonetary Assets.* As at the beginning of the year, nonmonetary assets include fixed assets, depreciation, and stock. Assuming the CPI rises from 110 to 130 during the year, these are converted to current purchasing power figures as follows.

*Fixed Assets.* Fixed assets are converted in exactly the same way as on the balance sheet at the beginning of the year:

$$\$500 \times 130 \div 110 = \$590$$

*Depreciation.* Likewise, cumulative depreciation is converted in the same way as on the opening balance sheet. Assuming that the balance sheet at the beginning of the year carried depreciation to date on a fixed asset at $500 and the profit and loss account for the year showed depreciation as $100, these historic figures would be combined and converted to a year-end current purchasing power figure as follows:

$$\$600 \times 130 \div 110 = \$709$$

*Stock.* Stock at the end of the year has already been converted in the profit and loss account (see above).

*Monetary Items.* As outlined earlier, monetary items at the end of the

**Table 32  Conversion of Historic Dollars ($H) to Dollars of Current Purchasing Power at Year End ($C) (thousands of dollars)[a, b]**

| | $H | Conversion Factor × | Conversion Factor ÷ | $C (December 31) |
|---|---|---|---|---|
| **Balance sheet (January 1)** | | | | |
| Fixed assets | 700 | 120 | 100 | 840 |
| Less depreciation | 280 | 120 | 100 | 336 |
| Net | 420 | | | 504 |
| Stock | 440 | 120 | 115.5 | 457 |
| Debtors | 290 | 120 | 116 | 300 |
| Cash | 100 | 120 | 116 | 103 |
| Current assets | 830 | | | 860 |
| Less creditors | 270 | 120 | 116 | 279 |
| Net current assets | 560 | | | 581 |
| Net assets = total equity interest | 980 | | | 1085 |
| **Profit and loss account for year** | | | | |
| Sales | 2000 | 120 | 118 | 2034 |
| Stock at beginning of year | 440 | | | 457 |
| Purchases | 1200 | 120 | 118 | 1220 |
| | 1640 | | | 1677 |
| Stock at end of year | 480 | 120 | 119.5 | 482 |
| Cost of goods sold | 1160 | | | 1195 |
| Gross profit | 840 | | | 839 |
| Expenses | 500 | 120 | 118 | 508 |
| Depreciation | 70 | | | 84 |
| Monetary items | — | | | 10 |
| | 570 | | | 602 |
| Net profit | 270 | | | 237 |
| **Balance sheet (December 31)** | | | | |
| Fixed assets | 700 | 120 | 100 | 840 |
| Less depreciation | 350 | 120 | 100 | 420 |
| Net | 350 | | | 420 |
| Stock | 480 | | | 482 |
| Debtors | 330 | | | 330 |
| Cash | 390 | | | 390 |
| Current assets | 1200 | | | 1202 |
| Less creditors | 300 | | | 300 |
| Net current assets | 900 | | | 902 |
| Net assets = total equity | 1250 | | | 1322 |

[a] *Source: Accounting for Inflation,* London, 1973, Part II, p. 5. Adapted and reproduced by permission of The Institute of Chartered Accountants in England and Wales.

[b] Consumer Price Index: January 1 = 116, December 31 = 120.

year are already expressed in terms of current purchasing power and need
not be converted.

*Total Equity Interest.*   As at the beginning of the year, total equity interest
is determined at the end of the year by subtracting liabilities from assets
after the conversion of both into dollars in terms of current purchasing
power.

### CONCLUSION

The conversion examples outlined are, of course, extremely simplified, and
in actual practice such items as the "lower of cost or net realizable value"
rule and the acquisition/disposal of fixed assets must be taken into detailed
account. Specifics and examples for the conversion of all aspects of
financial reports can be found in any good working guide to inflation
accounting, together with completed sample financial tables.

Table 32 sets out conversions similar to the ones outlined above, assuming that the Consumer Price Index rose from 116 to 120 during the reporting year.

(Also see *Net Change Method,* p. 236, and *Columnar Worksheet
Method,* p. 57).

### SUGGESTED FURTHER READING

*Accounting for Inflation,* Institute of Chartered Accountants in England and Wales, London,
1973.

Burton, J. C., "Financial Reporting in an Age of Inflation," *Journal of Accounting,* February
1975, pp. 68–71.

"How to Report Results in Real Dollars," *Business Week,* May 5, 1975, pp. 72–74.

King, A. M., "How Good Is Price Level Accounting?" *Financial Executive,* February 1975,
pp. 16–20.

Revsine, L. and J. J. Weygandt, "Accounting for Inflation: The Controversy," *Journal of
Accounting,* October 1974, pp. 72–78.

Russell, T. A., "Application of Price Level Accounting," *Financial Executive,* February 1975,
p. 21.

# SECTION

# 43

## INFLATION AND DEBT

*Analyzes the premise that businesses that are net debtors benefit from an inflationary environment.*[1]

It is a commonly held belief that companies that are net debtors benefit from unanticipated inflation because they pay back their obligations with "cheap" dollars—dollars with less purchasing power than the borrowed ones.

For example, assume a firm is financed half by debt and half by equity, of $50,000 each. If asset value doubles (from $100,000 to $200,000) equity value triples, from $50,000 to $150,000:

### Balance Sheet 1

Assets: $100,000    Debt:   $50,000
                              Equity: $50,000

### Balance Sheet 2

Assets: $200,000    Debt:   $50,000
                              Equity: $150,000

In this example it is assumed that the firm's asset values go up commensurately with prices of items purchased by the company. If asset values in the example were to only double while consumer prices quadrupled, the owners would be in a weaker position. For multiasset firms, however, asset values probably go up at nearly the same pace as other prices, and the generalization is valid.

A firm, then, can benefit from inflation if it is a net debtor. But how much a net debtor need the firm be? Merely offsetting monetary assets with

---

[1] Adapted from Joseph A. Lavely, "Inflation: Does the Firm Benefit?" *Management Accounting,* June 1975, pp. 16–18.

monetary liabilities is not enough. This can be shown with the following income statement:

| | |
|---|---:|
| Cash revenues | $200,000 |
| Cash costs | (80,000) |
| Depreciation | (20,000) |
| Income | $100,000 |
| Taxes @ 50 percent | (50,000) |
| Income after taxes | $50,000 |

The total cash flow to owners is $50,000 from income after taxes plus $20,000 from depreciation. Depreciation is a tax-deductible expense, but it requires no cash outlay in the current period. It represents a return of investment to owners rather than a return on investment. Thus owners can withdraw the difference between the $200,000 cash inflow from revenues and the $130,000 cash outflow from cash costs and taxes, or $70,000 (the sum of $50,000 from income after taxes plus $20,000 from depreciation).

Next, assume that inflation has increased revenues and costs by 10 percent. The income statement becomes:

| | |
|---|---:|
| Cash revenues | $220,000 |
| Cash costs | (88,000) |
| Depreciation | (20,000) |
| Income | $112,000 |
| Taxes @ 50 percent | (56,000) |
| Income after taxes | $56,000 |

Owners can now withdraw $56,000 from income after taxes plus $20,000 from depreciation for a total of $76,000. But since inflation has driven up prices 10 percent, the owners need $77,000 to maintain their purchasing power.

How could owners have lost ground when revenues and costs both increased in the same proportions? Because depreciation did not increase along with other expenses. Depreciation is based on past (historic) costs, not current (economic) costs. If depreciation were based on current costs and had increased 10 percent, to $22,000, the income statement would read:

| | |
|---|---:|
| Cash revenues | $220,000 |
| Cash costs | (88,000) |
| Depreciation | (22,000) |
| Income | $110,000 |
| Taxes @ 50 percent | (55,000) |
| Income after taxes | $55,000 |

Cash available to owners would have been $55,000 from income after taxes, plus $22,000 from depreciation, for a total of $77,000—exactly offsetting the 10 percent increase in prices.

Thus if the firm is to be protected against unanticipated inflation, it must be indebted at least to the extent of monetary assets, plus depreciation. But this hedge will be effective only if the interest rate charged on the indebtedness remains fixed. If, on the other hand, the interest rate on debt correctly anticipates future inflation and/or fluctuates with inflationary changes, no gain from inflation accrues to the debtor. To further complicate the situation, if current interest rates overanticipate inflation, the firm would have to be a net lender—to the extent of depreciation—in order to protect itself.

Some firms try to use debt to offset profit losses that frequently occur during inflation. It has been assumed that prices and costs increase equivalently. Recent experience indicates, however, that some of the burden of fighting inflation—by holding back price increases—falls on the firm in the form of pressure from consumers and/or the government. Firms are pressured to fight inflation by reducing profits. Many firms have, in fact, absorbed cost increases. Such companies might be tempted to exercise liability management to help offset some of this decline in profitability. It would be unwise to endanger the firm's liquidity position just to offset a temporary decrease in profits, however.

The premise that businesses that are net debtors benefit from inflation is more complex than it first appears. During unanticipated inflation, taxes siphon off some of the inflation-induced increase in revenues. To protect itself against this inflation, a company must be indebted at least to the extent of monetary assets, plus depreciation, as previously stated. Careful study indicates that so long as the actual rate of inflation continues to be unanticipated, firms should consider utilizing more debt in financing assets.

## SUGGESTED FURTHER READING

Lavely, Joseph A., "Inflation: Does the Firm Benefit?" *Management Accounting,* June 1975, pp. 16–18.

## INFLATION SELLING

*Using inflation to advantage when selling products or services.*

Inflation selling is the use of inflation as a selling tool—showing the prospective buyer that it is to his or her advantage to buy now to avoid higher prices later. The sales manager who realizes that rising prices can operate to advantage and puts inflation to work often can gain a competitive edge over marketers who continue to adhere to more traditional selling techniques.

A reluctance to buy often accompanies inflationary periods, especially after accelerating rates have been experienced for a prolonged period of time. Rapidly rising prices and high financing charges combine with the uncertain economy to make firms and individuals put off intended purchases. If the economic environment has not created materials shortages and if a company can continue production at normal levels, it is up to the firm's sales force to overcome this increased buyer resistance and continue to move goods. Inflation selling can help.

### WHAT CAN BE SOLD WITH INFLATION SELLING?

Inflation selling can be used to help sell any product or service that will continue to rise in price at a rate equal to or exceeding the rate of inflation. This applies to major purchases and investments—a new plant, houses, automobiles, real estate—as well as to products for the buyer's more immediate needs. All types of markets can be approached: manufacturers can be sold extra raw materials, homeowners can be sold repair services, housewives can be shown the advantages of stockpiling food or household supplies.

Products or services that decrease in value as inflation grows should be adapted to the inflationary environment if possible. For example, insurance becomes more difficult to sell during inflationary periods because the dollar protection it provides shrinks as inflation continues. Product changes can help overcome this disadvantage. A few insurance companies have now put indexed endowment policies on the market. Payment on maturity is tied to a major index, usually the Consumer Price Index. A ceiling of increased value, such as 25 percent over 3 years, may be placed on the face amount of the policy to protect the selling company. Using the indexed feature, salesmen can call the prospective buyer's attention to inflation and their firm's competitive advantage, rather than avoiding the issue.

Similarly, in some countries savings associations are using indexed interest rates to attract deposits. Savers are assured of a base rate, plus an indexed rate to keep pace with inflation. The method has been instrumental in creating a strong inflow of savings. Previously deposits had been falling off because savers were actually losing money in terms of real value: the 5 percent interest rate was being outstripped by 10 percent inflation.

## USING INFLATION SELLING TECHNIQUES

The first step in successful inflation selling is showing the prospective purchaser how buying now can save him money in the long run. This can usually be done most effectively by graphic means—putting it down in black and white. It is best to use printed bochures or price sheets with figures showing anticipated inflationary increases for each product you sell. Table 33 represents a typical inflation sales sheet using such figures.

**Table 33   Typical Format for Inflation Selling Cost Table**

Today ABC's turret lathe costs $26,000. Here is what inflation alone will do to raise this price over the next decade.

| | ABC lathe price, including inflation factor | | |
| | Annual inflation rate (%) | | |
| Year | 5 | 10 | 15 |
|------|---|----|----|
| 1976 | $27,300 | $28,600 | $ 29,900 |
| 1977 | 28,665 | 31,460 | 34,385 |
| 1978 | 30,098 | 34,606 | 39,542 |
| 1979 | 31,602 | 38,066 | 45,473 |
| 1980 | 33,182 | 41,872 | 52,294 |
| 1981 | 34,841 | 46,059 | 60,138 |
| 1982 | 36,583 | 50,664 | 69,158 |
| 1983 | 38,412 | 55,730 | 79,531 |
| 1984 | 40,332 | 61,303 | 91,460 |
| 1985 | 42,348 | 67,433 | 105,179 |

In computing a similar chart for your products or services, assume that production costs remain stable in real terms. The price is multiplied by the projected rate of inflation to find the first year's increase. This increased price is then multiplied by the same factor for each succeeding year.

As can be seen, compounded inflation increases a product's price dramatically in just a few years. By graphically demonstrating this to prospective buyers, salesmen can reinforce the idea that *now* is the time to buy. The concept can also be used to advantage in direct mail campaigns and certain other types of advertising.

But the yearly inflationary increase in a product's or service's price is only one side of the inflation selling coin. It should also be remembered that the value of money in real terms is *decreasing* each year. Thus if a prospective buyer's company is in a strong cash position, it is again beneficial for him to buy *now* because his cash on hand declines in value the same amount as the rate of inflation, as shown below:

Cash on hand January 1, 1976 = $50,000

| | Real value of $50,000 on January 1 | | |
|---|---|---|---|
| | Annual inflation rate (%) | | |
| Year | 5 | 10 | 15 |
| 1977 | $47,500 | $45,000 | $42,500 |
| 1978 | 45,125 | 40,500 | 36,125 |
| 1979 | 42,869 | 36,450 | 30,707 |
| 1980 | 40,726 | 32,805 | 26,101 |
| 1981 | 38,690 | 29,525 | 22,186 |

The same situation obtains, of course, with consumers; the longer they hold cash, the more it declines in value. Even if the money is on deposit in an interest-bearing account, the real value of the money is going down unless the interest paid is higher than the inflationary rate.

By demonstrating to company buyers or consumers that it is financially unwise to hold cash for anticipated future purchases, inflation selling techniques can help unlock many types of sales.

### FINANCING

If a product being purchased must be financed, there is often reluctance to buy during inflationary periods because interest rates are generally higher than normal. Here, too, inflation selling techniques can be used to advantage by demonstrating to prospective buyers that their financing payments will decrease in real or purchasing power terms each month over the period of their loan, according to the rate of inflation. As Table 34 shows, a monthly repayment of $211 is actually costing the borrower just $145 in current purchasing power value in the thirty-sixth month of the loan, assuming a 12 percent inflationary rate. Printed charts similar to Table 34, which can be used by salesmen to demonstrate how financing payments for their company's products go down in real value, are another effective tool for inflation selling.

### CREDIT

During inflationary periods it is especially important to qualify customers carefully regarding credit status and to protect yourself if payment is not prompt. Payments lose real value every day they are late, and a customer who habitually stalls on settling his accounts can be costly, as outlined below:

Payment due January 1 = $25,000
Rate of inflation = 15 percent

| Date | Real value of payment when received: |
|------|------|
| February 1 | $24,688 |
| March 1 | 24,375 |
| April 1 | 24,062 |
| May 1 | 23,750 |
| June 1 | 23,437 |
| July 1 | 23,125 |

Be sure sales contracts call for late payment penalties that are at least equal to the rate of inflation, plus reasonable interest. Some American firms are now charging 5 percent of each 28-day period between delivery and payment. In other countries increasing use is being made of indexed invoices, with prices that go up each 28 days in proportion to the rise in a major economic indicator, such as the Wholesale or Consumer Price Index.

### TRAINING SALESMEN

An essential element in successful use of inflation selling is training all company salesmen in its methods. It is important to remind them that the technique is the one positive way to approach inflation in their selling efforts.

**Table 34   Typical Format of a Reduced Real Value Payments Chart for Inflation Selling Use**

| | Real value of monthly payments of $211.11 each | | |
| | Annual inflation rate (%) | | |
| Month | 6 | 12 | 18 |
|---|---|---|---|
| 1 | $210.05 | $209.00 | $207.94 |
| 2 | 209.00 | 206.91 | 204.82 |
| 3 | 207.96 | 202.79 | 198.72 |
| 4 | 206.92 | 200.76 | 195.74 |
| 5 | 205.89 | 198.75 | 192.80 |
| 6 | 204.86 | 196.76 | 189.91 |
| 7 | 203.84 | 194.79 | 187.06 |
| 8 | 202.82 | 192.84 | 184.25 |
| 9 | 201.81 | 190.91 | 181.49 |
| 10 | 200.80 | 188.00 | 178.77 |
| 11 | 199.80 | 186.12 | 175.91 |
| 12 | 198.80 | 184.26 | 173.27 |
| 13 | 197.81 | 182.42 | 170.68 |
| 14 | 196.82 | 180.60 | 168.12 |
| 15 | 195.84 | 178.79 | 165.70 |
| 16 | 194.86 | 177.00 | 163.21 |
| 17 | 193.89 | 175.23 | 160.73 |
| 18 | 192.92 | 173.48 | 158.35 |
| 19 | 191.96 | 171.75 | 155.97 |
| 20 | 191.00 | 170.03 | 153.63 |
| 21 | 190.04 | 168.33 | 151.33 |
| 22 | 189.09 | 166.65 | 149.06 |
| 23 | 188.04 | 164.98 | 146.82 |
| 24 | 187.10 | 163.33 | 144.62 |
| 25 | 186.16 | 161.70 | 142.45 |
| 26 | 185.23 | 160.08 | 140.31 |
| 27 | 184.30 | 158.48 | 138.21 |
| 28 | 183.38 | 156.90 | 136.14 |
| 29 | 182.46 | 155.33 | 134.10 |
| 30 | 181.47 | 153.78 | 132.09 |
| 31 | 180.56 | 152.24 | 130.11 |
| 32 | 179.66 | 150.72 | 128.16 |
| 33 | 178.76 | 149.21 | 126.24 |
| 34 | 177.87 | 147.72 | 124.35 |
| 35 | 176.99 | 146.24 | 122.48 |
| 36 | 176.11 | 144.78 | 120.64 |

Instruction should be given in useful details for sales areas already discussed. Salesmen should learn to compute charts similar to Tables 33 and 34 to show advantages of immediate purchasing and/or financing. Even if charts are preprinted, learning to compile inflation-related data will enforce the gains possible for prospective buyers— and it is important to sell those gains in addition to goods or services.

Inflation selling probably was not included in your employee's original sales training, and in this case practice sessions using the company's products or services can help individuals learn to make effective inflation selling presentations. New salesmen should learn techniques in initial training classes.

Ask salesmen to make new inflation selling suggestions as they use the method in the field, and incorporate the best ideas in future marketing and training programs.

Also see *Sales Force Efficiency* (p. 339).

## SUGGESTED FURTHER READING

Hammil, Vince, "To Reach Survival, Change Here," *Sales Management,* August 6, 1974, pp. 28–29.

"How To Find Your Best Markets in an Inflationary Economy," *Sales Management,* October 14, 1974, p. 10.

"Making the Profitable Sale," *Sales Management,* May 19, 1975, pp. 3–45.

"Marketing: Pricing Strategy In an Inflationary Economy," *Business Week,* April 6, 1974, pp. 42–49.

# 45

## INVERSE BONUSES

*Outlines an incentive technique that reduces a preset bonus to penalize materials waste caused by careless work.*

Inverse bonus techniques are being used with increasing frequency in Europe as a means of helping stem wastage of high-priced materials and other commodities. If materials prices continue to rise because of inflation, various inverse bonus applications will undoubtedly spread.

An employee working under an inverse bonus program has a pre-established bonus reduced for each item of wastage he causes. The technique was orginally developed in the tannery industry as a means of reducing careless cutting that ruined expensive hides. A bonus schedule was set up based on a percentage of the total cuts an employee performs on an established number of skins, and a certain percentage of the bonus was subtracted for each skin that was ruined. Thus a preset bonus of $100 a week would be reduced by $40 if a worker ruined five hides with a penalty value of $8 each.

The inverse bonus concept can be adapted in other ways. In many manufacturing applications, inverse bonus plans can help reduce careless materials waste, especially in machining and tooling operations. In sales, preset bonuses can be reduced if quotas are not met. In offices, bonuses can be established that are distributed only if certain energy- or supply-saving goals are met, or if preestablished work standards are achieved.

### SUGGESTED FURTHER READING

Neal, A. W., *Industrial Waste,* Business Books, Ltd., London, 1971.

# SECTION 46

## INVESTMENT FURNISHING

*Discusses the purchase of office furnishings likely to appreciate in value during inflation.*

Investment furnishing is the business equivalent of "flight-into-goods" hedging recommended by many investors to offset the devaluating effects of inflation on money. Since the value of money goes down during persistent inflation, many investors switch into tangibles such as gold, diamonds, paintings, antiques, and objets d'art, which have traditionally risen in value or at least have not depreciated significantly under inflationary conditions.

With investment furnishing—which is mainly confined to small, privately owned operations—the offices of executives are furnished with antique furniture, paintings, Oriental rugs, and so on, bought on the premise that the items will go up in value. Additionally, such furnishings provide a pleasant and impressive working environment. The extent to which the furnishings actually appreciate depends on their scarcity, age, design, market, and other factors. A seven-piece office suite designed by Carlo Bugatti in the nineteenth century recently sold for $67,000 at auction in London, having appreciated 1000 percent in just a few years.

Experts say that twentieth-century furnishings by well-known designers currently hold the best investment potential. Cubist and surrealistic paintings are said to be the canvases most likely to increase rapidly in value.

### SUGGESTED FURTHER READING

Field, J., "Furniture with Investment Appeal," *Financial Times,* London, July 23, 1974.

*Times-Sotheby Index,* London, 1975.

"Bargain Hunter May Find Some Super Buys," *Business Week,* December 21, 1974, pp. 158–159.

Berton, L., "Antiques Creak Under Selling Pressure," *Financial World,* November 20, 1974, pp. 26–27.

"Crosscurrents in the Art Market," *Forbes,* October 1, 1974, p. 58.

Winjum, J. O., and J. T. Winjum, "Art Investment Market," *Michigan Business Review,* November, 1974, pp. 1–5.

# **47**

## LEADS AND LAGS

*Two methods importers can use to protect themselves against foreign currency exchange rate fluctuations during inflation.*

During inflationary periods currencies of countries with high inflation rates tend to lose value against currencies of countries doing a more effective job of controlling inflation. Although this is not the only cause of foreign exchange currency fluctuation, it is generally conceded that "much more often than not, inflation is the basic cause of foreign currency crises."[1] Since it is not unusual for the currency of a country experiencing rapidly accelerating inflation to lose 10 percent of its value against a more sound currency in just a matter of weeks or months, the *leads and lags techniques* help assure the importer that these fluctuations work to his advantage, or at least not to his disadvantage.

### LEADS TECHNIQUE

The *leads technique* is designed to protect the importer when his home currency is *losing* value or is likely to lose value against the currency of his trading partner in a foreign country. To safeguard against foreign exchange loss, the importer orders needed goods or materials for future delivery and buys the required amount of foreign currency to pay for the goods *at the same time he places the order.* In this way he will have the full amount needed for payment when delivery is made, and it will cost him exactly what he anticipated, regardless of subsequent fluctuations in the money market.

As an example, consider the situation in early November 1974. The dollar was starting to come under pressure on foreign exchanges, especially against the currencies of West Germany and Switzerland, countries that seemed to have their inflationary problems under control. There was every indication the dollar would continue to lose value against these currencies.

For an American manufacturer who needed DM1,000,000 in West German products delivered in March, 1975, the situation was ideal for use

[1] Paul Einzig, *Foreign Exchange Crises,* St. Martin's Press, New York, 1970.

of the leads techniques. Using the November 1 exchange rate of 39¢ for the mark, he could have purchased DM1,000,000 for $390,000 in anticipation of the March payment date. By March 1, the value of the mark had jumped to more than 43¢, a rise of about 10 percent, and DM1,000,000 now cost $430,000. By anticipating this increase instead of waiting until delivery to make the monetary exchange, the importer's "lead" currency purchase saved $40,000, a considerable sum even after expenses of the advance purchase transaction were deducted.

## LAGS TECHNIQUE

The *lags technique* is the opposite of the *leads technique*. It allows an importer to benefit from foreign exchange fluctuations when his home currency is *strengthening* against his trading partner's currency. Using the technique, he delays payment for goods or materials received as long as possible while the foreign currency is going down in value. If the timing is right, the gains in the exchange rate more than offset any allowances for prompt payment of the invoice.

Using another example, inflation of 20 percent was weakening British sterling against other currencies early in 1974. By letting his payments "lag" for 2 months—during which the pound dropped from $2.40 to $2.21 against the dollar—an American importer could have saved 8 percent, or $40,000 on a $500,000 order.

Use of leads and lags techniques during an inflationary period depends, of course, on the relative strengths of currencies on the foreign exchange at any given or anticipated time. If inflation is running at a high level simultaneously in most trading countries, the relative values of their respective currencies usually fluctuate little. If some countries bring their inflation under control, however, or if individual countries lose control and their inflationary rates leap above average, the disequilibrium generally causes buying or selling pressure on foreign exchanges. In this situation, leads and lags techniques can be brought into play advantageously by anyone importing foreign products or materials.

## SUGGESTED FURTHER READING

Davis, William, *Money Talks,* Coronet Books, London, 1974.

Einzig, Paul, *Foreign Exchange Crises,* St. Martin's Press, New York, 1970.

Einzig, Paul, *Leads and Lags,* St. Martin's Press, New York, 1971.

Shepherd, Sidney A., *Foreign Exchange and Foreign Trade in Canada,* University of Toronto Press, Toronto, 1973.

# 48

## LEASING

*Discusses leasing as a method of achieving expansion without large cash outlays.*

During inflationary periods firms are often faced with the three-pronged problem of rising material costs, dwindling customer demand, and the drying up of traditional money sources. Not only does the resulting credit squeeze make it difficult to maintain adequate cash flows, in many cases expansion becomes impossible. This is especially true for smaller firms that discover capital financing has nearly disappeared and, if found, is excessively expensive.

Many firms unable to find adequate expansion financing during the recent inflationary spiral discovered an option: long-term equipment leasing. The result is that leasing has gained in popularity, with the value of goods under lease in the United States increasing from $20 billion to $46 billion between 1968 and 1975. Some experts predict a $100 billion industry in the near future.

Companies hard-pressed for capital during inflationary periods may find that leasing holds certain advantages. First, payment is made only for the use of the equipment. The user is under no obligation to obtain equity in the asset or to buy it on lease. Of course the lessor retains ownership of the equipment and is entitled to any residual asset value at the termination of the lease.

Second, leasing companies often have stronger lines of credit than their lessees. Lending institutions generally regard leasing companies as good credit risks because their investments are spread over a broad range of industries. Additionally, leasing firms are in a better position to use a combination of short- and long-term financing.

Third, recent inflationary developments have closed the gap between leasing and financing costs. This is especially noticeable when we consider the earning power of funds some lending institutions require to be held on deposit for the duration of the loan. As this gap narrows, advantages of leasing become more attractive.

In some types of leases, no down payment or deposit is required. In others, the only payment is the first year's leasing cost in advance. These minimum cash outlays free important capital for day-to-day cash needs, especially important during the critical liquidity periods that may be part of an inflationary environment.

There are also important tax considerations. Leasing can often help a small company make use of investment tax credit, even though the company's profits and tax liabilities may have decreased. This is accomplished by assigning the tax credit to the leasing company, since it is legal owner of the asset. The leasing rate can be lowered in return. Arrangements of this type allow companies to benefit from tax credits that would be impossible under other types of financing plans.

In contrast to normal financing sources, leasing companies in some cases can write leases for up to 20 years. Commercial loans are usually extended from 3 to 5 years. The leasing term is restricted only by the asset's useful life, not a bank's standard loan period.

Payment methods are generally more flexible in leasing. Although most standard lease plans specify level payments from the beginning, deferred payments often can be arranged, especially for new businesses. These deferred payments have the advantage of letting a company generate money before paying the first lease costs.

In recent years leased equipment has become more readily available, as cost of capital financing has grown more expensive. Leasing firms tend to specialize, and types of equipment available vary from company to company. Some common types include construction equipment, printing presses, medical equipment, corporate aircraft, drilling rigs, helicopters, work boats, rail cars, and industrial or other machinery.

Here is an example of how leasing helped one company:[1]

An Alaskan air service wanted to expand its helicopter fleet to service pipeline construction and offshore oil rigs in Cook's Inlet. It had assets of $800,000, but required four new helicopters worth $1.5 million to handle the extra business.

The company needed 100 percent financing, but banks were unable to provide it. Based on the firm's sound management and the expanded potential the new helicopters would provide, a lessor of equipment bought the helicopters and arranged 100 percent financing on a long-term lease.

Because the financing required no cash outlay, the Alaskan company preserved its working capital and could use short-term bank financing to meet its payroll and other increased operating expenses.

Obviously, there are many cases in which leasing is not advantageous or leased equipment simply is not available. During inflationary periods,

[1] Donald B. Romans, "Why Leasing Is Becoming So Popular." Reprinted by permission from NATION'S BUSINESS, June, 1975. Copyright 1975 by NATION'S BUSINESS, Chamber of Commerce of the United States.

however, when capital financing is not only expensive but also difficult to obtain, there are many instances in which leasing can allow immediate expansion without large outlays of cash.

## SUGGESTED FURTHER READING

"Leasing Makes Major Inroads; Growth Unaffected by Inflation," *Industry Week*, April 14, 1975, pp. 49–50.

Minicucci, R. "Rather Try than Buy? You Can Do It with Leasing," *Administrative Management*, June 1974, pp. 26–27.

Redfield, P., "Leasing: A Way to Fill Capital Gap?" *Commercial and Financial Chronicle*, March 17, 1975, p. 8.

Romans, Donald B., "Why Leasing Is Becoming So Popular," *Nations's Business*, June 1975, p. 75–76.

Rutley, G., "New Lease on Corporate Life," *Industrial Management*, December 1974, p. 21.

Singhvi, S. S., "Lease or Buy Decision: A Practical Approach," *Journal of Commercial Bank Lending*, October 1974, pp. 60–65.

# SECTION 49

## LIFO

*Outlines the inherent advantages of Last In, First Out (LIFO) inventory valuing during an inflationary environment.*

Since the Internal Revenue Service changed its regulations in 1939 to permit the last in, first out method of inventory flow, proponents of LIFO and first in, first out (FIFO) have been both vocal and convincing in arguing which is the more appropriate method.

The basic distinction between the two is that FIFO bases ending inventory value on the price of the last units purchased, whereas LIFO values ending inventories according to the price of units purchased at the beginning of the year. The distinction can have significant effects on profits, as shown in the following description.[1]

The value of even a constant inventory is likely to change over time.

For example, suppose a company's inventory both at the beginning of the year and at the end of the year is one million units of the same product, but that each unit cost only $1.00 a year ago and now costs $1.05—a 5 percent increase. How is the value of this inventory to be reckoned for the year as a whole?

To identify the price paid for each specific item in the ending inventory would be an onerous task, at best. To avoid such tasks, accountants have established simplified conventions to handle the flow of inventory values.

One accountant might assume that a first-in, first-out model of inventory flow (FIFO) is appropriate. Accordingly, he assumes that the ending inventory consists entirely of units purchased at the current price of $1.05 and that its value is $1,050,000 (see Section 2 in Table 35).

He theorizes that these goods will be sold next year, and therefore *this* year's cost increase of 5 percent will work to increase *next* year's cost of goods sold and thus to decrease *next* year's profits. Hence he does not charge any of the difference in the values of the beginning and ending inventories—$50,000—against the company's current profits.

Equally, another accountant might assume that the last-in, first-out (LIFO) flow model is appropriate—that is, he considers the ending inventory consists entirely of units purchased at the old price of $1.00 each. Accordingly, he charges the $50,000

[1] Ronald M. Copeland, Joseph F. Wojdak, and John K. Shank "Use LIFO to Offset Inflation," *Harvard Business Review,* May/June, 1971, p. 92.

**Table 35    Inventory Pricing Methods and Reported Profits**[a]

|                        | Section 1: LIFO |             | Section 2: FIFO |             |
| ---------------------- | --------------- | ----------- | --------------- | ----------- |
| Sales revenue          |                 | $3,550,000  |                 | $3,550,000  |
| Cost of goods sold     |                 |             |                 |             |
|   Beginning inventory | $1,000,000 |         | $1,000,000      |             |
|   Purchases  | 3,500,000       |             | 3,500,000       |             |
| Goods available for sale | 4,500,000     |             | 4,500,000       |             |
| Ending inventory       | (1,000,000)     | (3,500,000) | (1,050,000)     | (3,450,000) |
|     Profits before tax[b] |  | $50,000  |                 | $100,000    |

[a] *Source:* Copeland, Wadjak, and Shank, "Use LIFO to Offset Inflation," *Harvard Business Review*, May/June, 1971, p. 92.
[b] Negative profit difference = $100,000 − $50,000 = $50,000.

cost increase against this year's profits, as a cost of goods sold this year. Note that the cost of goods sold in Section 1 of Table 35 is $3,500,000.

As Table 35 shows, accounting profits of either $100,000 or $50,000 can be reported from the same set of economic facts. If LIFO is used for tax reporting, then profits—and consequently tax liability—are halved, an obvious advantage. On the other hand, some (including stockholders) might feel that the LIFO method understates the company's real performance.

While both methods are widely used and fully accepted by the accounting profession, LIFO has inherent advantages in offsetting the negative effects of an inflationary environment, especially in industries most sensitive to rising costs. The following[2] outlines these advantages, and discusses some of the difficulties encountered in switching from FIFO to LIFO.

## THE ADVANTAGES OF LIFO

The basic advantages of LIFO are that during inflationary periods the method helps reduce tax dollars and improves cash flow. The opposite is true during a deflationary environment, but it would take a brave economist or businessman to predict that the upward price spiral that has characterized the economy in recent decades will reverse itself in the years ahead. In light of recent inflationary trends, adoption of LIFO is not particularly risky.

[2] Adapted from Orville R. Keister, "LIFO and Inflation," *Management Accounting*, May 27, 1975, pp. 27–30.

The basic advantages of LIFO can be clearly seen in Table 36, if we assume that the two companies used as examples are completely identical except that one uses FIFO and the other LIFO.

Beginning inventory for both was 100 units at $1 each. Purchases during the year equaled 200 units at $1.50. Sales during the period amounted to 150 units at $3. Thus by selecting LIFO over FIFO, one firm pays $24 less taxes than the other. This gives the firm using LIFO $24 more for immediate use simply by its selection of accounting alternatives.

Another important consideration is the cash flow improvement possible with LIFO. Tight money markets that accompany inflation often make it impossible to find money for expansion or other purposes. Or, if capital can be found, interest rates are usually exorbitant. By using the LIFO method, dollars are freed that can be used internally, forestalling borrowing needs.

Another advantage of LIFO involves disposable income. With double-digit inflation, FIFO or similar inventory methods produce income figures that simply are not accurate, either for external reporting or internal

**Table 36  FIFO Versus LIFO**[a]

|  | FIFO | LIFO |
|---|---|---|
| Beginning inventory (100 @ $1.00) | $100 | $100 |
| Purchases (200 @ $1.50) | 300 | 300 |
| Goods available | $400 | $400 |
| Sales (150 @ $3.00) | $450 | $450 |
| Cost of sales: |  |  |
|   FIFO = 100 @ $1.00 + 50 @ $1.50 | 175 |  |
|   LIFO = 150 @ $1.50 |  | 225 |
| Income before income taxes | $275 | $225 |
| Income taxes (48%) | 132 | 108 |
| Net income | $143 | $117 |
| Cash position, end of period |  |  |
|   Sales | $450 | $450 |
|   Less purchases | (300) | (300) |
|   Less income taxes | (132) | (108) |
| Cash available | $ 18 | $ 42 |

[a] *Source:* Keister, "LIFO and Inflation," *Management Accounting,* May 27, 1975, p. 28.

management purposes. With inflationary prices rises, FIFO accounting results in paper profits.

| | |
|---|---|
| Inventory cost | $30 |
| Sales price | 50 |
| Latest purchase price | 40 |
| FIFO profit | 20 |
| LIFO profit | 10 |
| Dollars available after unit replacement | 10 |

As this example shows, the $20 FIFO profit is not usable profit. Part of it is not an actual monetary return but exists only on paper. On a larger scale, use of misleading FIFO profits may be costly in union negotiations, dividend declaration decisions, expansion decisions, and so on, since the company appears to have earned more money than it actually has. LIFO profits are much more realistic, in that they more closely represent true disposable income.

Thus LIFO can save dollars for a company using the method during inflationary periods—by lowering tax payments, by improving cash flow and reducing interest payments, and by preventing distorted wage claims based on nonexistent profits.

## DISADVANTAGES OF LIFO

If LIFO has the inherent advantages just outlined, why has it not been universally accepted in light of recent inflationary trends? A 1973 report by *Accounting Trends and Techniques* revealed that of 600 companies surveyed, 377 used FIFO and only 150 used LIFO in whole or in part. Also in 1973 a survey by Arthur Young & Company of 247 American and New York Stock Exchange companies found only 10 percent using LIFO. (Significantly, however, 20 percent of these had switched to LIFO within the preceding 12 months). Since companies seem reluctant to adopt LIFO, what are its negative factors?

The key disadvantage is that profits reported under LIFO are generally lower, sometimes significantly so. When duPont adopted LIFO, the company's earnings per share dropped from $6.27 to $5.10 during the first 6-month period. Firestone's earnings per share were reduced by $0.87, to $1.53 for the first 9 months after LIFO was installed. Such dramatic reductions in earnings are difficult for management to explain to an investing public that is not educated in differences in inventory accounting. The apparent earnings drop could result in lower stock prices, corporate takeover bids, difficulties with bonus plans, and so on.

Conversely, however, it can be argued that a company is better managed if it ceases reporting false, inflated profits and starts doing something about decreasing tax payments, decreasing borrowing needs, and improving cash flows.

Another disadvantage of using LIFO also occurs in the first year of its adoption. Theoretically, funds flow should improve when using LIFO. Yet because of lower inventory balances on the statement of changes in financial position, it will appear that LIFO has caused a deterioration of the working capital position. This is, of course, only a bookkeeping effect and the actual cash-dollar position has improved, despite the misleading drop in inventory balances.

The point at which LIFO is introduced can also be a possible disadvantage. If the LIFO base is adopted when inventories are higher than normal, it may be necessary to dip into base inventory when supply shortages develop. Matching current revenue with early costs may grotesquely bloat profit figures.

Increased clerical work that may be required by LIFO can also be a disadvantage. Keeping strict LIFO flow records on an inventory of 1000 different items is obviously a laborious task. Procedures, such as dollar-value LIFO, have been developed to ease bookkeeping burdens considerably. These techniques are detailed in most LIFO accounting texts.

There is some concern that if LIFO is adopted, it will be difficult to get government approval to change to some other system. Experience does not seem to confirm this fear. Change permission is applied for on form 3115, and permission has been granted in most cases to date.

If LIFO is used for tax purposes, it must be used for company books and for financial reporting. Conceivably, this tax provision could have some impact on credit arrangements or ability to raise equity capital. Taxpayers with low profit margins or operating loss to carry forward could experience adverse tax effects, too.

Do these disadvantages outweigh the advantages of switching to LIFO? It depends on the individual company and the timing involved. There is little question, however, that by electing not to use LIFO in an inflationary period, many companies are choosing to pay higher taxes and to have inferior cash flows. The advantages of the method warrant management investigation to help cope with the inflation-prone years ahead.

## SUGGESTED FURTHER READING

"Adoption of LIFO and Disclosure of Financial Statements Clarified by IRS," *The CPA Journal,* May 1975, p. 48.

Auerbach, N. E., "Switching to LIFO," *Financial Executive,* February 1975, pp. 42–44.

Bahin, J. M., "We Switched to LIFO," *Financial Executive,* February 1975, pp. 45–50.

Copeland, Ronald M., Joseph F. Wojdak, and John K. Shank, "Use LIFO to Offset Inflation," *Harvard Business Review,* May/June, 1971, pp. 91–98.

Keister, Orville R., "LIFO and Inflation," *Management Accounting,* May 1975, pp. 27–30.

"Recent LIFO Developments," *The CPA Journal,* May 1975, pp. 53–54.

## LONG–TERM CONTRACT COSTS

*Outlines a method of "deflating" current costs to original bid prices in long-term contracts.*

Cost control on long-term contracts through budgetary control is a traditionally accepted management tool. Variances from the original budget estimate were determined and incorporated into expected final cost of the project and simultaneously evaluated when the commitments were made.

In an inflationary environment, however, the conveniences and effectiveness of budgetary control are substantially lessened. When inflationary pressures were minimal, it was possible for management either to ignore variances between estimated and actual cost caused by inflation, or to compensate for such discrepancies by one lump sum contingency assessment against all costs of the contract. Today, however, the size of variances between actual and estimated costs resulting from inflationary increases in prices of almost all commodities—including labor costs—make it impossible to continue control by these methods. The following outlines a method of "deflating" current costs to restore the efficiency of budgetary control on long-term contracts.[1]

### DEFLATION OF CONTRACT COSTS

In today's economy management often seeks to protect profits through escalation clauses added to the body of contracts. Although use of such clauses is satisfactory in terms of profit maintenance, the method is not adequate for reliable evaluation and control. Management should not accept inflationary cost change as the perennial justification for contract cost overruns. Poor performance should not go unrecognized under the guise of cost inflation.

The budgetary control problem stems from difficulty of evaluating the difference between costs estimated months—perhaps years—ago and costs

[1] Adapted from Jaroslav P. Bures, "Deflating Long-Term Costs," *Management Accounting,* August 1975, pp. 43–44.

incurred today. To maintain effectiveness of budgetary control, a rapid correlation between the two is needed. The most efficient way of doing this is by discounting or deflating current costs to their equivalents at the budget time.

In recent years most industries have changed their pricing policies. Purchases and acquisitions today often include terms such as "price in effect at time of shipment" or "with current price subject to escalation based on a price index." Firm price commitments are becoming increasingly rare, and when such commitments are made, they are pegged on prices inflated to the level expected at the time of shipment.

The process of deflating depends on the type of price involved. If the commitment is of a "firm price" type, the deflation must cover the period from the time of expected future delivery to the time of the original estimate. A "current price" (with index escalation or price at the time of shipment provision) must be deflated from the current date back to the time of the original estimate. The first type of deflation requires estimating the change of price levels between now and the expected delivery time. The second type deals with known changes.

In either case the vehicle of deflation is an appropriate price level index selected from the official table of wholesale price indexes, or in some instances from the table of average hourly earnings of production workers. Selection of specific index or rate will depend on the kind of business in which the company and the vendor or subcontractor is engaged, and on the expenditure involved. Frequently the index selected to analyze cost commitments is the same as the index used by the company to protect its prices to the customer against the impact of inflation.

## THE DEFLATION WORKSHEET

The mechanics of deflation are relatively simple (Tables 37 and 38). Table 37 is a worksheet giving the computations for commitments with a firm price at delivery time. Table 38 shows the application of either index-escalation or price-at-delivery provisions to current prices. The following assumptions have been used in both tables:

• The item is fabricated structural steel having an estimated cost in January 1974, of $500,000.
• Fabricated structural steel fits the U. S. Department of Labor Wholesale Price Index Code 10-7 (1967 = 100).
• Analysis is performed in November 1974, and the firm price offered by the vendor for delivery in June 1975 is $675,000. (In Table 38 a current

**Table 37  Deflation Computation Worksheet—Firm Price at Delivery Date**[a]

| Line | Firm price at delivery date | Value |
|---|---|---|
| 1 | Index value at original estimate or budget time (Index code 10-7) | 135.4 |
| 2 | Current index (Date November 74) | 182.5 |
| 3 | Expected inflation per month as percent of current index | 0.5 |
| 4 | Number of months from date in line 2 to expected delivery date this line (Date June 15) | 8 |
| 5 | Estimated percent increase in current index from date in line 2 to date in line 4 (line 3 times line 4) | 4 |
| 6 | Estimated index level at delivery time (line 5 in decimal plus 1) times current index line 2 (182.5 × 1.04) | 189.8 |
| 7 | Vendor's quote divisor (line 6 divided by line 1) | 1.402 |
| 8 | Vendor's quote (firm or estimate) | $675,000 |
| 9 | Equivalent estimated cost (line 8 divided by line 7) | $481,533 |
| 10 | Original estimated or budgeted cost | $500,000 |
|  | Budget or purchase price variance—to requisition (line 9 less line 10) favorable | $18,467 |

[a] *Source:* Bures, "Deflating Long-Term Costs," *Management Accounting,* August 1975, p. 44.

**Table 38  Deflation Computation Worksheet—Index-Escalation or Price-at-Delivery Provisions**[a]

| Line | Current price level, quote at "price at delivery" or index escalation | Value |
|---|---|---|
| 1 | Index value at original estimate or budget time | 135.4 |
| 2 | Current index | 182.5 |
| 3 | Vendor's quote divisor (line 2 divided by line 1) | 1.348 |
| 4 | Vendor's current price | $650,000 |
| 5 | Equivalent estimated cost or budgeted cost (line 4 divided by line 3) | $482,196 |
| 6 | Original estimated or budgeted cost | $500,000 |
|  | Budget or purchase price variance—to requisition (line 5 less line 6) favorable | $17,804 |

[a] *Source:* Bures, "Deflating Long-Term Costs," *Management Accounting,* August 1975, p. 44.

price of $650,000, also subject to escalation based on Code 10-7, has been assumed to be available from another vendor.)
• In January 1974 the Index for Fabricated Structural Metal Products was 135.4.
• By November 1974 the index rose to 182.5.
• It is further projected that the index will continue to rise through the first 6 months of 1975 at an average rate of 0.5 percent per month.

The worksheet allows the analyst to arrive at the equivalent (deflated) cost which is eventually compared to the original budgeted (estimated) cost. The variance between the final actual cost and the originally budgeted cost of the item is thus segregated into its true components: variance caused by inflation and variance related to performance (in this case, a purchase price variance).

## ADDITIONAL BENEFITS

Two additional benefits are available to the company that employs the deflation method. The comparison between the equivalent estimated cost (line 9 in Table 37, line 5 in Table 38) can serve as an indicator for relative preference in selection of a vendor. Furthermore, the difference between the respective equivalent estimated cost and the final actual cost (the inflation variance) can be matched against the recoveries from the company's escalation provisions in the contract with the customer. Adequacy of escalation provisions incorporated in a company's contracts with customers obviously has a significant impact upon profits. This secondary benefit may even become a primary consideration in adoption of the method.

## SUGGESTED FURTHER READING

Bures, Jaroslav P., "Deflating Long-Term Contract Costs," *Management Accounting,* August 1975, pp. 43–44.

## MANAGEMENT COMPENSATION

*Sets out the inequities placed by an inflationary environment on management compensation programs and provides guidelines for flexible plans to help alleviate the problem.*

Executive compensation programs can be seriously disrupted by periods of persistent inflation. The erosionary effects of steadily rising prices mean that deserving management personnel often receive a lower increase in real terms than they should. Additionally, the government takes a greater proportion of any increased salary as the executive is forced into higher tax brackets. The result is that executives are often little better off financially after receiving what appear to be sizable salary increases, and they may have less actual buying power. Over a period of time, this aspect of inflation can have a serious demoralizing effect on management motivation.

The following examines the negative effects of inflation on management compensation and suggests guidelines for meaningful alternatives.

### THE PROBLEMS

#### Taxation

One of the most serious threats to fair salary increases is the existing system of taxation. Even if pay increases are tailored to match inflationary rises in the cost of living, an employee can lose money by being pushed into a higher tax bracket, increasing his effective rate of tax. In this way both federal and state governments are prime beneficiaries of the high inflation rate. When pay levels increase in real or inflationary terms, tax revenues also go up. To alleviate this problem, Canada instituted an indexed tax structure that automatically raises the tax liability threshold as salaries are pushed up by inflation.

#### Deferred Compensation

A decade ago, deferred compensation plans became a popular way of beating the tax man. A portion of total compensation was deferred until after retirement; thus taxes were paid on income only when it was included in the lower retirement tax bracket. Today such programs have waned considerably in popularity. The following example outlines the difficulties.[1]

Suppose that a 40-year-old executive earning $40,000 in current compensation has an additional $10,000 deferred and paid after his retirement. Given a continued hefty rate of inflation, we might find that our executive was earning $100,000 per year immediately prior to retirement, even though he was still in the same job he held 25 years ago. Because he retires with a $50,000-a-year pension, he ends up in a tax bracket that is higher than the one he was in at the time his $10,000 was originally deferred (unless our politicians . . . adopt an indexed tax structure). So his $10,000 deferred payment turns out to be more heavily taxed than would have been the case had it been paid currently. And what's more, inflation has terribly eroded the purchasing power of whatever is left.

### Stock Options

From the end of World War II until 1970, gains from stock options provided an even greater share of total executive compensation than bonuses.

Today, following the recent inflation-caused depression of the stock market, stock options have declined in popularity. In addition to the disadvantages posed by the volatility of stock prices, studies have shown that the inflation-adjusted value of shares represented by the Dow Jones Industrial Average was about the same in real money terms in early 1975 as it was 20 years earlier. Not surprisingly, many executives now have little interest in stock option agreements.

### Inequalities

Coupled with the problems just mentioned, companies are forced to give union-represented workers pay increases of 10 to 12 percent to match inflationary rates. Following this outlay, they are reluctant to grant similar proportionate pay raises to middle- and top-management personnel. This may not create undue hardship at the highest pay levels, but it can put a severe strain on middle-management incomes. Caught in the crunch between militant union leaders, reticent board members, and the tax man, middle-level managers are forced to take cuts in purchasing power that do not represent merely investable funds but are needed income for day-to-day living expenses.

### Merit Pay

Last, the principle of merit pay has been seriously affected by inflation. In stable economic periods a firm that gave average increases of 6 percent

[1]Graef S. Crystal, "Compensation—Less From More," *Financial Executive,* February 1975, p. 74.

might reward outstanding performance with a 10 percent hike. Employers today are forced to give 10 to 12 percent increases just to keep salaries abreast of inflation. A 20 percent increase should be awarded under the old yardstick for exceptional performance, but very few managements have the money or the courage to approve such large hikes. Consequently merit pay—and its intrinsic motivational value—have become victims of inflation.

## THE FLEXIBLE COMPENSATION APPROACH

Although there are no quick answers to many of the problems already outlined—other than perhaps a government turnaround on indexed tax thresholds—there are ways to alleviate some of the compensation burdens caused by inflation.

One of the best methods is use of a performance bonus incentive plan coupled with a flexible compensation program. The method is being used increasingly by industrial firms to not only reward executives according to the quality of their on-the-job performance but to give them individual choice about the form their incentive compensation takes. In this way each executive has more flexibility in tailoring income to meet his own financial and tax situation.

The first part of the approach—performance bonuses—has been in use for some time but is now gaining significantly in popularity. Industrial giants like Exxon, U.S. Steel, and IBM have all installed or improved performance bonus plans in recent years. Such programs are also gaining acceptance in banks, insurance companies, and other large institutions, in which individual executive performance is more difficult to measure. Most of the plans offer management personnel incentive bonuses for outstanding performance in helping the company achieve predetermined goals in such areas as sales, profits, or cost control.

Inflation has been largely responsible for bringing on the second part of the approach—the coupling of performance bonuses with flexible compensation plans. Flexible compensation plans, which give the individual some choice regarding the form of his incentive pay, can provide some or all of the bonus in nontaxable form, yielding greater buying power to the executive. The following example illustrates the principle.[2]

Two executives each have a base salary of $30,000 and nontaxable fringe benefits of $5,000. Each files a joint return in Illinois with $10,000 deductions and exemptions. The impact of a $10,000 cash bonus versus a $10,000 bonus in nontaxable benefits is

[2]John O. Todd, "Cafeteria Compensation: Making Management Motivators Meaningful," *Personnel Journal*, May 1975, p. 275. Reprinted with permission, *Personnel Journal*. Copyright May 1975.

**Table 39    Net per Dollar of Compensation**[a]

| Executive Doe | | Executive Roe |
|---|---|---|
| $30,000 | Salary | $30,000 |
| 10,000 | Cash bonus | — |
| $40,000 | Total cash | $30,000 |
| 5,000 | Noncash benefits | 15,000 |
| $40,000 | Taxable | $30,000 |
| 7,880 | Taxes—federal | 4,380 |
| 950 | Taxes—state | 700 |
| | | 5,080 |
| 8,830 | | $39,920 |
| $36,170 | Buying power | |

Executive Roe has 60% higher net nonsalary benefits than Executive Doe.

[a] *Source:* Todd, "Cafeteria Compensation," *Personnel Journal,* May 1975, p. 276. Reprinted with permission, *Personnel Journal.* Copyright May 1975.

illustrated in Table 39. Executive Roe's buying power is $3750 greater than that of Executive Doe. In effect, Executive Doe lost almost half of his bonus.

Since the primary goal of any compensation plan is to place *net* dollars in the executive's hands, it is easy to see why flexible compensation is gaining in popularity as inflation becomes more persistent. Executives are not all alike, nor do they have the same financial requirements. Executive Doe, for example, might prefer the extra cash, even though its total value is diminished by taxes.

The following examples from flexible plans are samples of what is currently being offered by companies.[3]

Automobile.
Automobile expenses and insurance.
Deferred compensation.
Disability insurance (supplemental).
Dues (professional, business, athletic, and so on).
Estate planning services (help integrating noncash company plans).
Excess major medical.
Group life insurance (supplemental).

[3] Todd, "Cafeteria Compensation," *Personnel Journal,* May 1975, p. 276. Reprinted with permission, *Personnel Journal.* Copyright May 1975.

Loans at favorable interest rates.
Medical-dental reimbursement (supplemental).
Phantom split-dollar life insurance.
Phantom stock plans.
Physical examinations.
Restricted stock purchase plans.
Reverse stock options.
Sabbatical leaves.
See-saw stock options.
Split-dollar life insurance.
Stock options—qualified.
Stock options—nonqualified.
24-hour accident insurance.
Travel accident insurance.
Vacation.

Most firms have provided one or more of these "fringes" to executives for some time as part of regular compensation. In total, fringe benefits amount to more than a quarter of the total labor cost in American businesses. Since most of these benefits have definable costs, the company incurs no economic penalty by allowing two equally paid executives to adopt entirely different compensation plans.

Thus, properly presented, such flexible compensation packages not only encourage executive performance and help avoid unfair taxation but also constitute a powerful recruiting tool, maximizing the incentive of a performance bonus plan.

## SUGGESTED FURTHER READING

Crystal, Graef S., "Compensation—Less From More," *Financial Executive,* February 1975, pp. 74–76.

Todd, John O., "Cafeteria Compensation: Making Management Motivators Meaningful," *Personnel Journal,* May 1975, pp. 275–281.

Wolfe, A. V., "Managerial Approach to Compensation," *Personnel Journal,* April 1975, pp. 212–216.

# 52

## MARKET SHARE/PROFITABILITY RELATIONSHIPS

*Discusses ways in which market share affects profitability.*

According to a recent study,[1] market share is one of the key areas determining profitability, and firms striving to maximize profits during persistent inflation will do well to analyze their market positions and potentials. Many firms could profitably divest themselves of secondary product lines, even if the products are selling well. This move allows the company to concentrate efforts on capturing larger market shares with their major, more profitable, products.

At Table 40 shows, there are four important differences among companies commanding a large market share and those with relatively small shares.

### PROFIT MARGINS

As the share of the market rises, turnover on investment increases slowly, but profit margins on sales rise sharply. As the table demonstrates, the main reason for the return on investment/market share relationship is the large difference in pretax profit margins on sales. Companies with the lowest market shares (under 10 percent) had average pretax losses of 0.16 percent. The average return on investment for these companies was about 9 percent. To determine why profit margins on sales increase so sharply with market share increases, we must examine in detail differences in prices and operating expenses.

### PURCHASES-TO-SALES RATIO

The principal difference in costs with respect to market share is the purchases-to-sales ratio. Table 40 reveals that in businesses enjoying market

[1] Robert D. Buzzell, Bradley T. Gale, and Ralph G. M. Sultan, "Market Share—A Key to Profitability," *Harvard Business Review,* January/February, 1975, pp. 129–140.

Table 40   Relationships of Market Share to Key Financial and Operating Ratios.[a]

| Financial and operating ratios | Market share | | | | |
|---|---|---|---|---|---|
| | Under 10% | 10–20% | 20–30% | 30–40% | Over 40 |
| Capital structure | | | | | |
| Investment/sales | 68.66 | 67.74 | 61.08 | 64.66 | 63.98 |
| Receivables/sales | 15.52 | 14.08 | 13.96 | 15.18 | 14.48 |
| Inventory/sales | 9.30 | 8.97 | 8.68 | 8.68 | 8.16 |
| Operating results | | | | | |
| Pretax profit/sales | −0.16 | 3.42 | 4.84 | 7.60 | 13.16 |
| Purchases/sales | 45.40 | 39.90 | 39.40 | 32.60 | 33.00 |
| Manufacturing/sales | 29.64 | 32.61 | 32.11 | 32.95 | 31.76 |
| Marketing/sales | 10.60 | 9.88 | 9.06 | 10.45 | 8.57 |
| R & D/sales | 2.60 | 2.40 | 2.83 | 3.18 | 3.55 |
| Capacity/utilization | 74.70 | 77.10 | 78.10 | 75.40 | 78.00 |
| Product quality | | | | | |
| Average of percents, superior minus inferior | 14.50 | 20.40 | 20.40 | 20.10 | 43.00 |
| Relative price[b] | 2.72 | 2.73 | 2.65 | 2.66 | 2.39 |
| Number of businesses | 156 | 179 | 105 | 67 | 87 |

[a] Source: Buzzell, Gale, and Sultan, "Market Share—A Key to Profitability," Harvard Business Review, January/February, 1975, p. 132.
[b] Average values on 5-point scale: 5 = 10% or more below leading competitors' average, 3 = within 3% of competition, 1 = 10% or more above the competition.

shares exceeding 40 percent, purchases represent just 33 percent of sales, whereas in small-market-share companies (under 10 percent) the ratio is 45 percent. One reason for this difference is that companies with large market shares are generally more vertically integrated—they tend to "make" rather than "buy"—and they often manage their own distribution facilities. Probably more important, however, is the decline in costs of purchased materials that comes through a combination of economies of scale in buying and increased bargaining power in dealing with suppliers.

## MARKETING-TO-SALES RATIO

As market share increases, the marketing-to-sales ratio declines somewhat—about a 2 percent difference between the smallest and largest market-share groups. Primarily this is the result of scale economies—the spreading of fixed marketing methods by large-share businesses.

## PRICE PREMIUMS AND HIGHER QUALITY

Market leaders are in a position to develop unique, competitive strategies and to have higher prices for their higher-quality products than are small-share companies. In the survey figures in Table 40, it is impossible to determine which is greater—price premiums obtained by market leaders or differential in the quality of their products. It is clear, however, that the combination of higher prices and quality gives market leaders a unique competitive advantage.

## SUGGESTED FURTHER READING

Buzzell, Robert D., Bradley T. Gale, and Ralph G. M. Sultan, "Market Share–A Key to Profitability," *Harvard Business Review*, January/February, 1975, pp. 129–140.

## MATERIALS CONTROL CHECKLIST

*Provides nine key materials control elements to help offset the effects of materials price rises and/or shortages during inflation.*

A strong materials control program is important at any time but is especially critical during inflationary periods. Rapidly rising materials costs and the materials shortages that often accompany inflation can have a profound effect on profits. Firms that do not institute sound materials control programs are sure to find that wasteful production practices are costing them ever-increasing numbers of profit dollars.

Fortunately materials acquisition and utilization is an area over which management can exercise considerable control. Every manager, engineer, designer, buyer, and production and quality-control specialist can make a real contribution to limiting costs, controlling waste, and improving efficiency. Thus materials control takes on added importance during inflation. Properly administered, it can be instrumental in helping alleviate the profit squeeze.

The following checklist provides nine key elements in planning a better materials control program.

*Reexamine Product Design.* Ensure that products are being manufactured as inexpensively and efficiently as possible. Check that each quality specification is actually needed. Substitute less costly materials wherever possible. Make sure tolerances are not overspecified for the purpose of the product. Minimize the number of different kinds of materials in the product's design.

*Improve Production Methods.* Try to eliminate production steps wherever possible. Seek production-improving ideas from employees and/or outside consultants. Use flow charts to simplify assembly line steps and clarify production procedures.

*Maintain Tight Stock Control.* Establish realistic stocking levels and order in the most economic quantities. Establish procedures for moving old stock first if material is subject to deterioration.

*Analyze Quality Control.*    If products regularly fail to meet quality-control tests, consider making changes in materials, equipment, or tooling methods.

*Standardize Parts.*    If products manufactured by the company are closely related, study product lines to see whether parts of one product can be substituted at a cost savings for similar parts in another product.

*Ensure Proper Storage of Materials.*    Eliminate materials waste due to theft or contamination. Storage areas should be climatically controlled, secure, and centrally located.

*Reduce Production Overruns.*    Overruns drain company profits and eat up costly or scarce materials. Be sure that sales orders are accurate and adhere closely to them.

*Reduce Materials Handling.*    In addition to being expensive, handling exposes materials to the risk of damage and or contamination. Materials should not be moved until they are needed for immediate use in production.

*Improve Employees' Working Conditions and Motivations.*    Employee motivation is one of the key elements in any materials control program. Employees must be convinced that saving material at every opportunity is essential to make a better, more profitable product, thus stabilizing their jobs. Strive to improve employee motivation and production efficiency by making sure work areas are pleasant, safe, and stimulating for those who work there.

Get the whole company to work as a team in controlling materials costs. Failure by one division in its materials control methods can negate the positive efforts of several other divisions. Make certain all supervisors and managers stress the importance of materials control to their employees.


## SUGGESTED FURTHER READING

Kolbe, R. A., "Waging the War Against Scarcity," *Purchasing,* March 18, 1975, pp. 49–51.

Meitz, A. A. and B. B. Castlemen, "How to Cope With Supply Shortages," *Harvard Business Review,* January 1975, pp. 91–96.

Moskowitz, L., "Business Management in a Shortage Economy," *Credit and Financial Management,* December 1974, pp. 14–15.

Zeyher, L. R., "A Plan for Better Materials Control," *Advanced Management Journal,* Winter 1975, pp. 50–53.

# SECTION 54

## MAYNARD OPERATION SEQUENCE TECHNIQUE

*Outlines a new work measurement technique for improving productivity in manufacturing and nonmanufacturing jobs.*

Since the turn of the century, increasingly sophisticated work measurement techniques have been instrumental in saving millions of dollars for businesses, governments, and nonprofit institutions. Today work measurement—determination of the amount of time required to do physical work—is used throughout much of the industrialized world to establish wages, reduce costs, and increase productivity.

In recent years the inflationary environment has caused increased interest in fast, accurate, cost-effective work measurement techniques. Primarily these have been applied as a means of increasing productivity to help offset the effects of inflation. Secondarily, the techniques have been used for establishing work standards for the increasing use of monetary incentive programs.

The Maynard operation sequence technique (MOST) is a recent development in work measurement offering many advantages over traditional methods. The technique can be learned in a few days, is much faster to apply than most widely used systems, requires fewer specialists, produces less paperwork, and can be used to measure a wider range of work. Standards based on MOST are now in use in the electronics, automotive, power generating, packaging, shipbuilding, and other heavy industries. Tests have indicated it can also be beneficial for measuring nonmanufacturing work, such as clerical and maintenance jobs.

The following outlines the basic concepts behind the MOST work measurement system and its use as a management tool for improving productivity in an inflationary environment.[1]

---

[1] Adapted from K. B. Zandin, "Better Work Management with MOST," *Management Review,* July, 1975, pp. 11–17.

**225**

### BACKGROUND

There are two basic ways to calculate time standards. The first, time studies, requires stopwatch studies by a trained observer of actual work situations. Because many observations must be made to establish valid averages, the method is often time-consuming. Additionally, workers frequently object to this type of subjective output measurement.

To help overcome these problems, various types of predetermined motion-time systems (PMTS) have evolved for calculating time standards. It has been found that times for basic human motions (turning the wrist, grasping, reaching) are fairly consistent, no matter who performs the action. By breaking work into small basic motions and assigning predetermined times, it is possible to set time standards without having to do time studies on each work situation.

Accurate as these systems are, they have the disadvantages of time-consuming calculations and voluminous paperwork. Additionally, they are mainly oriented toward mass-production operations and are less suitable for the majority of work situations. MOST has been developed to help alleviate these problems.

### THE MOST CONCEPT

MOST does not break an operation down as finely as PMTS. Rather, the technique groups together basic motions that frequently occur in sequence. Arriving at a standard time with one popular PMTS method for putting work into a drill press requires identification of 15 separate motions and assigning time values to each from a data card. With MOST, the same analysis requires the identification, directly from memory, of only seven motions.

#### How MOST Works

The MOST system uses three fundamental motion sequences to measure light manual work and three for heavy work in which lifting equipment is utilized. Additionally, specialized sequence models have been designed for job shop production on machine tools.

The sequences for measuring light manual work are *General Move, Controlled Move,* and *Tool Use. General Move* covers the moving of objects by hand or manually from one place to another, freely through the air. It is subdivided into four activities to cover various situations:

A = Action distance (mainly horizontal).
B = Body motion (mainly vertical).
G = Grasp.
P = Position.

Index figures are used to account for variations in these activities. Fully indexed a motion sequence becomes:

$A_6B_6G_1A_1B_0P_3A_0$

$A_6$ = Walk three to four steps to object location.
$B_6$ = Bend and rise.
$G_1$ = Grasp one object with one hand.
$A_1$ = Move within reaching distance.
$B_0$ = No bend.
$P_3$ = Position and adjust object.
$A_0$ = No return.

This example could represent a worker walking three paces to pick up a bolt from floor level, rising, and positioning the bolt in a hole.

To determine the time value of the move described, the index numbers are added and result multiplied by 10. Thus the time value in the example would be

$$6 + 6 + 1 + 1 + 0 + 3 + 0 = 17 \times 10 = 170 \text{ time measurement units (TMU)}$$

corresponding to 0.1 minute. Index figures and time values are determined in the same way for remaining sequence models, and the total time is computed by adding all time models together.

MOST's index values are taken from statistical formulas, backed by PMTS analysis, for precision and accuracy. The calculations take into account predetermined rules relating to frequency of occurrence of actual elements, length of leveling time (the number of observations required to remove random errors of observation and variability), and required system accuracy.

Preprinted standard calculation sheets list motion sequences. Use of the sheets guides analysts and helps eliminate errors, resulting in smaller deviations among analysts than other time measurement systems. Each calculation form provides space for a specially developed filing code, which simplifies handling of the time data and assures rapid retrieval from a firm's standard-times data bank. A typical filing code would read as follows:

| Code category | Coded event | Code number |
| --- | --- | --- |
| Activity | Set up and tear down | 103 |
| Object group | Holding devices | 03 |
| Object | Vice | 10 |
| Occurrence frequency group | | 4 |
| Running number | | 1 |

| 1 | 0 | 3 | 0 | 3 | 1 | 0 | 4 | 0 | 1 |
| --- | --- | --- | --- | --- | --- | --- | --- | --- | --- |

## RESULTS

Results achieved through the use of MOST have been highly effective in increasing productivity, improving utilization of facilities, calculating accurate work costs, establishing realistic work targets, scheduling workloads, and improving planning. One company using the system increased productivity 45 percent, yielding savings of $2.86 million each year. In nearly all 50 installations to date, MOST has paid for itself in less than a year.

## SUGGESTED FURTHER READING

Zandin, K. B., "Better Work Management with MOST," *Management Review,* July 1975, pp. 11–17.

# SECTION 55

## MONEY SUPPLY

*Discusses the monetary growth cycle and its effects on inflationary rates.*

A broad definition of "money supply" is the amount of money that exists in an economy at any given time. Notes and coins, being accepted means of payment, clearly are part of the money supply. Additionally, demand accounts at banks that can be drawn on by checks must be considered part of the supply. These two together most narrowly define "the money supply."

Theoretically savings accounts cannot be used as money because checks cannot be drawn on them to settle debts. However it is a simple matter in most cases to transfer money from savings accounts into checking accounts, and a broader definition of money supply therefore must include deposit accounts. It can be argued that other types of liabilities such as bills of exchange and deposits in building societies are so liquid that they should be considered part of the money supply, but generally they are excluded.

An argument began in the late 1960's between two camps of economists regarding the effect of money supply on the rate of inflation. On the one side were the advocates of government fiscal policy (taxes, controls, interest rates, etc.). Opposing them were the monetarists, who advocated greater concern with the quantity of money that exists at any given point in time. Led by Milton Friedman, this side held that the money supply can and should be controlled, that it has a bigger effect on total expenditure than tax changes, and that government authorities should aim at a fixed and steady growth in the quantity of money—such as 5 percent a year—rather than drastically increasing or decreasing the supply according to their reading of the economic barometer.

In the industrialized countries, much attention is now paid to the monetary theory of inflation, although even Friedman warns that it should not be viewed as a cure all:[1]

We are in danger of assigning to monetary policy a larger role than it can perform, in danger of asking it to accomplish tasks that it cannot achieve, and, as a result, in danger of preventing it from making the contribution that it is capable of making. A

[1] Quoted in William Davis, *Money Talks,* Coronet Books, London, 1974, p. 159.

**229**

steady rate of monetary growth at a moderate level can provide a framework under which you can have little inflation and much growth. It will not produce perfect stability, it will not produce heaven on earth. It will make an important contribution to a stable economic society.

Perhaps most important, Friedman's arguments have led to a general awareness that fiscal policy and changes in money supply should reinforce each other, not pull in opposite directions.

## MONEY SUPPLY AND INFLATION

Economists have shown that there is a direct correlation between the monetary growth cycle and the inflation cycle. Increases in monetary

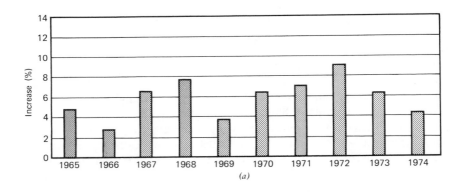

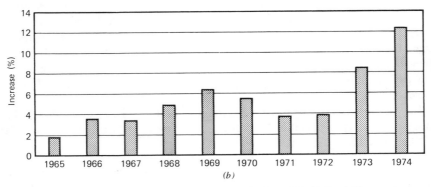

**Figure 7**   United States money supply/inflation correlation, 1965–1974. (*a*) Changes in money supply. (*b*) Rate of inflation (Consumer Price Index.) (*Source:* U.S. Department of Commerce.)

Table 41   Changes in Money Supply, 13 Industrialized Countries[a]

| Country | 1971[b] | 1972[b] | 1973[b] | 1974[b] | 1975 January[c] | 1975 February[c] | 1975 March[c] |
|---|---|---|---|---|---|---|---|
| Austria | 10.2 | 16.6 | 12.9 | 6.5 | 8.4 | 9.8 | 11.6 |
| Belgium | 10.1 | 12.4 | 12.8 | 8.7 | 8.3 | 9.3 | 3.7 |
| Canada | 21.2 | 25.9 | 12.0 | 12.4 | 16.2 | 16.2 | 13.4 |
| Denmark | 4.2 | 10.9 | 12.0 | 5.2 | 5.0 | 7.0 | 9.1 |
| France | 13.8 | 13.0 | 10.0 | 10.9 | 12.4 | 11.0 | 10.0 |
| Germany (West) | 12.3 | 13.6 | 5.6 | 5.9 | 12.0 | 11.6 | 12.3 |
| Italy | 22.8 | 18.6 | 20.4 | —[d] | —[d] | —[d] | —[d] |
| Japan | 25.3 | 22.2 | 26.4 | 13.3 | 10.9 | 11.6 | 9.8 |
| Netherlands | 16.7 | 17.7 | 7.7 | 3.3 | 12.2 | 10.8 | 12.3 |
| Norway | 15.0 | 11.2 | 12.8 | 12.6 | —[d] | —[d] | —[d] |
| Sweden | 9.6 | 10.6 | 7.9 | 6.3 | 11.5 | 12.2 | —[d] |
| Switzerland | 18.5 | 13.6 | -4 | -1.9 | 0.1 | 0.5 | 2.6 |
| United Kingdom | 12.8 | 16.7 | 9.5 | 4.3 | —[d] | —[d] | 15.4[e] |

[a] Source: U.S. Department of Commerce.
[b] Annual figures = averages of monthly changes.
[c] Monthly figures = percentage change in 12 months.
[d] Not available.
[e] Quarterly average.

growth cause increases in the inflationary rate, and decreases in the money supply result in a slowing of the inflationary rate. In both cases the time lag is about 2 years. Thus the significant increase in the money supply in the United States between 1971 and 1972 was instrumental in causing the sharp inflationary increase experienced during the 1973–1974 period. Figure 7 shows this correlation for the years since 1965.

Given this knowledge, businessmen can use the monetary growth cycle to project future inflationary rate increases and decreases. Other factors enter the picture, of course—materials shortages, government actions, oil price rises—but government monetary policy has proven to be the most reliable indicator of future inflationary rate changes. For example, the increase in money supply has averaged about 6½ percent annually in the United States over the past 3 years. Accordingly, the domestic rate of inflation should not rise sharply for some time—late 1976 at the earliest.

On an international level, Table 41 shows changes in the money supply of 13 industrialized countries since 1971.

## SUGGESTED FURTHER READING

Bannock, G., R. E. Baxter, and R. Rees, *Dictionary of Economics,* Penguin Books, Baltimore, 1972.

Davis, William, *Money Talks,* Coronet Books, London, 1974.

Greenwood, J., "How Japan's Tight Money Policy Really Worked," *Banker,* August 1974, p. 995.

Harvey, J. C., "Curing Monetary Inflation," *Financial Executive,* February 1975, pp. 22–25.

*International Financial Statistics* (monthly), International Monetary Fund, Washington, D.C.

Klein, R. and W. Wollman, *The Beat Inflation Strategy,* Simon & Schuster, New York, 1975.

*Monetary Trends* (monthly), Federal Reserve Bank, St. Louis.

*National Economic Trends* (monthly), Federal Reserve Bank, St. Louis.

"Recovery Breaks Through the Financial Clouds," *Fortune*, June 1975, pp. 11–12.

*Statistical Abstract of the United States* (yearly), U.S. Bureau of the Census, Washington, D.C.

## MOTIVATION CHECKLIST

*Provides 10 key elements that should be present in employee motivation programs to help assure widespread acceptance of company goals and a desire to work toward them.*

Psychological motivation of employees takes on added significance during inflationary periods for a number of reasons. It is especially critical that employees be motivated to work toward company goals, since increased productivity is needed to help offset the effects of inflation. Second, inflationary price rises will negate pay increases in real terms, causing employee dissatisfaction unless workers are properly motivated through nonmonetary incentives. Additionally, internal disruptions that usually accompany persistent inflation—layoffs, increased automation, job switching—can have an adverse effect on employee attitude and morale unless management takes steps to maintain motivation toward achieving company objectives.

To help offset these problems, a sustained employee psychological motivation program should be instituted with the active support of top management. Particular attention should be paid to such areas as job security, fringe benefits, physical working conditions, and salaries and wages.

The following checklist[1] reviews the key elements necessary in establishing such a psychological motivation program or evaluating motivational programs already in use.

*Participation.*   Employees should be allowed to participate as much as possible in decisions regarding their work. Potentially, there are four levels at which they can participate:

- Making the actual decision.
- Providing recommendations to those who will make the decision.
- Learning the alternatives being considered from the actual decision maker.
- Learning of the decision after it has been made.

[1] From Ernest H. Ward, "Elements of an Employee Motivation Program," *Personnel Journal,* March 1975, pp. 205–208. Adapted with permission, *Personnel Journal.* Copyright March 1974.

The higher an employee participates in these decision levels, the greater he will be motivated.

*Performance Measurement.* Individual and/or group performance should be measured. This measurement, when coupled with knowledge of results and recognition, can be a strong motivator. Measurement should evaluate job performance factors according to importance in meeting departmental or company goals.

*Knowledge of Results.* Employees should be kept informed of their progress, as measured by job performance factors. It is difficult for an employee to be consistently motivated when he is in the dark about his past and current performance. Performance tends to improve when employees are regularly informed of their progress.

*Recognition.* Superior performance should be recognized through merit salary increases, promotions, or increased responsibility. To be motivationally effective, recognition must be based on valid performance measurement techniques; recognition that is considered unfair or not based on critical job aspects can have a negative motivational effect.

*Attitude Measurement.* Attitudes are closely related to motivation. To determine prevailing employee attitudes, comprehensive questionnaires should be used objectively, systematically, and periodically. Large, representative employee samples should be taken, and responses should be anonymous. A computer can be a valuable tool in this area; for maximum benefit, attitude measurement should include quick feedback to employees, and a computer program written for this purpose helps timing.

*Communication.* Two-way communication should be developed between top management and employees. Employees must know company objectives if they are to be motivated to achieve them, and top management should communicate the goals through company newspapers, in-person talks, plant tours, and/or closed-circuit television. Conversely, employee ideas and feelings should flow upward to top management by means of employee suggestion systems and attitudinal measurement programs.

*Publicity.* Motivation to work toward company goals is influenced by the employees' image of the company. Toward this end, company and employee achievements should be publicized at every opportunity (e.g., by assuring that company accomplishments appear in local newspaper articles). Additionally, company and departmental objectives can be publicized internally by means of posters, badges, banners, company newspaper features, pamphlets, and so on.

*Work Assignment.* A work assignment system should be developed to ensure that individual employee capabilities match skills required by individual jobs. Motivation will halt if employees are put into jobs that are frustratingly difficult. Conversely, an employee properly matched to his assignment will often be highly motivated through the achievement of doing his job well.

*Work Research.*    Many studies have shown that workers are motivated when they are allowed to participate in various aspects of work research, such as working procedures and environment studies, even though the basis for the research is to improve worker efficiency. Through participation, their work is upgraded by a demonstration of management's concern for doing the job properly by providing the best procedures, tools, and work layout.

*Supervisor Motivation Training.*    The supervisor is the key to the success or failure of any motivation program, since he plays a role in nearly all the motivational aspects previously discussed. All factors can be negated through supervisory ignorance, disregard, or neglect of elements important to employee motivation. All supervisory personnel should be educated in important factors and practices that enhance employee motivation.

## SUGGEST FURTHER READING

Dermer, J., "Interrelationship of Intrinsic and Extrinsic Motivation," *Academy of Management Journal*, March 1975, pp. 125–129.

Rohan, T. M., "Building the Will to Work," *Industry Week*, April 28, 1975, pp. 42–43.

Rosenbaum, B. L., "New Approach to Changing Supervisory Behavior," *Personnel*, March 1975, pp. 37–44.

Tavernier, G., "Motivating Employees in Hard Times," *International Management*, April 1975, pp. 14–18.

Ward, Ernest H., "Elements of an Employee Motivation Program," *Personnel Journal*, March 1975, pp. 205–208.

White, R. D., "Democratizing the Reward System," *Public Personnel Management*, September 1974, 409–414.

# 57

## NET CHANGE METHOD

*Outlines the principles of a simplified inflation accounting technique.*

The net change method is an inflation accounting technique for converting historical dollar figures into "true value" dollars of current purchasing power. The method converts balance sheets at the beginning and end of the reporting period, but not the profit and loss account. Profits for the reporting period are calculated by determining the difference in total equity interest at the beginning and end of the year and adding back dividends. (Also see *Inflation Accounting*, p. 179).

As the method is explained,[1] it will be helpful to consult the following tables:

• Table 42 (the balance sheet of a company for its sixth year, with comparative figures for its fifth year).
• Table 43 (the company's profit and loss account during the same period).
• Table 44 (the balance sheets for the company at the beginning and end of its sixth year). Columns 1 and 3 show figures in historic dollars. Columns 2 and 4 convert these historic figures into dollars of current purchasing power at the end of the sixth year.

In the following explanations a Consumer Price Index figure of 129 is assumed at the end of the sixth year. For conversion purposes, it is therefore necessary to multiply historic dollar figures by 129 and divide by the index at the time of acquisition. Figures for the Consumer Price Index appear in Table 45.

Following is an outline of the methods used to convert the figures in Table 44.

---

[1] Adapted by permission from *Accounting for Inflation*, The Institute of Chartered Accountants in England and Wales, London, 1973.

**Table 42  Balance Sheet for Year 6$^a$ (thousands of dollars)**

| Year 5 | | | | |
|---|---|---|---|---|
| | | Share capital and reserves | | |
| 500 | | Ordinary share capital | | 500 |
| 246 | | Undistributed profit | | 309 |
| 746 | | Total equity interest | | 809 |
| | | Loan capital | | |
| 200 | | Debenture | | 200 |
| 34 | | Tax equalization account | | 39 |
| | | Current liabilities | | |
| | 270 | Creditors | 300 | |
| | 35 | Proposed dividend | 40 | |
| | 70 | Current taxation | 77 | |
| 375 | | | | 417 |
| 1355 | | | | 1465 |
| | | Fixed assets | | |
| | 100 | Property | 100 | |
| | 10 | Less depreciation | 12 | |
| 90 | | | | 88 |
| | 700 | Plant and machinery | 800 | |
| | 270 | Less depreciation | 350 | |
| 430 | | | | 450 |
| 520 | | | | 538 |
| | | Investments | | |
| | 10 | Fixed interest | 10 | |
| | 10 | Equity | 10 | |
| 20 | | | | 20 |
| | | Current assets | | |
| | 440 | Stock | 480 | |
| | 290 | Debtors | 320 | |
| | 85 | Cash | 107 | |
| 815 | | | | 907 |
| 1355 | | | | 1465 |

$^a$ Source: Accounting for Inflation, Part II, p. 10. Adapted and reproduced by permission of The Institute of Chartered Accountants in England and Wales.

# Table 43  Profit and Loss Account for Year 6[a] (thousands of dollars)

| Year 5 | | | | | Year 6 |
|---|---|---|---|---|---|
| 1750 | | Sales | | | 1920 |
| | | Cost of sales | | | |
| | 400 | Stock at beginning of period[b] | 440 | | |
| | 1090 | Purchases[b] | 1190 | | |
| | 1490 | | 1630 | | |
| | 440 | Stock at end of period[b] | 480 | | |
| | 1050 | | | 1150 | |
| | 431 | Expenses (other than depreciation) | | 471 | |
| | 72 | Depreciation | | 82 | |
| 1553 | | | | | 1703 |
| 197 | | Operating profit | | | 217 |
| 2 | | Investment income | | | 2 |
| 199 | | | | | 219 |
| 14 | | Debenture interest | | | 14 |
| 185 | | Profit before tax | | | 205 |
| 74 | | Tax | | | 82 |
| 111 | | Profit after tax | | | 123 |
| 190 | | Balance at beginning of year | | | 246 |
| 301 | | | | | 369 |
| | | Dividends | | | |
| | 20 | Ordinary—interim | 20 | | |
| | 35 | —final | 40 | | |
| 55 | | | | | 60 |
| 246 | | Balance at end of year | | | 309 |

[a] *Source: Accounting for Inflation*, Part II, p. 11. Adapted and reproduced by permission of The Institute of Chartered Accountants in England and Wales.

[b] These items would not normally appear in the published accounts of a company. They are included to help clarify this example.

# Table 44 Conversion of Balance Sheets at Beginning and End of Year 6[a, b]

| Item | Balance sheet at beginning of year ($H) | ($C) (12/31/6) | Balance sheet at end of year ($H) | ($C) (12/31/6) |
|---|---|---|---|---|
| | (1) | (2) | (3) | (4) |
| Fixed assets | | | | |
| Property | 100 | 129.0 | 100 | 129.0 |
| Less depreciation | 10 | 12.9 | 12 | 15.5 |
| Net | 90 | 116.1 | 88 | 113.5 |
| Plant and machinery | 700 | 857.7 | 800 | 960.6 |
| Less depreciation | 270 | 339.3 | 350 | 435.5 |
| Net | 430 | 518.4 | 450 | 525.1 |
| Total | 520 | 634.5 | 538 | 638.6 |
| Investments | | | | |
| Fixed interest | 10 | 10.6 | 10 | 10.0 |
| Equity | 10 | 12.9 | 10 | 12.9 |
| Total | 20 | 23.5 | 20 | 22.9 |
| Current assets | | | | |
| Stock | 440 | 468.2 | 480 | 483.4 |
| Debtors | 290 | 307.4 | 320 | 320.0 |
| Cash | 85 | 90.1 | 107 | 107.0 |
| Total | 815 | 865.7 | 907 | 910.4 |
| Loan capital | (200) | (212.0) | (200) | (200.0) |
| Tax equalization account | (34) | (36.0) | (39) | (39.0) |
| Current liabilities | | | | |
| Creditors | (270) | (286.2) | (300) | (300.0) |
| Proposed dividend | (35) | (37.1) | (40) | (40.0) |
| Current tax | (70) | (74.2) | (77) | (77.0) |
| Total | (375) | (397.5) | (417) | (417.0) |
| Net assets | 746 | 878.2 | 809 | 915.9 |
| Share capital and reserves | | | | |
| Ordinary share capital | 500 | | 500 | |
| Undistributed profit | 246 | | 309 | |
| Total equity interest | 746 | 878.2 | 809 | 915.9 |

[a] *Source: Accounting for Inflation,* Part II, p. 12. Adapted and reproduced by The Institute of Chartered Accountants in England and Wales.
[b] $H = thousands of historic dollars, $C = thousands of dollars of current purchasing power at the end of Year 6.

Table 45    Consumer Price Index$^a$ (January 1 of Year 1 = 100)

| Year | Average | End | Percentage increase during year |
|------|---------|------|------|
| 1 | 102.0 | 104.0 | 4 |
| 2 | 106.2 | 108.2 | 4 |
| 3 | 110.5 | 112.5 | 4 |
| 4 | 114.8 | 117.0 | 4 |
| 5 | 119.4 | 121.7 | 4 |
| 6 | 125.4 | 129.0 | 6 |

$^a$ Source: Accounting for Inflation, Part II, p. 17. Reproduced by permission of The Institute of Chartered Accountants in England and Wales.

### PROPERTY

The property listed was bought when the CPI was 100. Therefore the current purchasing power figure is obtained in the following manner:

$$\$100 \times 129 \div 100 = \$129$$

Since no other property was acquired or sold during the reporting year, the figures remain the same on the balance sheet at both the beginning and end of the year.

Depreciation on the property is converted by the same factor. The cumulative depreciation of $10 at the beginning of the year becomes

$$\$10 \times 129 \div 100 = \$12.9$$

The $12 at the end of the year becomes

$$\$12 \times 129 \div 100 = \$15.5$$

### PLANT AND MACHINERY

Since plant and machinery were purchased at different times, various indexes must be used in conversion. These are set out in Table 46.

### FIXED INTEREST INVESTMENT

As a monetary asset, the fixed interest investment at the beginning of the year must be converted into year-end purchasing power dollars. This is done

**Table 46  Analysis of Cost and Cumulative Depreciation**[a, b]

| Year of acquisition | Cost ($H) | Cumulative depreciation to end Year 5 ($H) | Cumulative depreciation to end Year 6 ($H) | Factor | Cost ($C) | Cumulative depreciation to end Year 5 ($C) | Cumulative depreciation to end Year 6 ($C) |
|---|---|---|---|---|---|---|---|
| Property Beginning of Year 1 | 100 | 10 | 12 | 129.0/100.0 = 1.290 | 129.0 | 12.9 | 15.5 |
| Plant and Machinery Beginning of Year 1 | 400 | 200 | 240 | 129.0/100.0 = 1.290 | 516.0 | 258.0 | 309.6 |
| 2 | 50 | 20 | 25 | 129.0/106.2 = 1.215 | 60.8 | 24.3 | 30.4 |
| 3 | 100 | 30 | 40 | 129.0/110.5 = 1.167 | 116.7 | 35.0 | 46.7 |
| 4 | 50 | 10 | 15 | 129.0/114.8 = 1.124 | 56.2 | 11.2 | 16.9 |
| 5 | 100 | 10 | 20 | 129.0/119.4 = 1.080 | 108.0 | 10.8 | 21.6 |
| Subtotal | 700 | 270 | 340 | | 857.7 | 339.3 | 425.2 |
| 6 | 100 | | 10 | 129.0/125.4 = 1.029 | 102.9 | | 10.3 |
| Total | 800 | | 350 | | 960.6 | | 435.5 |

[a] *Source: Accounting for Inflation*, Part II, p. 13. Adapted and reproduced by permission of The Institute of Chartered Accountants in England and Wales.

[b] $H = thousands of historic dollars; $C = thousands of dollars of current purchasing power at the end of Year 6.

by multiplying the investment by the year-end index and dividing by the index at the beginning of the year:

$$\$10 \times 129 \div 121.7 = \$10.6$$

No conversion is needed for monetary assets at the end of the year because they are already expressed in terms of current purchasing power.

### EQUITY INVESTMENT

Equity investment, a nonmonetary item (a claim on the resources of another company), was acquired when the index was 100. The conversion is therefore

$$\$10 \times 129 \div 100 = \$12.9$$

### STOCK

The firm acquired all the $440 worth of stock held at the beginning of year 6 evenly during the last quarter of year 5. To determine its value at the beginning of the sixth year, the index at the midpoint of the last quarter of year 5 must be calculated. This is done in two steps, as follows:

1. Index July 1 (Year 5)                      = 119.4
   Index December 31 (Year 5)          = 121.7

   Average (midpoint) July–December = 119.4 + 121.7 = 120.6

2. Index October 1 (Year 5)              = 120.6
   Index December 31 (Year 5)          = 121.7

   Average (midpoint) fourth quarter = 120.6 + 121.7 = 121.2

Using this midpoint index figure, the true value of the stock held at the beginning of year 6 becomes

$$\$440 \times 129 \div 121.2 = \$468.3$$

The stock at the end of the year was acquired evenly over the fourth quarter of that year. The index for the midpoint of the quarter, calculated as previously, was 128.1, and the true year-end value of the stock thus becomes

$$\$480 \times 129 \div 128.1 = \$483.4$$

### DEBTORS, CASH, LOAN CAPITAL, TAX EQUALIZATION ACCOUNT, AND CURRENT LIABILITIES

These items are all converted in the same manner as "Fixed Interest Investment."

### TOTAL EQUITY INTEREST

Since all the items on the balance sheets have been converted to dollars in current purchasing power at the end of the reporting year, the assets are added together and the liabilities subtracted from the total to obtain the net asset figures for both the beginning and end of the year:

Net assets, beginning of Year 6 = $878.2
Net assets, end of Year 6 = $915.9

By definition, total equity interest at the beginning and end of the year is equal to the net assets at the beginning and end of the year.

### CALCULATION OF RETAINED PROFIT

Since no new equity capital was introduced during the year, the retained profit is the difference between the total equity interest at the beginning and end of Year 6:

$$\begin{array}{r} \$915.9 \\ \underline{878.2} \\ \$\ 37.7 = \text{retained profit} \end{array}$$

### CALCULATION OF PROFIT FOR THE YEAR

To calculate profit for the year, simply add (in dollars of current purchasing power) any dividends paid to the retained profit figure (here, $37.7). The tax charge is the same in both the historic and current purchasing power accounts, as it is assumed to occur at year's end. These steps are shown in Table 47.

(Also see *Columnar Worksheet Method*, p. 57).

Table 47   Calculation of Profit for Year[a, b]

| Item | $H | Factor | $C |
|---|---|---|---|
| Dividend paid (6/30/6) | 20 | 129.0/125.4 | 20.6 |
| Dividend proposed | 40 | 1.000 | 40 |
| | 60 | | 60.6 |
| Retained profit | 63 | | 37.7 |
| Profit for year after tax | 123 | | 98.3 |
| Tax | 82 | 1.000 | 82 |
| Profit before tax | 205 | | 180.3 |

[a] *Source: Accounting for Inflation,* Part II, p. 15. Adapted and reproduced by permission of The Institute of Chartered Accountants in England and Wales.
[b] $H = thousands of historic dollars; $C = thousands of dollars of current purchasing power at the end of Year 6.

## SUGGESTED FURTHER READING

*Accounting For Inflation,* Institute of Chartered Accounts in England and Wales, London, 1973.

Frey, K. M., "Survey of Price Level Accounting in Practice," *The CPA Jornal,* May 1975, pp. 29–33.

Hamway, J., "Taking Account of Inflation," *Director,* March 1975, pp. 384–386.

"Juggling the Books, Allowing for Inflation," *Industry Week,* May 12, 1975, pp. 35–37.

Sterling, R. R., "Relevant Financial Reporting in an Age of Price Changes," *Journal of Accountancy,* February 1975, pp. 42–51.

# SECTION 58

## NEW SELLING ENVIRONMENT

*Discusses the effects of an inflationary environment on the selling of goods and services.*

An inflationary environment, often accompanied by price controls and/or buyer reluctance to accept higher prices, usually puts a severe strain on profits. As a result, much more consideration must be given to stressing profit growth as well as volume growth, with emphasis on maintaining profit margins, holding down costs, and pricing for profit as well as making sales.

One of the key areas affecting profitability is the cost of sales. During strained economic periods companies should take a harder-than-usual look at such factors as selling to marginal accounts, sales force compensation, expense ratios, relative product profitability, customer service, and product lines, to make certain that all these important areas are being managed profitably. In an inflationary economy profit should be stressed as a measurement of performance, rather than as an end in itself.

### THE NEW SELLING ENVIRONMENT

The economic realities of most inflationary periods result in higher costs, lower profits, and many new constraints for most businesses. Indeed, many economists predict that we will be faced with the following problems for at least the next decade.

*High Rates of Unemployment.* The 8 percent unemployment rate forecast by the government for the next 2 years will be nearly double the average for the 1960's.

*Continued Inflation.* The 7.1 percent average annual rate predicted for the 1975–1980 period will be double the annual rate of the 1960's.

*Lower Standards of Living.* Increased costs will cause a slowdown in the rise of living standards. Lifestyles will change.

*Oil.* Supplies will remain tight and prices high, affecting the entire business and consumer spectrum.

*Raw Materials.* Shortages will remain critical in many areas, and costs in other areas will rise, pushing up prices.

*Capital.* The cost of borrowing money will remain high, curtailing business growth and new markets.

## THE NEED FOR CHANGING SELLING TECHNIQUES

In light of these predicted difficulties, the selling environment will change marketing techniques over the next decade; indeed, it is changing them already. Based on sharply reduced future sales projections, one major automobile manufacturer has initiated a long-term program to cut capital overhead by one-third. Airlines are consolidating their route structures. Retail chains are contracting, both in marketing areas and in numbers of outlets. *Sales Management* magazine has reported how companies are reacting—and will increasingly react—to this new selling environment by listing management trends in a number of key areas (Table 48).

As a result of these trends, sales managers over the next decade will face an inflationary selling environment characterized by the following conditions.

*Fewer Products to Sell.* With profitability the key word and materials shortages continuing, companies will concentrate on best-selling, high-profit products. Marginal or low-profit items will be dropped or deemphasized, permitting the concentration of costly labor, materials, and energy sources on turning out products with the highest return.

*Concentrated Markets.* Emphasis will be placed on serving key customers as it becomes less profitable to sell to smaller buyers. When manufacturers contract product lines and put emphasis on key accounts, smaller companies will find it increasingly difficult to buy what they need.

*Fewer New Products.* Confronted with the costly risks inherent in introducing new products, firms will concentrate on updating existing lines and will curtail new product development.

*Profit Improvement Selling.* Contracting markets will force manufacturers to concentrate on reducing costs and lowering break-even points to increase their profits. Raw materials purchases will be made from salesmen who are instrumental in showing buyers how to cut costs, and this contribution to customer profit improvement will become an important basis for selling.

*Reduced Sales Staffs.* Once most sales efforts are concentrated on key accounts, fewer salesmen will be needed. Training will be more result oriented. Top producers will be retrained to sell in the new environment, and marginal salesmen will be dismissed. In some cases sales forces may be

**Table 48 Probable Reaction to the Changing Sales Environment**[a]

| The trend will be toward . . . | . . . And away from |
|---|---|
| 1. Consolidation of company and division size | 1. Emphasis on being or becoming the biggest |
| 2. Short-term, cyclical ups and downs | 2. Reliance on long-range planning or commitments |
| 3. Emphasis on profits | 3. Emphasis on volume (unless it contributes directly to profit) |
| 4. Insistence that each account make its maximum contribution to your profit | 4. Large numbers of customers solicited or served |
| 5. Insistence that each salesman make his maximum contribution to profit | 5. Large sales force |
| 6. Insistence that each product and product line make its maximum contribution to profit | 6. Full product lines |
| 7. Insistence that each channel of distribution make its maximum contribution to profit | 7. Multiple distribution channels and large numbers of distributors and dealers |
| 8. Renovated products and acquired products | 8. Entirely new products |
| 9. Systems selling | 9. Interest in single-unit sales |
| 10. Emphasis on applying products and services to improve customer profit and promoting that effect as the prime benefit | 10. Product-benefit selling |

[a] *Source: Sales Management,* May 19, 1975, p. 4. Reprinted with permission from *Sales Management, The Marketing Magazine,* Copyright 1975.

set up as subsidiaries of their parent companies to handle related lines from other manufacturers.

*Slower Growth.* Sales increases will follow the slowdown in Gross National Product growth, and smaller sales objectives will be set. Objectives will increasingly stress profits on sales, rather than total sales volume. Special emphasis will be put on maximizing profits per market share.

## CONCLUSIONS

The company preparing for selling in the inflationary environment ahead should take the following measures: set up a lean, highly motivated sales force, set objectives in terms of increased profits, concentrate on big-selling, profitable product lines, zero in on key accounts, and trim overhead costs to the bone. These are all basic principles of good management that often go slack during the heady periods of a buoyant economy.

### SUGGESTED FURTHER READING

Hanan, Mack, "Welcome to a New World Where Profits Come Harder," *Sales Management,* May 19, 1975, pp. 3–4.

Deutsch, L. L. and P. J. Miranti, *The Use of Profitability in Managing Field Sales Operations,* Sales Executive Club of New York, 1974.

Goodman, S. R., *Techniques of Profitability Analysis,* Wiley, New York, 1970.

Henry, P., "Manage Your Sales Force as a System," *Harvard Business Review,* March/April, 1975, pp. 85–95.

Mossman, F. H., "New Approaches to Analyzing Marketing Profitability," *Journal of Marketing,* April 1974, pp. 43–48.

"Toward Higher Margins and Less Variety," *Business Week,* September 14, 1974, pp. 98–100.

# SECTION 59

## OFFICE COMMUNES

*Sketches a method of offsetting rising office space and furnishings costs by sharing facilities with other companies.*

Increasing numbers of firms are making use of office communes to help offset inflationary increases in the cost of office space and furnishings.

Office communes are fully equipped offices set up by a company, trade organization, or government and shared by several firms to spread and reduce overhead costs. Generally the companies sharing space are in related but not competitive fields, permitting joint use of specialized equipment and services that normally would have to be purchased or leased individually. The method has been particularly successful when expensive electronic data processing equipment has been shared.

Considerable cost reductions are possible if suitable business "partners" can be found. An office commune in California provided individual facilities to 12 companies at a cost to each of just $6000 per year. Office specialists estimated that it would have cost each company nearly $60,000 annually for comparable facilities if they had acted individually.

In addition to office space and furnishings, many communes share services such as secretarial help, photocopying, Telex equipment, accounting, warehousing, and distribution facilities.

### SUGGESTED FURTHER READING

Paulden, S., "Office Communes," *Financial Times,* August 12, 1974, London.

# SECTION 60

## OFFICE ENERGY CONSERVATION

*Sets out a number of energy-saving ideas that can be used by office operations to offset price increases.*

Users of electricity, coal, natural gas, oil, and other petroleum products will be plagued by rising fuel costs for at least the next decade, the result of recurring shortages, international cartels, and persistent inflation.

To help offset these cost increases, firms should institute energy-conservation programs aimed at holding fuel costs to a minimum. Various overall approaches to the problem are discussed in *Conservation of Energy* (p. 89) and *Energy Analysis* (p. 129).

The following presents a variety of energy-saving ideas that have been used by companies to cut fuel costs in office operations.[1] Most of the methods are applicable to any office situation. Collectively, they hold good potential for reducing energy use in administrative and service organizations.

### HUMIDIFICATION

Humidifying the air in an office can counteract lower temperatures. For example, a temperature of 68 degrees in a room with a relative humidity of 50 percent is just as comfortable as a temperature of 70 degrees with a relative humidity of 30 percent. An office without a humidifying unit normally has a rating of 20 percent.

### INSULATION

If a building is poorly insulated, 20 to 30 percent of the heat supply can be lost. This is one of the key areas in which significant cost savings can be

---

[1] Adapted from Dwayne Meisner, "The Whole Office Catalog," *Administrative Management,* February 1974, pp. 29–32. Copyright © 1974 by Geyer-McAllister Publications, Inc., New York.

realized. By installing better insulation in existing buildings and offices and using modern insulating techniques in new-office construction, dramatic savings can be achieved over a period of years.

## MEASURED LIGHTING

Many offices contain too much lighting. Employees in average work situations are very comfortable with a lighting level of 80 foot-candles, yet 100 and even 150 foot-candles are common in many offices today. Studies have shown that reducing levels of lighting actually improves most office environments. Under more restrained lighting, most offices appear more human, less sterile. Work performance is usually smoother without the desk and fixture glare that often accompany maximum lighting.

## LAMP TYPE

The choice of lamp type in office lighting can affect electricity consumption. Incandescent lamps are less efficient on a watt-for-watt basis, and since they give off more heat, more air conditioning is required, consuming more energy.

A number of newly developed lamps provide the same illumination previously available while consuming less energy. For example, normal size bulbs that use krypton gas are available in ratings of 54, 90, and 135 watts. These provide the same light output as conventional long-life bulbs with 60, 100, and 150 watt ratings.

## LIGHTING ZONES

Lighting systems in many offices are controlled in large zones. This prohibits the turning off of lights in office units that are not being used, or, conversely, necessitates lighting a whole area if just one person is working late. The zone system also provides the same amount of lighting to outside offices with windows as to interior windowless spaces.

The energy waste in such systems is enormous, and many firms have initiated changeovers to individually controlled, local illumination.

## MAINTENANCE

The practice of maintaining services throughout a building for 5 or 6 hours beyond the normal business day to accommodate cleaning staff is an unnecessary expense. By using time clocks or other devices, energy can be devoted to office space as needed. To keep all the areas lighted while the maintenance staff proceeds from floor to floor is extremely wasteful.

## AUTOMATED DIMMING

Automatic dimmers now on the market can be connected to an existing lighting fixture to produce energy-conserving, automated, programmed dimming. The systems utilize low-voltage programming signals, which affect the lighting cues. These controls can also be used with time clocks to dim lights automatically during off hours.

## LIGHT-CONSERVING ENVIRONMENT

Light can be conserved by using suitable color finishes on ceilings, walls, floors, and furnishings. Dark finishes absorb light, whereas finishes that are too light can cause glare. In selecting a light finish for offices, reflection should be in the following ranges:

| | |
|---|---|
| Ceiling finishes | 80 to 90% |
| Walls | 40 to 60% |
| Furniture | 25 to 45% |
| Office machines | 25 to 40% |
| Floors | 20 to 40% |

These upper limits have been selected to avoid excessively bright surfaces that make people uncomfortable or reduce visibility by producing too much glare.

In one typical installation featuring light-conserving finishes, the average illumination level increased from less than 10 foot-candles to more than 40 foot-candles.

## LUMINESCENT SIGNS

Many firms have replaced illuminated exit signs and other energy consuming hall guides with luminescent signs that need no electricity. They are fully visible under normal daytime conditions and glow for up to 8 hours at night. They are activated and reactivated by light, requiring no electricity.

## MICROPROCESSORS

Microprocessors are low-cost minicomputers on an $8\frac{1}{2} \times 11$ inch circuit card that permit room-by-room heating and lighting system controls for large buildings, resulting in much more efficient use of power than large-area thermostatic methods. Newly developed microprocessors will play an increasingly important role in reducing energy costs in the future.

## COMPUTER APPLICATIONS

Computers are gaining in popularity for controlling energy use. A typical application is the programming of EDP equipment to check power demand at frequent intervals (e.g., every 30 seconds). As demand approaches a predetermined limit, the computer systematically begins to cut back on power consumption, preventing the company from being charged penalty rates for excess usage.

In another application, the Grumman Corporation harnessed the heat from its computers to keep its plant warm. The heat given off by the firm's nine computers was intense enough to provide 83 percent of the heat needed to warm the four-story plant.

## THERMOSTAT GUARDS

Inexpensive lock and key thermostat protectors are available to prevent major temperature control changes by employees. The devices can be installed in minutes, need no changes in wiring, and permit only authorized persons to make adjustments.

## ENTRIES

The installation of a double entry wherever doors open to the outside can result in significant heat savings in northern climates.

### OUTDOOR LIGHTING

Outdoor parking lot illumination often utilizes more light than is really needed for security purposes. The same is true for building and landscape illumination.

### SUGGESTED FURTHER READING

Meisner, Dwayne, "The Whole Office Catalog," *Administrative Management*, February 1974, pp. 29–32.

# SECTION 61

## OFFICE MAINTENANCE

*Presents methods to offset inflated costs of office maintenance without sacrificing standards.*

Office maintenance is an expense common to nearly every business. Because it relies largely on human labor, it is especially susceptible to inflationary wage increases. In some large firms—financial institutions, insurance companies—the costs of office maintenance can run into millions of dollars. The figures for manufacturing companies are lower but can still be significant.

The following outlines a variety of techniques that can be utilized by most companies to reduce office maintenance costs without affecting overall standards of building cleanliness and safety.

### SAVINGS POTENTIAL

Savings in office maintenance can be direct or indirect. Direct cost efficiencies usually come through a reduction in staff.

Indirect savings, which can result from improved performance, include conservation of a building's facilities (furniture, flooring, carpeting, etc.), better employee relations, reduced safety and fire hazards, improved administrative operations, and a more healthful environment. Indirect savings might also encompass savings that accrue from avoiding penalties relating to equal opportunity laws and other laws governing employment of custodial workers. Such penalties can be costly.

### COST REDUCTION TECHNIQUES

Here are some of the most cost-effective ways—both direct and indirect—for lowering the expense of office maintenance.[1]

[1] Adapted from Edwin B. Feldman, "12 Ways to Save on Maintenance and Still Do a Good Job," *Administrative Management,* June 1973, pp. 30–32. Copyright © 1973 by Geyer-McAllister Publications, Inc., New York.

### Equipment

The typical custodial department is usually underequipped in terms of size, type, and amount of necessary gear. In the long run, this practice does not pay. It is common, for example, for two custodians to share one floor-cleaning machine. In normal operations they will both need the machine at the same time. Time is lost waiting and transporting the one machine back and forth.

Greater automation generally means higher productivity. For example, an automatic scrubbing machine for cleaning floors can double output; the same is true of a wet vacuum for speeding wax removal. In reviewing equipment, upgrade and equip workers with the right kind of tools for greater productivity and higher worker morale.

### Contract Cleaning

Contract cleaning is not a cure all, but in some situations it may offer economic advantages. If contract cleaning is selected for certain operations, make sure to provide for a contractural arrangement and job specifications that are clear and productive. In comparing costs of contract cleaners with in-house custodial services, remember that the company's staff should be supplied with adequate equipment, support, training, and so on, if comparisons are to be valid.

### Supervision

Adequate supervision should be provided to ensure that custodians are motivated, assignments are understood, procedures are correct, conditions are safe, and supplies and equipment are adequate. Supervision that is firm but not overbearing usually results in productivity increases that outweigh the supervisory cost. Even if it is necessary to reduce staff to pay for additional supervision, the results usually justify the step.

### Scheduling

For greatest productivity, as much work as possible should be performed on the shift of least activity. This is affected, of course, by the local labor market, transportation problems, security, and supervision, but maintenance work is most productive when there are the fewest other employees on the premises.

### Training

On-the-job training should be supplemented with classroom instruction. This may sound like an additional expense, but studies have shown that well-prepared training classes pay for themselves by improving productivity, increasing quality, and reducing absenteeism and turnover.

### Preventive Devices

Use should be made of preventive devices that eliminate or lessen the frequency of difficult cleaning jobs. For example, a grating placed at a major building entrance to catch soil, sand, water, and other dirt will prevent the material from being tracked onto thousands of square feet of floor area. Since in some conditions it costs $50 to $100 per pound to remove soil from building interiors, the dirt is best kept outside.

Other preventive devices include waste receptacles, cigarette urns, elevator carpeting, and plastic liners for waste receptacles.

### Built-in Maintenance

Most often, maintenance costs are not a basic concern of architects or interior decorators who are assigned to design or renovate offices. For this reason the maintenance supervisor should be called in to recommend changes in preliminary building plans and specifications that can result in operating cost reductions. Architects should be given guidelines for locations, size, and equipment required for custodial closets, spacing and sizing of electrical outlets in corridors and stairwells, suitable surfaces for ceilings, color limitations for carpets and resilient flooring, types of lighting fixtures, proper wall mounting for rest room fixtures, and scores of other considerations that can lead to major reductions in maintenance costs over the years.

### Chemicals and Maintenance Materials

It is poor economy to perform maintenance with inferior products. For example, artificial economies from use of a cheap floor finish will negate the considerable time required to strip and refinish a floor because the material scratches, powders, scuffs, and marks quickly. The type of chemicals and materials used can save 25 to 40 percent in time and expense associated with flooring maintenance. Additionally, maintenance workers feel that if management is unable to provide them with workable materials, their jobs must not be important, and performance suffers accordingly.

**Floor Surfaces**

Economies may be possible through the changing of floor surfaces. Carpeting, for example, can be less expensive than certain types of tile in many situations because of the ease of maintenance.

**Measured Assignments**

In most cases custodians should be given measured assignments, based on reasonable time allowances for given procedures and use of specific materials and equipment. In this way maintenance workers know exactly what is expected and can work toward standards.

**SUGGESTED FURTHER READING**

Feldman, Edwin B., "12 Ways to Save on Maintenance and Still Do a Good Job," *Administrative Management,* June 1973, pp. 30–32.

# SECTION 62

## OVERSTAFFING

*Discusses the importance of holding staff to minimum levels during inflation and sketches staff reduction techniques.*

It has been estimated that the average business can save 10 to 50 percent of its wage cost by thoroughly analyzing staff size and making suitable reductions. Overstaffing, one of business's most common money-wasters, increases in importance during inflationary periods because of disproportionately high wage increase demands. With profits under pressure, managements should be diligent in pruning staff to the optimum working level and taking steps to assure that the level is maintained.

Unfortunately overstaffing is one of the most difficult costs to analyze and bring under control. Supervisors can hardly be expected to be cooperative, since reductions in their staffs limit their respective spheres of responsibility and importance. Remaining employees complain about the increased workload that has fallen on their shoulders. Trade unions generally oppose staff reductions without sizable tangible benefits for the employees remaining, and attempts by management to carry out cuts often result in strikes.

One of the primary reasons for overstaffed conditions is that companies hire on the basis of the number of persons needed to handle the workload during peak periods. If these periods fluctuate or are seasonal, many employees are left with little to do during normal periods. Work gets spread around to fill the vacuum, and soon a whole department is engaged in work that could be handled by relatively few people. Part-time workers that are utilized only during peak periods can help alleviate this problem (see *Part-Time Employees,* p. 261).

Another cause of overstaffing, especially during inflationary periods, is reduction in the workload. In the poor business climate that often accompanies inflation, sales and production fall off and fewer staff are needed. Often, however, management is reluctant to let employees go, fearing that the company will be undermanned in the event of a business upturn. Again, part-timers can be profitably utilized in filling gaps.

To reach the optimum-sized staff, thorough analysis should be carried out in each work area in which overstaffing is suspected. Such analysis should be based on such factors as time- and work-study techniques, volume analysis, peak load conditions, standards, and workloads (past, present, and projected). Guidelines such as the following should be used.

*Establish Job Time Standards.*   For example, determine the amount of time it takes to type one invoice. Then multiply this figure by the average number of invoices generated daily. Thus if typing each invoice takes an average of 20 minutes and 200 invoices are generated daily, a total of 66 hours of typing would be required each day. Based on a 7-hour work day, 9 or 10 typists should be able to handle the daily workload. Part-time or temporary help could be brought in during peak periods.

*Analyze Job Procedures.*   Often job procedures grow haphazardly, based more on habit than efficiency. In analyzing staff, determine whether unnecessary, wasteful steps are included in job tasks. Would doing the job in a different way result in reduction of employees or in time savings? Can reductions or efficiencies be realized by rearranging the office or plant? Would new work flow methods result in fewer employees or less overtime?

*Peak Loads.*   Peak loads can best be handled by anticipating when they will fall and gearing for the rush by controlling vacation schedules, arranging for part-time or temporary help, asking existing staff to work harder, using overtime if necessary, and other measures.

## SUGGESTED FURTHER READING

*Cost Control and the Supervisor,* American Management Association, New York, 1966.

# SECTION 63

## PART–TIME EMPLOYEES

*Outlines cost savings and productivity increases that can result from using part-time employees during inflationary periods.*

Proper utilization of manpower takes on added meaning during inflationary periods. With profits under pressure, salaries and wages must be kept to a minimum, even though employees will be pushing for pay increases to help offset the rising cost of living. At the same time, productivity must be maximized to negate the effects of inflation on the firm. Management is faced with the task of getting the most work from the smallest number of people at the least cost.

Proper structuring of manpower utilization programs can be instrumental in meeting these objectives, and in many cases these programs can be enhanced through the intelligent use of part-time employees. Housewives and retired persons make up a huge reservoir of largely untapped part-time skills in nearly every community, and recent studies have shown that their productivity and reliability records are often better than those of full-time employees.

The following[1] discusses the use of part-time employees during inflationary periods as a method of holding down wage costs and increasing productivity.

### AVAILABILITY

One of the most persistent myths regarding part-time workers is that they are not readily available. In fact, it is the other way around; it is the part-time jobs that are not available.

One study has shown that there are at least 4 million housewives in the United States who would be willing to work part-time. This number would reach 10 million if employers were to make childcare facilities available.

[1] Adapted by permission from William B. Werther, Jr., "Part-Timers: Overlooked and Undervalued," *Business Horizons,* February 1975, pp. 13–20. Copyright 1975 by the Foundation for the School of Business located at Indiana University.

Inflation, unemployment, and social pressure to become more than a homemaker have all combined to bring increasing numbers of women into the labor market. Currently, more than half of all women of working age are employed at some time during the year; a third of them (13.4 million) are part-timers.

Added to these millions, there are the increasing numbers of retired persons—the fastest growing segment of the population. Even after subtracting those over 65 who are already employed or unable to work, there are still 17.2 million retired persons in the United States potentially available for employment. With inflation eroding their fixed incomes, increasing numbers of retirees are anxious to supplement incomes through part-time jobs.

These two sources alone, then, represent more than 27 million potential part-time employees, a vast labor pool for firms willing to make part-time jobs available.


### RELIABILITY

Another myth regarding part-time employees concerns reliability. Recalling experiences with unskilled and unreliable teenagers, many employers are reluctant even to investigate the potential of part-time workers.

Generally part-timers *have* been teenagers, and since they lack needed work skills, they have most often been relegated to menial jobs at menial wages. Since neither the job nor the pay offers much incentive to perform well, their attitude toward work is usually one of indifference.

A marked improvement is usually seen in performance, however, when skilled housewives or retired persons are recruited as part-time workers and put into responsible positions with meaningful pay and opportunities. Housewives are used to the responsibility of a home, and the retiree's track record is usually one of a lifetime of responsible employment. When part-time workers are recruited from these sources, the problem of immaturity is side-stepped and unreliability should be no worse than that of full-time employees. Even given repetitive tasks, part-timers are not exposed to the job as long as full-timers and are less frustrated.


### ABILITY

The number of skills possessed by retired workers is virtually unlimited, and their ability to use those skills is easily verifiable through employment history records. Their ranks include craftsmen, technicians, professionals, and managers—all with years of valuable experience. Part-time accountants can be used at tax time, experienced salesmen during a peak sales period, or retired managers to conduct orientation or training programs.

Housewives also possess a variety of abilities, although less comprehensive in range. Clerical and typing proficiencies are most common. However every year increasing numbers of women graduate from colleges with various degrees, meaning that employers can more readily recruit mature, college-educated women for part-time work. Even when the education and job do not match, housewives are at least as trainable as full-time recruits. And as sex-based discrimination is eliminated, women will possess a wider diversity of skills.

A balanced recruitment program provides unskilled part-timers to handle clerical tasks or highly repetitive assembly jobs. Skilled workers can be put on the payroll for their specific abilities. Almost all areas of the organization's employment needs can be met through part-time personnel.

## PRACTICAL ADVANTAGES

In addition to availability, reliability, and ability, part-time manpower presents employers with some distinct advantages. These benefits, moreover, are not limited to some operations within the firm or some companies; the advantages can accrue to all organizations.

### Scheduling Flexibility

If a proportion of the workforce is part-time help, managers can achieve greater scheduling flexibility in allocating human resources. This flexibility permits work schedules to be optimized in relationship to demand, equipment utilization, and employee wishes.

For example, if part-time personnel are introduced into a bank's workforce, the increased numbers of customers and mail-in transactions that normally occur on Fridays, Mondays, and the first of the month can be dealt with on a part-time basis. Part-timers can be scheduled for "minishifts" of 4 or more hours to supplement the full-time workforce during periods of peak business activity. Additional tellers' windows can be opened, and transactions can be handled more quickly and efficiently. All this occurs with a minimum of full-time staff.

In factories, full-time employees can select preferred schedules and any gaps in the schedule can be covered by part-timers. Or, if a plant decides to operate a 12-hour shift, two 6-hour minishifts of part-time workers can be used instead of extending the hours of already- fatigued workers.

When variable work hours are installed part-timers can be effectively used to staff switchboards, office phones, customer service counters, and so on, to smooth out early morning and late evening gaps in manpower. Staffing demands that result from vacations, short leaves of absence, seasonal surges in workload, and terminations can be met by part-timers. Even unexpected absences can be handled by using the roster of part-timers as a call list.

### Lower Labor Costs

Part-time manpower should be paid rates commensurate with those of full-time personnel; employees who are paid lower wages are only marginally attached to the workforce. Since most part-time jobs pay wages below those of full-time positions, little company loyalty is generated and turnover is usually high. By paying a more realistic wage, looking for alternatives in part-time employment is less attractive and turnover becomes minimal.

Even when paying wages comparable to full-time rates, however, firms utilizing part-timers can realize substantial savings in labor costs. These employees are not normally given the full range of fringe benefits—the fastest growing component of labor costs. This means that part-timers who are absent are not paid; employer contributions for health, life, and other forms of insurance are saved; and outlays for time off with pay (holidays or vacations) are not made. Even without these fringe benefits, part-time workers are usually satisfied because they are receiving wages that are high compared with typical part-time pay.

If one-fourth of an employer's workforce is replaced by part-time help, a reduction in fringe benefit costs of 25 percent is realized. Overtime can be substantially pared—even eliminated—by variable minishifts of, for example, 3 hours a day. Increased work loads can be met by expanding the hours of part-time help without the expense of overtime.

### Performance

Highly repetitive assembly jobs, monotonous clerical work, or demanding customer contact positions are fatiguing. Whether caused by boredom or inconsiderate customers, fatigue leads to errors. The degree of exasperation or boredom and the associated fatigue is less for the part-time employee, who therefore makes fewer errors. Thus properly trained and experienced part-time personnel are more likely to produce higher quality work.

Because the fatigue is less and because the part-timer's shifts are shorter, it is reasonable to expect quantity of output to be greater also. Knowing that the workshift will be completed in 3 or 4 hours, the part-timer has less reason to pace his work, and he can give the task his all. Productivity may be even further enhanced if the higher output of part-timers is effectively used as a target for full-time personnel. One study in Massachusetts showed that 50 married women hired as social workers on a half-time schedule by the Massachusetts Department of Welfare handled an average of 89 percent of the cases handled by full-time workers. Moreover, their turnover rate was one-third that of their full-time colleagues.

### Reducing Turnover Rates

Each time an employee resigns, the company loses several hundred dollars—sometimes several thousand. The cost of recruiting, screening, and training each worker represents one of the most significant business expenses. This amount is lost when turnover occurs.

It is possible that the company can retain or recapture the skills of proven workers with a program of part-time positions. When an employee leaves because of health, inadequate child care arrangements, or other conflicting demands, the skills (and the corporate investment) may be retained in the form of part-time work compatible with personal desires and company needs. Even if such an arrangement is not immediately feasible, a change in the individual's status may result in an application for part-time work in a few weeks or months. The potential savings alone—especially to companies in which turnover is high—justifies consideration of part-time manpower.

### Employment Stability

Part-time employees can be valuable in ensuring overall company employment stability. By adjusting the hours that such employees work, swings in demand often can be met effectively. This technique gives the company greater latitude in coping with economic changes without costly layoffs, crash recruiting campaigns, or radical changes in inventory.

Most companies strive for stability in employment, not only to maintain a favorable experience rating for unemployment tax contributions but also because of the potential difficulties full-time workers encounter when they suddenly become unemployed. With a proportion of the workforce composed of part-timers, reductions in manpower are less traumatic. The situation is unpleasant, of course, but the temporary displacement of part-time employees is often less crucial because their earnings are usually not the primary source of family income.

Furthermore, if a part-time employee is separated from the company, he is normally ineligible for unemployment compensation. To be covered, he must show that he is ready and willing to accept full-time employment. Unless covered, the layoff of a part-timer will not be included in the company's experience rating, and the unemployment compensation contribution (the payroll tax) paid by the employer remains unchanged. For firms that typically have wide variations in employment levels, the utilization of part-time personnel can lead to significant reductions in this employer tax.

### Affirmative Action

To qualify for federal funds, many employers are operating under affirmative action plans that contain employment objectives. Whether those goals are an increase in the employment of minorities, the handicapped, Vietnam veterans, or women, the use of part-time personnel provides a method of attracting members of these groups without head-on wage competition from other employers. Most organizations attempt to meet the objectives of their plans by competing for full-time employees; astute managers obtain significant economies in wages and recruitment by seeking out part-timers who possess the desired characteristics.

### SUMMARY

Companies that systematically make use of part-time employees during inflationary periods can benefit through lower labor and turnover costs, greater scheduling flexibility, and improved performance. In light of recent positive experiences in many areas, management should explore more fully this often-neglected source of employees. If part-timers are employed over a period of time, perhaps as replacements for terminated full-time workers, disruptions and transition costs should be minimal. Moreover, part-timers may help to achieve other goals—affirmative action objectives, improved employment stability, and more efficient manpower utilization.

### SUGGESTED FURTHER READING

Greenwald, Carol S. and Judith Liss, "Part-Time Workers Can Bring Higher Productivity," *Harvard Business Review,* September/October, 1973, pp. 20–22.

"Part-Timers in the Managerial Ranks?" *Industry Week,* October 14, 1974, pp. 40–41.

Werther, William B. Jr., "Part-Timers: Overlooked and Undervalued," *Business Horizons,* February 1975, pp. 13–20.

# SECTION **64**

## POWER DEMAND SYSTEMS

*Discusses a method of lowering energy expenses by use of a monitoring system to lower peak demand.*

Power demand systems are being increasingly used to help offset inflationary price increases in energy sources.

In most cases utility companies bill for the maximum demand placed on their distribution and generation system during a given time. If a company's peak power demand reaches a certain level during one of these periods, however, the firm is billed at the peak demand rate as if it had used that rate consistently. Power demand systems, generally monitored by computer, avoid the higher rate by anticipating power use and holding total consumption below a predetermined level.

For example, the system might anticipate a furnace being turned on. As the temperature in the furnace begins to use more power and threatens to exceed a predetermined level of demand, the system might turn off the air conditioning. Since in a well-programmed system the air conditioning would be off for only a matter of minutes, the temperature in the plant would not be affected. By avoiding a demand peak, however, the system prevents the company from being charged at the higher demand electricity rate.

Properly conceived and monitored, power demand systems can effect significant cost savings in manufacturing facilities and offices that are large energy users.

### SUGGESTED FURTHER READING

"The Do-It-Yourselfers Tackle Inflation," *Industry Week,* June 24, 1974, p. 42.

# 65

## PRICING

*Outlines pricing strategies for maintaining adequate margins during inflationary periods.*

Prolonged periods of spiraling inflation can upset traditional methods of pricing products or services.

The constant and rapid erosion of the value of money means that a product's selling price may be too low in just a matter of weeks or months. During a 12 percent inflationary period, for example, currency is losing value at the rate of 1 percent a month, and a product selling for $1000 in January will be actually selling for $940 in real money terms just 6 months later, unless inflationary increases are taken into account by raising the price.

Additionally, there are constantly increasing prices of raw materials. Assuming the 12 percent inflationary rate, a product that cost $1000 to manufacture in January would cost $1060 to produce—in real money terms—after half a year. Unless the price tag is raised, these higher manufacturing costs will eat significantly into profits.

To further complicate the situation, consumer groups and government bodies backing antitrust laws become especially vigilant during inflationary periods, and each price hike must be able to withstand the most probing scrutiny.

To ensure that a product's selling price is fair, accurate, and profitable, an inflationary environment demands better, faster, and more frequent pricing decisions than are called for during more stable periods. The following guidelines, used by various international companies, should be kept in mind when deciding a product's price.

### RETAIN PROFITABILITY

There is a tendency during stable economic periods to attempt to build volume by letting prices and profit margins slip for the sake of making sales. The uncertainties that accompany an inflationary environment, however, cause many companies to shift their thinking to putting *more* emphasis on profits and less on expanded volume. In highly competitive selling or bidding situations, many firms have found it better to withdraw product lines with a thin profit margin than to risk inflationary-erosion losses.

## FORMALIZE PRICING POLICIES

When unstable costs and fluctuating margins prevail, it is better to put tighter controls on the ways prices are established. In an effort to curtail shading by overenthusiastic salesmen, some firms remove pricing responsibility from the field and place it higher in management structure—sometimes to the level of chief executive officer. In such cases no deviation from book price is allowed in the field.

Another possible control is the hiring of full-time pricing specialists for important areas that affect profitability. These areas include production, marketing, financial, and market research. The specialists carry responsibility for reviewing pricing frequently and for maintaining adequate profit margins.

## CONSTANT UPDATING

If products are to be priced profitably, all factors affecting pricing must be updated regularly. Such factors include labor costs, raw material costs, selling costs, and overheads. Firms that have found 6-month budgets and quarterly cash projections adequate during normal times may have to begin to budget quarterly and project weekly during inflationary periods.

The computer is the primary tool used for increased price and cost analysis. Properly programmed, it can deliver information flows that allow revision of prices weekly or daily. Some firms program their EDP systems to issue warnings when costs have increased and margins need to be reexamined. At the ultimate level of such a system, a daily computer printout automatically shows updated relationships between cost and margin on all inventories.

## ESCALATOR CLAUSES

As a hedge against rapidly rising raw materials costs during inflationary periods, firms may incorporate escalator clauses in pricing of long-term contracts. Such clauses stipulate that the selling price of products be determined by production cost at time of delivery, rather than at the time of order. Buyers are often reluctant to enter into such agreements during stable economic periods. But materials shortages often accompany inflation and usually provide the seller with a wedge for insisting that production cost increases be added to a contract. Most often, deferred pricing systems are tied to one of the standard indexes, such as the Wholesale Price Index, the Gross National Product Implicit Deflator, or the wholesale price for a specific commodity used in production. Labor cost increases may also be included, although this is less common. The delivered price is thus a combination of the price at order, plus increases in raw materials and/or labor costs.

## ELIMINATION OF "FREE" SERVICES

Another pricing area to be examined during inflationary periods is the so-called free service. "Free" services may include special packaging, free delivery, warehousing, and other concessions. These should no longer be provided gratis but should be billed separately, in addition to the straight invoice price. Customers who want these services are made to pay for them and, more importantly, customers who do not want a particular service are spared the expense. Separate accounting or elimination of such services can be instrumental in helping to reduce costs and provide a more accurate picture of pricing and profitability.

## NEW PRODUCTS

Pricing of new products presents special problems during an inflationary period. Uncertain economic conditions, price fluctuation in raw materials, volatile demand, and other factors may be responsible for difficulties in arriving at prices.

In the past most companies priced new products on a cost-plus basis and made periodic adjustments with respect to competition. Today there is a trend toward pricing new products along market- or value-oriented lines, rather than using cost orientation. Two schools of thought are emerging; both have their strong proponents, and both can show remarkable success examples.

On the one hand, there are firms that advocate "skimming"—charging as much for any new product as the market will bear. This philosophy is based on unveiling a new product and making as much profit from it as quickly as possible, before similar but lower-priced products are introduced by competitors. The high initial price, of course, encourages rapid entry of competition in the market, and the "skimming" company must count on high, short-term initial profits before prices are driven down. The key to this strategy is careful analysis of how high a product can be priced without pricing itself out of the market.

At the other extreme are advocates of "penetration" pricing. These firms begin with a low price for a new product. Their goal is instant dominance of a market, with a goal of long-term leadership in sales of the product. Such firms believe that if enough of the market is captured initially, customers can be persuaded to "trade up" to higher prices later. Additionally, proponents of penetration pricing believe that low initial pricing can unlock markets that would never respond to higher prices. A good example is the huge consumer market that emerged when $25 hand-held calculators appeared.

Although small profit margins used in penetration pricing are instrumental in discouraging potential competition, care must be taken during inflationary periods not to cut margins *too* thin. Unexpected rises in labor or material costs can quickly render a low-margin product unprofitable.

## DE-MARKETING

Since statutory price controls may accompany inflationary periods, preventing price increases, many firms concentrate only on their most profitable lines. They "de-market" products that return negligible income. This can be accomplished in various ways: by entirely removing low-profit items from the line, by telling salesmen not to push such products, by offering salesmen bonuses for selling high-profit items, and so on.

"De-marketing" has taken on even broader meaning in some industries in which demand now exceeds supply (e.g., oil and power). Faced with critical or anticipated shortages, some of these industries have begun to "sell" the idea of decreasing consumption. If demand persists, higher prices can be used in these and other industries to bring consumption into line with supply.

## SUGGESTED FURTHER READING

Brooks, D. G., "Cost-Oriented Pricing: A Realistic Solution to a Complicated Problem," *Journal of Marketing*, April 1975, pp. 72–74.

Fuss, N. H., Jr., "How to Raise Prices—Judiciously—To Meet Today's Conditions," *Harvard Business Review*, May 1975, p. 10.

Fuss, N. H., Jr., "Pricing in an Unsettled Economy," *Advanced Management Review,* September 1975, pp. 26–36.

McManus, G. J., "Pricing Process: Facts—Or the Flip of a Coin," *Iron Age,* April 28, 1975, pp. 32–34.

"Pricing Strategy in an Inflationary Economy," *Business Week,* April 16, 1974, pp. 43–49.

# 66

## PRODUCT DISCONTINUANCE CHECKLIST

*Provides guidelines and checklists to aid in product elimination decisions during inflation.*

During the past 20 years the number of products manufactured by American companies has grown enormously, and today it is not uncommon for a firm to carry several thousand products. Given the established principle that 20 percent of a company's products usually generate 80 percent of its profits, it is likely that most firms are carrying product lines that if not unprofitable, are at least not generating an adequate return on investment.

During inflationary periods unprofitable products become especially critical. Given increased labor and materials costs, as well as tight money, added inventory expenses, and an overall squeeze on profits, the retention of unprofitable product lines can have costly financial consequences.

The following outlines overall considerations for product discontinuance during an inflationary period and provides checklists to aid in product elimination decisions.

### BENEFITS OF A PRODUCT ELIMINATION PROGRAM

In addition to improving profits, systematic product elimination brings about a number of other advantages. These include improving sales, reducing inventory levels, freeing executive time for more profitable products, and making important and scarce resources—such as raw materials and energy—available for more promising projects. Additionally, the product elimination process forces management to concern itself with the reasons for the product's failure, leading to guidelines for decisions about future new product introductions.

Surprisingly, a recent study showed that "the product elimination policies and practices of 96 of the nation's largest manufacturing firms are for the most part unstructured, unsophisticated, and ineffective."[1] The five major

[1] Stanley H. Kratchman, T. Richard Hise, and Thomas A. Ulrich, "Management's Decision to Discontinue a Product," *The Journal of Accountancy*, June 1975, p. 51. Copyright © 1975 by the American Institute of Certified Public Accountants, Inc.

**Table 49    Basic Accounting Data Required for All Products in Product Elimination Decisions**[a]

1. An estimate of the developmental costs germane to that product. These include those expenditures required to initially investigate the feasibility of producing and marketing the item, research and development costs, expenditures for test markets, costs of producing models and pilot plants, etc. These costs can and should be considered investment expenditures; they should not be confused with, and should be separated from, the variable expenses allocable each time period to that product.
2. An estimate of those variable expenses that can be directly applied to specific products, including costs of production and marketing.
3. An indication of the number of units of the product or service sold in past time periods.
4. Total sales revenues accounted for by each product.
5. Estimates of sales revenues for competitive products.
6. Estimates of the number of units sold by competitive products or services.
7. Current and past pricing structure for the product, including list price and discount policies.
8. Inventory turnover per time period.
9. Competitive pricing policies. Especially important is the average price obtained for competitive products or services.
10. Indication of total company sales volume for past periods.
11. A projection of future sales for each product carried. This projection can be an extrapolation of past sales based on regression analysis, but other, more sophisticated procedures may be employed.
12. An estimate of the number of executive man-hours devoted to each product.

[a] *Source:* Kratchman, Hise, and Ulrich, "Management's Decision to Discontinue a Product," *The Journal of Accountancy,* June 1975, p. 52. Copyright © 1975 by the American Institute of Certified Public Accountants, Inc.

findings were as follows:

• Only one-third of the firms had a formal discontinuance program in writing.
• Only 13 companies used the computer in making product elimination decisions.
• One-half of the firms had discontinued five or fewer products in the year under study, despite having sizable product lines.
• More than one-third of the companies had not assigned a specific individual responsibility for product discontinuance.
• The typical company had eliminated fewer than 20 products during the previous 5-year period.

## REQUIRED DATA

Intelligent product discontinuance decisions cannot be made unless sufficient and reliable data are available for all product lines. Primarily it is the responsibility of the marketing manager, working with the management accounting staff, to determine data required for a successful product elimination program. Table 49 is a checklist giving the basic accounting data usually required for all products. Most often, computerization is desirable, if not absolutely necessary, in this information-gathering function.

## USE OF DATA "WARNING SIGNALS"

Once the basic data on products are compiled, "warning signals" will appear—that is, signs that a product should be considered for discontinuance. Table 50 outlines a number of warning signals that can be derived from the data included in Table 49. Using these signals, management can make decisions about a product's future viability. Of course there are other considerations, such as the possible adverse effect of a product's elimination on sales of other company products; but at least an accurate picture of a product's profitability status will be revealed.

The warning signal data can be used in several ways.

*Standards can be developed from the warning signs.* Failure of existing

**Table 50  Summary of Warning Signals That Mean a Product May be in Trouble**[a]

1.  Declining absolute sales volume.
2.  Sales volume decreasing as a percentage of the firm's total sales.
3.  Decreasing market share.
4.  Past sales volume not up to projected amounts.
5.  Expected future sales disappointing.
6.  Future market potential for products or services of this type not favorable.
7.  Return on investment below minimally acceptable level.
8.  Variable costs exceed revenues.
9.  Various costs as a percentage of sales consistently increasing.
10.  Increasingly greater percentage of executive time required.
11.  Price must be constantly lowered to maintain sales.
12.  Promotional budgets must be consistently increased to maintain sales.

[a] *Source:* Kratchman, Hise, and Ulrich, "Management's Decision to Discontinue a Product," *The Journal of Accountancy,* June 1975, p. 53. Copyright © 1975 by the American Institute of Certified Public Accountants, Inc.

products to meet these standards should be an area of management concern.

*Standards can be computerized.* Once standards are set, they can be computerized so that products failing to meet any standard can be "red-flagged" as soon as possible.

*Priorities can be set.* Management can decide which of the warning signals should be given greatest emphasis for each individual product. In some cases profitability and financial returns will be the all-important factors; in others, marketing considerations may get priority.

*Product improvement.* If properly evaluated and interpreted, the warning signals can be instrumental in pointing out what steps should be taken to improve a product to make it more competitive.


## SUGGESTED FURTHER READING

Fiedler, J. A., "Choosing A Remedy for Sick Sales: Product Change or Advertising Change," *Journal of Marketing,* April 1975, pp. 67–68.

Kratchman, Stanley H., Richard T. Hise, and Thomas A. Ulrich, "Management's Decision to Discontinue a Product," *Journal of Accountancy,* June 1975, p. 51.

"Toward Higher Margins and Less Variety," *Business Week,* September 14, 1974, pp. 98–100.

## 67

# PRODUCTIVITY BARGAINING

*Outlines the basic principles behind bargaining agreements to increase productivity during inflation; sketches case histories.*

Productivity is especially important during inflation because increasing productivity offsets the degree at which inflation expands. Productivity must match public spending and private consumption to achieve a zero inflationary rate.

Productivity in the United States is lagging. From 1970 through 1974 it rose only 8.4 percent, compared with an increase of 43 percent during the same period in Japan. Moreover, productivity actually showed a decline in the United States in 1974, the first decrease in 27 years.

The Japanese government, with a national budget of $65 billion, spends $13 million on productivity improvement. The United States, on the other hand, spends only $2 million of its $313 billion budget to finance the National Commission on Productivity and Work Quality.

In recent years several Western European countries have also outstripped the United States in productivity. By the end of 1974 the United States had dropped to ninth place among the top 12 industrialized countries in the rate of productivity increase. Part of the reason is that the other countries are more positive in encouraging private investment in plants and equipment. Currently, about 16 percent of our GNP is being spent on capital investment; in Germany, France, and Japan, these expenditures are 26, 28, and 36 percent, respectively.

## REASONS FOR DECLINE IN NATIONAL PRODUCTIVITY

One reason for decreasing productivity in America is the use of outdated equipment. Studies have shown that 20 percent of all American industrial equipment is more than 20 years old and should be replaced. One estimate has put a price tag of $200 billion on updating the country's industry with the best modern equipment. The steel industry, for example, will have to spend $14.3 billion; machinery makers, $13.6 billion; and the aerospace industry, $1.3 billion.

Other reasons for the drop in productivity are open to argument. Some critics accuse management of complacency and lack of foresight. Others see the problem stemming from increased labor union power. A third group holds that the free enterprise system is being bogged down by ever-increasing numbers of government regulations, stifling the incentive for efficiency.

Whatever the causes, the drop in productivity has had a marked impact on the inflationary environment of the United States. When wage and materials costs rise without comparable increases in productivity, cost-push inflation results. As the Republican Conference of the Senate has observed, "Increasing the productivity of American industry and labor is critical in order to raise output, combat inflation, and provide additional real purchasing power for the nation's workers."

Productivity bargaining is one approach to increasing efficiency in industry. More widely practiced in Europe than in the United States, the approach goes well beyond the normal bounds of collective bargaining, since labor and management not only create the productivity agreement, they work together to ensure a cooperative environment in which the changes called for in the agreement can be carried out.

## THE CONCEPT

Like collective bargaining, productivity bargaining is used to determine wages, hours, and working conditions. In addition to these functions, however, productivity bargaining sets goals for greater worker efficiency and offers incentives to the workforce in return for achievement of projected productivity increases. The ideal result of productivity bargaining should be a written agreement outlining "a continuing, constructive collaboration between labor and management for increasing work achievement over time, and for sharing the gains in profits this increased productivity will bring."[1]

In productivity bargaining management defines changes in work operations that will be beneficial to the company and presents them to labor. Labor, in return, responds with modifications and tradeoffs until a suitable bargain, acceptable to both parties, is reached. In most cases the agreement covers a whole plant, although specific functions or departments can be emphasized.

Generally the work changes specified in the agreement are major and diverse. Therefore the entire package of interrelated changes in work or

[1] Jerome M. Rosow, "Now Is the Time for Productivity Bargaining," *Harvard Business Review*, January/February, 1972, p. 79.

production methods must be spelled out in the agreement. "The gains must tempt both parties; everybody must play the game, and everybody must win."[2]

In Europe the most common work changes relate to five key areas: modifications of existing incentive plans, wage structure reform through more effective use of job evaluation, flexibility of labor, elimination of open-end contracts, and changes in working methods (such as shift work). Elimination of overspecialization of work and excessive rigidity in skill lines have been key management concerns in productivity bargaining.

## GENERAL PRINCIPLES

European experience has provided a number of guidelines that management can use in achieving successful productivity bargaining agreements. It has been found that management must take action as follows:

- Accept a commitment to fundamental change and invest the necessary time, energy, and patience to effect the change.
- Appoint executives who are personally motivated to make the agreement work and to pursue the issues to conclusion (managers who have a drive for recognition and leadership).
- Accept full responsibility and initiative for changing existing work patterns and achieving needed reforms.
- Be fully responsive to the ideas, needs, and desires of the workers, shop stewards, and labor union representatives.
- Provide valid, worthwhile incentives in return for changes, such as greatly reduced working hours, much better pay, and so on.
- Meet workers' psychological needs for job security.
- Share credit with union leaders for getting the agreement negotiated, signed, and working.

### Need

Productivity bargaining seldom results from a natural extension of collective bargaining. It occurs most often when there is a strong management need for far-reaching changes in production methods and rapid increases in productivity. Motivation for such changes usually occurs when sales, profits, and capital investment are under pressure during periods of rising costs or increased competition.

[2] Rosow, "Now is the Time for Productivity Bargaining," *Harvard Business Review,* January/February 1972, p. 79.

The principles of productivity bargaining are applicable to nearly every industry or business. It has usually been assumed that companies in labor-intensive industries can benefit more by using the technique than firms in capital-intensive industries, but experience shows this is not necessarily true. Companies in the capital-intensive chemical industry, for example, have displayed significant productivity increases through using the technique, and similar results have been achieved by oil-refining companies. By adapting productivity bargaining principles to suit individual company needs, nearly every management should be able to benefit.

### Commitment

Success with productivity bargaining relies heavily on trial and error, time, patience, and an aggressive but flexible management. This is because such agreements are generally tailored to fit individual companies and plants within the company; there are set basic formulas, but each application is different.

This being the case, strong management motivation and commitment are prerequisites of a successful program.

Management controls the money, the machines, the materials, and the men; it alone has the power to initiate the radical and costly changes that follow implicitly from productivity bargaining. The managers must face the decisions, the problems, and the hard and long efforts necessary to improve an entire productive system. As well as weighing the value of this approach objectively, management must be prepared to commit itself strongly if it commits itself at all. Managers at all levels—whether members of the board or first-line supervisors in the plant—must be brought to believe in, or at least support, the necessity for change.[3]

### Costs

In costing out a productivity improvement program, management must project relevant economic data for 5 to 10 years ahead.

A price must be paid for improved efficiencies—mainly in increased wages. Additionally, there may be lump sum, one-time buyout costs, and certain fringe benefits may have to be conceded in the bargain.

These costs must be weighed against the labor cost and output per man-hour before and after the productivity agreement goes into effect, taking into account future inflationary projections. If accurate data are obtained, management should be able to study the economic gains objectively, plan

[3] Rosow, "Now Is the Time for Productivity Bargaining," *Harvard Business Review*, January/February, 1972, p. 86.

budget targets, and decide on the price it can pay to bring about desired changes.

### Job Security

One of the key elements in productivity bargaining is the problem of job security. No worker can be expected to accept a program that may eliminate his job, no matter how tempting the wage improvement.

In many instances productivity bargaining is unsuccessful if management is unwilling to write "no redundancy" clauses into the agreement. This is a high price to pay for change, but sometimes it is the only alternative and must be taken into account in savings forecasts.

This problem is alleviated somewhat in companies with a high rate of attrition; agreement is made not to hire replacements. In other instances the anticipated higher rate of production and sales may offset the costs of keeping surplus employees.

[However,] companies must bear in mind the fact that once they bring up the subject of a productivity bargain, they must expose the nerves of job security. Management must face the issue before the fact and scrutinize its manpower redeployment options before it even begins to calculate possible benefits.[4]

New manpower policies are usually a necessity when entering productivity bargaining agreements. Displacement of existing workers should be kept to a minimum to ensure that workers feel secure in their jobs. Toward these ends, provisions should be made for new manpower planning programs, retraining programs, in-company transfer programs, and worthwhile options for redundant workers. Options can take many forms, including the following:

- Severance pay.
- Severance pay coupled with retraining and assistance in external job placement.
- Retraining and assignment to a new job within the company.
- Early retirement. When this option is used, it is usually necessary to adjust pension payments upward to an adequate level.

These options are costly, and one of management's most crucial jobs in formulating a productivity agreement is to balance natural attrition rates as closely as possible with manpower requirements. Where this is impossible, decisions regarding the cost effectiveness of productivity agreements must

[4] Rosow, "Now Is the Time for Productivity Bargaining," *Harvard Business Review*, January/February 1972, p. 87.

be based on the long-term cost of invoking these options for greater efficiency versus the cost of continued low productivity in the future.

### Worker Attitude

Productivity bargaining offers an excellent opportunity for management to explore ways of improving worker job attitude. If the bargaining is carried out in an atmosphere of mutual cooperation by labor and management, the environment created is ideal for exploring and rooting out sources of worker frustration. This area is critical, because even high wages and standards of living cannot overcome deep-seated employee frustration, and productivity will suffer accordingly.

Job frustration has several characteristics.

- The quality of work becomes inferior.
- The quantity of work does not meet standards.
- The rates of tardiness, absenteeism, and accidents are higher than normal.
- Wage demands are excessive—especially during inflationary periods.
- Moonlighting is commonplace.
- Grievances, work stoppages, and strikes occur frequently.
- Opposition is expressed to existing work schedules.

To alleviate the frustrations of low- and middle-income workers, new policy decisions must be initiated by management. When such policies are formulated, they can be an integral part of bargaining, or they can be offered independently of the contract as reinforcement for the overall spirit and terms of the final agreement. The following four areas offer good opportunities for relieving worker frustration.

*Upgrading.* Nearly all workers desire an opportunity to expand as individuals. Wherever possible, upgrading to more responsible positions should be included in the productivity bargain. In addition to stimulating greater employee effort through more job responsibility, upgrading provides a buyout for surplus low-skill jobs. Additionally, a comprehensive upgrading program often reduces redundancy fears, making the new program easier to implement. When upgrading is impractical, job rotation programs can help stem worker frustrations by increasing job interest and reducing boredom and monotony.

*Work Organization.* Over a period of time, work patterns and rules in any company become static—accepted through tradition. Jobs become specialized. Such rigidity provides little individual challenge and often prevents achievement of company goals.

To overcome this stagnation, all phases of work should be examined in an attempt to reinvigorate the organization. Traditional methods should be questioned, customs probed, and patterns broken. Toward this end, job enrichment, job redesign, and participative management may be used to advantage. Coupling upgrading with reorganization can sometimes help achieve both labor and management goals in productivity agreements.

*Incentives.* Knowledge that they will share in the profits derived from productivity increases can have a marked effect on worker efficiency and the elimination of frustrations. Well-formulated incentive programs such as profit-sharing plans or the Scanlon plan should be tied formally or informally to productivity bargaining agreements (also see *Productivity Incentives,* p. 287).

*Health and Safety.* Increased production efforts, including the use of new work methods, raise worker concern with health and safety standards. Management must realize that these cares are valid and must initiate reforms to ensure maintenance of high standards of worker health and safety.

### CASE HISTORIES

In recent years productivity bargaining has made impressive headway in the United States. Inflation, foreign competition, and slumping domestic productivity have all been instrumental in prompting management and labor to look more closely at productivity problems. This trend will doubtless continue.

There have been some notable success stories as a result of these agreements. The following examples[5] illustrate the wide variety of forms that productivity bargaining can take.

• Management and labor of the Rushton Mining Company introduced an autonomous work concept that lets teams of nine men take responsibility for production in their mine section. Each team member learns all jobs used in the section, permitting job rotation. Additionally, each team member receives training in state and federal safety regulations.

[5] Adapted by permission from NATION'S BUSINESS, July, 1975 ("Productivity: How to Beat Inflation and Boost Earnings," pp. 21–25). Copyright 1975 by NATION'S BUSINESS, Chamber of Commerce of the United States.

The results are higher productivity, increased worker satisfaction, lower absenteeism, reduced accident rates, and higher profitability for the company.

• In 1972 the business climate of the city of Jamestown, New York, was in critical condition. With a reputation as a bad labor town, the city had not attracted a major new business for 50 years. Unemployment stood at 10 percent, the number of industrial jobs had been declining for 20 years, needed skills were decreasing, and young workers and factories were moving to greener pastures.

Faced with impending disaster, the mayor initiated a Labor-Management Committee consisting of 15 executives from local manufacturing companies and 15 labor leaders. The committee drew up a list of four goals: improvement of labor relations, manpower development, assistance to industrial development programs, and productivity gains in existing industries. To carry out these goals, in-plant committees were set up to bring management and workers together.

The results in improved plant performance, labor relations, and productivity have been dramatic. Productivity has increased in virtually every industry that has adopted the new program. Unemployment has dropped to 4.2 percent. New industry is being attracted. Only five minor strikes have occurred in 3 years, with a total loss of 41 days; in the previous 3 years, 302 days had been lost. The skill upgrading program has produced 162 graduates from 15 companies.

Overall, the program has been so successful that it has been able to attract federal financial assistance to further its goals.

• Scanlon plans have been installed in seven of the Dana Corporation's 70 plants, with goals of improving efficiency and employee morale.

In one example (the firm's Spicer Axle Division), time cards have been eliminated and 57 percent of employees have invested in company stock through a stock purchase program.

When the plan is in operation a base labor cost is expressed as a percentage of sales. All savings achieved above the base are distributed as a bonus, 75 percent to workers and 25 percent to the company. Workers participate by making money-saving suggestions to plant committees consisting of management and employee representatives.

The Scanlon plan was introduced at Spicer in March 1973. Bonuses for the first 6 months averaged 7.8 percent; for the next 12 months, 13.2 percent; and for the next 9 months, 22.8 percent. From management's point of view the improved bonuses have been more than offset by improved efficiency. Absenteeism has dropped to 2.5 percent and turnover is less than 1 percent. At the end of the trial period, employees voted overwhelmingly to continue the plan.

- R. G. Barry Corporation, a footware manufacturer, organized its workforce into teams into 1969. Each team was given a great deal of responsibility in organizing its work and making decisions that affected its area of activity.

Between 1969 and 1974 the new team approach cut employee absenteeism and turnover in half. During the same period, total production kept pace with wages—both increased 35 percent—and the number of product rejects was cut by two-thirds. Downtime diminished significantly, and training costs were reduced by 50 percent. According to Barry's president, the team concept has created "conditions under which most of the people, most of the time, care enough to do what has to be done for the enterprise to succeed."

- Productivity per employee has more than doubled through the use of participative management in recent years at Donnelly Mirrors, Inc., a manufacturer of automotive mirrors.

Production line employees participate in a wide variety of management decisions. When a new piece of equipment is being considered, for example, a machine operator is called in to help an engineer and a purchasing agent evaluate it.

Employees also have a voice in setting salary levels, but if they recommend pay rises, they must also initiate ideas to increase productivity or cut costs to offset the pay increases. Almost half the cost savings go into a bonus pool. Time clocks have been eliminated at Donnelly, and absenteeism has dipped significantly.

## MANAGEMENT RESPONSIBILITY

As indicated earlier, there is a variance of opinion regarding the causes of falloff in the nation's productivity. As many industry spokesmen have pointed out, however, the responsibility rests with individual managements to isolate and tackle the problem within their own spheres of operation.

Management consultant John Patton, who has been studying the problems of productivity for 30 years, sums up the current situation as follows:[6]

Declining productivity is not entirely the fault of organized labor, even though the average stockholder does not realize that unions have more to say about day-to-day operations than management does in many companies.

It is not entirely the fault of our patronizing, interfering government, which con-

---

[6] Reprinted by permission from NATION'S BUSINESS, July, 1975 ("Productivity: How to Beat Inflation and Boost Earnings, p. 25). Copyright 1975 by NATION'S BUSINESS, Chamber of Commerce of the United States.

tinually keeps extending its tentacles of red tape to enmesh and throttle our free enterprise system.

It is not entirely the fault of the shifting attitudes of our younger generation, many of whom have rejected the materialism, work ethic, and institutional loyalties of their forebears.

The real fault lies squarely at the feet of management, for not seizing the initiative to take remedial action.

## SUGGESTED FURTHER READING

"Disaster in Productivity," *Fortune,* December 1974, p. 24.

Giges, N., "Retailers Share Profits in New Incentive Plan," *Advertising Age,* October 7, 1974, p. 75.

Hill, R., "Working on the Scanlon Plan," *International Management,* October 1974, pp. 39–41.

"Labor, Management Get Together, Swap Productivity Success Stories," *Commerce Today,* July 21, 1975, pp. 5–7.

"Productivity: How to Beat Inflation and Boost Earnings," *Nation's Business,* July 1975, pp. 21–25.

Rosow, Jerome M., "Now Is the Time for Productivity Bargaining," *Harvard Business Review,* January/February, 1972, pp. 78–89.

# 68

## PRODUCTIVITY INCENTIVES

*Discusses the use of monetary incentive plans as a means of combating inflation through increased productivity.*

One of the best ways to overcome the effects of inflation on business operations is to increase productivity. Thus all avenues should be explored that hold promise of increasing the output per employee per hour. If the same number of employees using the same equipment can increase their production rate significantly, the beneficial effect on profits can be quite dramatic, since overheads remain relatively constant.

There has been a recent trend away from the use of monetary incentive programs because of union pressures or because of automated manufacturing processes that make it impossible for the individual worker to increase production. Recent studies have shown, however, that paying monetary incentives for increased output is still one of the most effective ways to encourage productivity. Some very dramatic results have been achieved when such programs have been installed.

### A CASE HISTORY

As long ago as 1911 scientific management pioneer H. I. Gantt observed[1]

While men prefer as a rule to sell their time, and themselves determine the amount of work they will do in that time, a very large number of them are willing to do any reasonable amount of work the employer may specify in that time, provided only they are shown how it can be done, and paid substantial additional amounts of money for doing it.

Based on this premise, monetary incentive programs have found acceptance with managements in America since the early decades of this century. Moreover, "the fact that incentive pay is still used extensively seems to

[1] H. I. Gantt, "Work, Wages, and Profits," *The Engineering Magazine,* New York, 1911, p. 39.

argue that this means of motivating workers is still quite effective in spite of past abuses and increasing line- and machine-paced types of production."[2]

To be effective, the gains achieved by a monetary incentive program must, of course, outweigh the costs. Incentive payments are designed to induce workers to increase their output during a specified period of time. This results in the lowering of direct per-unit labor costs. Additionally, since higher production is achieved in the same factory and with the same equipment, the overhead cost per unit is reduced as well as the direct labor cost.

In a rigidly controlled study, business professors Donald L. McManis and William G. Dick set out to record precisely the effects installation of a monetary incentive program had on a typical business concern—the Hoerner Waldorf Corporation, a manufacturer of corrugated shipping containers. The study compared productivity before and after introduction of incentive pay.

Production standards in the corrugated shipping container industry have been developed by the Technological Association of Pulp and Paper Industries (TAPPI). The standards allow each company to compare its performance with that of others in the same business. The standards also provided a good basis for comparing productivity before and after monetary incentives were introduced.

At Hoerner Waldorf, 18 different manufacturing operations were studied. It was found that in 10 of the 18, the *lowest* monthly output after incentive payment installation was equal to or greater than the *highest* monthly output prior to the program. In total, 16 of the 18 operations "displayed statistically significant increases in productivity after monetary incentives were installed" and "the total evidence overall for these individual operations clearly and overwhelmingly supports the theory that monetary incentives used to increase productivity can be effective."[3]

Table 51 breaks down each of the 18 operations studied, showing the percentage change in productivity after the incentive program was installed. Increases ranged from 18 to 597 percent, with only one operation showing a decrease, tentatively attributed by the authors to frequent change of personnel and/or product mix variations.

---

[2] Donald L. McManis and William G. Dick, "Monetary Incentives in Today's Industrial Setting," *Personnel Journal,* May 1973, p. 388. Reprinted with permission, PERSONNEL JOURNAL, Copyright May 1973.

[3] McManis and Dick, "Monetary Incentives in Today's Industrial Setting," *Personnel Journal,* May 1973, p. 389. Reprinted with permission, PERSONNEL JOURNAL, Copyright May 1973.

Table 51   Percentage Change in Productivity After Incentive Program Installation[a]

| Operation | Mean before incentives (% of TAPPI standards) | Mean after incentives (% of TAPPI standards) | Change (%) | Direction of change in output |
|---|---|---|---|---|
| Corrugator | 60.7 | 90.6 | 50 | Increased |
| Press, 70-inch | 49.4 | 74.3 | 50 | Increased |
| Press, 120-inch | 49.9 | 73.2 | 47 | Increased |
| Rotary slotter | 77.5 | 113.2 | 46 | Increased |
| Die mounting | 83.9 | 141.3 | 68 | Increased |
| Slit and score | 22.3 | 90.9 | 307 | Increased |
| Up-and-down slotter | 69.3 | 43.5 | 37 | Decreased |
| Die cut, semiautomatic | 50.6 | 62.4 | 23 | Increased |
| Band saw | 32.4 | 47.2 | 46 | Increased |
| Folder-taper | 46.4 | 54.3 | 18 | Increased |
| Taper, semiautomatic | 44.9 | 78.6 | 103 | Increased |
| Stitcher, semiautomatic | 43.3 | 70.8 | 63 | Increased |
| Waxing | 86.6 | 135.7 | 57 | Increased |
| Floor bundling | 9.1 | 54.3 | 597 | Increased |
| Strapping, automatic | 43.0 | 67.1 | 56 | Increased |
| Shipping | 64.7 | 94.3 | 46 | Increased |
| Materials handling | 38.3 | 80.5 | 110 | Increased |
| Repair and maintenance | 83.3 | 108.4 | 30 | Increased |
| Overall plant | 53.3 | 84.4 | 58 | Increased |
| Output in MSF[b] per employee | 251 | 440 | 75 | Increased |

[a] Source: McManis and Dick, "Monetary Incentives in Today's Industrial Setting," Personnel Journal, May 1973, p. 390. Reprinted with permission, PERSONNEL JOURNAL, Copyright May 1973.
[b] MSF = Mean Square Feet.

### Average Plant Efficiency

A test was also devised to measure average overall plant efficiency at Hoerner Waldorf, before and after introduction of the incentive system. To do this, efficiency figures for the 10-month period preceding program installation were compared with plant figures for the 10 months following program introduction. "The postincentive period averaged 58 percent greater efficiency, as measured against TAPPI standards, than the preincentive period."[4] Equally significant, labor costs were reduced by 21

[4] McManis and Dick, "Monetary Incentives in Today's Industrial Setting," Personnel Journal, May 1973, p. 390. Reprinted with permission, PERSONNEL JOURNAL, Copyright May 1973.

percent *even after an estimated bonus of 25 percent was paid for increased productivity.* At the same time, the fixed or overhead cost per unit dropped by 37 percent.

Prior to the introduction of monetary incentives, the *highest* monthly average efficiency was 59 percent of the TAPPI standard. After installation, the *lowest* monthly average was 71 percent.

### Productivity per Production Employee

Perhaps the most meaningful test carried out by the study's authors was one designed to determine whether output per production employee per unit of time increased after monetary incentives were installed. The investigators compared output in terms of thousands of square feet of corrugated board per production employee per month before and after introduction of incentive pay. Output increased 61 percent, using the same production facilities, while fixed costs were lowered by 38 percent.

Prior to initiating the incentive pay system, the average number of production workers employed was 80.5. After the system was installed, the average was 72. When this decrease in the number of workers was combined with the increase in output, the result was an increase in average output per month per employee of 75 percent—from 252 to 440 MSF. This reduced direct labor time per unit by about 43 percent. At the same time, the average bonus for production workers was 25 to 30 percent. The net direct labor savings ranged from 26 to 29 percent. Thus as the study's authors point out, "When the direct labor savings is combined with the 38 percent reduction per unit in overhead costs, there can be very little doubt that the savings far exceeded the cost of the plan."[5]

The study also showed that the highest average monthly output per employee prior to the incentive program (314 MSF) was lower than the lowest monthly average per employee once the program was installed (332 MSF). Significantly, output exceeded 300 MSF in only one month during the first period and fell below 400 MSF in only one month after the program was installed.

### Study Conclusions

The strong statistical evidence gather at Hoerner Waldorf seems to offer convincing proof that properly conceived incentive systems can be highly

[5] McManis and Dick, "Monetary Incentives in Today's Industrial Setting," *Personnel Journal,* May 1973, p. 391. Reprinted with permission, PERSONNEL JOURNAL, Copyright May 1973.

instrumental in raising productivity and lowering costs. As the study's authors themselves conclude,

Each of the three tests clearly supports the theory that monetary incentives can be effective in increasing productivity in many firms today. With the increasing investment per worker and the consequent rise in overhead costs, the value of effective monetary incentives is ever more important, since a greater part of the savings remain with the employer, while the risk of loss from loose standards is reduced.

There has been no intention [in the study] to state or imply that monetary incentives will always increase productivity. Some types of work or work situations are not suited to the application of monetary incentives. An inappropriate plan or one that is improperly introduced or administered is doomed to failure. If the workers have been well motivated by nonmonetary incentives, the possible gains may be somewhat less. A monetary incentive plan should not be expected to compensate for poor management practices or an inadequate pay scale. But monetary incentives *do* remain a very powerful management tool—one that should not be overlooked by modern management." [6]

## TYPES OF MONETARY INCENTIVE PLANS [7]

A company wishing to investigate various options in monetary incentive plans has a broad range from which to choose. Many plans devised during the last century are still in use, with slight modifications. Additionally, modern incentive plans have been introduced to meet today's manufacturing requirements.

Generally, monetary incentive plans are those in which the worker's remuneration is directly related to the amount of his output. These plans fall into two primary categories: individual incentive plans and group incentive plans. In the individual plans the worker's remuneration is based solely on his individual productivity. In group plans the amount of incentive pay is dependent on total output of two or more workers. Individual plans have been favored by industry in recent years because group effort is difficult to increase and/or prolong. Most experts say that greater productivity and more significant cost savings stem from individual plans, and they suggest that group programs should be installed only in work situations that prohibit measurement of individual effort.

Most popular individual plans can be grouped under two general head-

[6] McManis and Dick, "Monetary Incentives in Today's Industrial Setting," *Personnel Journal,* May 1973, p. 392. Reprinted with permission, PERSONNEL JOURNAL, Copyright May 1973.
[7] Adapted from Niebel, *Motion and Time Study.* Copyright 1972 by Richard D. Irwin, Inc., Homewood, Ill.

ings: (1) plans in which the employee participates in all gains due to productivity increases and (2) plans in which the employee shares productivity gains with his employer.

### Employee Participates in All Gains

*Piecework.*   In traditional piecework plans the worker was paid in direct proportion to his productivity—so much per item produced. No minimum was guaranteed. When legislation required guaranteed minimum hourly wages, piecework, as originally conceived, was not practicable. Even updated piecework plans that include hourly base rates have declined in popularity since World War II. Primarily this is because all standards are expressed in terms of money. Since postwar base hourly rates have often changed, the amounts of paperwork required to revise standards to reflect rising base rates makes the system unwieldy.

*Standard Hour Plan.*   Standard hour plans are similar in concept to piecework plans, but *time* is used as a standard rather than *money*. Thus there is no need to change standards when base rates are changed. As in traditional piecework plans, workers are paid in direct proportion to their productivity. Largely because of the inherent clerical advantages, use of standard hour programs has increased significantly in recent years and they are the most popular incentive plans today.

*Taylor Differential Piece Rate.*   The Taylor plan establishes two piece rates in terms of money: a lower rate that is paid in proportion to a worker's output up to a set standard of production, and a higher rate paid on output above this standard. The plan is designed to encourage productivity by generously rewarding operators who exceed standards.

*Merrick Multiple Piece Rate.*   Similar in concept to the Taylor plan, the Merrick plan establishes three piece rates rather than two: one for new employees, one for average workers, and one for experienced operators. The plan was devised to help offset disproportionately low rates paid under the Taylor plan to workers who did not achieve the standard.

*Measured Daywork.*   Using measured daywork plans, base rates are established; standards are then set for a particular job using work measurement studies. A record is kept of each operator's job efficiency for a period of time, usually 1 to 3 months. At the end of this period the worker's efficiency (percentage above standard) is multiplied by the base rate to form his guaranteed base rate for the next time period. Many modifications of measured daywork plans are in use. Because they take daily pressure off the worker, who knows his base rate will be paid even if he falls below standard for short periods of time, the plans have become quite popular.

### Employee Shares Gains with Employer

The following are examples of incentive plans in which employees share productivity gains with their employers.

*Halsey Plan.* The Halsey plan was developed as an alternative to piece-work. Unlike piecework programs, the Halsey plan guarantees a base rate. Additionally, a worker who performs above the set standard receives 30 to 50 percent of the value of time saved. Because these programs do not reward the worker in direct proportion to increased output, labor is not generally receptive to them.

*Bedaux Point System.* Similar to the Halsey plan, the Bedaux point system guarantees an hourly rate up to standard performance, then rewards output beyond this point by sharing the value of any time saved. Workers are expected to earn a certain number of "points" each hour, expressed in "B's." Points earned above standard are shared between worker and em-ployer, the worker receiving 75 percent of the extra points earned.

*Emerson Plan.* Like the systems already covered, the Emerson plan guarantees workers a base rate and sets standards using work study methods. However at $66\frac{2}{3}$ percent of standard, an incentive is introduced that increases in size as the standard is approached. Beyond the standard, the operator is paid in direct proportion to his output plus 20 percent.

*Profit Sharing.* Profit sharing has been described as "any procedure under which an employer pays to all employees, in addition to good rates of regular pay, special current or deferred sums based not only upon individual or group performance, but on the prosperity of the business as a whole."[8]

Profit sharing plans take a broad range of forms, but most fall into one of three headings: cash plans, deferred plans, or combined plans. As the names imply, cash plans distribute money from company profits directly to em-ployees, deferred plans invest the money for distribution to employees at a later date, and combined plans divide shared profits between the two dis-tribution methods.

Labor officials tend not to favor profit sharing plans as a monetary incen-

---

[8] Council of Profit Sharing Industries, *Profit Sharing Manual,* Akron, Ohio, p. 3.

tive because the role of unions is negated when such plans are operated fairly. During periods when profits are low, moreover, such programs may have a demoralizing effect on employees because they are receiving no monetary incentives.

Profit sharing is successful, however, in many cases. Increased productivity, reduced costs, less waste, and marked improvement in employee attitudes and efficiency have been the results of profit sharing plans in many firms. Properly conceived, there is good evidence that plans designed for labor-management harmony can be highly beneficial to company productivity.

## INSTALLING AN INCENTIVE PLAN

Monetary incentive programs have been introduced in nearly every type of business. Incentive principles can be applied in small-, medium-, or large-sized businesses in the manufacture of nearly any product, whether production work is direct or indirect. Service industry incentive plans have also been used widely.

The advantages to both labor and management are self-evident. Workers can immediately increase their pay in proportion to their output, resulting in higher morale, less turnover, and decreased absenteeism/tardiness. In turn, management receives higher productivity, lower costs, and increased profits.

In general, industries that have historically paid good wages should have no trouble in introducing equitable, easily measurable monetary incentive plans to increase worker productivity. However experience has revealed that in companies where employees are forced to work at an incentive pace simply to earn a living wage, there is little enthusiasm for incentive systems.

To begin incentive plan installation, management should be sure that production facilities are adequate for a wage incentive program. Standardization of work methods must be used in production to ensure that work measurement studies will be accurate. Work scheduling must provide operators with a constant backlog to prevent their running out of work. Adequate inventories must be maintained for the same reason. Machines must receive proper maintenance to prevent breakdowns. Base rates should be fair, preferably established over a period of time using job evaluation techniques.

Perhaps most important, fair standards of production performance must be determined. It is critical that standards be based on time studies or work sampling procedures, rather than merely relying on past experience or supervisory judgments. Work measurement specialists should be consulted to establish valid standards. As a rule of thumb, the operator should be able to earn about 25 percent over his base rate if he is conscientious in his work.

Since all parties involved—workers, unions, and management—must fully understand the implications of the wage incentive plan if it is to be successful, the plan should be simple.

A fair hourly base rate for each operation should be determined by job evaluation. The worker should be rewarded with an incentive payment in direct proportion to his output beyond standard production. To make sure that the employee is aware of the monetary benefits of his high productivity, his incentive earnings should always be separated from regular wages on his paycheck stub.

Grievances can be alleviated by providing efficient systems for accurate piece counts and for taking into account unavoidable loss of time. When grievances do occur, careful problem analysis should be made and prompt steps should be taken to remove problems. This does not mean, however, that program changes should be made without valid proof that aspects of the plan need to be changed. It is especially important not to compromise on standards. Once established on a fair, scientific basis, work standards should remain rigid. Unless methods and equipment have been changed, liberalizing standards will erode the entire incentive program.

No incentive program can successfully operate without an involved management team. Management must accept the responsibility of constantly evaluating and maintaining the plan once it is introduced.

## REASONS FOR FAILURE

A monetary incentive plan has failed when it costs more to operate than it saves—that is, when the cost of maintenance exceeds its benefits.

In nearly all cases the cause of incentive program failure is poor management. The usual reasons given for failure (bad employee attitude, high costs, liberal standards, poor scheduling, etc.) all reflect management's operation of the plan without proper planning and controls.

Failure of a well-planned program is sometimes caused by a breakdown in industrial relations.

In a study made of 246 monetary incentive program failures, Bruce Payne, president of Bruce Payne & Associates, Inc., discovered three key contributing factors: fundamental deficiencies in the plan, 41.5 percent; inept human relations, 32.5 percent; and poor technical administration 26.0 percent.

The following elements contributed to failure in each of these three categories.

*Fundamental deficiencies*
| | |
|---|---|
| Poor standards | 11.0% |
| Low incentive coverage of direct productive work | 8.6% |
| Ceiling on earnings | 7.0% |
| No indirect incentives | 6.8% |
| No supervisory incentives | 6.1% |
| Complicated pay formula | 2.0% |

*Inept human relations*
| | |
|---|---|
| Insufficient supervisory training | 6.9% |
| No guarantee of standards | 5.7% |
| A fair day's work not required | 5.0% |
| Standards negotiated with the union | 4.8% |
| Plan not understood | 4.1% |
| Lack of top management support | 3.6% |
| Poorly trained operators | 2.4% |

*Poor technical administration*
| | |
|---|---|
| Method changes not coordinated with standards | 7.8% |
| Faulty base rates | 5.1% |
| Poor administration (i.e., poor grievance procedure) | 4.9% |
| Poor production planning | 3.2% |
| Large group on incentive | 2.8% |
| Poor quality control | 2.2% |

### FIFTEEN FUNDAMENTAL PRINCIPLES

At the second annual Time Study and Methods Conference in New York, John W. Nickerson, speaking on "The Importance of Incentives" set out the following 15 fundamental principles to aid in installing and managing an effective monetary incentive program.[9]

*Agreement of General Principles.* Management and labor should be in real agreement on the general principles involved in the relationship between work and wages.

*A Foundation of Job Evaluation.* There should be a sound wage rate structure, based on an evaluation of the skill, responsibility, and working conditions inherent in the various jobs.

*Individual, Group, or Plant-Wide Incentives.* It is generally conceded that standards applied to individuals or to small integrated groups are most effective. Such standards need to be set with the utmost care and undoubtedly tend toward the lowest unit cost. At times difficulties in record-

[9] From Benjamin W. Niebel, *Motion and Time Study,* Irwin, Homewood, Ill., 1972, pp. 629–632, with the permission of the publisher.

ing individual production or the existence of possibilities of teamwork make group standards advisable. The larger the group, the less the individual response. With plant-wide incentives, some of the jealousies and transfer difficulties often inherent in group plans are eliminated, but without an unusual degree of leadership and cooperation, the incentive effect is greatly diluted.

*The Production-Incentive Relationship.* When production standards are properly set and based on well-engineered conditions, good practice has demonstrated the desirability of adopting an incentive payment in which earnings above the established standard are in direct proportion to the increased production.

*Simplicity.* The plan should be as simple as possible, without causing inequities. Workers should be able to understand the effect of their own efforts on their earnings.

*Quality Control and Improvement.* The desirable and economical degree of quality should be determined and maintained, tied in with bonus payment where advisable.

*Improved Methods and Procedures.* To secure the lowest costs and to prevent uneven standards and inequitable earnings, which lead to poor labor relations, the establishment of production standards should be preceded by basic engineering improvements in design equipment, methods, scheduling, and material handling.

*Based on Detailed Time Studies.* Standards should be developed from detailed time studies. A permanent record of standard elemental times for each unit of an operation eliminates the occasion for many arguments. A table of basic standard times prepares the way for proper introduction of technological improvements.

*Based on Normal Operation Under Normal Conditions.* In general, the production standard should be established by management setting up the amount of work performed per unit of time by a normal qualified operator under normal conditions.

*Changes in Standards.* The plan should provide for the changing of production standards whenever changes in methods, materials, equipment, or other controlling conditions are made in the operations represented by the standards. To avoid misunderstandings, the nature of such changes and the logic of making them should be made clear to labor or its representatives, who should have the opportunity to appeal through the grievance machinery.

*Considerations in Changing Standards.* Except to correspond properly with changed conditions, production standards once established should not be altered unless by mutual agreement between management and labor representatives.

*Keep Temporary Standards at Minimum.* The practice of establishing temporary standards on new operations should be kept at a minimum. In any event it should be made clear to all that the standards are for a reasonably short period only.

*Guarantee of Hourly Rates.* Under ordinary circumstances the employees' basic hourly rates should become guaranteed rates.

*Incentives for Indirect Workers.* Effective standards may be established for most indirect jobs in the same manner as for direct jobs. If the exigencies of a situation demand that some form of incentive payment be applied to indirect workers as a whole or in groups, the indirect man-hours should be correlated to some measurable unit, such as production or direct employee hours, permitting indirect labor cost to be kept under control.

*Thorough Understanding of Human Relations Involved.* Finally, it should be emphasized that unless management is prepared to work on the problem with a thorough understanding of the human relations involved, it had better have no incentive plan. Whereas such a plan may be a progressively constructive force for increased production, it may also be a means of disrupting labor relations and of actually lowering production. While necessarily retaining its functions, management should take into account labor's point of view. It should impart to labor a complete understanding of the plan and should patiently consider grievances, in whatever manner may be agreed upon.

## SUGGESTED FURTHER READINGS

Fan, L. S., "On the Reward System," *American Economic Review,* March 1975, pp. 226–229.

McManis, Donald L. and William G. Dick, "Monetary Incentives in Today's Industrial Setting," *Personnel Journal,* May 1973, p. 388.

Niebel, Benjamin W., *Motion and Time Study,* Irwin, Homewood, Ill., 1972, pp. 623–632.

# SECTION 69

## PRODUCTIVITY LINKING

*Discusses a wage practice that ties pay increases to increases in productivity.*

Productivity linking is a pay practice that links all wage increases to productivity increases, although a minimum standard rate is usually established to protect workers during a recession or from shortages of raw materials or energy. If management is successful in negotiating productivity linking pay agreements, the technique can offset significantly the effects of inflation, since wage increases are limited to output increases. Use of the technique was increased significantly in small industry applications throughout Europe in recent years. Application in larger firms has been less widespread because unions are generally opposed to the method.

On a larger scale, some American economists have recommended the use of productivity linking to overcome the effects of inflation on our economy. Pointing to recent drops in the nation's productivity, they argue that if wage rates rise 15 percent and productivity increases only 5 percent, a 10 percent inflationary rate is inevitable. Government-enforced productivity linking would tie wage increases to productivity increases (in this instance, 5 percent), and the inflationary rate should theoretically drop to zero, provided government spending does not exceed income.

### SUGGESTED FURTHER READING

Secretan, L., "More Pay for More Production," *Financial Times,* London, August 20, 1974.

# SECTION 70

## PROFIT CONTRIBUTION REPORTS

*Outlines a method of creating profit awareness among sales managers.*

Since profit improvement takes on greater than usual significance during inflationary periods, some managements believe that it is highly important to create profit awareness at various corporate levels. On the sales level, sales departments and branches that formerly thought only in terms of volume are being taught to think in terms of profitability of sales.

Toward this end, one large international business equipment firm has initiated a profit contribution reporting system that extends to the level of branch manager. The system features a monthly computer-generated Financial Contribution Report (Figure 8), which plays the dual role of pinpointing the profit margin the manager achieves on his business and changing the manager's perspective from volume to profits. According to company management, use of the report was the key factor in raising pretax profit margins from 7.3 percent in 1972 to 11 percent in 1974. At the same time, the report was instrumental in lowering the ratio of selling and general administrative expenses to sales volume from 54.8 to 52.6 percent.

The Financial Contribution Report in Figure 8 shows sales income for products and services and segregates costs into two areas—variable (over which the branch manager has limited control) and manageable (those he can control).

Three financial contributions can be derived from the report, as follows:

- *Marginal contribution,* reflecting sales income less variable costs.
- *Gross contribution,* derived by subtracting manageable costs from marginal contribution.
- *Net contribution,* obtained by deducting certain corporate overheads allocated to the branches (taxes, insurance, and depreciation) from gross contribution.

In addition to being an effective means of creating branch profit contribution awareness, the report provides insights into relative branch performance and quickly identifies cost factor trouble spots.

| Dollars this month | | | Description | Dollars year to date | | | Annual Budget |
|---|---|---|---|---|---|---|---|
| Actual | Budget | Variance | | Actual | Budget | Variance | |
| | | | Income<br>    Mailing equipment sales<br>    Copier equipment sales<br>    Copier supplies sales<br>    Rental income<br>    Service income<br>    Service parts and supplies sales<br>        Total income | | | | |
| | | | Variable costs<br>    Direct cost of equipment,<br>    rentals, parts, and supplies<br>    Salesmen's compensation<br>    Service travel<br>    Freight<br>        Total Variable Costs<br>        Marginal Contribution | | | | |
| | | | Manageable costs<br>    Other compensation<br>    Supplies, equipment under $100<br>    Utilities, rent, maintenance<br>    Travel, related<br>    Branch freight<br>    Recruiting, hiring<br>    Training<br>    Demonstration supplies<br>    Debit write-offs<br>    Inventory adjustments<br>        Total Manageable Costs<br>        Gross Contribution | | | | |
| | | | Allocated costs<br>    Taxes, insurance, depreciation<br>    Net contribution | | | | |

**Figure 8**   Branch Financial Contribution Report. (*Source: Sales Management,* May 19, 1975, courtesy Pitney Bowes.)

## SUGGESTED FURTHER READING

"Pitney Bowes Promotes Profit Awareness for Branch Managers," *Sales Management,* May 19, 1975, p. 43.

# SECTION 71

## PROFIT DOLLAR PER EMPLOYEE

*Outlines the use of PDPE to increase worker cost consciousness during inflation.*

The concept of profit dollar per employee (PDPE) can be especially useful during inflation in comparing a company's productive efficiency with that of competitors in the same industry. It can also create greater cost consciousness among workers.

Although PDPE varies among industries, within an industry it can be used as a figure of merit that employees can readily understand. In most companies the profit dollar per employee is a relatively small figure. Thus it is much easier for workers to assimilate than are overall company profit figures, which sometimes are expressed in millions of dollars. By showing a worker earning $12,000 to $15,000 a year that the profit dollars generated per employee only amount to a few hundred dollars—less than their salaries for a month—greater cost consciousness can be achieved. Workers are more easily convinced that their individual contributions can have an effect on company profitability.

One firm that has a worker-oriented PDPE program publishes profit dollar per employee figures quarterly, including the performance of its competition. Managers discuss with workers ways to improve the figures, and workers are encouraged to respond with suggestions. As a result, the company's management believes that employees now think they can double their PDPE; most believe they are capable of saving $400 or $500 more during the year, regardless of their position within the company.

### SUGGESTED FURTHER READING

"The Do-It-Yourselfers Tackle Inflation," *Industry Week,* June 24, 1974, p. 40.

# SECTION 72

## PROFIT–BASED SALES COMPENSATION

*Describes sales incentive programs based on profitability of sales.*

Inflationary periods usually cause problems with the pay structures most companies use to compensate salesmen. Primarily this is because the majority of salesmen are paid on a commission basis, and in an inflationary environment the upward trend of prices lets them earn higher commissions than were intended when the compensation programs were established.

Second, inflationary periods are usually accompanied by a shift in management thinking away from volume and growth and toward maximization of profitability. Since most sales incentive programs used during stable economic climates are based on volume, these have to be restructured during inflationary times to pay out for sales contributions to the bottom line.

The following[1] sets out guidelines for evaluating various types of sales compensation programs during inflationary economies and outlines methods for setting up profit-oriented compensation plans.

### GOALS

In setting up the most effective sales compensation plan during an inflationary period, the first step is to establish goals the plan should accomplish. If management emphasis is to stress profits over volume, a profit-rewarding program should be tailored. In certain situations, however, other goals may be even more important for particular companies. Such factors as improving cash flow, increasing market share, retaining established business, selling new accounts, reducing selling costs, increasing sales calls, and introducing new products, are key sales elements and can be used as bases for incentive programs. All these elements should be evaluated and the most important ones selected as goals. When goals have been established, incentive plans can be designed to accomplish objectives.

[1] From Don Korn, "Paying Off for Profits," *Sales Management,* May 19, 1975, pp. 5–8. Adapted with permission from *Sales Management, The Marketing Magazine.* Copyright 1975.

## THE BASIC PLAN

Once goals are established, the next step is to set up a basic compensation plan. Some firms pay salesmen straight salaries or straight commissions, but these are in the minority today. Commonly, total compensation consists of a basic salary plus some kind of incentive—a bonus, a commission, or income from prize points earned.

If an incentive system is to be used, how much of the salesman's total compensation should be earned through incentives? This amount varies widely from industry to industry, but as a general rule the amount should be large enough to give the plan teeth but not so large that it causes salesmen to neglect paper work, customer service, and other duties.

Sales management consultants Richard Smyth and Matthew Murphey recommend that to be most effective, sales incentive plans should offer salesmen at least 30 percent of their salary or 25 percent of their gross earnings. For example, a salesman earning a $24,000 salary should have at least $7200 (30 percent of his salary) in potential incentive payments to make the program worthwhile.

Most sales executives agree that best results are achieved when incentive commission schedules are progressing, with the rate increasing with volume. For example, a plan might pay 2 percent on the first $50,000 in sales, 3 percent on the next $50,000, and so on. Regressive programs (the rate goes down as volume goes up) are sometimes used by firms to keep salesmen's earnings from going too high.

Some companies place arbitrary limits on the total amount of compensation a salesman can earn. This practice is especially sensible during inflationary periods when earnings can soar out of proportion to the original plan. Such limits should be carefully drawn—high enough to be a worthwhile incentive, but low enough to provide a meaningful target.

Frequency of incentive earnings payment varies widely among companies, ranging from monthly to yearly. Psychologists have shown that the shorter the time between performance and reward, the greater the incentive. Thus there has been a tendency recently to pay at shorter intervals. Additionally, a salesman who misses his quota one month knows he has a new chance the following month; if he is well behind his quota after 8 months of a yearly program, he may give up during the last 4 months.

One disadvantage of short-interval incentive payments is the higher cost of administering the program. A line should be drawn to balance cost effectiveness with psychological motivation when deciding on frequency of payment.

## PROFIT INCENTIVES

If it has been decided that increased profitability is to be the primary goal of a company's sales incentive program, a number of factors should be considered.

*Is the incentive to be based on product profitability or account profitability?* One method frequently used is to determine a gross margin value for each product and pay the salesmen a commission based on the total gross margin (dollar sales minus cost of production) of all products sold. This encourages the sales of the most profitable product lines and provides an incentive for salesmen to seek new accounts to purchase these lines. The primary disadvantage of this type of program is the limited scope afforded many salesmen in switching accounts from one product to a more profitable one; often the first product is best for the buyer. In such cases the salesman's incentive may be based on how he improves the profitability of each of his accounts. For example, a gross margin figure for each customer can be determined (the company made 20% on sales to account X) and that figure can be multiplied by the volume for the account.

*Are cost allocations accurate?* To have a meaningful incentive program based on gross margin percentages, costing procedures must be reliable. These should be reviewed and pinpointed with as much accuracy as possible. Costs should be updated as raw materials and/or other prices change. Paying compensation based on a gross margin of 40 percent is expensive if unattributed factors or changing costs cut the gross margin to 30 percent.

*Two-pronged Programs.* When profit-based incentive programs are desirable but volume must also be emphasized (i.e., when high volume must be maintained to absorb overhead, when product lines show no significant differences in profit margins, etc.), salesmen and sales managers can be given complementary goals to help ensure high performance in both areas. If salesmen are being given commissions based on increased profitability, for example, their sales managers might be given incentive payments based on volume increases. Conversely, when salesmen are rewarded for increasing volume, sales managers can push them toward more profitable products and accounts.

*Secondary Objectives.* Often secondary program goals can be worked into the basic incentive plan. For example, if the primary goal is to increase profitability, the basic plan might pay a commission based on gross margin per product. If, at the same time, a secondary goal is to open new accounts, the commission might be doubled on any new business. Thus two objectives are achieved under the same basic compensation plan.

### SETTING UP A PROFIT-BASED PAY PLAN

The factors to be considered in custom-designing a profits-based incentive plan include the following.

#### Should the Plan be Based on Dollars, Points, or Factors?

As outlined previously, one of the simplest methods is to set up a straight commission program based on gross margin. For instance, if a salesman moves $500,000 worth of goods that cost $400,000 to produce, the gross margin would be $100,000. If his commission rate is 10 percent, he would earn $10,000 in incentive pay. However certain problems exist in this type of plan. It is sometimes difficult to establish an accurate gross margin figure for every product.

Second, many firms are not anxious to divulge gross margin figures to their salesmen, being fearful of the consequences if any of the salesmen should go to work for competitors. In these cases it is often advantageous to group products into categories according to their relative profitability. For example, products grouped in category A might be the most profitable, group B the next most profitable, and group C the least profitable. The commission rates on each group would vary, depending on profitability: 3 percent commission might be paid on group A products, 2 percent on group B, and 1 percent on group C. For instance, if a salesman's total sales of $500,000 break down as follows:

Group A products = $150,000
Group B products = $200,000
Group C products = $150,000

then his commission would be determined in this manner:

$150,000 × .03 =   $4500
$200,000 × .02 =    4000
$150,000 × .01 =    1500
                   $10,000

Another method that is sometimes used to keep margin figures confidential is the assigning of factors to each product in the line. A firm, for example, might assign a factor value to each of 15 products it manufactures. The salesman's incentive is based on that factor, times the number of units sold, which converts into points: if he sells 5000 units with a factor of 0.5, he is awarded 2500 points. Commission payments are then based on the number of points accumulated during the incentive period.

### Quotas

Surveys have shown that the majority of firms installing incentive programs establish quotas for salesmen and pay commissions only after quotas have been reached. In most programs commissions are paid only on sales above the quota, although in some instances once a salesman's quota is reached, he receives the commission on his total sales.

### Secondary Bonuses

Programs can be tailored to pay bonuses for accomplishing secondary company goals. In a drive conducted to establish new accounts, for example, normal commissions might be doubled to encourage salesmen to bring in new business. Thus if one-third of the salesman's total sales of group A products was in new business, his commission would be superimposed on the basic profit-based plan as follows:

$$
\begin{array}{lll}
\$\ 50,000 \times 0.06 & = \$ & 3000 \\
\$100,000 \times 0.03 & = & 3000 \\
\$200,000 \times 0.02 & = & 4000 \\
\$150,000 \times 0.01 & = & \underline{1500} \\
& & \$11,500
\end{array}
$$

Additionally, sales contests can be set up to pay extra bonuses for selling certain product lines during specific time periods. Care should be taken, however, to ensure that such contests do not create peak and valley situations that put a great strain on manufacturing and shipping during contest periods. Uneven ordering can cut sharply into the profits the program was designed to create.

### Other Factors

Salesmen can directly affect profitability by means other than pushing profitable lines and establishing new business. One big order is more profitable than three smaller ones because it involves fewer order processing steps, less order assembly time, and lower unit shipping costs. Salesmen should be aware of this and should educate customers who buy in small lots to purchase larger quantities. In the same way, orders for which there is plenty of lead time are more profitable because they can be taken into account when scheduling production, thus avoiding costly last-minute overtime production and premium shipping rates. Salesmen should advise customers to anticipate future needs and order well in advance. To encourage salesmen along these lines, some firms pay bonuses for achieving specific goals in these areas. Usually points are awarded and allowed to accumulate during each pay period. A typical program pays 1 percent of the salesman's base salary for each point earned, and a maximum number of points is set per pay period.

## PROBLEMS

Certain problems arise in trying to establish a profit-based commission plan. The most common ones can be dealt with as follows.

### Team Commissions

In many situations, especially in industrial selling, sales are made by a team rather than individual salesmen. This creates a problem in equitably dividing the commission on each sale. To overcome this, management can introduce group incentives, which are divided among various district or department representatives and are based on overall profitability for a certain time period.

### Price Discounts

Many firms give salesmen the authority to offer discounts from list prices when making sales. This, of course, has a marked effect on profitability. To avoid overcompensating for discounted sales, some firms adjust commissions by figuring the gross margin on the actual sale price rather than on the list price, paying the commission on the adjusted figure. Other companies simply reduce the commission scale according to the size of the discount: a 20 percent commission might be paid on a list price sale, but only 10 percent commission on a 10 percent discount, 5 percent on a 20 percent discount, and so on.

### Late Payments

The longer it takes a customer to pay for delivered goods, the less profitable the sale becomes. This is especially true during inflationary periods: with a 12 percent inflation rate, an unpaid invoice for $50,000 is worth just $49,500 in real money value terms a month after it is due, $49,000 the second month, and so on. To encourage salesmen to follow up with slow-paying customers, some firms credit the salesman with half his commission at the time of the sale, half when the bill is paid in full. This not only ensures his attention to credit problems but motivates him to devote his strongest efforts to selling prompt-paying accounts. Also, some companies deduct a percentage of a salesman's incentive if the sale requires costly warehousing for extended periods of time.

### Sales Managers

As outlined earlier, it is often advantageous to establish for sales managers an incentive plan that complements the program used for salesmen. For instance, if salesmen are rewarded for increasing profitability, the sales manager might receive commissions on increased volume. In this way attention is being paid to both key areas of the sales function. Another approach is to pay the sales manager a bonus based on the average commission earned by all the salesmen under his jurisdiction. Since his reward is based entirely on his salesmen's efforts to increase profitability, he has a real incentive to ensure that everyone under his control maximizes profits in every way possible.

## SUGGESTED FURTHER READING

Greer, W. R., Jr., "Sales Compensation: Conflict and Harmony," *Management Accounting,* March 1974, pp. 37–41.

Korn, Don, "Paying Off for Profits," *Sales Management,* May 19, 1975, pp. 5–8.

Winer, L., "Effect of Product Sales Quotas on Sales Force Productivity," *Journal of Marketing Research,* May 1973, pp. 180–183.

# SECTION 73

## PROFIT–IMPROVEMENT CHECKLIST

*Sets out a checklist of 80 techniques to help offset the erosionary effects of inflation on profitability.*

In an inflationary environment profits usually come under pressure because of increased labor and materials costs, slow-downs in sales, high interest rates, and at times government controls. Many sections in this volume deal at length with profit-enhancement methods for specific business areas during inflation.

The following checklist of 80 profit-improvement techniques, compiled by Lybrand, Ross Bros. & Montgomery, the international accounting firm, is based on many audit studies of corporate and operating controls. Each of the techniques listed has accomplished one or more of the objectives, but the chart should not be used indiscriminately because some techniques may be mutually offsetting. Rather, the list should serve as a starting point to stimulate profit-improvement thinking within a company or division. When an idea appears to hold potential for a company, it should be evaluated to determine how the new procedure can be most successfully implemented.

# Profit-Improvement Checklist

Objectives

| Techniques | Cut purchase costs | Cut freight costs | Maximize working capital | Cut scrap | Cut production interruptions | Cut labor costs | Improve equipment utilization | Cut administrative overhead | Increase revenues |
|---|---|---|---|---|---|---|---|---|---|
| 1. Determine optimum buying sizes for metals. | X | | | | | | | | |
| 2. Use rebuilding services for valves, instruments, and so on. | X | | | | | | | | |
| 3. Use nonoriginal equipment sources for spares. | X | | | | | | | | |
| 4. Circumscribe addition of new articles to stock. | X | | X | X | | | | | |
| 5. Correlate forecasting data for marketing and production. | X | | X | X | X | | X | | |
| 6. Control "off-sheet" discounts. | | | | | | | | | X |
| 7. Control application of freight terms to customers. | | | | | | | | | X |
| 8. Consider freight factor in setting selling prices. | | | | | | | | | X |
| 9. Develop standard routing guides for outgoing shipments. | | X | | | | | | | |
| 10. Signal "premium" freight for investigation. | | X | | | | | | | |
| 11. Establish timely control over freight claims. | | X | | | | | | | |
| 12. Negotiate favorable terms with freight audit agency. | | X | | | | | | | |
| 13. Highlight unprofitable territories, products, customers, warehouses. | | | | | | | | | |
| 14. Act as self-insurer on rental cars. | | | | | | | | | X |
| 15. Negotiate hotel rates on guaranteed basis. | | | | | | | | X | |
| 16. Use compacts rather than big cars. | | | | | | | | X | |
| 17. Use coach class on planes. | | | | | | | | X | |
| 18. Stratify salesmen's calls on basis of customer needs. | | | | | | | | X | |
| 19. Capture order information near source. | | | | | X | | | X | |
| 20. Use self-checking capabilities of computers. | | | | | | | | X | |
| 21. Check new-customer credit before shipment. | | | | | | | | X | |
| 22. Train order-input clerks to reduce need for editing. | | | | | | | | X | |
| 23. Signal costly "piecemeal" order releases by customers. | | | | | | | | | |
| 24. Invoice special warehousing or packaging services. | | | | | | | | | X |
| 25. Invoice cancelation charges, where practicable. | | | | | | | | | X |
| 26. Report physical percentage of contract completion vs. dollar percentage. | | | | | | | | | X |

## Profit-Improvement Checklist (*Continued*)

| Techniques | Cut purchase costs | Cut freight costs | Maximize working capital | Cut scrap | Cut production interruptions | Cut labor costs | Improve equipment utilization | Cut administrative overhead | Increase revenues |
|---|---|---|---|---|---|---|---|---|---|
| 27. Reduce delays before production order reaches "floor". | | | | | X | X | | | |
| 28. Avoid emergency inventory transfers from plant to plant. | | X | | | | | | | |
| 29. Eliminate duplications on operating and accounting records. | | | | | | | | X | |
| 30. Take inventory cycle counts at "low" of stocks. | | | | | | | | X | |
| 31. Consider adaptability of current stocks when planning engineering changes. | | | | X | | | | | |
| 32. Substitute second shift for overtime. | | | | | | X | | | |
| 33. Avoid "split" labor assignments of high-rate men to low-rate jobs. | | | | | | X | | | |
| 34. Monitor machine running speeds and breakdowns. | | | | | X | | X | | |
| 35. Stabilize labor force by "level loading." | | | | | | X | | | |
| 36. Plan maintenance jobs. | | | | | | X | | | |
| 37. Reduce fire insurance premiums by complying with inspection reports. | X | | | | | | | | |
| 38. Sell used EDP cards to scrap-paper dealers. | | | | | | | | | X |
| 39. Make secured short-term loans of excess cash. | | | X | | | | | | |
| 40. Monitor unemployment insurance claims if experience rating is factor. | | | | | | X | | | |
| 41. Negotiate interruptible rates with utilities where practicable. | X | | | | | | | | |
| 42. Reduce numbers of different types of articles in stock. | X | | X | | | | | X | |
| 43. Standardize "preferred" items. | X | | | | | | | X | |
| 44. Define roles of purchasing personnel at different levels. | X | | X | | X | | | X | |
| 45. Evaluate vendor quality, delivery, and cost performances. | X | | X | | X | | | | |
| 46. Provide enough time to "shop the market." | X | | | | | | | | |
| 47. Centralize negotiations for major items, including freight. | X | X | | | | | | | |
| 48. Use traveling requisitions. | | | | | | | | X | |
| 49. Give purchasing personnel a free hand in vendor selection, using "specs." | X | | | | X | | | | |

The following is a checklist of items (numbered 50–80). X marks appear in several unlabeled columns (the column headings appear on the facing page).

| No. | Item | | | | | |
|---|---|---|---|---|---|---|
| 50. | Issue complete purchase orders for significant transactions. | X | | | | |
| 51. | Reduce "rush" procurement. | X | X | | X | X |
| 52. | Prescribe preferred routing for incoming bulk items. | | X | | X | X |
| 53. | Seek competitive bids for significant transactions. | X | | | | |
| 54. | Establish floor below which bids will not be obtained. | X | | | | X |
| 55. | Subject all buying contracts to periodic review. | X | | | | |
| 56. | Develop approved vendor list for highly technical purchases. | X | | | X | X |
| 57. | Combine related items on purchase orders. | | | | | X |
| 58. | Conduct make-or-buy studies. | X | | | X | X |
| 59. | Use purchase order copy as receiving report. | | | | | X |
| 60. | Test weigh bulk commodities. | X | | | | X |
| 61. | Authorize telephone releases for minor items bought on contract. | | X | | X | X |
| 62. | Eliminate useless copies made by receiving clerks. | | | | X | X |
| 63. | Stage incoming loads to eliminate demurrage and shipping overtime. | X | X | X | | |
| 64. | Speed up invoice processing to avoid discount losses. | X | | X | | |
| 65. | Set up plant delivery system. | X | | | X | |
| 66. | Signal vendor overshipments to buyers for bargaining purposes. | X | | | | |
| 67. | Negotiate with suppliers terms affecting packaging, pallets, and so on. | X | | | | |
| 68. | Reduce distance between receiving and storage facilities. | | | X | | |
| 69. | Establish incoming inspection to minimize damage from defects. | X | X | X | X | |
| 70. | Set up billing to vendors of "rework." | X | X | | X | |
| 71. | Bill freight to vendors on rejected shipments. | | X | | | |
| 72. | "Pass" minor invoice discrepancies. | X | | | | |
| 73. | Control slow-moving inventories and initiate timely disposal actions. | X | X | | | X |
| 74. | Establish reorder points and economic ordering or production quantities. | X | X | | X | |
| 75. | Plan use of inventory space. | X | | X | X | X |
| 76. | Maintain current locator files in storerooms. | | | X | | |
| 77. | Establish technologically significant materials codes. | X | | X | X | |
| 78. | Shift burden of carrying inventory to suppliers. | X | X | | X | |
| 79. | Introduce "self-help" storeroom bins for inexpensive items. | X | | | X | X |
| 80. | Install storeroom facilities to cut metal on site. | X | | | | X |

*Source:* Lybrand, Ross Bros. & Montgomery, New York.

## 74

## PROFITABILITY

*Provides statistics showing the negative effects of inflation on
the profitability of business corporations in the United States
between 1965 and 1974.*[1]

Critics of big business sometimes assert that corporations actually benefit
from periods of inflation. This belief is held for three reasons:

• Inventories increase in value during inflationary periods, thus generating
additional income.
• Price increases outstrip wages increases; that is, businesses gain because
they raise prices before they raise wages.
• Businesses are net debtors, and debtors gain during inflationary periods
because they repay their obligations in "cheaper" dollars.

Any harassed controller who has struggled with the complications caused
by spiraling inflation can refute all three arguments. The increase in inventory values is largely illusory, consisting mainly of paper profits (see *LIFO*,
p. 205). The contention that wages lag behind price increases is extremely
difficult to test and has never been adequately proven.[2] The complex question of businesses benefiting by being net debtors is treated in *Inflation and
Debt* (p. 189.)

Periods of prolonged inflation place a severe strain on profits. Moreover,
there is strong evidence that American business does not yet know how to
shield itself against an inflationary environment. During recent inflationary
periods the majority of American companies were unable to maintain
normal margins even in the overstated profits of conventional accounting.
In terms of real profits in dollars of current purchasing power, company
performance was distressingly poor.

The following outlines the pitfalls of reporting profits based on traditional
accounting methods during inflationary periods, showing where and how

[1] Adapted from George Terborgh, "Inflation and Profits," *Financial Analysts Journal,* May/
June 1974, pp. 19–23.
[2] See Reuben A. Kessel and A. A. Alchian, "The Meaning and Validity of the Inflation-
Induced Lag of Wages Behind Prices," *American Economic Review,* March 1960, pp. 43–66.

businesses are misled into believing they are faring better than they really are.

## THE PROBLEM

Profits are generally overstated during inflationary periods because of the practice of charging only the historic cost of physical asset consumption (fixed assets and inventory). Given the constant erosion of the purchasing power of the dollar, historical costs are insufficient, reflecting as they do earlier (lower) price levels, not the costs required for restoration of real assets used in production. To be meaningful, previously incurred costs should be restated in the dollars of realization—revenue dollars against which they are charged. If costs and revenue are not measured in the same dollars, the difference between them (profit) cannot be accurately determined.

Indexes of the general purchasing power of the dollar are used to convert historic costs into current costs. These are Department of Commerce conversions by means of replacement cost indexes, which are applied to both fixed-asset consumption (depreciation adjustment) and inventory consumption (inventory valuation adjustment). The Commerce Department's conversions are used in the following examples, which compare current-cost with historical-cost depreciations and current-cost with historical-cost inventory consumption to show effects on profits.

### Fixed Assets

Each year the Department of Commerce computes current-cost depreciation on fixed assets of nonfinancial (business) corporations, using two writeoff methods—straightline and double-declining (DDB) balance—and a variety of service life assumptions. Table 52 compares the department's computation of current-cost, double-declining-balance depreciation with its estimate of the depreciation allowed for income tax purposes for the years 1965–1974. It is easy to see that the excess of current-cost DDB over tax depreciation grew from a negligible amount in 1965 to $13.3 billion in 1974.

### Inventory

The conversion of inventory consumption charges from historic-cost to current-cost equivalent is computed by the Department of Commerce as the Inventory Valuation Adjustment (IVA). This allows calculation by LIFO

**Table 52** **Comparison of the Current-Cost Double-Declining-Balance Depreciation of Nonfinancial Corporations with the Depreciation Allowed Them for Income Tax Purposes (billions of dollars)**

| Year | (1) Current cost DDB[a] | (2) Income tax depreciation | (3) Excess of 1 over 2[b] |
|---|---|---|---|
| 1965 | $35.8 | $35.4 | $ 0.4 |
| 1966 | 39.7 | 38.4 | 1.4 |
| 1967 | 44.4 | 41.7 | 2.7 |
| 1968 | 49.0 | 45.4 | 3.6 |
| 1969 | 54.7 | 50.1 | 4.6 |
| 1970 | 60.6 | 54.0 | 6.6 |
| 1971 | 65.7 | 58.2 | 7.5 |
| 1972 | 70.6 | 63.6 | 7.0 |
| 1973 | 77.4 | 68.1 | 9.3 |
| 1974 | 86.5 | 73.2 | 13.3 |

[a] The Commerce Department's "Current-Cost 2." This employs a more conservative index of construction costs than "Current-Cost 1."
[b] Differences may not check exactly because of rounding.

**Table 53** **Inventory Valuation Adjustment for Nonfinancial Corporations**

| Year | IVA (billions of dollars) |
|---|---|
| 1965 | $ 1.7 |
| 1966 | 1.8 |
| 1967 | 1.1 |
| 1968 | 3.3 |
| 1969 | 5.1 |
| 1970 | 4.8 |
| 1971 | 4.9 |
| 1972 | 7.0 |
| 1973 | 17.6 |
| 1974 | 35.1 |

for inventory currently charged for income tax purposes and converts only the balance using historical costing systems. This adjustment covers only costs charged to "cost of sales." For all nonfinancial corporations, these amount to only 70 to 75 percent of total costs. The results appear in Table 53.

There is a gradual rise in the excess of current-cost over historical-cost charges, ending with a sudden surge to $35.1 billion in 1974.

### Adjustment of Profits

Adjusting profits as reported for income tax purposes, the picture in Table 54 emerges. Adjusted after-tax profits in 1965 were not far below the reported figure. In 1974 their real value was less than a third as large as

**Table 54   Adjustment of Reported Profits of Nonfinancial Corporations (billions of dollars)[a]**

| Year | (1) Profits before tax as reported | (2) Income tax liability | (3) Profits after tax as reported 1 − 2 | (4) Understatement of costs[b] | (5) Profits before tax as adjusted 1 − 4 | (6) Profits after tax as adjusted[c] 3 − 4 |
|---|---|---|---|---|---|---|
| 1965 | $ 65.8 | $27.6 | $38.2 | $ 2.1 | $63.7 | $36.1 |
| 1966 | 71.2 | 30.1 | 41.2 | 3.2 | 68.0 | 38.0 |
| 1967 | 66.2 | 28.4 | 37.8 | 3.8 | 62.4 | 34.0 |
| 1968 | 72.4 | 34.0 | 38.3 | 6.9 | 65.5 | 31.4 |
| 1969 | 68.0 | 33.7 | 34.3 | 9.7 | 58.3 | 24.6 |
| 1970 | 55.7 | 27.6 | 28.2 | 11.4 | 44.3 | 16.8 |
| 1971 | 63.2 | 29.8 | 33.4 | 12.4 | 50.8 | 21.0 |
| 1972 | 76.3 | 33.4 | 43.0 | 14.0 | 62.3 | 29.0 |
| 1973 | 95.8 | 40.7 | 55.0 | 26.9 | 68.9 | 28.1 |
| 1974 | 110.1 | 45.6 | 64.5 | 48.4 | 61.7 | 16.1 |

[a] Figures may not check exactly because of rounding.
[b] The sum of the excesses of current costs over historical costs shown in Tables 52 and 53.
[c] Since this is a retrospective recomputation of profits, it takes as given the corporate income taxes actually paid. If tax liabilities had been figured on the adjusted pretax profits, the after-tax effect of the adjustment would, of course, have been reduced by the tax saving resulting therefrom. But since they were actually figured on the reported profits throughout, there were no such tax savings. Adjusted after-tax profits are simply adjusted pretax profits minus actual taxes on reported profits.

reported. Moreover, their absolute amount was only one-half the 1965 figure.

### Restatement of Retained Earnings

An even more startling picture results when dividend payments are subtracted from adjusted after-tax profits to find adjusted, retained earnings (Table 55).

From 1969 to 1974, adjusted, retained earnings were negligible—in two cases they were negative. Nonfinancial corporations have been distributing almost all their adjusted earnings, their reported savings representing little more than the amount required to cover the understatement of costs. In 1974 the deficit was more than $10 billion.

### Adjusted Profits and Retained Earnings in Constant Dollars

Since inflation has been shrinking the dollar's value over the interval, it is necessary to restate the results in constant dollars (Table 56). The private GNP deflator has been used for this purpose (1965 = 100).

As these figures indicate, adjusted earnings in 1974 were less than one-third the earnings of 1965 when stated in constant dollars. Retained earnings, as already noted, were negative.

**Table 55   Adjusted Retained Earnings of Nonfinancial Corporations (billions of dollars)**

| Year | (1) Adjusted after-tax profits | (2) Dividend payments | (3) Adjusted retained earnings |
|---|---|---|---|
| 1965 | $36.1 | $16.9 | $19.2 |
| 1966 | 38.0 | 18.2 | 19.8 |
| 1967 | 34.0 | 18.9 | 15.1 |
| 1968 | 31.4 | 20.9 | 10.5 |
| 1969 | 24.6 | 20.7 | 3.9 |
| 1970 | 16.8 | 20.0 | −3.2 |
| 1971 | 21.0 | 20.2 | 0.8 |
| 1972 | 29.0 | 22.2 | 6.8 |
| 1973 | 28.1 | 23.7 | 4.4 |
| 1974 | 16.1 | 26.2 | −10.1 |

Table 56  Adjusted Profits and Retained
Earnings of Nonfinancial Corporations
(billions of 1965 dollars)

| Year | (1)<br>Adjusted<br>after-tax<br>profits | (2)<br>Adjusted<br>retained<br>earnings |
|------|------|------|
| 1965 | $36.1 | $19.2 |
| 1966 | 37.3 | 19.4 |
| 1967 | 32.1 | 14.2 |
| 1968 | 28.8 | 9.6 |
| 1969 | 21.6 | 3.4 |
| 1970 | 14.0 | −2.7 |
| 1971 | 16.8 | 0.6 |
| 1972 | 22.6 | 5.3 |
| 1973 | 20.7 | 3.2 |
| 1974 | 10.7 | −6.7 |

### Effective Income Tax Rates
### on Adjusted Profits

Since the income tax liability (federal and state) is computed on overstated historical-cost profits, the effective rate on profits adjusted for the overstatement is higher than the rate reported.

Table 57 reveals that effective tax rates on real profits have moved away from those on reported profits. From 1970 to 1974 they averaged 61 percent against 45 percent. By 1974 the rate had reached 74 percent.

## THE IMPLICATIONS

Tables 52 to 57 make it clear that businesses have an uphill battle to protect profits against the eroding effects of inflation. It is extremely difficult to protect even nominal profit margins because unit costs tend to increase faster than realized prices. Prices are often frozen for substantial periods: catalogs may be issued only annually or semiannually, seasonal merchandise may be priced months in advance of delivery, and long-cycle production may be quoted before work is started. Even when prices are more easily raised, there is a tendency to lag behind the upward thrust of costs.

Table 57   Effective Tax Rates on the
Pretax Profits of Nonfinancial Corporations
as Reported and as Adjusted[a]

| Year | (1)<br>On profits<br>as reported<br>(%) | (2)<br>On profits<br>as adjusted<br>(%) |
|------|------|------|
| 1965 | 41.9 | 43.3 |
| 1966 | 42.3 | 44.3 |
| 1967 | 42.9 | 45.5 |
| 1968 | 47.1 | 55.3 |
| 1969 | 49.4 | 57.7 |
| 1970 | 49.6 | 62.3 |
| 1971 | 47.2 | 58.7 |
| 1972 | 43.8 | 53.6 |
| 1973 | 42.5 | 59.1 |
| 1974 | 41.4 | 73.9 |

[a] Column 2 of Table 54 as percentage of
Columns 1 and 5, respectively.

Part of the answer lies in pricing policy. Management must learn how to price products in an inflationary economy (see *Pricing,* p. 268). This means not only anticipatory pricing (pricing in expectation of cost increases prior to sale), but also using a proper accounting of costs themselves. If all competitors target their prices on fully stated costs rather than competing on understated costs, there is a better chance that prices can be held at a profitable level.

Perhaps even more important, however, is the need for new methods for the accounting of costs and profits. If high rates of inflation persist, business management, the accounting profession, regulatory agencies of the government, and tax authorities must band together for action. If they do not, company profitability needed for expansion of productive investment will be seriously, perhaps disastrously, threatened.

## SUGGESTED FURTHER READING

Callaway, S. R., "Inflation Makes Profits More Illusory than Real," *Commercial and Financial Chronicle,* November 4, 1974, p. 9.

"Inflation: The Taxman's Favorite Pickpocket," *Monthly Economic Newsletter,* First National City Bank of New York, January 1975, pp. 9–12.

Linden, F., "Budgeting for Inflation," *Conference Board Record,* December 1974, pp. 18–21.

Manus, P. C. and C. F. Phillips, Jr., "Earnings Erosion During Inflation," *Public Utilities Fortnightly,* May 8, 1975, pp. 17–22.

Terborgh, George, "Inflation and Profits," *Financial Analysts Journal,* May/June, 1974, pp. 19–23.

## 75

## PURCHASING

*Sets out 25 alternative actions the purchasing function can use to cope more effectively with an inflationary environment and materials shortages.*

There is a disagreement among economists regarding the exact causes of critical materials shortages that often coincide with inflationary periods. Are inflationary price escalations the result of shortages, or do shortages occur because inflation creates an unstable business environment? This "chicken/egg" situation will undoubtedly be debated by economists for some time.

There is almost universal agreement, however, that companies will be faced with continuing price increases and short supplies of some materials (see *Alternate Materials and Designs,* p. 1).

For several years price escalation has been the rule, rather than the exception. As Wholesale Price Indexes (p. 417) show, wholesale prices in the United States have risen 60 percent since 1970 alone. Wholesale prices of fuel, power, and lighting have risen 135 percent; iron, steel, and lumber have gone up 75 percent.

While prices have been rising, productive capacity has not expanded sufficiently, largely because of inadequate rates of return realized by industrial firms. Since output has not been sufficient to meet demand, additional upward pressure has been placed on prices by demand-pull inflation.

The end result is that over the coming decade, the purchasing executive will be faced with the double problem of trying to hold down purchase prices while attempting to obtain items that are in short supply.

The following[1] outlines 25 methods to help the purchasing function contribute more effectively to organizational profit and service goals. The methods are grouped under three headings, as follows:

• Internal actions relating to product specifications and improved material requirements knowledge.
• Changes that focus primarily on buyer-supplier relationships in the external environment.

[1] Adapted from Robert M. Monczka and Harold E. Fearon, "Coping with Material Shortages," *Journal of Purchasing,* May 1974, p. 5–19.

• Changes that focus primarily on internal purchasing and other organizational systems.

## INTERNAL PRODUCT SPECIFICATION AND MATERIAL ACTIONS

Methods involving internal product specification and material actions deal mainly with increasing knowledge of specific items purchased.

### Buy the End Product

Vendors of end products, services, or components are often rather well placed with respect to raw materials and prices because of size, ownership interest, commercial contracts, or geographical location. Thus it is often more advantageous to buy a needed item than to manufacture it yourself.

### Long-Term Commodity Studies

Sound purchasing decisions are dependent on a realistic assessment of current and intermediate- to long-term supply, demand, and price situations. Such studies provide the basis for decisions on matters including plant location, product design, vendor selection, make or buy, and long-term purchasing strategy. Thorough investigations into these areas should allow the purchaser to anticipate price/supply problems and to take action to alleviate them. Areas to be studied include the following:

• Current status: description of the item to be purchased, how used, how purchased, and current contracts, prices, and expiration dates.
• Production process: how the item is made, material and labor used in manufacturing, price/availability forecasts, and possibility of making the item.
• Uses of the item: primary and secondary uses, possible substitutes, and economics of substitution.
• Demand: demand for the item, current and projected; competing demand, current and projected.
• Supply: current producers and their situation, aggregate supply situations, import potential and problems, potential new suppliers, and political trends.
• Price: history and trends, factors determining price, transportation costs, profit margins, pricing system used, and relation to other products.
• Purchasing strategy: methods that might be used to gain better value per dollar spent.

### Value Analysis/Value Engineering (VA/VE)

VA/VE has been defined aş "An organized, systematic study of the function of a material, part, component, or system, with the objective of identifying areas of unnecessary cost, so that total product or operating cost can be minimized without impairing the ability of the item to satisfy its established objectives."[2]

If applied systematically, VA/VE can be instrumental in alleviating price/shortages problems by the following methods.

• Standardizing materials in ample supply, thus eliminating need for expensive and/or unavailable items.
• Eliminating certain materials not essential to the product's function.
• Substituting obtainable items for expensive or critical supply items.

Concentrated VA/VE studies are almost certain to uncover material savings or substitution alternatives overlooked by casual analysis.

## EXTERNAL ACTIONS FOCUSING ON BUYER–SUPPLIER RELATIONSHIPS

Current price/shortages problems should dictate a continuing evaluation of buyer-supplier relationships with an eye toward more profitable purchasing practices. The following methods are key elements in maximizing purchasing.

### Examine and Evaluate Vendor Relations

In an inflationary economy, purchasers should make sure that supplying firms give them preferential treatment if they buy regularly. This includes on-time delivery of short-supply materials, as well as price advantages.

### Buy Out Vendor

The company may consider buying out a vendor who is supplying a scarce and/or expensive product or material. Instead of receiving only one allocation of the material, the firm can then utilize all the needed material or product, usually at a lower cost.

---

[2] Monczka and Fearon, "Coping with Material Shortages," *Journal of Purchasing,* May 1974, p. 11.

### Emphasize Worldwide Source Development

The purchasing department should examine the feasibility of obtaining materials and products from sources outside the United States. Prices and availability should be the major considerations in considering foreign sources.

### Supplier Development with Long-Term Vendors

Vendors currently supplying some products may have the technical and managerial skills necessary to produce hard-to-find supplies, particularly if raw material needs overlap their current product line.

### Establish Vendor Buying Cooperatives

Purchasing departments can alleviate shortage problems by helping vendors establish buying cooperatives for high-volume purchases. This practice makes the cooperative a more attractive customer than single purchasers, and the joint vendor group is more likely to receive preferential treatment. This advantage, in turn, can be passed along to the firms supplied by the co-op.

### Long-Term Purchase Agreement Guarantees

The use of long-term purchase agreements guarantees that the buying firm will continue to purchase from the vendor for a specified period of time (e.g., 5 years). This reduces uncertainties facing the seller, who may be willing to accord preferred customer treatment in return.

### Require Customer to Find Suppliers

A company's customers may have access to firms controlling raw materials or products the company needs. Customers often can ensure supply of needed materials or products from these primary vendors, especially if the customer is connected with governmental bodies.

### Arrange for Transportation

If vendors do not have adequately staffed traffic departments or appropriate transportation equipment, the purchaser may prefer to handle transportation of materials bought. In addition to prompt delivery, this practice can provide lower materials cost.

### Joint Purchasing

Feasibility of joining with another firm to purchase needed materials or products should be evaluated. The combined volume of two firms entering into a joint purchasing agreement may give those companies the buying power needed to obtain scarce materials and products on a preferred customer basis, or to qualify for lower prices.

### Trading Capability

Some firms may have a trading capability that should be exploited. For example, one firm may have an excess of, or access to, a material or product needed by another firm, while the second company may have materials or products required by the first firm. Such bartering took place under many guises in 1974 when oil was in short supply.

### Reverse Reciprocity

The company should adopt an attitude of reverse reciprocity: "I'll sell to you if you'll sell to me" or "I'll sell to you if you'll sell to my supplier." The legality of formal or informal agreements of this type may be open to question, but until a legal precedent has been established, the method can be helpful in coping with supply shortages.

### Eliminate Single Sourcing

If the company has had a policy of single sourcing its purchased products and materials, reconsider the policy. A single supplier, because of his own shortage problems or inefficiencies, may not be able to meet supply requirements or to give the best price. In some cases multiple sourcing may be the only way to obtain certain needed materials. Since availability of supplies is the key to profitable operations, some firms even incur the expense of tooling and interface for suppliers to obtain needed items from multiple sources.

### Buy from the Black Market

Market dislocations resulting from governmental attempts to control supply and demand have led to the development of a "black market" in many materials that come from smaller, noncontrolled producers, from foreign suppliers who are not regulated as closely as domestic producers, or from brokers of scarce materials who are looking for large profits on higher-than-normal commissions. Although black market purchasing is a questionable practice, it is an alternative to be considered, at least on a temporary basis, if the only other option is to close a production line.

## INTERNAL PURCHASING AND ORGANIZATIONAL SYSTEMS' ACTIONS

Possible actions of organizational systems and internal purchasing departments focus on the need to examine business philosophy, policy, and procedure as they relate to internal operations of purchasing and other departments. During periods of inflation and/or materials shortages, effects of outside changes on internal organizational and operating systems should be constantly reevaluated.

### Process Scrap

Often scrap material (rejects that cannot be reworked or normal machinery scrap) can be made ready for reuse through an agreement with a scrap processor, or by in-house refining, if possible. In critical materials situations this practice can save supplies that would be lost if the material were placed on the scrap market.

### Change Inventory and Forward Buying Policies

If there is uncertainty of particular commodities' supplies, consider increasing the average amount of inventory carried and extending forward buying commitments. Although such policy changes may reduce profits, closure of critical operations or extensive rescheduling of production might be even more costly.

### Offer More than the Going Price

Quite often there is material in the supply marketplace, but the normal supply and demand mechanism is not working because the material is being artificially withheld by some suppliers. A buying firm may have to let it be known that it is willing to pay more than the going price for the item. This harsh alternative should be considered when critical operations will be affected if supplies are not obtained.

### Increase Expediting Efforts

Increased expediting can be used to follow up on purchased items to ensure availability when needed. It is no longer good enough to expect suppliers to meet volume, quality, and time requirements. Contracts have to be followed through regularly in a shortage economy.

### Develop a Centralized Information and Resource Allocation Office

Consideration should be given to establishing a centralized information-allocation office to serve two basic purposes.

• The office becomes the repository for information on all purchases. The purchasing department can then effectively utilize buying power of total corporate requirements.
• The office is responsible for allocating available materials and products to the uses that are most profitable to the total organization.

### Improve Purchasing/Engineering Coordination

Improvement should be made on the interface between purchasing and engineering. In a shortage economy the purchasing department requires "early warning" of material and product requirements needed to meet production schedules. Engineering will find it increasingly dangerous to specify items with relatively short lead times, expecting purchasing to meet delivery needs.

### ABC Analysis of Critical Items

Classify commodities or products by their shortage criticality (e.g., most severe, moderately severe, and least severe). Then efforts can be concentrated on items in most severe shortage and in terms of importance to current and future operations. Obviously this type of analysis is not static and must be continually revised as conditions change.

### Select and/or Develop Inflation-Conscious Personnel

Increasing emphasis must be placed on providing the purchasing department with skills necessary to manage materials and suppliers in an inflationary environment. Purchasing personnel who are mere "order takers" cannot make a meaningful contribution to organizational profitability.

They must be innovative and willing to take more risks than would be advisable in normal economies. Characteristics that define the successful, inflation-conscious purchasing agent are leadership skill, innovative insights, analytical ability, ambition, and persuasiveness.

## SUGGESTED FURTHER READING

Bird, M. M., "Time Reciprocity: A Possible Answer to Shortages," *Journal of Purchasing and Materials Management,* November 1974, pp. 46–50.

"Cost Cutting: Small-Time Costs Yield Big-Time Savings," *Purchasing,* March 4, 1975, pp. 55–56.

Hakansson, H. and B. Wootz, "Supplier Selection in an International Environment," *Journal of Marketing Research,* February 1975, pp. 46–51.

Monczka, Robert M. and Harold E. Fearon, "Coping with Material Shortages," *Journal of Purchasing,* May 1974 p. 5–19.

Tavernier, G., "Rising Importance of the Purchasing Manager," *International Management,* September 1974, pp. 42–43.

SECTION

# 76

## REPLACEMENT COST ACCOUNTING

*Outlines an accounting technique that includes technological advances as well as inflation in the calculation of depreciation.*

Replacement cost accounting, a technique developed in the Netherlands, recognizes technological advances as well as inflationary increases in the calculation of the depreciation of assets such as plant or equipment. The method substitutes replacement cost values for fixed currency cost values, thus reducing tax obligations by depreciating assets at the higher replacement cost rate. Although currently prohibited for accounting purposes in the United States, the method is spreading in popularity in Europe, and the use of the technique will undoubtedly be adopted in other areas if persistent inflation continues.

Assume that a new piece of equipment costs $25,000. Using historical accounting methods the asset probably would be depreciated over a 10-year period—$2500 a year. During periods of double-digit inflation and rapid technological change, however, the 10 percent depreciation rate is obviously too low. When the asset must be replaced, inflation will have pushed up the price, and technological advancements in the assets' performance will also have added to the cost. To overcome this disadvantage, replacement cost accounting is used instead of historical accounting as follows.

In calculating depreciation all price changes at the close of the accounting period are taken into consideration. If the average inflation rate for the period was 6 percent (12 percent annually) and the average price rise due to technological advancement was 8 percent (16 percent annually), the valuation of the asset for depreciation purposes is adjusted by 14 percent, or $3500. Depreciation for the year is then calculated on $28,500, rather than $25,000. Depreciation for the period is thus $2850 instead of $2500.

In succeeding years adjustments are made to the recalculated value of the preceding accounting period.

## SUGGESTED FURTHER READING

Brittan, Samuel, "Living With Inflation—The Key Points," *Financial Times,* London, May 13, 1974, p. 25.

*Guide to Current Purchasing Power Accounting,* Price, Waterhouse, and Co., New York, 1974.

Morris, Richard, "Replacement Cost Accounting," *Accounting and Business Research,* January 1975, pp. 37–50.

# ROLLING FORECASTS

*Outlines periodic projections as a complement to the use of budgets in coping with problems due to inflation.*

During inflationary periods many companies help forestall unpleasant surprises in the area of earnings by using rolling forecasts, which lessens the need for hastily developed solutions that may compound rather than solve problems.

Rolling forecasts are projections that are not confined to a calendar or fiscal year and are updated periodically—often quarterly. They are not designed to replace the budget as a detailed control mechanism but rather to complement it as a more general planning tool. Use of rolling forecasts, consequently, keeps top management informed about current deviations from budgetary goals.

Obviously the use of rolling forecasts places an extra burden on operating management, which must assist in preparation. But the tool is almost indispensable in providing management with information necessary to anticipate inflation-connected problems and to develop plans to cope with them.

**SUGGESTED FURTHER READING**

Grose, Robert W., "Fighting Inflation: A Management Overview," *Industry Week,* March 3, 1975, p. 43.

# SECTION 78

## SALARY ADMINISTRATION

*Provides guidelines for cost-of-living salary adjustment practices during inflationary periods.*

Since World War II employers have generally held the position that rises in the cost of living, as measured by the Consumer Price Index, seriously affect only hourly wage earners and low-income families, and that only these employees need cost-of-living wage increases. This idea was based on the premise that only those who consumed all their incomes felt the full effect of CPI rises.

Since 1972, however, annual inflationary rates averaging 10 percent have created serious problems in management of salaries between $15,000 and $30,000. Employees in this range have become increasingly reluctant to accept the traditional concept of CPI application and have pushed for pay raises to at least match index rises.

The problem of double-digit inflation creates a number of salary difficulties. What should be the correct distribution of corporate profits to wage and salary increases? Should corporate policy strive to increase employee purchasing power during periods of rapidly rising costs, or merely ensure that employee purchasing power is maintained? In fact, can the company afford to maintain employee purchasing power? Should employees be asked to accept a reduced pay level to support the company's capital investment needs, which have also been affected by rising costs?

The following discusses these problems and sets out guidelines for cost-of-living salary administration during an inflationary period.

### COST-OF-LIVING BACKGROUND

The key to establishing salary administration policies is knowledge of the methods used by the Department of Labor in compiling the Consumer Price Index and family budget statistics. The index is a compilation of the cost of a "market basket" of goods and services "usually bought by urban wage earners and clerical workers" in 23 urban areas. It is based on roughly 400 items (see *Consumer Price Index*, p. 94).

**333**

The CPI has risen rapidly over the past several years, but significantly there has been little variation in the rate of rise between traditionally high-cost and low-cost cities. By the end of 1974 the rise of prices as measured by the CPI was not much greater in the highest-ranked metropolitan area (New York) than in the lowest (Seattle).

To more accurately gauge comparative living costs, the Labor Department devised an Urban Family Budget Index, which reflects living costs for an urban family of four with one breadwinner. Using these statistics, much wider variations become apparent in living costs in different urban locations. For example, there is a 33 percent cost-of-living spread between a "high-income family" in the most expensive area (New York) and the least expensive area (Bakersfield). Spreads of 15 percent are common, depending on the areas measured. These variations are seen when living costs are expressed in dollars. A family of four living in Boston in 1974, for example, would have had to pay $21,986 for the same goods and services that could be purchased in Seattle for $17,924. The Urban Family Budget Index is based on identical consumption from area to area. The higher cost of housing ($1500) and taxes ($2000) account for most of the difference between the costs of living in Boston and in Seattle.

## GUIDELINES FOR SALARY ADMINISTRATION

By making use of available statistical data, a company can formulate a comprehensive strategy for salary administration in an inflationary environment. The following seven steps should be taken.[1]

### Determine the Basic "Cost Index" for Your Company's Geographical Area

Using published Consumer Price Index and Urban Family Budget data, general cost-of-living guidelines can be drawn for any location. These should be refined, however, to make an index truly applicable to a given locality. The following example shows how thorough analysis can pay in saved costs.

Armed with press clippings describing Boston as one of the highest-cost areas in the United States, a group of area employee representatives accused management of failing to take these data into account when setting salary levels of employees transferred into Boston or hired from elsewhere.

[1] Adapted from Richard J. Bronstein, "The Cost of Living and Salary Administration," *Personnel,* March/April, 1975, pp. 11–18.

Before responding, management contacted the Department of Labor and found that the firm's location—25 miles from Boston—was in fact just outside the basic index area. Likewise, it was determined that most of the firm's employees lived beyond the region's prime population concentration, and like the company itself, were outside the Standard Metropolitan Statistical Area (SMSA) boundary. These nonmetropolitan areas are at or near the bottom of the statistical Family Budget figures.

Using this data, the company was able to formulate its own cost index. Although based in large part on the Boston SMSA figures, the new index was adjusted downward to reflect the fact that housing, taxes, and some "market basket" costs were traditionally lower than in the Boston region. Significantly, the company's employees did not disagree with the findings.

### Establish Specific Salary Policies
### for Transferred Employees and Newcomers
### Hired from Other Areas

Regardless of where employees move in urban America, living costs associated with transfers are particularly high.

Employees transferring from high-cost to low-cost areas should not be expected to take a downward salary adjustment, even though their cost-of-living expenses appear to decrease. Generally such an employee must replace his old 5 to 7 percent mortgage with a new (and probably larger) one at rates of 8 to 10 percent. Or he must rent a new apartment at 1976 prices. Costs of new home furnishings have also skyrocketed because of inflation.

For employees moving in the opposite direction, from low-cost to high-cost areas, the expenses of moving and increased living costs are staggering. Often upward salary adjustments of 20 to 30 percent are required just to allow the employee to break even. This often hurts recruitment programs because firms are reluctant to hire newcomers from other areas or to transfer employees. Another problem arises with respect to existing employees. If they find that a transferred newcomer is drawing a higher salary (justified because of relocation expenses) for doing the same work, they often push for pay increases themselves.

To counteract these problems firms should face the fact that living costs and salary expenses will continue to rise and design a compensation plan or long-term relocation cost allowance. The action should be carefully explained to others in the group, outlining reasons for higher salaries paid to transferred newcomers. Regardless of where an employee is transferring, he will experience higher costs than employees already at the location; thus a higher salary or allowances will be required to offset those costs.

**Utilize the CPI as an Index for the
Rate of Pay Increase Required
to Protect Employee Purchasing Power,
but do Not Apply it as an Unadjusted Factor**

The Consumer Price Index should not be the sole basis for adjusting wages and salaries. Although the CPI is valuable in helping establish wage adjustment and "merit increase" or "grade step progression" systems, competition must also play a major role in compensation decisions. The competitive price of similar jobs performed in the same labor market is a key factor in setting rates and establishing the level of across-the-board pay increases. Careful monitoring of competitive conditions in a company's labor market is essential, and data obtained should be combined with CPI information in determining wage and salary adjustments. Any other process involves the risk of over or underpaying.

**Define Specific Standards for
Overall Wage and Salary Increases**

After taking cost-of-living and company economic conditions into account, firms should set standards for salary increases. These standards should be used when determining the combined size of across-the-board pay adjustments and discretionary "merit" increase budgets.

When firms' salary administration practices have historically been based on discretionary pay increases, it is advisable to continue the practice. It should be remembered, however, that a "no raise" decision during a period of rampant inflation will result in serious deterioration in employee purchasing power, affecting worker morale.

**Set a Definite Policy for Applying Cost-of-Living Increases to
Various Salary Levels, and Follow It**

Cost-of-living increases drastically affect most employees' salaries up to about $20,000. The impact of higher living costs is lessened, however, above the $10,000 level; and the purchasing-power value of income increases significantly above $14,000 when social security taxes of almost 6 percent are eliminated.

Because of this factor, it is not necessary to adjust salaries in strict accordance with increases in the Consumer Price Index to offset cost-of-living erosion. The following adjustments should be reasonable in most firms.

• If the CPI rises 10 percent in a given year, a 10 percent pay boost is fully adequate to hold the purchasing power of a $14,000 salary.

• For an $18,000 salary, an 8.7 percent adjustment would be justified (10 percent of the first $14,000, plus 4 percent of the next $4000).
• At the $22,000 level, an adjustment of 7.8 percent should be applied (10 percent of the first $14,000, 4 percent of the next $8000).
• At some point, income should be considered out of range for cost-of-living adjustments. In most firms the cutoff point should be set between $20,000 and $30,000.

## Maintain Employee Purchasing Power Where Possible

With double-digit inflationary rates, simply maintaining the purchasing power of employees can put a severe strain on company profitability. It is usually unwise to try to increase employee purchasing power under these circumstances, except in very special instances of increased responsibility or exceptional performance. Rather, salary guidelines should be set that merely keep employee pay from falling behind in real terms. The corporation's first social responsibility is to pay for the cost of the capital employed in its business.

## Explain your Policies to Company Managers and Through Them, to All Employees

During periods of heavy inflation it is difficult for employees to understand the complex issues involved in administering salaries. For this reason it is highly important that managers and supervisors be kept aware of the reasons behind wage and salary adjustment policies.

Advise key personnel of the company's interpretations of CPI fluctuations and how changing economic and cost factors are reflected in compensation practices. Most important, know where your company is "located" for economic measurement purposes and pass this along to employees. If your company finds itself on the edge of a defined economic area and you interpret your cost position differently from the publicized SMSA indexes for the region, show employees why and how this interpretation was made.

Finally, be sure that at least the top and upper-middle management levels are aware of and understand the economic principles being followed. During spiraling inflation employees will have more economic questions than ever before. It is up to management to answer these questions by providing a basic understanding of the statistics of inflation, backed by logic, intelligence, and facts.

## SUGGESTED FURTHER READING

Barry, B., "Poor Little Rich Men," *Personnel Management*, February 1975, p. 3.

Bronstein, Richard J., "The Cost of Living and Salary Administration," *Personnel*, March/April, 1975, pp. 11–18

Kraus, D. and S. Patrick, "International Executive Compensation—Unmanaged or Unmanageable?" *Business Horizons*, December 1974, pp. 45–55.

Perham, J. C., "Compensation," *Dun's Review*, January 1975, pp. 32–35.

"Soaring Cost of Employee Compensation," *Business Week*, September 7, 1974, p. 42.

Wolfe, A. V., "Managerial Approach to Compensation," *Personnel Journal*, April 1975, pp. 212–216.

# SECTION 79

## SALES FORCE EFFICIENCY

*Discusses tactical changes to improve selling efforts during inflationary periods.*

A prolonged period of spiraling inflation creates innumerable problems for most businesses on the selling side.

On the one hand, customers are experiencing shortages of cash and/or exorbitant borrowing rates and are reluctant to buy anything that is not absolutely necessary. At the other extreme, inflationary economies are often accompanied by materials shortages, meaning that production must be curtailed. In this instance the salesman has little or nothing to sell. Between these extremes, selling costs soar as travel and entertainment expenses go up and sales per call go down.

During the 1973–1974 worldwide, double-digit inflationary period, most firms had their first real taste of problems a 15 percent inflationary rate causes in sales functions. A variety of cost-saving ideas were tried in an effort to overcome such difficulties. Many of these proved effective and were often retained by sales management after the inflationary rate had dropped.

Following is a summary of some of the most successful of these ideas, grouped under headings common to the sales activities of most companies.[1]

### AUTOMOBILE EXPENSES

Assuming that salesmen have something to sell and that regular calls on customers are to be maintained, automobile travel costs can be shaved by switching from standard-sized cars to smaller models. Today's medium-sized cars are as large as standard models of 6 years ago, currently cost about $350 less, and generally have a higher resale value. Additionally, they get 2 to 3 miles more per gallon of gasoline, an important consideration

---

[1] From "How to Keep a Sales Force Running in a Crunch Economy," *Sales Management,* January 21, 1974, pp. 3–39. Adapted with permission from *Sales Management, The Marketing Magazine.* Copyright 1974.

when fuel prices are rising. If cars are leased, switching from standard to medium-sized models will lower costs about $8 a month per car.

Successful use of this method is reflected in changing fleet market figures. In 1974, for example, intermediate models held 58 percent of the fleet market, compared to 49 percent the previous year. One typical large corporation's fleet was changed to 65 percent intermediate models, having previously consisted of 65 percent standard models. Companies that normally upgraded salesmen from intermediate to standard models after an established length of employment reduced costs by discontinuing the practice.

Greater savings can be realized by switching to compact or subcompact models in some cases. One company test showed that operating costs were reduced 8¢ a mile on smaller cars, since mileage was increased from 11 to 18 miles per gallon—an increase of up to 65 percent. The smaller models, however, may not withstand the hard driving of salesmen covering large areas, and operating savings may be offset by repair costs and low resale value. The best overall plan is to fit the car to individual sales requirements; larger models for on-the-road salesmen, compacts for city driving.

When choosing the type of car, a firm must also consider the samples and equipment salesmen carry. Some products require the space of a station wagon. Even here, money can be saved by shipping samples from the plant or designing special small-car roof racks for samples.

Mileage allowance increases for salesman-owned cars should be based on total costs of owning a car, not just gasoline costs. Thus if gas prices go up 15 percent in a year and all other costs are constant, the total cost of owning an average car increases by about 5 percent. When allowance increases do not appear to match retail gasoline price increases, this fact should be pointed out to salesmen, to prevent them from curtailing calls because of the belief that excess costs are coming out of their own pockets.

When rapidly rising gasoline prices were coupled with shortages of supply in 1974, *Sales Management* magazine surveyed a cross section of American marketing executives to determine how long-term gasoline shortages or rationing would affect their sales operations. The results of this survey (Table 58) provide a guide to management thinking about which sales functions should and should not be curtailed to save automobile travel expenses.


## LONG-DISTANCE TRAVEL

When dramatic hikes in air fares appeared during recent inflationary periods, many firms sharply cut back or eliminated air travel by salesmen and managers. This is not always possible or profitable. Costs can be cut in

**Table 58  Results of Automobile Travel Expense Survey**[a]

In the event of severe gasoline shortages or rationing, how likely is it that you will resort to the following measures?

| | Very likely (%) | Likely (%) | Not very likely (%) | In force now (%) | No answer (%) |
|---|---|---|---|---|---|
| Eliminating calls on all but key accounts | 15 | 37 | 43 | — | 6 |
| Eliminating calls on small accounts | 25 | 49 | 15 | 4 | 7 |
| Eliminating or drastically reducing calls on new prospects | 21 | 33 | 38 | 2 | 6 |
| Eliminating calls on customers in remote areas | 40 | 38 | 12 | 8 | 2 |
| Closing down district sales offices | 6 | 6 | 72 | 2 | 15 |
| Reducing the size of sales territories | 7 | 17 | 70 | 1 | 6 |
| Rearranging territories along geographic rather than industry lines | 6 | 16 | 51 | 19 | 9 |
| Setting new sales quotas | 13 | 35 | 44 | 2 | 6 |
| Establishing new incentive programs | 15 | 33 | 45 | 1 | 7 |
| Switching to smaller sales cars | 22 | 24 | 28 | 10 | 16 |

[a] *Source: Sales Management*, January 21, 1974, p. 27.

other ways, such as making all trips regional rather than using a number of separate trips. For example, the whole west coast might be covered in one swing instead of using separate flights to Los Angeles, San Diego, and San Francisco.

Some firms find that best savings come through arbitrarily cutting air travel expenses by a specific percentage (e.g., 50 percent). Salesmen know they have to stay within the new figure and schedule themselves accordingly.

As a rule, most companies have found it best not to reduce air travel arbitrarily but to make certain that all trips are absolutely necessary.

In some regions savings can be made by switching from air travel to trains and buses for relatively short trips. In the Northeast, for instance, the city center to city center Metroliner service in the New Haven–Washington corridor is somewhat cheaper than air fare and requires little if any additional travel time. Bus fares, including the new VIP service for businessmen, are considerably less expensive.

## TERRITORIES AND ROUTES

During inflation, sales territories can be realigned to effect as many economies as possible. Vertical (industry-wide) coverage can be switched to geographical coverage, consolidating sales forces from various corporate divisions. However the best salesmen should continue to call on key accounts. Travel expenses can be reduced by limiting calls on less profitable customers. Additionally, a firm appointment should always be made with customers before any calls are scheduled.

Another method is to reduce the size of sales territories, again lowering travel expense. These steps are often accompanied by a letter to customers outlining the need to cut down sales calls in order to keep prices as low as possible, and asking for their cooperation.

Savings can also be achieved by adjusting sales routes. Circular routing patterns can be used to avoid doubling back. Sales trips can be lengthened to reduce travel to and from the home base. Trips to district sales offices can be reduced or eliminated by having salesmen work from their homes, which can be equipped with telephone-answering devices that allow salesmen to phone in and monitor calls recorded during the day.

An additional way to reduce the cost of covering a territory is "car pooling" with salesmen from other companies. This is possible when product lines are not in conflict, yet areas or buyers overlap.

Similarly, pooling may be carried out within the company. Several salesmen in a food brokerage firm, for instance, had customers within reasonable proximity of one another. The salesmen were driven to their respective accounts by the sales supervisor. After a specified period of time, the supervisor doubled back, picked them up again, and eliminated several individual trips.

In certain situations, particularly in rural areas, sales calls can be reduced or eliminated by asking customers to do the traveling. Special showings at hotels or regional offices can be used to display product lines. All accounts from the area are invited to visit the one central location.

When drastic reductions must be made in territories and/or routes, it is often possible to make better use of catalogs to maintain sales. Well-conceived catalogs have saved calls and have also made sales to new accounts. The key ingredient is research. Successful salesmen are trained to be aware of, and sensitive to, needs of prospective customers. Research is needed to turn out catalogs that are effective in the same ways. Sales files and sales personnel should be consulted to plan a printed material program and to see that it continues as an up-to-date customer/company communications system solving customer problems, providing product applications information, and so on.

## SHORTAGES AND THE SALES FORCE

Inflationary periods can mean shortages. Shortages generally occur as rising costs force manufacturers to limit the quantity of raw materials bought for production. In demand-pull situations (when customers buy as much as possible before prices rise again), production simply cannot keep pace with demand. Either shortage cause can present sales managers with a two-pronged dilemma; they may be deluged with orders but have no products to deliver, or they may have a sales force that is largely reduced to a group of order takers trying to meet customer demands. Some guidelines have been developed to combat these problems.

*Generally, companies should not curtail sales efforts, even during the most critical shortages.* If they do, they may find that their sales base has slumped dramatically when supplies come into line with demand. The rule is especially important in handling key accounts—the 20 percent of customers who provide 80 percent of sales.

*It is important to keep major accounts abreast of supply situations, remain informed of their needs, and help them adjust their operations to fluctuating lines of supply.* This holds true even when shortages necessitate putting customers on an allocation basis.

*Sales staffs should be cut only as a last resort.* In the opinion of some marketers, numbers of salesmen should even be increased as a means of obtaining business from competitors who do cut back on major customer contact.

*Salesmen should be kept fully informed of supply and delivery situations.* This ensures that they do not promise customers orders that cannot be filled. Additionally, salesmen can work with buyers in adapting operations to permit the use of available products wherever possible. In some cases it is even advantageous from a goodwill point of view to assist customers in locating alternate sources of supply.

*Customers should be encouraged to allow as much lead time in ordering as possible.* Some firms supply bulletins to their sales force to inform them of competitors' problems in filling orders and meeting delivery dates. This provides a weapon when complaining customers imply that the salesman's firm is the only one with shortage problems.

*Some firms concentrate on building markets for secondary products if primary products are in short supply.*

*Sales meetings should be continued.* More than ever, salesmen need training and guidance to service customers. The meetings also boost morale, for which salesmen will be grateful when they have little to sell. Costs can be cut, however, by holding regional or local rather than national sales meetings. A business survey conducted during 1974 shortages showed that nearly one-third of the companies questioned planned to make such location changes. Savings from use of local meetings as compared to national ones were estimated at about 25 percent.

*An air of crisis can lead to innovation.* Customers hurting for supplies are often more receptive to salesmen's ideas about their own products and processes. Additionally, as the shortage crisis passes, buyers will be especially receptive to the salesmen who helped most when the going was rough.

## COMPENSATION

When shortages in supplies and manufactured goods create a seller's market, most sales managers take a hard look at their manpower requirements and review their salesmen's compensation programs. This is especially true when economic difficulties change customer buying patterns and motivation, causing shortages in product lines and altering the number of prospects a salesman can handle.

In making manpower or compensation changes, however, it is important to remember that the company will be in business after the economic upheaval has passed. For this reason salesmen are every bit as important as customers. This lesson was learned the hard way by some in past inflationary periods. When profits slipped, annual bonuses and other incentive payments were dropped—and the salesmen dropped the companies just as promptly. This behavior affected business during the crisis by making it difficult to service established customers and also led to very real problems when the economy brightened. Entire new sales teams had to be hired and trained.

Good management will realize the short-sightedness of arbitrary compensation cuts and will take other steps to weather economic difficulties. Compensation specialists recommend that firms continue to pay salesmen their normal salaries regardless of their productivity during supply shortages. This includes commissions that they would normally be earning, regardless of whether they are selling.

Alternatively, firms may be able to use salesmen in other capacities during the slow-down, even if their actual productivity is low compared with normal sales activities. Depending on current government regulations, it may be necessary to notify the Pay Board and obtain its approval of compensation that is to be paid to salesmen for other than normal selling activities.

Generally the most successful solution is to continue paying salesmen normal compensation while stepping up efforts to increase their productivity. A key ingredient is to develop innovative incentive programs geared to the existing economic situation. When acute product shortages exist, programs cannot be built primarily on traditional goals of achieving higher volume or adding new accounts. Rather, programs should be devised that will benefit the company in areas that are ignored in normal times. For example, during inflation some firms developed incentives to stimulate salesmen to sell old inventories or to concentrate only on products that are highly profitable. Another incentive goal is to encourage lowest possible selling costs. Some firms reward salesmen who set up sales training sessions with dealers, are successful in getting better local retail and wholesale advertising support, or provide increased sales service. Self-training and salesman recruiting programs can be formulated to teach the sales force to make better sales reports.

Rewards can be given for an exceptional job of helping worried customers get through the crisis or for coming up with innovative selling tactics in the emergency environment. Incentives can also be used to achieve higher volume per sales call and/or better route-area structuring.

If wives have not been involved in previous incentive programs, this may be the time to begin, since salesmen will probably be making fewer but much longer road trips.

Times of chronic sales disruption provide the sales manager with a good opportunity to reexamine his entire manpower and compensation structure. Losing some salesmen through natural attrition may be beneficial, and replacements made only after the economy picks up. The interim period should always be used, however, for restructuring and gearing for the future.

### TELEPHONE SELLING

During times of inflationary traveling expenses and generally lower sales productivity per in-person call, special efforts may be made to use telephone sales techniques. Some new sales plans are built entirely around the telephone. At the very least, managers should require salesmen to phone for firm appointments with buyers and prospects to avoid wasted trips. The phone should also be used for follow-up activities, rather than another personal call.

Incoming Wide-Area Telephone Service (WATS) lines can be used to encourage customers to call in orders. Telephone-oriented customer service departments, with experienced inside salesmen, can handle service questions and also take new orders.

One large international firm was able to cut selling costs by taking its entire consumer sales force out of the field several times a year and concentrating efforts on saturation telephone sales campaigns. Generally their sales pitches were pegged to a significant event inside the company—an impending price increase, for example. Sales regions were pitted one against the other to see which could write the largest amount of business during the phone sales campaign. On one occasion shortly after Christmas, a 50-man telephone sales force wrote several million dollars worth of orders in one day by telephoning for restocking orders.

Several key points should be used in setting up a formal telephone selling campaign.

*Planning.* Detailed advance plans should be made by each salesman regarding which accounts he will phone and the frequency of his calls.

*Goals.* Objectives should be set, not only for each salesman or the program as a whole, but for each call. The program should be reviewed frequently to determine achievement of goals.

*Follow-ups.* Direct mail communications should be used to follow up all calls, not only to reinforce the sales effort but to confirm important aspects of the conversation.

*Technique Training.* All salesmen enlisted as part of the telephone force should receive thorough training in the latest sales techniques.

*Evaluation.* Periodically the entire telephone selling program should be reviewed and evaluated to pinpoint areas in need of improvement. The success of the program should be judged on the volume of business written.

### Telephone Sales Training

Because of their training, salesmen are accustomed to selling face-to-face with buyers. Although there are similarities between face-to-face and telephone selling, there are also marked differences, and these necessitate a structured training program in phone selling techniques. Often it is wise to engage a specialist to conduct the training program. The following suggestions should be considered.

*Voice.* Recordings should be made of each salesman's telephone voice during a simulated sales conversation. Recordings can be made on an inexpensive telephone pickup device. The simulated conversations should match actual sales calls as closely as possible, and the sales manager should play the customer's role. Tapes should be reviewed with each salesman, paying particular attention to voice pitch, volume, rate of speech, and the projection of enthusiasm in the individual's telephone approach.

*Coverage.* Each salesman should be instructed to outline exactly what he wishes to cover in various types of calls. Since the opening of the conversation is usually the most important, phone technique consultants recommend scripting it word for word.

*Role-playing.* Use sales meetings as opportunities to sharpen phone selling through role-playing techniques. Salesmen can be divided into three-man teams and alternately play the parts of salesman, customer, and objective observer. The observer critiques simulated sales conversations. Extension phones add to the authenticity, or participants can face in opposite directions during the conversation.

## SUGGESTED FURTHER READING

"How to Keep a Sales Force Running in a Crunch Economy," *Sales Management,* January 21, 1974, pp. 3–39.

"Pricing Strategy in an Inflation Economy," *Business Week,* April 16, 1974, pp. 43–49.

# SECTION

# 80

## SECURED FINANCING

*Discusses the use of secured financing as a means of improving cash flow in an inflationary environment.*

During inflationary periods the demand for growth capital usually outstrips the supply available from traditional sources. Many companies that normally would qualify for bank financing find that they are unable to get money at any price.

The problem is becoming more serious, largely because of persistent inflation and the resulting disruptions created in the money market. A serious cash flow gap has developed. In 1950 only 29 percent of the funds used in the financing of nonfinancial corporate businesses were raised externally. That ratio has risen steadily in virtually every year since, reaching the level of 85 percent in 1974. Estimates indicate that capital expenditures in 1974 exceeded internally generated funds by 58 percent. Primarily this is due to the narrowing of profit margins and the continuing pattern of inflation. Persistent inflation has rendered depreciation allowances for existing equipment inadequate to pay for replacement and modernization.

A shift has also taken place with respect to the character of external capital invested. The ratio between debt and equity has risen sharply in the last decade. This trend continues, and the New York Stock Exchange reports that new issues of corporate stock have fallen from a high of $15.2 billion in 1972 to $7.6 billion in 1974. Additionally, it is anticipated that the legitimate need for equity capital will continue to be much greater than the amount suppliers in the marketplace are willing to provide.

The gap between the demand for unsecured credit and the available supply should widen at an accelerating pace during the next decade. Those who lend such funds will choose with greater selectivity. More and more frequently, maximum unsecured credit being offered by the banking system will fall short of valid company requirements.

Faced with this situation, what can financial vice presidents and treasurers do to help meet the cash flow deficit? One tool that is increasingly used is secured financing—and the use of accounts receivable as collateral for continuous revolving credit is especially popular. The following discusses advantages of secured financing during an inflationary period and gives examples of how some companies have profited by the technique.[1]

## THE ADVANTAGES

Secured financing has long been relied on for a major portion of growth capital by some industries, yet thousands of companies have never utilized this alternate, highly flexible source of working funds. For these companies, secured financing will represent an increasingly important means of obtaining capital in the critical years ahead.

Ordinarily a secured financing program can provide a company with more money than it can obtain through other financing techniques. Its use results from simple logic regarding the actual credit capacity of a prospective borrower. To illustrate, consider the analogy of a home mortgage. Few lending institutions would hand over $25,000, unsecured, to a young family who wanted to buy a new home. However the same family usually has little difficulty in obtaining the same amount in the form of a long-term mortgage. The only difference is collateral. The mortgage lender has the asset (the home, in this case) as security and can extend credit that he would refuse to offer on an unsecured basis.

In much the same way, businesses can make use of secured financing. The existence of collateral makes it possible for lending institutions to extend substantial credit to a greater range of borrowers than would otherwise be possible.

The secured lending approach is especially valuable because it is a method of utilizing a company's full financial capacity to meet all circumstances that take place during a company's lifetime; unusual growth, an acquisition, plant modernization, a downturn in business, perhaps even the need for a turnaround from severe financial problems.

One of the most typical examples is a manufacturing company whose current bank credit lines do not cover funds needed for continued growth. A secured borrowing package is set up based primarily on accounts receivable financing, and the major portion of the loan is generated by the borrower's own receivables. The receivables serve as collateral for continuous revolving credit, in contrast to bank loans, which must be renegotiated and renewed. In other words, an availability is created by the borrower's regular assign-

---

[1] From J. Allen Kerr, "Secured Financing for Improved Cash Flow," *Credit and Financial Management,* September 1975, pp. 30–32. Adapted with the permission of Credit and Financial Management (September 1975). © 1975 by the National Association of Credit Management.

ment of receivables, against which he draws. As his customers pay him, he repays the secured lender. Interest is charged only on the money actually in use, for the time it is in use, on a daily-usage basis.

When a borrower is in a very seasonal business and must build inventory in advance of his heavy shipping months, money can be supplied for labor and materials through a supplemental loan. The collateral is finished inventory, increasing in amount as the borrower builds toward his peak. He can repay the loan, separately from the accounts receivable loan, as his customers pay him during his busy period.

As another example consider a manufacturing company that wanted to purchase several new punch presses because cost reductions were mandatory to increase profits and meet competition. The machines represented a major capital investment. Ordinary financing meant making a very substantial down payment, and the company did not want to strip itself of cash for that purpose, despite projected savings. In fact, it did not wish to make any down payment at all.

The solution was a loan to cover the full purchase price, using as collateral both the machines to be acquired and some of the company's existing machines. Repayment was geared to the company's normal cash flow, minimizing any future squeeze on working funds as the payments were met.

In another instance an old-line consumer products manufacturer was unable to compete in a volatile but still attractive market. Strong competition had emerged from new companies, new products, new manufacturing methods, and new marketing ideas. Demand for the company's principal products had declined so rapidly that management had neither the time nor the surplus funds to cope with competition. The company's financial position was deteriorating rapidly. During a 5-year period earnings dropped from a substantial six-figure amount to an even larger deficit; and net worth dropped to only two-thirds as much as the firm's outstanding bank debt. The bank, of course, asked the company to pay the loan; yet the overriding need was for additional credit to reverse the downward trend.

Looking into the situation at the request of the bank, a commercial finance company found that sufficient credit could be extended on the basis of available collateral. The only question was the ability of the firm to make money on the funds it sought to borrow. A thorough study of the company and its market position indicated favorable prospects for the future.

Based on the study, funds were advanced to pay the bank, augment working cash, and proceed with marketing plans. In less than 2 years the company's net worth increased sevenfold. It was solidly in the black and earning well. The secured lender had been repaid, and the company was back with the original bank.

### COSTS

One of the most frequent misconceptions about secured financing relates to its cost. Often this is because insufficient cost analysis is applied. For example, a 7 percent preferred stock issue would tempt many companies as a device to add to equity base, and it would be a good financial move if the stock was intended to provide the basis for additional borrowing leverage. However the issuance could be a very expensive commitment for the future if the financial need was temporary. A stock issue at 7 percent has to be measured against the pretax equivalent of 14 percent interest on a short-term accommodation that can be retired when the need has passed.

Likewise, a company can regret the sale of common stock if it does not increase its after-tax earnings with the new capital to maintain its preissuance earnings per share. When common stocks of average companies have low price/earnings ratios and no real prospect for a return to favorable ratios in the foreseeable future, the issuing of stock at such prices is equivalent to borrowing at tremendous cost. Selling at five times earnings, for example, is equivalent to borrowing at a cost of 40 percent per year. The company would have to earn 20 percent after taxes to sustain the return of original shareholders.

### SOURCES

Secured financing is provided by commercial financing companies directly to their clients, by banks that staff themselves appropriately to offer the service, and by commercial finance companies and banks working coopera-tively through participation agreements. In a participation loan the administration and management of the credit, as well as a portion of the funds (generally 50 percent) are provided by the finance company. The bank supplies the balance of the funds. The entire loan, however, is secured.

The choice of a bank or a commercial finance company depends on the borrower company's position; either one could provide the better choice. Factors include the availability of lendable funds, the lender's policies and limitations, and promptness in coming to a decision regarding the loan request.

Now that better capitalized finance companies are acquiring funds on the commercial paper market, and commerical banks are increasing acquisi-tions of incremental funds through certificates of deposit, cost differentials between the two are seldom significant. Often companies end by working with both a bank and a finance company. Some banks with secured loan departments continue to participate with finance companies when specialized experience is required in a given industry or when unusual servicing features are needed. Additionally, banks that do not wish to fully staff for secured lending use finance company administrative assistance through participation arrangements.

## SUGGESTED FURTHER READING

"Bright Spot in Business Loans: Commercial Finance and Factoring," *Banking,* March 1975, pp. 33–34.

Kerr, J. Allen, "Secured Financing for Improved Cash Flow," *Credit and Financial Management,* September 1975, pp. 30–32.

Wilson, R. A., "Secured Lending Gets New Lease on Life," *Iron Age,* March 31, 1975, pp. 27–28.

## 81

## SELLING ORGANIZATION

*Discusses sales force organization and profitability during inflation.*

How does a sales manager know that his sales force is organized to return maximum profits on sales during an inflationary period? If he is setting up a new sales force, how can it most profitably be organized? If he heads an existing sales staff, what organizational changes can be made to increase profitability?

Profitability is the key word in an inflationary environment (see *New Selling Environment,* p. 245), and every sales manager should evaluate his organization periodically to ensure that it is achieving the highest possible returns. The following outline and flow chart constitute guidelines for establishing the most profitable type of sales force.[1]

Figure 9 shows the steps required in one method of (1) determining the type of sales force that can return the highest profits, (2) deciding on the number of salesmen needed and the management structure required to administer them, and (3) calculating maximum profitability of each of the various sales force options evaluated.

In measuring relative profitability in each alternate type of sales force, *contribution to operating margin* is the distinguishing factor. This is defined as follows:

$$COM = GM - SC$$

where $COM$ = contribution to operating margin

$GM$ = gross margin (net sales less manufacturing cost of products sold)

$SC$ = selling costs (direct costs of sales force)

In setting up the organization the types of sales territories to be evaluated should be defined. Most often these fall into two major areas: (1)

---

[1] From "Getting Organized, Step by Step," *Sales Management,* May 19, 1975, p. 27. Adapted with permission from *Sales Management, The Marketing Magazine.* Copyright 1975.

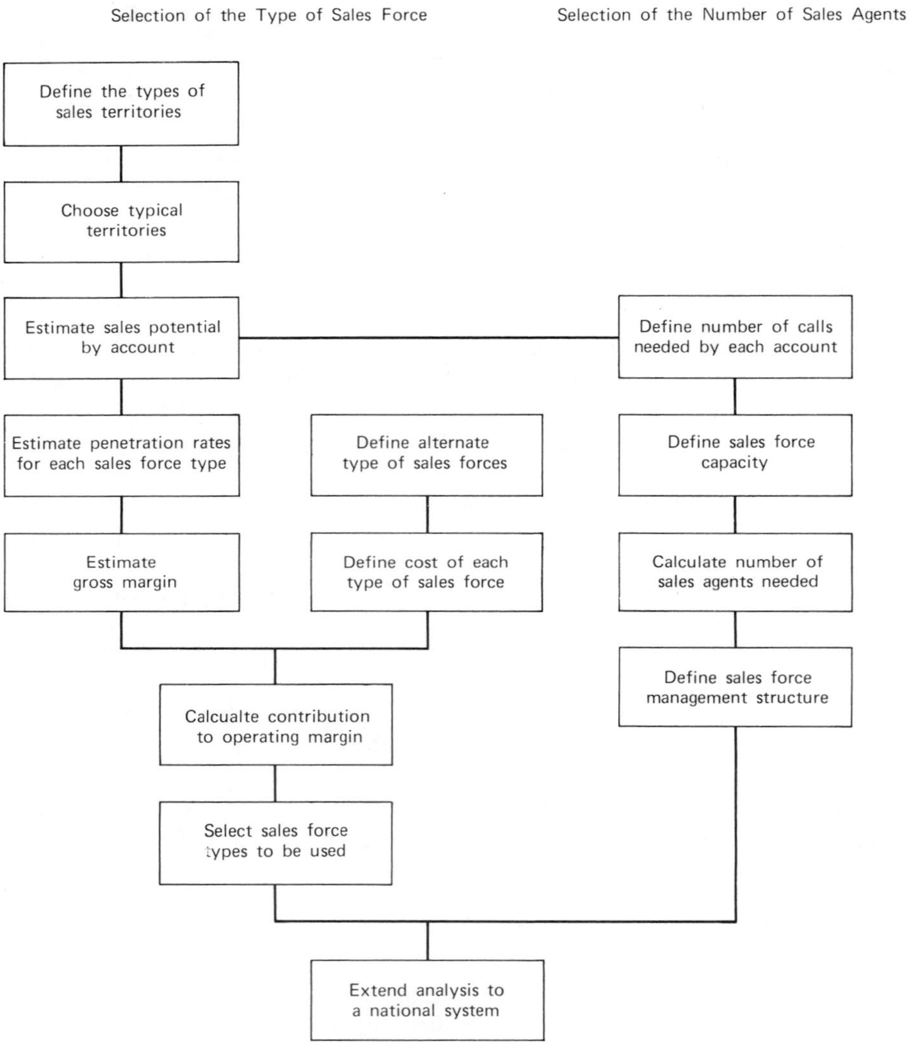

Selection of the Type of Sales Force                    Selection of the Number of Sales Agents

**Figure 9** Flow chart with guidelines for establishing most profitable type of sales force. (*Source: Sales Management,* May 19, 1975.)

concentrated territories in which large numbers of high-potential customers are located in a compact geographical area, and (2) broad territories in which small numbers of potential customers are spread over a wide geographical area.

Once the types of sales territories to be covered have been clearly defined, one representative territory of each type should be chosen for further analysis. All potential accounts in the sample territory should be identified, and an estimate should be made of sales potential for each account. Potential can be based on current data and/or potential future sales based on historical figures and projections.

When territories and their potential have been established, the next step is to evaluate various types of sales forces available. For example, should direct factory salesmen be used, or would commissioned manufacturers' representatives get the job done more effectively? In making this decision, the sales manager should estimate performance of alternate kinds of sales forces in selling specific types of accounts, determining the cost of each type of sales staff considered.

Next estimates should be made of the gross margin for each product to be sold at various volume levels. Once these estimates are determined, contribution of each type of sales staff to operating margin can be calculated. The type of sales force that makes the maximum contribution to operating margin should be chosen.

The following factors should be considered in selecting the number of sales agents required.

*Account Needs.*   Determine time and calls per week required by each account

*Sales Force Capacity.*   Determine time available and geographic coverage of salesmen.

*Numbers.*   Calculate the number of salesmen of each type required.

*Management.*   Define the structure needed to manage a typical territory.


## SUGGESTED FURTHER READING

Easingwood, C., "Heuristic Approach to Selecting Regions and Territories," *Operational Research Quarterly,* December 1973, pp. 527–534.

Fogg, C. Davis and Josef W. Rokus, "A Quantitative Method for Structuring a Profitable Sales Force," *Journal of Marketing,* July 1973, pp. 8–17.

"Getting Organized, Step by Step," *Sales Management,* May 19, 1975, p. 27.

Lodish, L. M., "Sales Territory Alignment to Maximize Profit," *Journal of Marketing Research,* February 1975, pp. 30–36.

Morris, J. H., Jr., "How to Organize Yourself for National Accounts Selling," *Sales Management,* December 9, 1974, pp. 29–31.

# SECTION 82

## SERVICE DEPARTMENT PRODUCTIVITY

*Outlines a three-step analysis program for measuring and improving productivity in internal service departments during inflationary periods.*

In most business organizations internal service departments are normally classified as expense centers or cost centers, and invariably they receive less management attention than profit centers. As a result, costs incurred by these departments usually represent a neglected area of cost control. Some of the key reasons for the relative lack of attention to these operations include the following:

• The expenses incurred by service departments are in most cases relatively small.
• Service department expenses are often allocated to the various line or product departments.
• Some expenses incurred by these departments are considered uncontrollable.
• Managerial attention tends to focus on the quality of the service rather than cost control.

During an inflationary period, when all costs should be carefully examined and all areas probed for productive efficiency, internal service departments should be scrutinized closely. Often a relatively simple and inexpensive analysis program uncovers many areas in which cost-effective efficiencies can be implemented to reduce expenses and improve productivity, thus helping to offset the effects of inflation.

The following three-step analysis program can be used to measure and improve productivity in nearly any internal service department.[1]

---

[1] Adapted from Shu S. Liao, "Three-Step Analysis Measures Productivity," *Management Accounting,* August 1975, pp. 25–28.

## THREE-STEP ANALYSIS

A three-step analysis program should be used to develop and implement improvements in service department operations. The three steps are systems analysis, individual task analysis, and optimal-level analysis.

### Systems Analysis

Systems analysis is the selection of elements, relationships, and procedures to achieve a specific purpose, such as the use of a road map to reach a specific geographical location. In evaluating existing service department productivity, simple systems analysis techniques should be used to determine whether the department's methods are appropriate.

In examining the efficiency of an internal printing department, for example, the analysis would logically follow two steps. First, printing requirements should be reviewed to eliminate unnecessary printing requests. In most businesses, line departments typically make service requests for their own convenience, without regard to the overall effect on the company. By having the systems analyst review requests with line management, related costs can be brought into focus.

Second, individuals and work flow should be evaluated to pinpoint bottlenecks and eliminate nonproductive slack time. This is necessary to prevent work standards from being established for inefficient methods. Elimination of nonproductive slack time always results in cost reductions, even before a work measurement program is undertaken.

PERT networks are a useful approach in systems analysis. The PERT technique, although mainly used in engineering and research scheduling, can be an effective aid in regulating work flow in most internal service departments, especially with large and complex work procedures. In small, simple projects, the critical path and bottlenecks in the work flow often can be determined by visual inspection or actual work observation. Figure 10 is a simplified flow chart for the printing department already discussed.

### Individual Task Analysis

After productivity improvement opportunities have been found through streamlining work procedures, the next step is to analyze individual job tasks through work measurement.

Several preliminary steps must be taken before the work measurement program starts.

• The tasks to be measured must be determined.

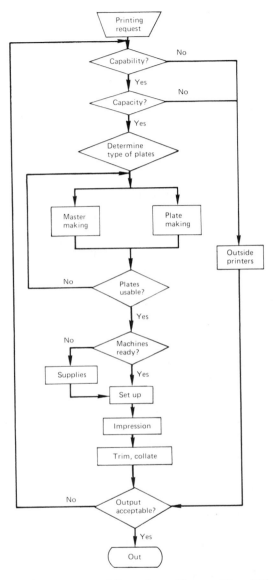

**Figure 10** Printing department workflow chart. (*Source:* Liao, "Three-Step Analysis Measures Productivity," *Management Accounting*, August 1975.)

- The measurement techniques must be selected.
- A unit of measurement for reporting purposes must be established.

In determining the tasks to be measured, the beginning and ending points for each job must be defined and a description of each task must be drawn up. It is not necessary to measure each job step involved, only relatively time-consuming functions. In a print shop, for example, plate making, machine set up, and impressions account for the bulk of the work. Standards should be developed for these three key functions. Once the beginning and ending points for each job step are defined, each motion element involved in the performance of the job should be listed in motion-flow sequence.

The technique to be used for measurement is determined by the type of task to be measured, the intended use of the measurement data, and the relevant cost factor. Simple techniques are frequently best, since they require less cost and effort. More precise standards can be established for more important tasks, and cheaper techniques can be used for less critical operations. No single measurement technique is suited to all types of tasks; some are most appropriate for clerical work, others for man/machine operations. Highly accurate predetermined elemental time standards are commercially available and can be used to advantage. For small-scale operations, stopwatch time studies are relatively inexpensive and offer a wide latitude for adjustment as circumstances dictate.

After the technique of measurement is selected, a unit of measurement must be established according to the ultimate use of the measured data. If mathematical models are to be used in the analysis, a more detailed unit of measurement may be justified, depending on the cost factor. For other uses of data, such as feedback, different units of measure can be applied. In the printing operation, for instance, standards for each job step should be established and communicated to the printing department manager. Actual performance of each employee's work then can be measured.

### Optimal-Level Analysis

It is important to keep fixed costs as low as possible in a productivity improvement program. The minimum acceptable level of fixed costs, however, depends on the optimal conditions of the work center. Use of standards established through work measurement can produce a theoretical optimality, but actual conditions are usually somewhat below this because of quality demands, deadlines, and other conditions.

In addition to the time standards for each task, work volume and peak load periods should be projected with a reasonable degree of accuracy. Usually this information can be obtained from historical records. A programming model then can be developed to determine the most effective level of staff and equipment to meet the needs of the department at the lowest fixed cost.

In the printing department example, projected volume might show that anticipated printing requirements exceed machine capacity. The alternatives might be to buy additional machines and hire operators for them, or to hire operators for a second shift. After taking into account additional salaries, fringe benefits, machine usage, unsatisfied printing demand, and so on, it might be determined that the best level of staffing necessitates three additional operators for a second shift.

### IMPLEMENTATION

Implementation of a productivity improvement program depends on the specific conditions of the internal service department involved. Administrative policies sometimes alter the solution obtained from the analysis of optimal-level operations. The important factor in implementation is to keep fixed costs at the lowest level consistent with the company's goals. If a fixed-cost item is subject to management's discretion, it should be examined to see whether the cost can be reduced without affecting expenses elsewhere. Once accepted, the optimal level of operations should be used as the basis for measuring the performance of the service department.

A good record-keeping system is an indispensable part of the program. Without accurate, timely feedback, time standards developed under the program become meaningless and the benefits of the program are negated. Two reporting systems are required.

• The supervisor of the service department must have reports of his employees' performance as sources of reliable information on which to base necessary corrective actions. The reports should be so designed that information is presented in a manner enabling the user to identify and solve the problems.
• A reporting system is needed relating to the transfer pricing method, which can be full-cost, cost-plus, or agreed-upon-price. Most internal service departments are organized as a cost or service center in a decentralized structure of operation. This is why expenses incurred in a service department most often should be charged to other departments in a

manner that will motivate affected individuals to act in the best interests of the company.

## SUGGESTED FURTHER READING

Liao, Shu S., "Three-Step Analysis Measures Productivity," *Management Accounting,* August 1975, pp. 25–28.

## SERVICE OF CUSTOMERS

*Recommends methods of increasing the profitability of the customer service function.*

The variable costs that fall under the general heading of "customer service" can have a serious affect on profitability, especially during inflationary periods. These costs—like most others—rise because of inflation, and firms that do not periodically analyze the costs of servicing their accounts will find profits eroding. Even in stable economic situations, customer service costs on individual accounts should be tabulated at regular intervals to determine how profitable each customer *really* is.

Customer service costs include such areas as order and billing costs, shipping costs, warehousing and order-assembly costs, inventory costs, returned goods, and freight loss and damage. Collectively they can often spell the difference between a highly profitable account and one that produces minimal returns or even a loss.

One aspect that is frequently overlooked in trying to lower customer service costs is the salesman's ability to influence positively or negatively the amount of time and money spent servicing each account. Following are recommendations for increasing the profitability of the customer service function in this key area.[1]

### FACTORS INFLUENCING CUSTOMER SERVICE COSTS

Let us assume that a firm has two accounts of roughly the same size— $100,000 a year. On the surface they may appear to be equally profitable, but the most basic analysis reveals a wide variation in returns.

Suppose, for example, that Company A orders 4 times a year in truckload lots of 40,000 pounds, at $25,000 an order. Company B, on the other hand, orders 30 times a year in lots ranging from 50 pounds upward. These two ordering patterns can spell the difference between profit and loss on the

[1] Adapted from Warren Blanding, "Customer Service: Writing a Happy Ending for the *Titanic*," *Sales Management*, May 19, 1975, pp. 32–34.

accounts. The large orders from Company A result in many economies of scale:

• Truckload lots have lower-cost transportation rates.
• Order processing costs are the same for a 40,000-pound order as for a 50-pound order.
• The full truckload can be locked and sealed at its point of origin, reducing chances of loss and/or damage through intermediate handlings.
• Regular, anticipated ordering results in efficient, anticipated warehouse scheduling.
• Tracking is simplified, since the order moves directly from point of origin to destination.
• Since only four orders are placed each year, customer service representatives must trace, expedite, or deal with complaints (if any) on these four occasions only.

On the other hand, the sporadic ordering of Company B creates a broad range of profit-diminishing problems. Often the small orders are emergency calls, necessitated because the company does not maintain proper inventories. This results in the following conditions:

• Small shipments transported at high penalty rates.
• More likelihood of delay, losses, and damage due to intermediate handling. This, in turn, leads to increased customer complaints, phone calls, tracing, expediting, and so on.
• Adjustments; damaged or lost goods must be salvaged and claims filed. Replacements must be shipped.
• Increased order processing and order-assembly costs, the result of 30 shipments of varying sizes.
• Increased warehousing costs. Because many of the orders are on an emergency basis, warehouse crews may have to be paid overtime and/or other customer orders will be delayed.
• Inefficient handling. Palletization, possible with larger orders, is much more profitable than handling small, individual orders manually.

A more thorough analysis (Table 59) clearly demonstrates the marked difference that order size can make on profitability. For the purpose of this analysis, it has been assumed that order processing costs are constant and that other order costs vary with number of units.

Most firms have a pricing scale that theoretically accounts for the increased costs of handling small orders, but it is seldom reliable or realistic, since it is nearly impossible to cost analyze all aspects of customer service operations.

**Table 59  Order Size/Profitability Relationship**[a]

|  |  | 20 Units | 40 Units | 100 Units | 200 Units |
|---|---|---|---|---|---|
| 1. | Sales per unit | $40.00 | $80.00 | $200.00 | $400.00 |
| 2. | Cost of goods sold | 30.00 | 60.00 | 150.00 | 300.00 |
| 3. | Difference | 10.00 | 20.00 | 50.00 | 100.00 |
| 4. | Order processing | 3.00 | 3.00 | 3.00 | 3.00 |
| 5. | Order assembly | 1.20 | 1.23 | 1.72 | 2.37 |
| 5a. | Checking | 1.00 | 1.10 | 1.40 | 1.90 |
| 6. | Packing | 2.60 | 2.87 | 3.68 | 5.03 |
| 7. | Total | $ 7.80 | $ 8.20 | $ 9.80 | $ 12.30 |
| 8. | Profit/overhead contribution (line 3 minus line 7) | $ 2.20 | $11.80 | $ 40.20 | $ 87.70 |
| 9. | Profit/percentage of gross sales (line 8 divided by line 1) | 5.5% | 14.8% | 20.1% | 21.9% |

[a] *Source:* Blanding, "Customer Service," *Sales Management,* May 19, 1975, p. 33.

Having pinpointed problem customers—such as Company B—what can be done to make the accounts more profitable? In some cases there is strong justification for dropping the accounts entirely and concentrating salesmen's efforts on expanding volume with smaller, but potentially highly profitable customers. More often, however, it is better to attempt to educate erratic buyers to ensure that ordering goes more smoothly for both parties.

Here the salesman is in a make-or-break position, and his attitude is often the determinant in the account's profit contribution. Sales training should constantly stress profitability of accounts, not merely the need for volume increases (see *New Selling Environment,* p. 245). Once salesmen have been profit educated, they, in turn, must carry the word to problem customers, keeping in mind the following key areas when making sales calls.

### Economic Order Sizes

Sell your company's sales units and persuade customers to make purchases in units that are economical for you as well as for him. Know how many units of your product are in each carton, each masterpack, each pallet—

whatever applies to your goods. Know truckload unit numbers and recommend them. It is natural for orders to be given in dozens, hundreds, or other round numbers, but these are not always the most profitable sizes for order handling or transportation. Learn your most economic order sizes and sell them.

### Lead Time

Refrain from using fast delivery or special attention as a sales tool. There will be occasional exceptions, of course, but make it a rule to sell standard lead time. Special promises run up costs and invite errors, often negating the good will you had hoped to achieve. Deemphasize hard selling at the end of a sales period; it brings a flood of orders, burying your customer service department. Explain to accounts that regularly scheduled buying in economical units will ensure the most reliable service.

### Substitutions

Get specific written instructions from customers on acceptable order substitutions. This facilitates order filling when it is impossible to meet specifications exactly. With this advance information, orders are less likely to be delayed while the customer is being tracked down and asked whether substitutions are acceptable. Additionally, problems of improper substitution will be avoided.

### Accurate Orders

Make certain that customers have and use exact product descriptions and codes on all orders. If order forms are incorrectly filled in, they will be put aside for handling later, sent back to the customer, or filled by guesswork. All these makeshift solutions cause delays, which can prove costly because of subsequent rush transportation and/or warehouse overtime, to say nothing of strained customer relations.

### Unprofitable Customers

Lay it on the line with unprofitable customers. There is nothing wrong with expecting to make profits, and most habitual offenders will listen if you sit down and go over the situation with them. They know that if you do not make sufficient profits, they will have to find a new supplier, which may not be easy if their reputation is industry-wide. At any rate, there is little to lose. If an unprofitable customer goes elsewhere, more sales time can be devoted to nurturing and expanding smaller, more profitable accounts.

## SUGGESTED FURTHER READING

Blanding, Warren, "Customer Service: Writing a Happy Ending for the *Titanic*," *Sales Management,* May 19, 1975, pp. 32–34.

# 84

## STOCK AND BOND PRICES

*Outlines cyclical trend analysis as a method of maximizing
profitability of financial investments in stocks and bonds in an
inflationary environment.* [1]

During inflationary periods interest rates on loans and bonds increase rapidly. These increases are the natural result of the supply and demand of available funds. As prices increase, consumers and businesses need more money to finance purchases and transactions. When inflationary price rises are anticipated, businesses borrow to invest in productive capacity, inventories, and durable goods before prices go even higher. At the same time, savings drop because interest rates paid are usually not high enough to compensate savers for the inflation-induced decline in the real value of money.

The nominal rate of interest on loanable funds is usually expressed by economists as the real rate of return plus the anticipated rate of inflation. Thus if inflation is expected to increase by 1 percent, the interest on loanable funds would go up by 1 percent.

The inflationary cycle has a marked effect on the availability of credit. The beginning of the cycle is generally characterized by significant increases in the money supply and credit, coupled with relatively low rates of interest. Loanable funds are readily available. However the subsequent rapid escalation in prices results in tight liquidity. Prices increase more rapidly than the money supply, causing the real supply of money to decline and interest rates to rise dramatically. Attempts by monetary authorities to correct the situation through faster monetary growth only result in a more intense liquidity problem at a later date. Until inflation is brought under control, tight liquidity will be part of the economy.

The relationship between bond yields and the length of maturity is also affected by these economic forces. Normally short-term notes have a lower interest rate than long-term bonds. This difference is instrumental in attracting long-term funds. During periods of rapid inflation, however, the situation is reversed. Short-term rates advance faster than rates on long-term bonds, and the yield curve is inverted. This is because borrowers

[1] Adapted from *Trust & Estates,* January 1975, p. 22; Copyright Communication Channels, Inc., 461 Eighth Ave., New York, N.Y. 10001 (1975).

anticipate that interest rates will drop to lower levels and they shorten their obligations, not wanting to pay high rates for extended periods. Also, lenders are attracted by the higher rates not usually available on short-term notes and, at the same time, are reluctant to lend for long periods because of possible losses if inflation accelerates. These factors combine to force short-term rates up sharply, while holding long-term rates down.

## EFFECTS ON STOCKS AND BONDS

Most financial assets are lowered in value in an economy characterized by tight liquidity and high interest rates. An existing bond's price reflects the discounted value of the interest and principal payments due in the future. The higher the interest rate, the lower the value of return expected in the future, as the following example indicates.

$100 to be received in one year is worth $95.24 today if 5 percent interest is to be earned over the next year, but only $90.91 at 10 percent interest. The decline in value is even greater for returns expected further in the future. A payment of $100 in five years is valued at $78.35 at 5 percent interest, but $62.09 if the rate of interest rises to 10 percent.[2]

Stock prices also react to short-term influences, but over time tend to reflect their fundamental values, as measured by the discounted value of dividends.

For these reasons prices of stocks and bonds often fall rapidly as inflation increases. A recent example was the sharp decline in values of stocks and bonds during the 1973–1974 spiral. However a different situation emerges once the rate of inflation plateaus or starts to go down, even if the rate of inflation remains high. After the rate of return has adjusted to reflect the inflation rate, stocks should behave normally in line with expected changes in dividends and earnings. At the same time, most corporations initially show higher profits due to inflation, the result of prices rising faster than costs.

The result, then, of an acceleration-deceleration inflationary cycle is a complementary cycle in stock prices. As inflation picks up and interest rates rise, the value of stocks declines. This decline slows down in tandem with a slowing of the inflation rate. Finally, lower interest rates and higher profits combine with deceleration of inflation to raise stocks from their depressed levels. Unlike fixed-rate bonds, stocks represent ownership of real

---

[2] Ben E. Laden, "The Impact of Inflation on the Investor," *Trusts & Estates*, January 1975, p. 23. Copyright Communications Channels, Inc., 1975.

assets and therefore can be expected to compensate for inflation eventually through increased earnings and dividends.

This cyclical reaction of stock and bond prices has occurred during each of the five major inflationary periods this century in the United States. In each instance bond yields increased during periods of rapidly accelerating inflation and prices of outstanding bonds dropped. Stock prices bottomed as inflation increased but recovered vigorously as the inflationary rate topped out and began its descent. "A comparison of trends in stock prices and bond prices indicates that when bonds were attractive for purchase, stocks were even more attractive as a hedge for the long-term investor.[3]

A recent study conducted for the National Bureau of Economic Research investigating the effects of inflation on stock values in 24 countries also supports the theory that periods of high inflation are followed by periods of improved stock prices.[4]

The implications of these cyclical patterns are obvious for executives charged with the responsibility of investing short- or long-term corporate funds in stocks and/or bonds during inflationary periods. By keeping abreast of Federal Reserve actions to increase or decrease the rate of money supply growth, inflationary upswings and declines can be anticipated. Changes in money supply tend to precede swings in the inflation rate by about 2 years (see *Money Supply*, p. 229).

At the first signs of persistent increases in the inflationary rate, stocks and bonds should be divested in favor of short-term "money market" investments, such as certificates of deposit, commercial paper, and U.S. Treasury bills. As the cycle progresses and the rate of inflation levels or begins to drop, these short-term investments should be converted into a portfolio of stocks and bonds, which should be held until the inflationary deceleration bottoms out and begins another upward spiral.

Thus by switching in and out of different investments at various stages in the inflationary cycle, the corporate investment officer can usually show a profit, even in periods of rapid inflation. Perhaps more important, the use of cyclical trend analysis can help prevent substantial investment losses.

## SUGGESTED FURTHER READING

Klein, Roger and William Wolman, *The Beat Inflation Strategy,* Simon & Schuster, New York, 1975.

---

[3] Laden, "The Impact of Inflation on the Investor," *Trusts & Estates,* January 1975, p. 23. Copyright Communications Channels, Inc., 1975.

[4] Philip Cagan, "Common Stock Values and Inflation—The Historical Record of Many Countries," National Bureau of Economic Reseach, Inc., New York, March 1974.

Laden, Ben. E., "The Impact of Inflation on the Investor," *Trusts & Estates*, January 1975, pp. 22–25.

Levey, M. S., "Bond Portfolio Management in an Inflationary Environment," *Best's Review* (Property edition), November 1974, p. 10.

Lintner, J., "Inflation and Security Returns," *Journal of Finance*, May 1975, pp. 259–280.

Shepherd, W. G., "Profits of Hindsight," *Business Week*, January 20, 1975, p. 65.

Siegelman, L., "Function of Interest Rates in the Super-Bear Syndrome," *Trusts & Estates*, September 1974, pp. 597–599.

Stinson, J., "Beating the Markets—Cyclically Speaking," *Financial World*, March 12, 1975, pp. 20–23.

# 85

## STRIKE LOSS COMPUTER

*Illustrates a device that can help forestall strikes by showing employees the pay losses they would incur, including an inflation factor.*

The strike loss computer is a personalized device that can be used by businesses and industries to graphically show employees exactly how much they would lose by striking during an inflationary period. The computer sets out the length of time needed to recover wages lost for each week off work, based on the hourly increase being demanded and the original take-home pay (Figure 11). Also included is a factor that takes into account the devaluation of money in real terms due to inflation.

Originally developed by the Republic Aviation Corporation, the basic format of the strike loss computer can be adapted to nearly all areas of business and industry. Use of the computer can be an important management tool in persuading employees that a strike would cost them more than the resulting gains.

Strike loss computer for _Employee's name_

| Weekly net pay | Weekly inflation loss | | | Total weekly net loss* | Length of time (weeks) to recover each week's loss if you strike for | | | | | |
|---|---|---|---|---|---|---|---|---|---|---|
| | 12% | 15% | 20% | | 0¢/hr | 3¢/hr | 6¢/hr | 9¢/hr | 12¢/hr | 15¢/hr |
| $300.00 | $0.69 | $0.87 | $1.14 | $300.87 | Never | 251 | 125 | 84 | 63 | 50 |
| 280.00 | 0.64 | 0.81 | 1.06 | 280.81 | Never | 234 | 117 | 78 | 59 | 47 |
| 260.00 | 0.60 | 0.75 | 0.99 | 260.75 | Never | 217 | 109 | 72 | 54 | 43 |
| 240.00 | 0.55 | 0.70 | 0.91 | 240.70 | Never | 201 | 100 | 67 | 50 | 40 |
| 220.00 | 0.51 | 0.64 | 0.84 | 220.64 | Never | 184 | 92 | 61 | 46 | 37 |
| 200.00 | 0.46 | 0.58 | 0.76 | 200.58 | Never | 167 | 84 | 56 | 42 | 33 |
| 180.00 | 0.41 | 0.52 | 0.68 | 180.52 | Never | 150 | 75 | 50 | 38 | 30 |
| 160.00 | 0.37 | 0.46 | 0.61 | 160.46 | Never | 134 | 67 | 44 | 33 | 27 |

*Assuming 15% inflation.

**Figure 11**   Typical format for strike loss computer.

## SUGGESTED FURTHER READING

Hutchinson, J. G., *Management Under Strike Conditions,* Holt, Rinehart, & Winston, New York, 1966.

## SUGGESTION SYSTEMS

*Outlines key elements in setting up employee suggestion systems to achieve inflation-offsetting goals.*

Cost savings that can come from effective employee suggestion systems have been well documented. Surveys conducted by the National Association of Suggestion Systems (NASS) have shown that on the average companies "realize $5.70 in tangible net cost savings for each $1 spent on running the suggestion system. Projecting aggregate savings of all 1000 NASS members, the figure is $470 million . . . in first-year savings alone."[1]

The cost savings that can accrue through suggestion systems are doubly significant during inflationary periods. Besides the profit improvement made possible by cost reduction and the more efficient use of assets, employee-generated ideas can result in many other inflation-offsetting benefits: increased productivity, waste reduction, lowered manufacturing costs, energy conservation, materials substitutions, and so on. When oil prices escalated, for example, a flight officer of a large United States air carrier had the idea of shifting cargo toward the back of the aircraft to change the plane's center of gravity. The result was a considerable saving on jet fuel at takeoff—an energy-conserving idea that saved the company $458,500 the first year.

The following outlines the key elements in setting up an employee suggestion system and supplies guidelines for making the system work.

### KEY ELEMENTS

At the outset management decisions are required in three key areas: system objectives, level of commitment, and system design and operation.

### System Objectives

The main thrust of the suggestion system must be precisely defined, as well as any secondary objectives. For example, is the suggestion system's

[1] Milton A. Tatter, "Turning Ideas into Gold," *Management Review,* March 1975, p. 5.

primary objective increased productivity? Or energy savings? Or cost reduction? Perhaps all these and other areas as well can be grouped under the primary objective of an overall company anti-inflation campaign.

In addition to defining objectives, management should set down the results desired and a time framework for achieving the results.

### Level of Commitment

Experience has shown that active, measurable, demonstrated commitment by management is one of the most important elements in achieving tangible suggestion system results. This means that executives must view the suggestion program as a part of business, on a par with sales, production, R & D, finance, and other functional elements. Additionally, top management must communicate the system's importance to other managerial levels through personal involvement, presence at awards presentations, adequate budgeting, and sustained enthusiasm.

### System Design and Operation

The suggestion system and its format must reflect awareness of the importance of the functional location of the system, the identity of the administrator, whether the system is to be centralized or decentralized, initial staffing requirements, budget allocations, report generation, and other matters. Figure 12 illustrates how a well-designed system might operate.

### ADMINISTRATING SUGGESTION SYSTEMS

The following 10 elements are among the most important in insuring maximum benefits from suggestion systems.

*Supervisory Involvement.* The hourly paid production workers in most manufacturing companies usually generate the most valuable ideas, simply because they know specific work problems better than anyone else. For this reason, first-line supervisors play a key role in helping workers generate ideas, modify concepts, and get them down on paper. This responsibility can be reinforced if top management uses it as a factor in supervisory job-performance evaluation.

*Timely Processing.* Suggestions should be processed in about 30 days, and in no case in more than 60 days.

*Promotion.* To sustain worker interest, the system should be highlighted using periodic contests and other means of recognition.

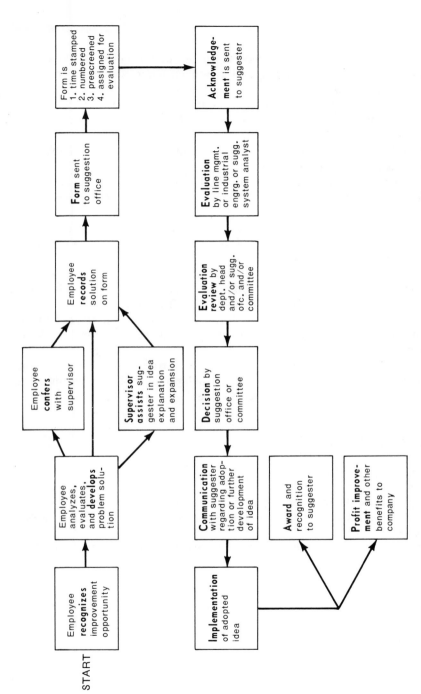

**Figure 12** Flow chart for well-designed suggestion system. (*Source*: Tatter, "How the Idea System Works." Reprinted by permission of the publisher from *Management Review*, March 1975. © 1975 by AMACOM, a division of American Management Assns.)

*Communication.* Quarterly reports on the performance of the system should be made to management, and an annual report should be compiled for management and all employees. The annual report should include total number of suggestions received, total number of ideas used, total awards paid, individual department performance, processing time, trends, and general commentary.

*Eligibility Standards.* The program should define *who* is eligible and *what* areas are eligible for improvement suggestions.

*Training.* Training programs should be incorporated to ensure that management, supervisors, and employees are informed of responsibilities and opportunities the suggestion system creates.

*Employee Recognition.* Full publicity should be given to award presentations, including presence of top management, coverage in the house organ, and even use of the local press.

*Accurate Evaluations.* To avoid misunderstandings that could undermine the system, the evaluation process should be spelled out in detail and fully understood. Evaluators should be qualified for the job.

*Forms and Printed Matter.* All forms and printed matter used in the system should be functional and graphically attractive and should facilitate the submission of ideas.

*The Administrator.* The choice of administrator is critical. As the program's sales arm, coordinator, and troubleshooter, he or she must be committed to planned, goal-oriented change.

**SUGGESTED FURTHER READING**

Clutterbuck, D., "Tractor Factory Ploughs a New Path," *International Management,* October 1974, pp. 54–55.

"Money Buys a Safe Plant," *Industry Week,* April 28, 1975, p. 49.

Oates, D., "Company Planning that Involves Everyone," *International Management,* January 1975, pp. 42–44.

Tatter, Milton A., "Turning Ideas into Gold," *Management Review,* March 1975, p. 4–10.

# SECTION

# 87

## TABLES FOR COMPUTING
## INFLATIONARY EFFECTS

*Sets out factors for quickly computing the effects of various projected rates of inflation.*

Being able to quickly calculate the impact of a given rate of inflation over a period of time can be helpful in many ways. Purchasing directors, for example, may want to project future prices of equipment or raw materials based on inflationary trends. Management may wish to construct models that require an estimation of the impact inflation will have on future wage costs. Salesmen often can make use of inflationary projections in convincing customers to buy now, rather than wait for inflationary increases.

Table 60 sets out factors that can be used to quickly calculate the impact of any rate of inflation up to 15 percent for any period of time up to 10 years. To determine how a given inflationary rate will affect future costs, the current figure is multiplied by the inflation factor for the number of years required.

For example, if a piece of machinery is selling today for $15,000 and a purchasing director wishes to forecast what the same piece of equipment will cost in 3 years, assuming a 9 percent annual inflationary rate, a factor of 1.2950 is used. The calculation is carried out as follows:

$$\$15,000 \times 1.2950 = \$19,425$$

Or, if certain workers are now earning $6.37 per hour and management wants to determine how much an 11 percent annual inflationary rate will increase these wages in 5 years, a factor of 1.6850 is used and the calculation is

$$\$6.37 \times 1.6850 = \$10.73$$

Conversely, it is often advantageous to be able to quickly calculate the devaluing effect of inflation on the purchasing power of money. Management may wish to determine how much will be lost in real terms if cash is held rather than invested, how this year's financial figures compare with last year's on a true value basis, or how much a long-term obligation will effectively be devalued because of inflation.

**377**

## Table 60 Inflation Factors—10 Years

| Annual Rate of Inflation (%) | Inflation factor at end of | | | | | | | | | |
|---|---|---|---|---|---|---|---|---|---|---|
| | Year 1 | Year 2 | Year 3 | Year 4 | Year 5 | Year 6 | Year 7 | Year 8 | Year 9 | Year 10 |
| 1 | 1.0100 | 1.0201 | 1.0303 | 1.0406 | 1.0510 | 1.0615 | 1.0721 | 1.0828 | 1.0936 | 1.1046 |
| 2 | 1.0200 | 1.0404 | 1.0612 | 1.0824 | 1.1040 | 1.1261 | 1.1486 | 1.1716 | 1.1950 | 1.2189 |
| 3 | 1.0300 | 1.0609 | 1.0927 | 1.1255 | 1.1593 | 1.1941 | 1.2299 | 1.2668 | 1.3048 | 1.3439 |
| 4 | 1.0400 | 1.0816 | 1.1249 | 1.1699 | 1.2167 | 1.2654 | 1.3160 | 1.3686 | 1.4233 | 1.4802 |
| 5 | 1.0500 | 1.1025 | 1.1576 | 1.2155 | 1.2763 | 1.3401 | 1.4071 | 1.4475 | 1.5514 | 1.6290 |
| 6 | 1.0600 | 1.1236 | 1.1910 | 1.2625 | 1.3382 | 1.4185 | 1.5036 | 1.5938 | 1.6894 | 1.7908 |
| 7 | 1.0700 | 1.1449 | 1.2250 | 1.3108 | 1.4026 | 1.5008 | 1.6059 | 1.7183 | 1.8386 | 1.9672 |
| 8 | 1.0800 | 1.1664 | 1.2597 | 1.3606 | 1.4693 | 1.5868 | 1.7137 | 1.8508 | 1.9989 | 2.1588 |
| 9 | 1.0900 | 1.1881 | 1.2950 | 1.4116 | 1.5386 | 1.6771 | 1.8280 | 1.9925 | 2.1718 | 2.3673 |
| 10 | 1.1000 | 1.2100 | 1.3310 | 1.4641 | 1.6105 | 1.7716 | 1.9488 | 2.1437 | 2.3581 | 2.5939 |
| 11 | 1.1100 | 1.2321 | 1.3676 | 1.5180 | 1.6850 | 1.8703 | 2.0760 | 2.3044 | 2.5579 | 2.8393 |
| 12 | 1.1200 | 1.2544 | 1.4049 | 1.5735 | 1.7623 | 1.9738 | 2.2107 | 2.4760 | 2.7731 | 3.1059 |
| 13 | 1.1300 | 1.2769 | 1.4429 | 1.6305 | 1.8425 | 2.0820 | 2.3527 | 2.6585 | 3.0041 | 3.3946 |
| 14 | 1.1400 | 1.2996 | 1.4815 | 1.6889 | 1.9253 | 2.1948 | 2.5021 | 2.8524 | 3.2517 | 3.7069 |
| 15 | 1.1500 | 1.3225 | 1.5209 | 1.7490 | 2.0114 | 2.3131 | 2.6600 | 3.0590 | 3.5179 | 4.0456 |

## Table 61 Devaluation factors—10 years

| Annual Rate of Inflation (%) | Devaluation factor at end of | | | | | | | | | |
|---|---|---|---|---|---|---|---|---|---|---|
| | Year 1 | Year 2 | Year 3 | Year 4 | Year 5 | Year 6 | Year 7 | Year 8 | Year 9 | Year 10 |
| 1 | .990 | .980 | .971 | .961 | .951 | .942 | .933 | .924 | .914 | .905 |
| 2 | .980 | .961 | .942 | .924 | .906 | .888 | .871 | .854 | .837 | .820 |
| 3 | .971 | .943 | .915 | .888 | .863 | .837 | .813 | .789 | .766 | .744 |
| 4 | .962 | .925 | .889 | .855 | .823 | .790 | .760 | .731 | .703 | .676 |
| 5 | .952 | .907 | .864 | .823 | .784 | .746 | .711 | .677 | .645 | .614 |
| 6 | .943 | .890 | .840 | .792 | .747 | .705 | .665 | .627 | .592 | .558 |
| 7 | .935 | .873 | .816 | .763 | .713 | .666 | .623 | .582 | .544 | .508 |
| 8 | .926 | .857 | .794 | .735 | .681 | .630 | .584 | .540 | .500 | .463 |
| 9 | .917 | .842 | .772 | .708 | .650 | .596 | .547 | .502 | .460 | .422 |
| 10 | .909 | .826 | .751 | .683 | .621 | .564 | .513 | .466 | .424 | .386 |
| 11 | .901 | .812 | .731 | .659 | .593 | .535 | .482 | .434 | .391 | .352 |
| 12 | .893 | .797 | .712 | .634 | .567 | .507 | .452 | .404 | .361 | .322 |
| 13 | .885 | .783 | .693 | .613 | .543 | .480 | .425 | .376 | .333 | .295 |
| 14 | .877 | .769 | .675 | .592 | .519 | .456 | .400 | .351 | .308 | .270 |
| 15 | .870 | .756 | .658 | .572 | .497 | .432 | .376 | .327 | .284 | .247 |

Table 61 sets out factors that can be used to calculate the loss in purchasing power of the dollar for inflationary rates up to 15 percent for any period of time up to 10 years. The current dollar figure is multiplied by the devaluation factor for the number of years required.

For example, if management wishes to see how this year's profits of $106,500 compare with last year's profits of $97,000 in real terms (assuming an 8 percent inflationary rate), the calculation is as follows:

$$\$106,500 \times .926 = \$98,619$$

# SECTION 88

## TRADE CREDIT TECHNIQUE

*Outlines the advantages of delaying payments for goods or
services during inflationary periods.*

The trade credit technique is the delaying of payment for purchased
materials or equipment, since normal credit terms are less costly than short-
term bank financing. The method can be especially advantageous during
inflationary periods when bank financing is more expensive than usual and
the money owed declines in real value almost weekly.

As an example, assume that a firm buys a piece of machinery for
$50,000. The seller offers a 2 percent discount for prompt payment. If the
company uses 12 percent bank financing to pay for the equipment, net
financing costs will be 10 percent per year (12% − 2%), or about $416 a
month. However, if the selling company will wait 90 days for payment, the
2 percent discount that is lost ($1000) is less costly than the bank interest on
money borrowed to settle the account ($1248). Additionally, assuming a 12
percent inflationary rate, the $50,000 obligation only costs the purchaser
$49,250 in real value because of devaluation in monetary purchasing power
that takes place during the 90-day period.

### SUGGESTED FURTHER READING

Samuels, J. M. and F. M. Wilkes, *Management of Company Finance,* Nelson Publishing Co.,
London, 1971.

# 89

## TURNOVER

*Outlines key areas in reducing employee turnover to hold down costs and improve productivity during inflationary periods.*

The problem of employee turnover is especially critical during inflationary periods. Costs involved in recruiting, selecting, and training become disproportionately high if profits are under pressure and/or declining. Even more important, however, high turnover means having large numbers of inexperienced people on jobs. During inflationary periods, when the maintenance of high productivity levels is critical, the inexperience of new employees can have a direct and profound effect on the success of the organization.

Turnover, like many business problems, has causes that are numerous and complex, and there are no simple cures to alleviate every situation. Research at many levels over a number of years, however, has led personnel specialists to believe that the basic causes of turnover can be traced to four critical functional areas: selection, job structure, supervision, and compensation. The following outlines steps that can be taken in each of these four areas to keep turnover rates to a minimum.

### SELECTION

The selection process is the key to countering turnover problems. If employees are not properly selected for the job to be filled, there is little likelihood of permanence.

In deciding on an applicant, the hiring officer should ask himself two basic questions. "Is the match between the job and the person reasonably close?" and "Is this person likely to stay with any job he takes?"

#### Matching Applicants to Jobs

The person being considered should not be grossly underqualified or overqualified for the position, and he should be interested in activities that are characteristic of the job. In tight labor markets there is often a tendency to fill positions with applicants who are only remotely qualified, simply to have someone on the job. Cost analysis would probably show, however, that using a "warm body" to fill a position is more detrimental to profits than leaving the job open.

The opposite problem can occur when the labor market is loose and applicants are plentiful. Then workers are often hired whose qualifications greatly exceed those needed for the job. There is justification for this practice if the employee can be moved up rapidly to higher levels, but most often the person becomes bored and the job receives minimal attention while the employee seeks more challenging work.

Another aspect of employee/job matching is the applicant's interest. Even if a worker seems to be qualified for a position, there is little point of putting an outgoing, extroverted person into a secluded job where he cannot fill his needs to be with other people. His interests will make him quickly dissatisfied with the position.

### Will the Person Stay with the Job?

Experience has shown that the best indicator of an applicant's future permanence is his past record. The stability of a person's life pattern may be determined from many sources, including job history, family status, and educational history. A reasonably stable past usually indicates that a similar stable pattern will be followed in the future.

### Screening Techniques

Another key element in the selection process is the use of application blank screening techniques, as outlined in the following.

Many organizations, in studying their regular application blank, have found that by scoring and appropriately weighing key elements they are able to achieve dramatic decreases in turnover using a quick and easily administered screening technique. Figure 13 indicates the results of such a study conducted among clerical employees of an insurance company. The application blank was analyzed and the scoring system developed to predict turnover. Applying this system to another group of employees, it was found that the average tenure of those scoring 0 or below was extremely poor, while those scoring 4 or above were highly likely to stay with the company more than two years. With this data, the company was able to set appropriate cutoff scores to assure enough employees to fill the required positions by taking only those who had a high probability of staying with the company.[1]

[1] George G. Gordon, "Putting the Brakes on Turnover," *Personnel Journal,* February 1974, p. 142. Reprinted with permission, PERSONNEL JOURNAL, Copyright February 1974.

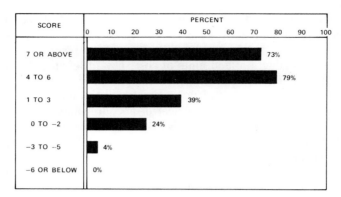

**Figure 13**  Percentage of employees at each score level surviving more than 2 years. (*Source:* Gordon, "Putting the Brakes on Turnover." Reprinted with permission of *Personnel Journal.* Copyright February 1974.)

### JOB STRUCTURE

The second critical element in employee turnover is poor job design. Employees need the opportunity to take on responsibility or to show their initiative, and there is documented evidence that "even at the simplest level of job content, employee involvement in restructuring a job or group of jobs can have dramatic effects on both productivity and turnover."[2] Numerous studies in job design and motivation have discovered a direct relationship between the extent of employee participation in job design and the rate of turnover. In one Bell System study[3] in which employees were instrumental in restructuring jobs, the turnover rate of service representatives dropped 13.1 percent in the restructured group. During the same period turnover in a control group increased 9.3 percent. With training costs of $2500 per man, cost savings of $225,000 could have been realized over 6 months if all jobs had been restructured.

The important aspect of job restructuring is that the talents and creativity of employees are channeled into making their work more meaningful to them. This results in workers who are committed not so much to activities but to working for the success of the company.

### SUPERVISION

Regardless of supervisory style, studies have revealed that one factor is absolutely essential for success: the supervisor must view employees as

[2] Gordon, "Putting the Brakes on Turnover," p. 143.
[3] Robert N. Ford, *Motivation Through the Work Itself,* American Management Association, New York, 1969.

human beings and must treat them with human dignity. Although this may seem elemental to modern supervisory management, there is still a widespread tendency to view workers in mechanistic terms, such as man-hours, units of production, and units of cost. Too little interest is shown in the proven psychological facts that each worker has his own degree of self-respect, and each responds differently from others to varying types of treatment. Some must be given a great deal of encouragement, some must be constantly challenged, some are motivated by a desire to be on a winning team, and others are motivated by a need to be "best." To be effective, a supervisor must know and recognize these different needs and motivations.

Unfortunately the supervisory role is not always as effective as it should be in reducing turnover and increasing productivity.

In recent years, the social sciences have produced a great deal of knowledge about the supervisor's role as well as a number of techniques for enhancing his effectiveness in that role. Yet, more often than not, a person is promoted from a nonsupervisory to supervisory position with no attempt by the organization to arm him with the knowledge and techniques that can facilitate his success in the new job. Yet to a large extent, the effectiveness of the supervisor will determine the success of those below him.[4]

### COMPENSATION

Motivational research has shown that the maxim of "pay high and employees will stay and produce well, pay low and they will either leave or not produce satisfactorily" is not entirely valid. The relationship between compensation and performance is much more complex than this. It is known that intrinsic aspects of the job are at least as important as pay. One study shows that overpaid workers often produce significantly less than workers paid a normal wage.[5]

Such findings point up the two critical compensation areas that are the keys to lowering turnover:

• Pay must be equitable; employees must believe that the compensation they are receiving for the work they are doing is equitable when compared with the pay of other company employees. If they believe otherwise, there will be dissatisfaction, turnover, and low productivity.

• Pay must be competitive; if a worker possesses good, marketable skills

[4] Gordon, "Putting the Brakes on Turnover," *Personnel Journal,* February 1974, p. 143. Reprinted with permission, PERSONNEL JOURNAL, Copyright February 1974.
[5] I. Wood and E. E. Lawler, III, "Effects of Piece-Rate Overpayment on Productivity," *Journal of Applied Psychology,* No. 54, 1970, pp. 234–238.

that can be sold at a much higher rate to competing firms, there is a good chance he will change employers, even if he is satisfied with his present job, his supervisor, and the company. There may be mitigating factors, of course, but they fade in importance when pay differentials reach major proportions.

An equitable, competitive compensation program is a major element in keeping turnover rates at low levels. However it is becoming more and more evident that compensation alone cannot overcome problems caused by bad selection, poor job design, and improper supervision.


## CONCLUSION

There is often an inclination to shrug off high turnover rates as a social problem—"People don't want to work any more." More often than not, this is an excuse for not taking the time or initiative to investigate and tackle the turnover problem. Research has provided management with an arsenal of hiring and motivational techniques that can make significant inroads into curbing the turnover problem.

When concerted efforts have been made, a number of dramatic success stories have been reported. On example: in the restaurant industry, where annual turnover rates of 300 percent are not uncommon, Howard Johnson's reduced turnover by 46 percent in pilot areas by installing a sophisticated selection and training program based on Activity Vector Analysis and Job Activity Rating. When these methods are in use throughout the system, annual savings in manpower replacement and training costs will exceed $1 million.[6]

In an inflationary environment even more than under other conditions, companies should take steps to pinpoint weaknesses in each of the four areas already outlined and should establish priorities for eliminating problems that contribute significantly to turnover. Once existing problems are eliminated, new measures can be adopted, aimed at keeping turnover rates within acceptable limits.


## SUGGESTED FURTHER READING

Gordon, George G., "Putting the Brakes on Turnover," *Personnel Journal,* February 1974, pp. 141–144.

---

[6] "Case Study of a Plan to Reduce Turnover," *Personnel Journal,* September 1974, p. 702.

## TWO–D PRINCIPLE

*Sketches a technique for maximizing profits per sales call during inflation.*

One of the best ways to increase sales profitably is improved utilization of salesmen's time, to maximize profits per sales call. Maximization is not difficult if the salesman handles only one type of product, but complications arise in allocating sales time if the salesman is expected to sell a variety of products to several types of customers. It is then necessary to determine which products can be sold most profitably to which customers, and sales efforts must be directed accordingly. The 2-D Principle, developed by Porter Henry, a sales management consultant, can be helpful in making the most of sales time.[1]

Let us assume that a company is selling various products to three types of customers, A, B, and C. Typically calls are planned according to the dollar volume generated by each of the three different customer categories—the higher the volume, the higher the percentage of sales calls. Alternately, and perhaps better, calls are allocated according to each customer's contributions to profits. In either case the salesman weighs current and probable future sales and profits. He plans his calls in each of the three categories to return the highest volume or profits. For example, he may decide that his call schedule should break out as follows, knowing that large customers require less sales and service time per dollar than smaller customers.

| Customer type | Present volume or profit | Sales calls |
|---|---|---|
| A | 60% | 40% |
| B | 30% | 35% |
| C | 10% | 25% |

Let us also assume that the company sells three products with three dif-

---

[1] From Porter Henry, "Use the 2-D Principle for Making the Most of Sales Time," *Sales Management*, May 19, 1975, pp. 25–26. Adapted with permission from *Sales Management, The Marketing Magazine.* Copyright 1975.

ferent profit contributions, and that sales time is allocated by product
volume or profitability.

| Product line | Present volume or profit | Sales calls on selling time |
|---|---|---|
| 1 | 20% | 10% |
| 2 | 50% | 60% |
| 3 | 30% | 30% |

To maximize the selling effort, allocation of time should not be made
solely on the basis of customer category or by product line; rather, the company should combine the two, since the salesman is actually confronted by a
two-dimensional grid (Figure 14).

Most firms assign sales time by using the totals. For example, salesmen
whose firms allocate sales time by *product* are told to use the totals across
the bottom of the chart in allocating time to spend on each product. Firms
that assign time by *customer type* use the right-hand column totals. Both
methods are at fault, however, in not fine-tuning the approach to take into
account the individual boxes within the grid. This results in salesmen putting the same emphasis on each product when calling on customers. In effect
they are filling in the grid in proportion to their row and column totals, as in
Figure 15.

For the most effective use of selling time, the opposite approach should
be chosen; instead of filling in the grid from the outside in, salesmen should

| | Percentage of sales effort | | | |
|---|---|---|---|---|
| | Products | | | |
| Customers | 1 | 2 | 3 | Total |
| A | | | | 40% |
| B | | | | 35% |
| C | | | | 25% |
| Total | 10% | 60% | 30% | 100% |

**Figure 14** Typical 2-D sales grid layout. (*Source:*
Henry, "Using the 2-D Principle for Making the Most
of Sales Time." Reprinted with permission from *Sales
Management, The Marketing Magazine.* Copyright
1975.)

reverse the process and work from the inside out. In other words, using their own judgment about profitability of sales calls, salesmen should allocate percentages of their effort to each of the boxes in the grid, building up totals from these. Each box then represents the amount of effort to be spent on one particular product with one type of customer.

In determining these allocations, a number of questions should be asked.

*Current Status.* What is the present volume and profitability of this line with this customer?

*Purchases.* What are the customer's total purchases of this particular product, both from our company and from competitors?

*Share.* What percentage of total business do we now hold?

*Product Profitability.* How profitable is this particular product for our company?

In using the superficial time-allocation method in Figure 15, the salesman would probably devote most of his sales efforts to Box A-2, which represents his biggest customer group and his hottest-selling product. Closer examination might show, however, that product 2 has a lower markup than the others or that the company already enjoys 80 percent of the potential business from that customer category, limiting additional sales.

Working from the inside out on the grid and analyzing each box individually, the salesman might decide that Box A-2 really deserves only 10 percent of his time, rather than 24 percent—just enough effort to maintain the firm's present share of business. The time "saved" (14 percent) could

| Customers | Percentage of sales effort | | | |
|---|---|---|---|---|
| | Products | | | |
| | 1 | 2 | 3 | Total |
| A | 4.0% | 24% | 12.0% | 40% |
| B | 3.5% | 21% | 10.5% | 35% |
| C | 2.5% | 15% | 7.5% | 25% |
| Total | 10.0% | 60% | 30.0% | 100% |

**Figure 15** Typical 2-D sales grid giving equal sales time to customers using specific products. (*Source:* Henry, "Using the 2-D Principle for Making the Most of Sales Time." Reprinted with permission from *Sales Management, The Marketing Magazine.* Copyright 1975.)

| Customers | Percentage of sales effort | | | |
|---|---|---|---|---|
| | Products | | | |
| | 1 | 2 | 3 | Total |
| A | 6.0% | 10% | 12.0% | 28% |
| B | 5.5% | 21% | 10.5% | 37% |
| C | 12.5% | 15% | 7.5% | 35% |
| Total | 24.0% | 46% | 30.0% | 100% |

**Figure 16** Typical sales grid allocating the most time to high-profit sales efforts. (*Source:* Henry, "Using the 2-D Principle for Making the Most of Sales Time." Reprinted with permission from *Sales Management, The Marketing Magazine.* Copyright 1975.)

then be put to use in more profitable ways, such as increased effort on product 1, which has a higher markup. Believing that customer group C offers the best potential for increased purchases of product 1, the salesman might devote 10 percent of his "saved" time to this group and 2 percent each to groups A and B. The new grid (Figure 16) reflects these changes, made in the appropriate boxes.

In making use of the 2-D grid principle, all the variables for establishing individual grids for specific salesmen should be considered. These variables include salaries, commissions, and expenses; markups, inventory costs, and receivable costs for each product line; and present and potential purchases of each product line by each customer category. Of course since these variables change periodically, individual grids should be updated on a regular, planned basis. A computer that has been programmed with needed basic information is a valuable tool in making updates.

How much will use of the 2-D grid increase profitability? It has been reliably demonstrated that if grids are accurately constructed and sales efforts diligently follow the time recommendations, sales managers can expect profit increases in the range of 10 to 12 percent—certainly a strong incentive for any firm during inflationary times.

## SUGGESTED FURTHER READING

Henry, Porter, "Use the 2-D Principle for Making the Most of Sales Time," *Sales Management,* May 19, 1975, pp. 25–26.

# SECTION 91

## UNIDENTIFIED MATERIAL LOSSES

*Provides a checklist of methods to determine causes of unidentified material losses.*

Studies have shown that unidentified material losses in both large and small manufacturing businesses have risen sharply in recent years. An unidentified material loss occurs when material disappears and its value is accounted for, but the cause of the loss is not determined.

Such losses take on increased significance during periods of inflation. First, materials costs are constantly rising, meaning that the erosionary effect of unidentified losses on profits is heightened. Second, materials shortages often accompany inflation, and substantial unidentified loss can affect availability of critical supplies. Additionally, price controls often are in effect during inflation, meaning that companies cannot cover such losses by simply raising prices.

With the expanded volume of materials flowing through the average manufacturing operation, it is seldom economical to check and verify each and every point at which losses can occur. However a recent study by Wilson and Hoitash uncovered the in-plant locations at which unidentified material losses are most likely to occur and recommended steps that can be taken to stem such losses. The following provides a detailed checklist of various methods that can be used to identify causes of material loss.[1]

### RECEIVING SUPPLIER SHIPMENTS

- Verify packing slips for number of containers, part number, and quantity of material noted on container.
- Verify quantity by hand count.
- Verify quantity by weight count.
- Verify quantity of samples by hand or weight count.

[1] Robert C. Wilson and Charles F. Hoitash, "Improving Inventory Control and Profit by Identifying the Causes of Material Losses," *Journal of Purchasing,* November 1974, pp. 68–78.

**390**

• Verify with supplier monthly to make sure his shipment accumulation is in agreement with total receipts.

### WAREHOUSING OF PARTS

• Make sure a designated area is assigned for each and every part number, and make sure parts are warehoused accordingly.
• Warehouse parts so that part numbers are readily visible, and ensure that stock is stored allowing space for aisleways.
• Segregate material by product-line usage.
• Check for physical damage to containers, which is a potential cause of leakage of parts.
• When disbursing parts to area of use, make sure only the parts designated for that area are sent.
• Keep float of parts from warehouse to the next point of use at a minimum, and distribute to a specific schedule.
• Review measures to prevent pilferage.

### IN-PROCESS

• Review to ensure that the bill of material includes the appropriate offal quantity.
• Make sure that processed parts are put into specified containers that are properly identified and counted.
• Verify that in a given lot of material to be processed, all material, when processed, is accounted for either as good parts or scrap.
• Verify counts on containers of processed parts by hand counting, weight counting, or machine counting, which may be checked for accuracy.

### SUBASSEMBLY

• Make sure the right parts are assembled in accordance with the process and bill of material.
• Make sure subassemblies are properly identified, counted, and packaged for the warehouse and/or the assembly line.
• Verify counts in containers.
• Make sure that parts and/or subassemblies are properly scrapped out by correct part number and quantity.
• Check assembly area for spillage, to make sure that all parts are picked up and disposed of properly.

### ASSEMBLY LINE

• Make sure the parts and usage are in accordance with the process and bill of material.
• Make sure parts and/or subassemblies are scrapped out properly, with appropriate part number and correct count.
• Make sure spillage is handled properly, through a salvage operation and/or scrap.

### FINAL PRODUCT PACKAGING

• Make sure specified containers and/or pallets are used.
• Make sure containers are properly filled with specified quantities.
• Make sure containers are identified properly with part number and count.

### FINAL PRODUCT WAREHOUSING

• Make sure warehousing is in accordance with the specified layout.
• Review warehousing area for potential pilferage.
• Make sure the packaging is correct and includes the appropriate part number and count.

### SHIPPING ACTIVITY

• Make sure the number of containers being shipped agrees with the invoice.
• Verify that the container has not been damaged and is properly secured to avoid possible spillage and/or pilferage.
• Verify counts by hand and/or weight counting.

### SHIPPING AND RECEIVING MATERIAL TO AND FROM A CONSIGNEE

• Follow items reflected under Shipping Activity.
• Follow items reflected under Receiving Supplier Shipments.

### RETURN SALES

• Supplier parts returned because of overshipment and/or quality defects should be reviewed as in Shipping Activity.
• Customer return of final products due to overshipment and/or quality defects should be reviewed as in Receiving Supplier Shipments.

### SCRAP

• Materials such as brass and aluminum must be properly segregated.
• Materials must be properly identified with correct part number and quantity.
• Check quantity of scrap by hand and/or weight counting.
• See that scrap and offal are not mixed.
• Review scrap to make sure that material actually is bad and not usable even with reasonable rework.
• Compare different classifications of scrap shipments to the theoretically generated offal and recorded scrap.

### SUGGESTED FURTHER READING

Wilson, Robert C. and Charles F. Hoitash, "Improving Inventory Control and Profit by Identifying the Causes of Material Losses," *Journal of Purchasing,* November 1974, p. 68–78.

# SECTION 92

## UNPROFITABLE PRODUCT LINES

*Presents guidelines for minimizing losses on unprofitable product lines that must be retained.*

Companies that market several lines know that some are more profitable than others. Sometimes it is difficult to pinpoint exact profitability. But even when profitability can be established, the sales force is often reluctant to drop low-margin or profit-loss products, which are part of the "full line" the salesmen need to effectively sell higher-priced items.

For this reason some unprofitable products must be retained. But it is especially important during inflationary periods to minimize losses from low-margin or profit-loss products. Following[1] are some guidelines for "de-marketing" these products during an inflationary environment and—in some cases—perhaps making them profitable.

### STOP ADVERTISING AND PROMOTING UNPROFITABLE PRODUCTS

If customers want products that are not profitable for you, make them available, but do not flaunt them.

### ESTABLISH MINIMUM ORDERS

Determine certain basic costs (order processing, order assembling, shipping, etc.) and establish minimum orders that will at least cover these costs. Alternatively, such costs can be recouped by adding a service charge to small orders.

### INCREASE PRICES

Do not enter price battles with competitors over products that are already losing money. If anything, increase markups and let your competitors have

[1] From "How to Prop Up Those Unprofitable Products You've Got to Keep," *Sales Management*, May 19, 1975, p. 45. Adapted with permission from *Sales Management, The Marketing Magazine*. Copyright 1975.

the less desirable business—so long as sales of the rest of the line are not affected.

### DEEMPHASIZE SALES

Instruct salesmen not to waste valuable selling time on profit-losing products. If customers ask specifically for the products, sell them; but keep salesmen's attention firmly glued to selling high-profit items. An effective way of accomplishing this is to cut commissions and/or bonuses on all unprofitable products (see *Profit-Based Sales Compensation,* p. 303).

### COMBINE LOSERS WITH WINNERS

If you make money on shirts but lose money on ties, put together a package deal that gives a good profit on the combination. There are endless variations in this type of marketing, and some of them may help your losing items turn a profit.

### MINIMIZE OPTIONS

If your unprofitable product comes in a wide variety of colors, packagings, and sizes, reduce these to a minimum—one color, one package, and a few standard sizes. Not only will this cut costs, it may be instrumental in maintaining customers that might be lost if the line were entirely abandoned.

### MULTIPLE SELLING

Emphasize to salesmen the importance of creatively selling additional profitable products every time they are forced to take an order for a loser. The combined order often puts the transaction in the black. Discourage selling to accounts that only purchase low- or no-profit items, or sell extra hard to upgrade them to the high-profit lines.

### ANALYZE THE REASONS FOR A PRODUCT'S UNPROFITABILITY

Perhaps analysis will unveil ways to make it profitable. For example:

• Are breakage and subsequent returns a costly problem? Investigate new packaging techniques.

• Are certain costs such as warehousing and shipping assigned to the product in an unfair way? Correct the situation to reflect actual costs.

• Do complaints about the product eat up too much of salesmen's valuable selling time? Eliminate causes of complaints by correcting the product, or, if this is impractical, assign complaints to a service department.

• Is the product valuable, increasing inventory taxes? Plan and manage inventories to minimize tax liabilities.

• Is the line small, valuable, and easily stolen? Increase security measures to safeguard against pilferage.

## SUGGESTED FURTHER READING

"How to Prop Up Those Unprofitable Products You've Got to Keep," *Sales Management,* May 19, 1975, p. 45.

# SECTION

93

## VARIABLE WORK HOURS

*Outlines a case study in variable work hours and recommends use of the technique as a means of increasing productivity to offset the effects of inflation.*

Persistent inflation has served to focus increased attention on bettering the productivity of clerical workers. Costs and wages must continue to rise as long as inflation continues, and some of the effects of inflation can be offset by increasing output per employee per day.

Computerization is the heart of increased office efficiency. With computer time-sharing, even small firms can afford to make use of EDP in handling greatly increased workloads without adding staff. Other methods in increasing office productivity include monetary incentives, work study techniques, psychological motivation, and job enrichment programs.

Variable work hours (VWH) have also been tried as a means of increasing employee morale, motivation, and productivity. There is still controversy about "flextime" and other VWH modifications, but the methods have been successful in many cases. There is strong evidence that the installation of variable work hours, properly implemented and managed, can result in increased production, fewer errors, improved employee morale, and a significant reduction in lateness and absenteeism.

The following[1] outlines the concept and results of a VWH program in a large New York life insurance company. The program has been highly successful from both management's and the employees' points of view and has greatly increased office efficiency. The program is being extended and will become standard procedure in a wide range of corporate areas, staff and line alike.

### THE CONCEPT

Like most large-city business operations, Mutual of New York's Group Insurance Transactions/Billing Department had the daily problem of

[1] From Cynthia J. Fields, "Variable Work Hours—The MONY Experience," *Personnel Journal,* September 1974, pp. 675–678. Adapted with permission, PERSONNEL JOURNAL, Copyright September 1974.

employees' tardiness. This was not generally due to indifference but was caused by unforeseen and uncontrollable delays in the city's mass transit system. Productivity was good once employees were on the job, but lateness caused lost production time that could not be recovered. The situation affected profitability. Additionally, employee morale suffered because habitual lateness prevented their receiving pay increases and promotions.

In response to the problem, MONY decided to set up a controlled experiment in variable work hours. A pilot group of 22 clerical employees was allowed to choose daily arrival times without advance notice. A core time from 9:15 A.M. to 4:00 P.M., when all employees should be present, was established. Workers could arrive any time after 8:15 A.M. and leave any time up until 5:00 P.M., after completing the normal $7\frac{1}{4}$-hour work day. Work began at 15 minute intervals; if an employee arrived at 8:22, work officially started at 8:30. Anyone arriving after 9:15 was marked late. Each individual maintained a daily record of hours worked and submitted it biweekly to the supervisor.

Over a period of time, production standards had been established in the Transactions/Billing area. This made it relatively easy to control the experiment because fluctuations from normal standards could be readily seen. Additionally, an average month prior to installation of the program (August) was picked as a control standard.

### THE RESULTS

The experiment found favor with both management and employees. At the end of 6 months the pilot program had been successful in meeting its twin goals of increasing employee productivity and upgrading morale.

Production during the 6-month period, measured in terms of transactions processed per day, increased an average of 9 percent above transactions in the control month (Table 62). By January and February the increase reached 17 percent. The actual increase in production hours was due to reductions in lateness and fewer requests to arrive late and leave early on personal business. During the trial period only four instances of lateness were recorded, and absenteeism was 7.6 percent lower than in the 6-month period before VWH was installed.

A statistically significant drop in errors was also recorded during the experimental period. Individual production standards were met or exceeded 85 percent of the time, and individual quality standards were met or exceeded 84 percent of the time.

To help evaluate the program from the workers' point of view, a questionnaire was distributed to employees at the end of the 6-month trial

Table 62  Variable Work Hours Production Figures[a]

| Month | Number transactions processed | Transaction average per day | Work days | Actual number of days worked in production by all employees |
|---|---|---|---|---|
| August (control) | 9,928 | 54.5 | 23 | 182 |
| September | 8,212 | 56.2 | 20 | 146 |
| October | 10,592 | 67.0 | 21 | 158 |
| November | 7,750 | 56.2 | 20 | 138 |
| December | 6,091 | 47.2 | 20 | 129 |
| January | 10,238 | 65.0 | 22 | 159 |
| February | 9,644 | 66.5 | 19 | 145 |

[a] *Source:* Cynthia J. Fields, "Variable Work Hours—the MONY Experience," *Personnel Journal,* September 1974, p. 676. Reprinted with permission, *Personnel Journal.* Copyright September 1974.

period. From responses, it was evident that the VWH program had been instrumental in the productivity improvements. Most of the staff felt the program had favorably changed their job attitude and positively affected section morale. Employees stated that choosing their own hours gave them a sense of responsibility, therefore a greater commitment to the job. Typical comments included the following:

"Since there is less of a rush to get here, I feel more relaxed when arriving; therefore I can work better. I like my job better; therefore, I do more work."; "I'm in a better mood for work if I don't have to rush or worry too much about being late"; "Since hours are adaptable, the job does not seem like a drawback on many occasions—I like my job much better."[2]

Because of the pilot program's success, variable work hours became standard in the Transactions/Billing Department, and MONY initiated the experiment in other areas of the company. In each case the results were the same: worker morale was heightened and productivity was increased. The key to the program's success was adjusting the variable work hours concept to specific needs of individual departments, after determining that both

[2] Quoted in Fields, "Variable Work Hours," *Personnel Journal,* September 1974. Reprinted with permission, PERSONNEL JOURNAL, Copyright September 1974.

management and staff were initially receptive to the VWH concept. Variations were devised in several cases. In some work areas, for example, employee coverage is needed at all times. Here tentative work schedules are informally arranged between supervisors and employees. Changes are acceptable if advance notice is given to the supervisor. If all area employees want an early arrival time (leaving a staff shortage at the end of the day), a rotation system is used to vary arrival times each week. This gives everyone a chance to choose his arrival time at regular intervals.

Supervisors as well as staff have responded favorably to variable work hours at MONY. The supervisory headache of monitoring lateness in both line and staff areas has been largely eliminated. Additionally, supervisors have found that production deadlines are more easily met and that morale has improved since VWH were implemented. An accounting executive said, "As a supervisor, I am delighted with the variable work hours. I find the employees are more congenial, have a better attitude in general, are willing to work when they arrive and until time to leave ... It certainly has enhanced working ... in my area."[3]

Fifty percent of MONY's New York home office staff is operating under VWH, ranging from line clerical operations to staff areas such as personnel and electronics research. The program varies according to area, but several factors are constant: starting times are always at 15 minute intervals, employees must record their hours for submission to supervisors, a monthly status report is submitted to personnel for each area, and the effect of VWH is evaluated in each work area after 6 months. The evaluation includes analysis of production and attendance figures, as well as administration of employee questionnaires. In every case to date the VWH experiment has been as successful as the original pilot study in the Transactions/Billing Department.

## SUGGESTED FURTHER READING

Busch, E. T., "Flextime—The New Work Schedule?" *The CPA Journal*, July 1974, pp. 57–59.

Fields, Cynthia J., "Variable Work Hours—The MONY Experience," *Personnel Journal*, September 1974, pp. 675–678.

Fields, Cynthia J., "Staggered Work Hours—A Roundtable Discussion," *Personnel Journal*, February 1975, pp. 80–82.

"Flexible Working Hours Find Favor in Europe," *Office*, March 1975, p. 66.

"Flextime Endorsed," *Monthly Labor Review*, January 1975, p. 85.

[3] Quoted in Fields, "Variable Work Hours," *Personnel Journal*, September 1974, p. 677. Reprinted with permission, PERSONNEL JOURNAL, Copyright September 1974.

# SECTION 94

## VARIANCE ANALYSIS

*Outlines an analysis system to pinpoint budgetary deviations and bring them under control during an inflationary period.*

Variance analysis is a proven management tool that takes on added importance during inflationary periods as a means of systematically checking all budgetary cost aspects that deviate from preset figures. In a volatile economy budgetary deviations are much more prevalent than during normal times, and variance analysis can play an important role in ascertaining why costs have varied, as well as in determining methods of controlling the deviance.

In general, variance analysis consists of the following steps:

• If actual costs differ from budgeted costs, a study should be initiated to find the *cause* of the deviation.
• After the cause of the variation has been pinpointed, the employee or employees responsible for that segment of work should be asked to explain in detail why the variance occurred and what steps could or should have been taken to avoid it.
• The manager or supervisor responsible for the deviant work area should meet with other managers involved to establish methods of controlling such costs in the future. These methods should be put in force immediately.
• A full report on the methods used to control the variance should be issued to the entire managerial staff, to allow all to share knowledge of the problem.
• If it is found that cost variations (e.g., increased taxation) cannot be controlled by individuals or the company, the budgeted figures must be changed.

In practice, variance analysis is usually broken down into two main areas of application: profit variance analysis and production variance analysis.

### PROFIT VARIANCE ANALYSIS

Since profits often are under pressure during inflationary periods, profit variance analysis can be an important tool in locating critical shortfalls, making it possible to attempt to correct the situation. In analyzing profit variance to determine why budgeted goals were not achieved, the following factors should be considered.

### Capital Return

Current return on capital should be compared with previous years and with that of other companies within the same industry. Reasons for upward or downward trends should be analyzed.

### Sales/Profit Ratios

Profit margins should be compared with margins achieved in previous years. For example, if a company showed profits of $800,000 on sales of $3.2 million 3 years ago but could only achieve the same profit on sales of $4 million this year, the main cause of the variance should be determined. Have recent sales allowances been too generous? Have prices become uncompetitive? Are selling and distribution costs out of line? Have market conditions changed? Are new production processes more costly?

### Sales Ratio Compared to Capital

As a rule, annual sales volume should be about twice the amount of capital investment. When this is not the case, sales and production should be analyzed to determine the area in which the problem is originating. Important factors in controlling this ratio include the lowering of production inventory, better utilization of equipment, and increased manpower efficiency. With persistent inflation, automation is increasingly being called on as the answer to these problems.

### Government Intervention

Often government is responsible for failure to achieve profit goals. Such intervening actions as increased taxation, price controls, and mandatory environmental programs are frequently blamed. Although many of these cannot be controlled by management, steps should be taken to ensure that governmental intervention is not used as an excuse for other inefficiencies.

### Sales Values

Profit is dependent on the pricing policies set by competitors as well as sales and production costs. Given the rapidly escalating materials costs characteristic of inflation, pricing procedures become even more critical and complex. Constant analysis should be made to ensure that current pricing is in line with costs. When competition must be met by lowering prices, meeting the budgeted figure depends on cutting production costs.

## PRODUCTION AND COSTS VARIANCE ANALYSIS

The following four areas should be taken into account when analyzing the deviation of production and cost figures from those budgeted.

### Labor

Analysis should be made to determine why labor costs are higher than budgeted, if this is the case. Are the number and type of workers in line with written job specifications? Do pay scales ensure payment commensurate with job skills required?

### Work Study

Have work study programs been carried out to ensure the most cost-effective use of workers, machines, and materials? If so, have new situations—caused by inflation—been affecting production costs since the work studies were conducted? For example, a materials waste level that was tolerable when the work study was conducted may no longer be practicable because of escalation in costs of materials.

### Materials

When a variance occurs in materials costs, usage and costs should be compared with previous production records to locate the cause. Standard materials prices should be set whenever possible. When these cannot be met, less expensive materials should be substituted where possible, or prices of goods should be increased. If deviations are caused by controllable factors such as last-minute buying or purchasing in uneconomical lot sizes, immediate steps should be taken to curtail these practices.

### Overheads

Overhead cost control presents difficulties, since it is often nearly impossible to pinpoint the exact nature of an overhead. For this reason many accountants recommend the use of flexible budget figures or two-tiered budget figures for overhead costs. Even so, detailed analysis of variances should be carried out when overheads deviate significantly from previous periods. In some instances overhead variances are uncontrollable. For example, if production takes longer than budgeted, overhead costs will increase proportionately. Such costs can be brought back into line only if production efficiency meets its budgeted goals.

## SUGGESTED FURTHER READING

Batty, J., *Corporate Planning and Budgetary Control,* MacDonald and Evans, London, 1970.

## 95

## WAGE ESCALATION CLAUSES

*Outlines recent trends in the use of cost-of-living adjustment contract clauses.*

In the recent inflationary environment both management and labor have shown renewed interest in wage escalation clauses. These clauses, also known as cost-of-living adjustments (COLAs), gear wage changes automatically to price changes, as measured by a recognized index.

From labor's point of view, COLAs protect worker's pay from the erosionary effects of inflation by automatically adjusting hourly rates upward to match cost-of-living increases. Because of recent inflationary trends, many labor negotiators are predicting a dramatic increase in the number of collective agreements featuring such adjustments. There are indications that the use of COLAs will also become more widespread in nonunionized and salaried areas.

Most managements have traditionally looked on COLAs with disfavor, fearing that they will increase inflation. In recent years, however, this attitude has been somewhat tempered by the presence of increased inflationary rates—especially in Europe. With workers pushing for exorbitant wage hikes that will cover all inflationary contingencies, many managements prefer to agree to indexed escalation clauses, which limit increases to inflationary levels. England, for example, had 20 percent inflation in 1974, and workers in large unions called for 30 to 40 percent increases, claiming that no one knew how high the inflationary level would climb. Obviously it was to management's advantage to introduce indexed COLAs rather than meet these extreme demands.

The following outlines major types of COLAs that have been used in the United States and covers recent trends evolving as a result of the new inflationary environment.[1]

### THE GM FORMULA

The agreement reached between General Motors Corporation and the United Auto Workers in 1948 has become the model for all major bargain-

[1] Adapted from Eileen B. Hoffman, "Adjusting Wages to Inflation via the Escalator Clause," *Conference Board Record,* August 1974, p. 57. Copyright The Conference Board.

ing situations. The agreement provides for wage changes in a precise ratio to relatively slight changes in the Consumer Price Index.

Under the terms accepted, GM agreed to maintain the existing ratio between the Consumer Price Index and the average hourly earnings then in effect. To do this, the company took the latest published index figure (April 1948) and divided it by the then-current average hourly rate of GM employees ($1.49) as follows.

$$\frac{169.3 \text{ points (CPI } 1935\text{--}1939 = 100)}{149\text{¢ (average hourly rate in cents per hour)}} = 1\text{¢ for each } 1.14 \text{ point change}$$

Thus when the CPI changed 1.14 points, a 1¢ change in hourly wages would be necessary to maintain a constant ratio. Such wage adjustments were to be made quarterly.

The 1948 agreement also provided another innovation—an annual improvement factor intended to raise real earnings as compensation for higher productivity. The estimated figure worked out to a 2 percent per year increase, and when applied to the existing average hourly wage rate (1.49), it meant a wage increase of 3¢ per hour per year.

### USE OF COLAS

Since the GM agreement, the use of COLAs has fluctuated depending on the economic environment. Widespread use during the inflationary Korean War period slacked off in 1952, only to resume in 1956 when inflation spiraled up again. Four million workers were covered by escalator clauses by 1958, but the number had dipped to just 1.85 million by 1963. This held fairly steady until inflation again took hold in the early 1970's, and the general trend has been upward since that time.

Today more than 5 million American workers are covered by COLA clauses of some kind, and several major unions plan to push for installing or regaining escalator clauses in upcoming collective bargaining sessions. The use of COLAs varies widely from industry to industry. Industries that traditionally have *not* used the concept include construction, finance, insurance, real estate, services, textiles, lumber, and public utilities. On the other hand, cost-of-living escalators have been an important part of bargaining in automobile, agricultural implements, aerospace, steel, can, aluminum, copper, electric equipment, meat packing, trucking, and communications industries. Major unions that have recently bargained for or are pursuing

COLA clauses include the United Mine Workers, the Glass Bottle Blowers, the International Brotherhood of Railway Workers, the Amalgamated Clothing Workers, the Oil, Chemical, and Atomic Workers, and several city employee unions.

## MAJOR QUESTIONS

When setting up wage agreements that adopt the principle of escalation, management and labor negotiators must resolve a number of major questions involving procedure or formulas to be followed.

### The Index To Be Used

Most contracts that include COLAs follow the lead of General Motors and use the Consumer Price Index to make escalation adjustments. Specifically, the U.S. City Average for Urban Wage Earners and Clerical Workers is used. This specialized segment of the CPI measures changes in prices of consumer goods commonly bought by moderate-income families in metropolitan areas. The index reflects changes in the price of a typical "market basket" of purchases.

In 1974 the Bureau of Labor Statistics announced that revisions would be made in compiling the index in April 1977, and a major controversy developed over the effect the new index would have on COLA agreements. Organized labor objected to the new index because it will be broader in scope, including professional, self-emplyed, retired, and unemployed persons; union belief was that the new index would not measure the effects of inflation accurately and that wage escalation agreements would be negated. A compromise was reached, and in 1977 the BLS will begin issuing two indexes—an updated version of the existing CPI for Urban Wage Earners and Clerical Workers and the new, broader CPI for all Urban Households.

A recent trend has been toward the use of local city indexes compiled by the BLS for use in high-cost metropolitan areas. For example, two major unions switched from the National Consumer Price Index to the San Francisco CPI in drawing up contracts in 1974. Similar concessions have been won by the Teamsters in Los Angeles and the Transit Workers in New York.

Of course any yardstick that both parties agree upon can be used as a basis for COLAs. Some agreements tie wage increases to the price of a company's product, company sales, or even the wage rates of competitors. The Homestake Mining Company ties increases to the price of gold.

### Choice of Base Period

The base reference year for the Consumer Price Index is 1967 = 100. Accordingly, if by December 1977 the CPI has reached 170, it will cost the average family 70 percent more than it did in 1967 to purchase the same amount of goods and services. From time to time the BLS introduces new base periods but continues to publish the older series as long as union agreements are still tied to it. Agreements tied to the CPI usually contain clauses that deal with index revisions, such as this example from the Postal Workers contract:

"Continuance of the cost of living adjustment shall be contingent upon the continued availability of the official monthly Index in its present form and calculated on the same basis as the Index for June 1973. If the Bureau of Labor Statistics changes the form or basis of calculating the Index, the parties agree to request the Bureau to make available, for the life of this Agreement, a monthly Index in its present form and calculated on the same basis as the Index for June 1973." [2]

### Frequency of Readjustment

Management and union negotiators often find themselves in disagreement over frequency of review, one of the key elements in establishing COLA contracts. This is because during periods of rampant inflation, the more frequent the adjustment, the greater the wage gains. Thus management usually argues for less frequent reviews, while labor is intent on achieving the greatest frequency possible.

Reviews can be established for any regular time period—monthly, quarterly, semiannually, annually, or once during the life of the agreement. Of the more than 3 million reviews that took place in the United States in 1974, 1.9 million were carried out quarterly, 93,000 semiannually, 987,000 annually, and the rest in other sequences.

Monthly reviews, in addition to allowing greater wage increases, are costly to administer and until recently were rare in the United States. Additionally, such reviews can show declines because of seasonal fluctuations in the CPI. Review frequencies are becoming increasingly shorter, however, and the 1974 monthly adjustment negotiated between the Oil, Chemical, and Atomic Workers and Lever Brothers Company may point to a new trend.

Adjustments made quarterly, semiannually, or yearly generally average the monthly figures for the time period involved. When inflation is accelerating, this results in a slightly lower adjustment figure.

[2] Quoted in Hoffman, "Adjusting Wages to Inflation via the Escalator Clause" *Conference Board Record,* August 1974, p. 58. Copyright The Conference Board.

### Floors and Ceilings

Another area in which labor and management often disagree is the establishment of floors and ceilings for wage fluctuations.

Using a pure escalation agreement, wages would follow the chosen index all the way up or down. In practice, however, labor leaders are reluctant to give up any wage gains achieved and are usually successful in negotiating a floor level. The floor is generally a specified index point below which no downward cost-of-living adjustments will be made. Sometimes the contract simply states that wage rates cannot be adjusted downward, regardless of index fluctuations.

A relatively new development is the inclusion of a guaranteed payout in contracts—regardless of the movement of the CPI. Under these agreements a minimum cents-per-hour adjustment is guaranteed and is, in effect, a deferred wage, since the amount is determined beforehand. More than 2 million workers in the United States have COLA clauses featuring guaranteed minimum increases.

Some contracts include a specific CPI number or percentage increase that must be reached before the escalator clause goes into effect. For example, a United Press International contract with the Newspaper Guild called for a January 1975 pay increase equal to any rise in the Consumer Price Index above 8 percent during 1974.

A company is equally anxious to ensure that wages cannot escalate disproportionately during rapidly accelerating inflation, and management often insists on a ceiling for wage increases under escalator clauses.

The type of "cap" put on agreements varies: it may stop cost-of-living increases after a certain point on the Consumer Price Index has been reached, it may set a limit on the cents-per-hour increase that can be achieved during any one adjustment period, or it may set a maximum adjustment over the life of the contract.

In 1973 about 40 percent of workers covered under COLA clauses had ceilings specified in their contracts, but recently union negotiators have been successful in getting rid of caps. In the last 2 years, ceilings have been removed in contracts for the auto, farm implement, can, steel, and aluminum industries.

A frequent COLA formula is a cents-per-hour change in wages for a specified point change in the CPI. The "cents-for-points" formulas in major agreements range from a 1¢ adjustment for each 0.3 point change in the CPI to a 1¢ increase for each 0.5 point movement.

Percentage change in wages for changes in the CPI is another formula. Under this approach the worker who earns a higher rate gets a higher cost-of-living increase than the worker at a lower hourly rate, thus maintaining the differential between jobs.

**Labor Costs**

In using COLAs as a tool to help overcome the effects of inflation on company wage costs, an all-important factor is whether the cost-of-living adjustment is merely a separate wage payment or bonus or whether it is deemed part of the employees' standard hourly rate. Many employers insist that increases derived from CPI adjustments be regarded as bonus or "float" rather than as part of basic wage rates.

In some agreements the adjustment is treated as a specific allowance separate from other aspects of pay. Often it is paid by separate check. In other cases cost-of-living increases are included in calculating overtime and other premium pay, and even vacation pay. The allowance is added to each employee's straight-time hourly earnings but not to the base rates.

The trend, however, seems to be toward including COLAs as part of standard pay:

During the recent round of negotiations, unions have insisted that a part of the float be incorporated into the basic wage structures. Indeed, the greatest change in COLAs in the past few years has been this fold-in of the float into the basic wage rates and the timing of the fold-in. The Machinists' bargaining goals for contracts in aerospace companies . . . call for annual fold-in of COLA floats similar to the arrangement in the 1974 Basic Steel contracts. On May 1, 1974, the steel industry incorporated the existing COLA float . . . into hourly rates for nonincentive workers and into hourly add-ons for incentive employees. The same procedure will be followed for future increases. . . .[3]

## SUGGESTED FURTHER READING

Hoffman, Eileen B., "Adjusting Wages to Inflation via the Escalator Clause," *The Conference Board Record,* August 1974, pp. 54–60.

Hughes, J., "Are Threshold Agreements Inflationary?" *Banker,* October 1974, pp. 1191–1195.

Mitchell, W., "Index Related Wages and the Threshold Syndrome," *Personnel Management,* October 1974, pp. 30–34.

Poulin, J., "COLA Clauses—Antidote to Inflation?" *Labour Gazette,* October 1974, pp. 718–720.

Schreiner, J., "Ounce of COLA Is Worth a Pound of Erosion," *Labour Gazette,* November 1974, pp. 782–785.

[3] Hoffman, "Adjusting Wages to Inflation via the Escalator Clause," *Conference Board Record,* The Conference Board.

# 96

## WAGES, PRODUCTIVITY, AND INFLATION

*Discusses inflationary pressures caused by union wage demands and labor power factors and outlines management responsibilities.*

Proponents of the "cost-push" theory of inflation place much of the blame for price increases on organized labor. These economists argue that wage increases negotiated by large unions in recent years have outstripped worker productivity increases and that prices rise to offset this imbalance (Table 63). To control inflation under the "cost-push" theory, increased wages must be matched by proportionate increases in productivity or union demands for sizable wage hikes must be curbed.

The following tells how the labor/inflation problem has evolved and what the future holds, supplying guidelines for management to use in more equitably balancing the collective bargaining system.[1]

### THE PROBLEM

Without question, labor unions have helped bring about many needed reforms. Over the years, the power of union organization has been instrumental in obtaining needed grievance and arbitration procedures, better working hours, improved working conditions, increased benefits, and higher pay levels for workers.

In recent years, however, there has been a marked strengthening of union power. Many economists feel that serious imbalances of bargaining power have evolved between labor and management and are weighted in favor of the unions. This has allowed organized labor to extract wage increases well in excess of productivity improvements. When these increases are conceded, the process is perpetuated; the much-publicized success of one union in gaining a sizable wage settlement encourages other unions to seek equal or

[1] Adapted from R. Conrad Cooper, "Management, Labor, and Inflation," *Advanced Management Journal*, October 1974, pp. 14–19.

**Table 63  Wages and Productivity Index**[a] **(by quarter, 1967 = 100)**

| Year and quarter | | Average hourly compensation, all employees, private nonfarm | Output per man-hour, total private nonfarm |
|---|---|---|---|
| 1973 | First | 145.3 | 114.1 |
|  | Second | 147.3 | 113.7 |
|  | Third | 149.7 | 113.6 |
|  | Fourth | 152.7 | 113.4 |
| 1974 | First | 156.0 | 111.6 |
|  | Second | 160.2 | 111.0 |
|  | Third | 163.9 | 110.3 |
|  | Fourth | 167.7 | 109.4 |
| 1975 | First | 171.6 | 108.9 |
|  | Second | 174.7 | 110.4 |

[a] *Source: Business Conditions Digest,* Bureau of Economic Analysis, U.S. Department of Commerce, Washington, D.C., September 1975.

higher increases. Pressures are put on union leaders, forcing them to deliver sizable settlements. These settlements, in turn, are instrumental in pushing up inflation, creating economic instability, and rendering American products less competitive in world markets.

A major part of the problem is that bargaining power has become more and more concentrated in the hands of a few large unions. Because of their concentrated strength, these unions have the strategic ability to create national emergencies by withdrawing their labor. When this occurs, government intervention is required and the labor-management balance in bargaining strength completely breaks down.

The large-union, industry-wide bargaining approach also creates problems at the local level. No two plants, companies, or groups of employees have identical problems, and there has been a pronounced increase in the rejection of industry-wide settlements by local union members.

## LABOR POWER FACTORS

The increasing power of large labor unions stems from four principal factors.

### Public Attitude

The relatively complacent public attitude toward labor unions can be seen in a number of ways.

• Strikers are increasingly sheltered from financial loss by means of unemployment compensation and public funds (food stamps, welfare payments, etc.)
• Public employee unionization has increased significantly over the last decade, including teachers, hospital workers, firemen, policemen, and other government employees at all levels.
• The public accepts strikes by government employees, albeit grudgingly, even though nearly all such strikes are illegal.
• There is little evident public concern over failures to apply statutory penalties to government employees engaging in illegal strikes. This encourages similar strike action by other employees.

### Legislation

Another important factor in labor union power involves government attitude. The legislative bodies that enact the nation's labor laws, the administrative agencies charged with the application of these laws, and many federal, state, and local judiciary bodies have often displayed a pro-labor bias. This stems, no doubt, from elected officials' interpretation of public attitudes. Additionally, labor unions have made good use of their vast financial and organizational strengths in political campaigns.

Evidence of this legislative bias can be seen in the following examples:

• The original National Labor Relations Act [1935] openly encouraged unionization of industrial workers.
• When the complicated procedures of the Railway Labor Act are invoked, pro-labor settlements nearly always result.
• The Full Employment Act enhances labor union influence in the labor market to the point of monopoly control in major employment segments.
• Labor union immunity under antitrust laws.
• The government's apparent reluctance to halt mass picketing and violence in illegal strike situations.

### Organizational Strength

Union leaders derive power from the organizational and constitutional framework on which unions are built. Occupying political positions in what are in effect one-party structures, union officials are able to keep tight control on union functions and operations.

A major concern of union leaders is self-perpetuation in office. Toward this end they must continually deliver wage and benefit increases to union members.

Their source of power can be seen in many ways: compulsory union membership; hiring hall arrangements; penalties and fines to discipline union members for crossing picket lines or exceeding union-established production quotas; control of the labor market by limiting entrants, as seen in the construction industry; and great financial wealth accumulations for political and strike-relief purposes.[2]

### Bargaining Procedures

Established bargaining arrangements are another element in the union power base. Often collective bargaining procedures are not the give-and-take tradeoffs visualized by outsiders. Holding the power to seek and impose, labor usually has a decided advantage over management, which must cooperate, defend, persuade, or resist. In recent years collective bargaining has been largely a one-way street, with the unions taking and management giving.

Labor power has been accentuated with the establishment of bargaining units, as seen in the following examples:

• Bargaining arrangements allow negotiations with a single craft or key production unit in one plant of one company. If negotiations break down, this unit alone often has the power to shut down the entire plant, perhaps several plants—an effect grossly disproportionate to the significance of the unit itself.

• Bargaining may be carried out simultaneously for all the production and maintenance employees in all the plants of all competing companies within an entire industry. In such cases a breakdown in negotiations can create a national emergency. The government, of course, exerts pressure for a peaceful settlement, and this usually means meeting union demands.

• Bargaining may be fragmented into local areas, tightly organized units of craft unions being solidly aligned with loosely organized groups of highly competitive companies. The construction and airline industries are examples.

---

[2] Cooper, "Management, Labor, and Inflation," *Advanced Management Journal,* October 1974, p. 18.

### SOLUTIONS

There are no easy short-term answers to the problems just outlined. In many cases unions have gained the upper hand, and the reestablishment of balanced collective bargaining practices would be a lengthly process.

However there are steps that managements can take now to begin the process. Most of these steps, if taken earlier, would have made it possible to avoid many of the problems apparent today.

#### Attention to Valid Grievances

Management should give more systematic attention to wages, hours of work, and other conditions of employment. Because this area was neglected in the past, workers turned to union organization as the only viable alternative. This basic set of conditions should not be allowed to cause further problems of the same kind.

#### Legal Procedures

Management should make increased use of the National Labor Relations Board and court procedures when unionization appears. Both are strong tools for blocking the establishment of improper bargaining units and unsound bargaining and strike procedures. In the past management has failed to take timely advantage of these procedures.

#### Communication

Management should initiate a concerted effort to make its case with employees, the public, and governmental leaders. Failure to do this has resulted in large groups of the public being either complacent or economically uninformed about the labor-management relationship. Strong efforts should be made to assert the management cause and the economic consequences of persistent wage increases without corresponding improvements in productivity.

#### Bargaining Representatives

Top management must recognize the importance, urgency, and difficulty of collective bargaining, appointing only trained, experienced executives to the management side of the table. Too often in the past this responsibility has been delegated to people not prepared to carry it out effectively. Labor negotiations are a specialized task, requiring unique skills, and the consequences of inadequate preparation can affect company operations negatively for years.

### Hard Bargaining

Management should cease making precedent-setting concessions on basic issues of principle in lieu of concessions in economic matters. Such concessions of principle have served to give the desired short-term gains, but at the expense of long-term injury. Examples include the union shop, dues checkoff, some forms of seniority, and inhibiting contracting-out clauses. A long view should be taken and carefully costed before any precedent-setting concessions are bargained away.

## SUGGESTED FURTHER READING

Cooper, R. Conrad, "Management, Labor, and Inflation," *Advanced Management Journal,* October 1974, pp. 14–19.

## WHOLESALE PRICE INDEX

*Sketches the purpose for and uses of the Wholesale Price Index and provides index statistics.*

The Wholesale (Primary Market) Price Index compiled by the Bureau of Labor Statistics is designed to show the general rate and direction of the composite of price movements in primary markets, as well as the specific rates and directions of price movements for individual commodities or groups of commodities. It is designed to measure "real" price changes between two periods of time; that is, to measure price changes not influenced by changes in quality, quantity, terms of sale, and so on.

The newly revised index, based on 1967 = 100, is the official Wholesale Price Index for January 1952 and all subsequent months. All sales of goods by or to manufacturers or producers (except sales that represent interplant transfers within the same company) are included in the base weights.

Beginning with January 1952, the index is based on prices for one day in the month—usually the Tuesday of the week in which the fifteenth day of the month falls. Generally the prices selected are f.o.b. production or central marketing points. Delivered prices are included only when it is the customary practice of the industry to quote prices on this basis.

The prices are collected from manufacturers and other producers. In some cases prices are secured from trade publications or from other government agencies that collect price quotations in the course of their regular work.

The various Wholesale Price Indexes have a number of uses, especially during an inflationary period. The indexes often forecast future increases in prices, since producers usually pass on increased wholesale costs to customers. Both buyers and sellers use the indexes in formulating contracts and escalation clauses that specify price increases tied to rises in wholesale costs. Engineers, designers, and purchasing directors watch for sharp wholesale price rises in specific commodities as a signal to substitute less expensive materials in their products. Industries that use large amounts of fuel can make energy-source decisions based on past and anticipated costs derived from the Wholesale Price Indexes for fuel, power, and lighting.

Table 64 shows the Wholesale Price Index for all commodities and all

**Table 64   Wholesale Prices of All Commodities and All Commodities Other Than Farm and Foods[a] (index: 1967 = 100)**

| Year and month | | All commodities | Industrial commodities |
|---|---|---|---|
| 1960 | | 94.9 | 95.3 |
| 1961 | | 94.5 | 94.8 |
| 1962 | | 94.8 | 94.8 |
| 1963 | | 94.5 | 94.7 |
| 1964 | | 94.7 | 95.2 |
| 1965 | | 96.6 | 96.4 |
| 1966 | | 99.8 | 98.5 |
| 1967 | | 100.0 | 100.0 |
| 1968 | | 102.5 | 102.5 |
| 1969 | | 106.5 | 106.0 |
| 1970 | | 110.4 | 110.0 |
| 1971 | | 113.9 | 114.0 |
| 1972 | | 119.1 | 117.9 |
| 1973 | | 134.7 | 125.9 |
| 1974 | | 160.1 | 153.8 |
| 1975 | January | 171.8 | 167.5 |
| | February | 171.3 | 168.4 |
| | March | 170.4 | 168.9 |
| | April | 172.1 | 169.7 |
| | May | 173.2 | 170.3 |
| | June | 173.7 | 170.7 |
| | July | 175.7 | 171.2 |

[a] *Source:* U.S. Department of Labor, Bureau of Labor Statistics.

**Table 65 Wholesale Prices of Fuel, Power, and Lighting Materials**[a]
(index: 1967 = 100)

| Year and month | Total | Coal | Gas fuel | Electric power | Petroleum products |
|---|---|---|---|---|---|
| 1960 | 96.1 | 95.6 | 87.2 | 101.2 | 95.5 |
| 1961 | 97.2 | 94.6 | 88.7 | 101.7 | 97.2 |
| 1962 | 96.7 | 93.7 | 89.2 | 102.1 | 96.1 |
| 1963 | 96.3 | 93.8 | 91.8 | 101.3 | 95.1 |
| 1964 | 93.7 | 93.8 | 90.7 | 100.4 | 90.7 |
| 1965 | 95.5 | 93.4 | 92.8 | 100.1 | 93.8 |
| 1966 | 97.8 | 95.5 | 96.7 | 99.6 | 97.4 |
| 1967 | 100.0 | 100.0 | 100.0 | 100.0 | 100.0 |
| 1968 | 98.9 | 103.7 | 92.7 | 100.9 | 98.1 |
| 1969 | 100.9 | 112.6 | 93.3 | 101.8 | 99.6 |
| 1970 | 105.9 | 150.0 | 103.3 | 104.8 | 101.1 |
| 1971 | 114.2 | 181.8 | 108.0 | 113.6 | 106.8 |
| 1972 | 118.6 | 193.8 | 114.1 | 121.5 | 108.9 |
| 1973 | 134.3 | 218.1 | 126.7 | 129.3 | 128.7 |
| 1974 | 208.3 | 332.4 | 162.2 | 163.1 | 223.4 |
| 1975 June | 243.0 | 385.9 | 220.0 | 190.6 | 252.2 |

[a] *Source:* U.S. Department of Labor, Bureau of Labor Statistics.

**Table 66    Wholesale Prices of Machinery and Motive Products**[a] **(index: 1967 = 100)**

| Year and month | Total | Con-struction machinery and equipment | Metal Working machinery and equipment | General purpose machinery and equipment | Elec-trical machinery and equipment | Motor vehicles |
|---|---|---|---|---|---|---|
| 1960 | 92.0 | 85.9 | 85.1 | 91.2 | 99.5 | 98.8 |
| 1961 | 91.9 | 87.3 | 85.9 | 90.5 | 98.2 | 98.6 |
| 1962 | 92.0 | 87.5 | 87.3 | 90.9 | 96.7 | 98.6 |
| 1963 | 92.2 | 89.0 | 87.6 | 91.4 | 95.7 | 97.8 |
| 1964 | 92.8 | 91.2 | 89.3 | 91.9 | 95.1 | 98.3 |
| 1965 | 93.9 | 93.6 | 91.8 | 92.5 | 95.1 | 98.5 |
| 1966 | 96.8 | 96.5 | 96.0 | 96.6 | 97.2 | 98.6 |
| 1967 | 100.0 | 100.0 | 100.0 | 100.0 | 100.0 | 100.0 |
| 1968 | 103.2 | 105.7 | 104.0 | 103.3 | 100.3 | 102.8 |
| 1969 | 106.5 | 110.4 | 108.0 | 107.0 | 102.9 | 104.8 |
| 1970 | 111.4 | 115.5 | 114.0 | 113.7 | 106.4 | 108.5 |
| 1971 | 115.5 | 121.4 | 117.3 | 119.1 | 109.5 | 114.7 |
| 1972 | 117.9 | 125.7 | 120.2 | 122.4 | 110.4 | 118.0 |
| 1973 | 121.7 | 130.7 | 125.5 | 127.0 | 112.4 | 119.2 |
| 1974 | 139.4 | 152.3 | 146.9 | 151.2 | 125.0 | 129.2 |
| 1975  June | 161.0 | 184.4 | 171.9 | 178.2 | 140.4 | 143.1 |

[a] *Source:* U.S. Department of Labor, Bureau of Labor Statistics.

commodities other than farm and foods (industrial commodities) since 1960.

Table 65 and 66 give two typical industry indexes, the Wholesale Price Index for Fuel, Power, and Lighting Materials, and the Wholesale Price Index for Machinery and Motive Products.

### SUGGESTED FURTHER READING

*Handbook of Basic Economic Statistics* (monthly), Economic Statistics Bureau, Washington, D.C.

*Statistical Abstract of the United States* (yearly), U.S. Bureau of the Census, Washington, D.C.

# SECTION 98

## WORKER ABSENTEEISM

*Reviews negative effects of absenteeism during an inflationary environment and traces causes and solutions.*

Absenteeism is very costly for businesses. One survey conducted by a New York telephone company disclosed that employee absences cost American companies at least $10 billion every year. Each day, about 2 million employees are away from work through absence. It has been estimated that absences cost the average company $300 per year for each person employeed.

The costs of absenteeism soar in an inflationary environment. Not only are absent employees being paid—at ever-increasing wage and salary rates—for not working, but productivity suffers when it is critically needed to offset inflationary pressures. The major costs attributable to absenteeism include the following.

*Disrupted Schedules.* A key person's absence can stop or slow down the flow of work, causing loss of time by other employees further down the schedule.

*Idle Machinery.* Whether it is a typewriter or a piece of production machinery, money is wasted if no one is operating equipment.

*Shipment and Invoice Delays.* When shipments are delayed because of absences, invoicing is also delayed. This has a negative effect on cash flows, a critical factor during inflation.

*Inventory Requirements.* Many companies are forced to carry higher-than-necessary inventories to protect themselves against production lags caused by absences. Again, pressure is put on cash flows.

*Overtime.* Overtime is premium time, and although remaining employees often can cover absences with overtime, the per-hour cost is greater. If more employees are hired to cover absences (and studies have shown that some companies hire as much as 14 percent in excess of needs for this purpose), higher recruiting and training costs result, as well as increased benefit expenses.

*Paperwork Costs.* Absenteeism causes additional paperwork and the accompanying clerical costs needed to perform it.

## CAUSES AND SOLUTIONS

Scores of studies have been carried out in attempts to isolate the primary causes of absenteeism and to provide solutions to the problem. It has been established that the rate of absenteeism varies greatly from company to company and is usually directly proportionate to the rate of turnover. It is evident, therefore, that certain elements are instrumental in causing high absenteeism and turnover rates, and that the elimination or lessening of these elements in company operations can be used to reduce the problem.

Surveys show that the following conditions are the prime contributors to high absenteeism.

*Poor Working Atmosphere.* Improper lighting, inadequate ventilation, unsatisfactory facilities (cafeterias, wash rooms, etc.) are prime offenders. Absenteeism can be improved significantly by correcting poor conditions in these areas.

*Worker Boredom.* The boring routine of many work processes is a prime contributor to absenteeism. When workers are given more responsibility and a greater chance to use their initiative, absentee rates are usually lowered. For example, when employees are assigned to assemble an entire product or component, rather than just adding a specific part, turnover and absenteeism usually drop.

*Work flow.* Uneven work flows that put pressure on workers one day and leave them with little to do the next create tension that leads to absenteeism. This is especially true on slack days, when employees feel they will not be missed. Whenever possible, work should be planned to keep employees busy without undue pressure.

*Conflicts.* Conflicts with co-workers also cause pressures and often result in employees staying home. The supervisor plays a key role in stemming this problem; disagreements should be uncovered, brought out into the open, and settled promptly.

*Transportation.* As urban transportation systems become more crowded, the difficulty in getting to work is increasingly responsible for absenteeism. Workers just do not want to "fight the crowds." There is little companies can do about this, although some firms hire their own buses to transport employees to and from central locations easily reached by employees. Company-coordinated car pools can help ease the situation in some cases. Flexible working hours that allow employees to arrive and leave at non-rush hours can also help alleviate the problem.

*Communication.* Absenteeism is significantly higher when there is a lack of communication between workers and their immediate supervisors. Supervisors must be trained in communication techniques and must be willing to use them. Significant drops in absenteeism have been achieved simply by changing supervisors.

*Lack of Recognition.*   Workers need to be told when they are performing their jobs well and to be recognized for their achievements; this is closely allied with communication. Recognition is one of the strongest psychological motivators and should be used by supervisors at every opportunity.

Various incentive plans can be instrumental in helping curb absenteeism. Wage incentives are effective because a worker's pay is directly dependent on how much he produces. Bonuses directly tied to attendance and punctuality can also be effective.

Absenteeism and tardiness can also be fought by judicious use of a prominently displayed chart listing names of employees and showing each individual's absence and tardiness record. The program should *not* be set up as an obvious attempt to keep tabs on worker habits; rather, it should be installed as a contest ending with prizes or bonuses for employees posting the best work attendance records.

## SUGGESTED FURTHER READING

Berger, P. D. and J. P. Monahan, "Planning Model to Cope with Absenteeism," *Journal of Business,* October 1974, pp. 512–517.

*Cost Control and the Supervisor,* American Management Association, New York, 1972.

Radke, Magnus, *Manual of Cost Reduction Techniques,* McGraw-Hill, New York, 1972.

Smardon, R. A., "Some Cures for Chronic Absenteeism," *Supervisory Management,* November 1974, pp. 12–15.

# 99

## WORLDWIDE INFLATION STATISTICS

*Provides statistics showing inflation rates of 50 countries from 1971 through mid-1975.*

Persistent inflation has become a worldwide phenomenon. In 1974 nearly every major country in the world experienced inflation of double-digit proportions. The rates ranged from 7 percent in West Germany to nearly 600 percent in Chile. The top 15 industrialized countries averaged 12.6 percent.

Table 67 sets out inflationary rates since 1971, as measured by changes in consumer prices, for a representative sample of 50 countries around the globe.

**Table 67   Worldwide Inflation as Indexed by Changes in Consumer Prices**[a, b]
(**annual figures = averages of monthly changes, monthly figures = percent change in 12 months**)

|  |  |  |  |  | 1975 | |
|---|---|---|---|---|---|---|
|  | 1971 | 1972 | 1973 | 1974 | March | June |
| World | 5.9 | 5.8 | 9.5 | 15.1 | 14.0 | — |
| Industrialized countries |  |  |  |  |  |  |
| United States | 4.3 | 3.3 | 6.2 | 11.0 | 10.3 | 9.3 |
| Canada | 2.8 | 4.8 | 7.6 | 10.9 | 11.2 | 10.4 |
| Japan | 6.3 | 4.8 | 11.7 | 22.7 | 14.0 | 13.7 |
| Austria | 4.7 | 6.4 | 7.5 | 9.5 | 9.2 | 8.4 |
| Belgium | 4.3 | 5.4 | 7.0 | 12.6 | 14.8 | 12.5 |
| Denmark | 5.9 | 6.6 | 9.3 | 15.5 | 13.4 | 10.7 |
| France | 5.4 | 6.0 | 7.4 | 13.6 | 13.5 | 11.7 |
| West Germany | 5.2 | 5.5 | 7.0 | 6.9 | 5.9 | 6.4 |
| Italy | 4.8 | 5.7 | 10.8 | 19.1 | 20.3 | 19.0 |
| Luxembourg | 4.7 | 5.2 | 6.1 | 9.5 | 10.5 | 10.7 |

[a] *Source: International Financial Statistics* (monthly), International Monetary Fund, Washington, D.C.
[b] Dash (—) indicates figures not available.

**Table 67**  (*Continued*)

|  | 1971 | 1972 | 1973 | 1974 | 1975 March | 1975 June |
|---|---|---|---|---|---|---|
| Netherlands | 7.5 | 7.8 | 8.1 | 9.6 | 10.3 | 10.3 |
| Norway | 6.3 | 7.2 | 7.5 | 9.4 | 11.0 | 12.0 |
| Sweden | 7.4 | 6.0 | 6.8 | 9.8 | 7.6 | — |
| Switzerland | 6.6 | 6.7 | 8.8 | 9.8 | 8.3 | 8.0 |
| United Kingdom | 9.5 | 7.1 | 9.2 | 15.9 | 21.1 | 26.2 |
| Other European countries |  |  |  |  |  |  |
| Finland | 6.3 | 7.4 | 10.7 | 17.0 | 18.6 | — |
| Greece | 3.1 | 4.3 | 15.4 | 27.5 | 14.2 | 12.9 |
| Ireland | 9.0 | 8.6 | 11.5 | 16.9 | 23.8 | 24.4 |
| Portugal | 11.9 | 10.8 | 12.9 | 25.1 | 12.4 | — |
| Spain | 8.2 | 8.3 | 11.4 | 15.6 | 19.6 | 17.2 |
| Turkey | 15.7 | 11.8 | 15.4 | 15.8 | 20.9 | 21.0 |
| Yugoslavia | 15.8 | 15.9 | 19.4 | 21.5 | 25.1 | 26.7 |
| Oceania |  |  |  |  |  |  |
| Australia | 6.0 | 5.9 | 9.4 | 15.1 | — | — |
| New Zealand | 10.4 | 7.0 | 8.2 | 11.1 | — | — |
| Oil-exporting countries |  |  |  |  |  |  |
| Indonesia | 4.3 | 6.7 | 31.0 | 41.1 | 20.1 | 18.3 |
| Iran | 4.2 | 6.4 | 9.8 | 14.1 | 18.4 | 15.8 |
| Iraq | 3.7 | 5.2 | 4.9 | 8.3 | 9.4 | 11.5 |
| Nigeria | 16.0 | 3.0 | 6.3 | 12.5 | — | — |
| Venezuela | 3.2 | 2.8 | 4.2 | 8.5 | 14.5 | 16.6 |
| Other countries in Western Hemisphere |  |  |  |  |  |  |
| Argentina | 34.7 | 58.0 | 62.3 | 23.3 | 68.5 | — |
| Bolivia | 3.6 | 6.5 | 31.5 | 64.0 | 6.0 | — |
| Brazil | 20.2 | 16.9 | 12.7 | 27.4 | 28.5 | 25.7 |
| Chile | 19.3 | 72.7 | 319.5 | 585.9 | 371.9 | — |
| Mexico | 5.8 | 5.0 | 11.2 | 22.4 | 17.8 | 17.6 |
| Panama | 2.0 | 5.4 | 6.9 | 16.2 | 10.6 | 6.6 |
| Peru | 6.8 | 7.3 | 9.5 | 16.9 | 21.7 | 21.1 |
| Other Middle East countries |  |  |  |  |  |  |
| Egypt | 3.2 | 2.1 | 5.1 | 10.1 | — | — |
| Israel | 12.0 | 12.9 | 19.9 | 39.4 | 44.0 | 38.7 |
| Jordan | 4.3 | 8.0 | 10.6 | 20.2 | 9.5 | 10.6 |
| Lebanon | 1.7 | 4.9 | 6.1 | 11.2 | 6.2 | — |
| Syria | 5.7 | 2.1 | 20.5 | 15.6 | 8.8 | — |

Table 67 (*Continued*)

| | 1971 | 1972 | 1973 | 1974 | 1975 March | June |
|---|---|---|---|---|---|---|
| Other Asian countries | | | | | | |
| China, People's Republic of | 2.9 | 3.0 | 8.2 | 48.1 | 2.8 | 7.8 |
| India | 3.1 | 6.4 | 17.0 | 28.5 | 16.9 | — |
| Korea | 12.1 | 11.8 | 3.1 | 23.6 | 21.6 | 26.0 |
| Malaysia | 1.6 | 3.2 | 10.6 | 17.5 | 5.3 | 4.8 |
| Singapore | 1.8 | 2.6 | 25.4 | 23.0 | 2.5 | 3.1 |
| Viet-Nam, Republic of | 18.9 | 25.3 | 43.6 | 56.5 | 30.7 | — |
| Other African countries | | | | | | |
| Ghana | 2.9 | 13.6 | 10.5 | 24.2 | — | — |
| South Africa | 5.7 | 6.5 | 9.6 | 11.6 | 13.6 | 14.1 |
| Tunisia | 5.8 | 2.1 | 4.7 | 4.3 | 7.9 | 8.7 |

## SUGGESTED FURTHER READING

Hackett, J. T., "Multinational Corporations and Worldwide Inflation," *Financial Executive,* February 1975, pp. 64–68.

"Inflation and Stagnation in Major Foreign Industrial Countries," *Federal Reserve Bulletin,* October 1974, pp. 683–698.

*International Financial Statistics* (monthly), International Monetary Fund, Washington, D.C.

Kaufman, R. H., "Inflation—A Global View," *Columbia Journal of World Business,* Winter 1974, pp. 135–138.

Mayer, L. A., "Bad Year for the Rich Countries," *Fortune,* August 1974, pp. 158–163.

"World Purchasing Power—Clobbered by Inflation," *Monthly Economic Newsletter,* First National City Bank of New York, September 1974, pp. 9–12.

# 100

## ZERO INFLATION CAMPAIGN

*Describes an employee awareness program to reduce effects of in-company inflation.*

Zero inflation campaigns are in-company drives to make employees aware of inflationary effects on company operations and to increase productivity, decrease materials' wastage, institute tighter work scheduling, and adopt other methods of meeting inflation that can be used to reduce the effects as nearly to zero as possible. Newsletters, meetings, and posters are means of calling attention to the problem and publicizing ways in which individual employees can help attack inflation at the company level. A contest may be established between departments, awarding prizes to the department that cuts inflation-connected costs most effectively. In a similar vein, employees who make suggestions that result in an inflation-connected cost reduction may be awarded a bonus of, say, 10 percent of the savings.

Success of the method depends on creating an awareness among workers of all the inflation-connected factors that increase costs, yet can be controlled at least partially by employee and company attention. For example, costs of materials made from oil, such as plastics, have risen more rapidly than costs of some alternate materials in recent years. Successful substitution of a lower-cost, less inflation-prone material would be an inflation-connected cost reduction.

Scheduling of purchasing and work to allow earliest feasible purchasing of materials and fastest completion of and billing for work could also reduce inflation-connected costs stemming from the decrease in purchasing power of money.

Increased productivity measures of all kinds should be included, and employees should be made aware of the favorable effect increased productivity could have on overall national inflationary rates.

### SUGGESTED FURTHER READING

Levy, M. E., *Containing Inflation in the Environment of the 1970s,* Conference Board, New York, 1971.

Morley, S. A., *The Economics of Inflation,* Dryden Press, Hinsdale, Ill., 1971.

# SUBJECT INDEX

- How can products be priced profitably when scores of costs are rising on an almost daily basis?
- Is a 10-percent annual salary increase adequate for motivating employees when inflation is spiraling upward at the same rate?
- How can budgetary controls be maintained when a piece of equipment quoted at $50,000 costs $55,000 by the time the purchase order is processed?

While economists argue over possible cures for inflation, businessmen must wrestle with its dislocating effects on company operations. INFLATION MANAGEMENT provides answers to these and many other business questions that have evolved with inflation. It sets forth 100 practical techniques to help businessmen adjust to it, learn to live with it, and maintain profitability in spite of it.

The techniques cover a broad range of sources representing the best and latest management thinking for combating inflation at the company level. Founded primarily on American business practices, the book also includes inflation-controlling techniques that have proven effective for businesses in Germany, Japan, Great Britain, Canada, the Netherlands, Brazil, and other countries.

The book will be of interest to any executive at any management level who wishes to gain an overall grasp of the business problems caused by inflation and measures that can be taken to alleviate them.